Gisela, Karen, Michael

It is my deepest pleasure
to know your wonderful
family, the Reinsessels.
My best wishes to you.
Arlene Roanhaus

THREADS OF MEMORIES

My Tragic But Fascinating Life

Arlene F. Roanhaus

Threads Of Memories
My Tragic But Fascinating Life

Copyright @ 1997
First Printing 1999

ISBN: 0-7392-0451-3

Printed in the United States by:
Morris Publishing
3212 East Highway 30
Kearney, NE 68847
1-800-650-7888

Dedication

To Barbie Lois who has been instrumental as my incentive and inspiration for writing this book. Writing this book, telling of my tragic but fascinating life, has been rewarding to me in so many ways of reminiscing my past and counting my blessings. Barbie, you have touched my life as much as I have touched yours. Best of luck and God's blessings to you in your dedicated and pivotal role as a teacher, fashioning and touching the lives of our youth today. You make me so very proud of your accomplishments!

Acknowledgments

My deepest thanks to my husband who has been so patient and understanding of all the hours that I have put into writing this book, for his loyalty and encouragement, and especially how he supported me in this two year long project.

My appreciation is extended to all my grown children who have been there for me all through this endeavor, and for listening to me during the many times that I expressed my feelings about this project. Many of the details that supported much of my writings are credited to them for enhancing my memory. I have honored some of their requests to omit narrating various incidents of their lives that they felt infringed on their privacy. I will support this appeal with the fact that these private incidents would by no means mar or discredit their personal attributes or their credibility, but in their own perspective I have deemed worthy not to include.

My loyal friends and neighbors are to be commended for their support in dealing with my excitement concerning this personal venture. My apologies to them if I have slighted mentioning their names because there are so many experiences in which they most likely were involved, many of which are in reference particularly to my days of school teaching.

My twenty-four grandchildren who have shared my excitement all during this process and I am grateful to them for the many times they contributed with, "Grandma, remember when....." The language I used in my writing is simple and readable so my young grandchildren are able to enjoy and comprehend within the realm of their ability to undertsand.

Special thanks to my daughter, Diane, who spent hours of proofing my manuscript and believed in my dream of seeing my life story in book form.

Special thanks to my grandaughter, Tanya for her help in collating and doing the final proofing of my pages for the publisher.

Thanks in advance to my daughter, Dolly, for promoting the sales of my book.

Thanks to a friend, Betty Noble, for promoting the sales of my book.

Special gratitude is extended to: The Kenosha News, Western Kenosha County Bulletin, 4-H Home Lite, Westosha Report, and PPS Spirit, for news atricles reprinted.

Thanks to all of the news reporters especially Jill Andersen for publicity coverage promoting my book.

Thanks to Mitch Mason for researching the R.O.P.E.S. information for me and to Diane Rusch for the R.O.P.E.S. training.

In loving memory of my wonderful parents, Joseph and Dorothy, and my two cherished brothers, Robert and Ardell.

Preface

Having an abundance of time during my recuperation from major surgery, many thoughts have just automatically proceeded to waltz through my mind. So I find myself sitting at my computer just reminiscing through the many stages of my life. Memorable as they are, there are some happenings in my life that I want to remember forever, and some of them I'd like to eradicate from memory as though they never happened. Well, such is life - God's will!

Threads of memories can become so precious after having just gone through this encounter at my tender age of seventy years. One's heart fills with joy at the fact that I really made it through that ordeal, and God has given me another opportunity in life to test my endurance and stamina to fight one of the many battles that He has chosen for me to bear.

My mother's words of wisdom have always stuck with me, "God only sends what He knows one can endure". So apparently I have been selected as one of those who can endure over and beyond the anticipated norms in existence.

It's the middle of May in the year of 1997, and some how or other, we're not having the typical spring weather that Wisconsin usually has. Instead, the season of spring seemed more like the season of autumn. Weather contributes to creating one's mood and feelings, and some days seem a little gloomier than others but perhaps in another month, we'll have the blazing heat of the solar sun that God so graciously put in the upper dome of the atmosphere.

Presently, I'm busy trying to help myself a little more each day, as well as doing a little more in the house while functioning from within a wheel chair. I've always had a flare for wheels during my life, but never before for this kind of wheels. But I'm confident that each day will bring about a little more progress until I can, hopefully, do everything that I did before this ordeal.

Recuperating isn't quite what it's cracked up to be! You see my mind instructs my body to do one thing but my body hasn't gained enough strength in response to cooperate. Two forces, such as these, that are not in unison can create a problem. But then we all live in a world of problems, a greater conglomeration than one can perceive. But if I live each day at a time, to the fullest extent, in the manner in which God intended, then I need not fear destiny, because my salvation will be God's reward, eternal happiness.

My life hasn't always been filled with excitement and adventure, at times I've experienced much joy, at other times I've felt the pain of sorrow and sadness. Even though I have had an abundance of worry, anxiety and stress, I some how always managed to find and maintain a feeling of peace and contentment, through a magnitude of strong will and energy that surpasses the given norm in life.

Though tragic at times, my life has given rise to greater character development due to associations of experiencing courage, fear, hope, and persistence, all of which added fascination to my life. I can only convey these attributes through the age old expression: "Been there, done that".

My heart has always been filled with love for my family and relatives, all the students I've ever taught, co-workers I've worked with, and those friends and neighbors around me.

This includes my love, faith, and trust in the Supreme Being, God, who gave me the precious gift of life along with its trials and tribulations. I have always tried to accept God's will, perhaps more graciously in my tender age than I did when I was in my youth. Life experiences make one wiser as time progresses on and the realization of the hand that is dealt to you must be played with common sense, faith, humility, and expertise.

This story of my life has become a realization in which I want to make known what a full, but tragic life can be. It is in accordance with my utmost dignity, integrity, and sincerity that I divulge my many very personal and touching happenings throughout my life, of which I hope will not offend or astonish anyone. All of my personal experiences will help to analyze my personality, my background, my dignity, and my self-worth.

The incentive for writing this book has been bestowed on me by a former student of mine. She was one of the students I taught in my last year of teaching in 1989, before retiring .

This particular class grew very fond of me as I did of them, and we enjoyed sharing experiences as much as enjoying the learning process. They were a good class, worked very hard, and when it was time to have fun, we all had fun together, being cautious never to neglect or interrupt the learning procedure. One day while discussing various current events around the world as well as the local community, I began relating some of my personal experiences involving circuit court jury duty to them. One of the girls in the class of 1989, Barbie Lois, said to me, "Mrs. Roanhaus, you should write a book, and don't forget to put us in it".

That thought always remained with me. It has taken me years just thinking about it, but now as many memories have flashed back to me, I have come to realize that my life memoirs could become a reality. I knew that I could not remember every little detail in the happenings of my life, just bits and pieces, so I thought of them as strands or threads, so this is how I arrived at the title of my book.

Now that my life is slowing down, I'm taking the time out of my still busy schedule to share my life experiences with you. Everything in this book is the absolute truth and not one bit of fiction, everything is exactly as it happened. I hope that you'll enjoy reading my book as much as I have enjoyed writing it. All I can say is that my life, as tragic and fascinating that you will find it to have been, is most enjoyable and I live each day to its fullest potential in gratitude to God.

TABLE OF CONTENTS

Dedication
Acknowledgments
Preface

Chapter 1
Threads of My Early Life

The house that I was born in was on one of the farms that had been in the Lenz generations for many years. In fact, this particular farm was over a hundred years old at that time, but all the buildings were very well kept and up to date with the times. There was no indoor plumbing and this caused much extra work for everyone involved, but was installed years later. Today this house and the other farm buildings would be about one hundred eighty years old.

At this time, I'd like to introduce myself. Hi, the name given to me by my parents was Arlene Florence and obviously my house name was Lenz. I was born on November 29, 1926, in a farmhouse on the farm I have just mentioned, which is located just about one-sixteenth of a mile east of our house now.

In those days women had their babies at home, and a nurse would come in for a few days to help out while the mother was in bed for nine days. You need to realize that in those days there was no such thing as a visiting nurse. A family would have to locate and hire a retired nurse who would just help people out for a limited period of time. My, how times have changed. My parents said that I was a healthy bouncing fatty baby. [To this day, I note no changes in regard to the description as a baby!]

My father's name was Joseph Bernard Lenz who was born in the township of Wheatland on November 5, 1895. As a boy, he lived at the bottom of the hill from the farm where I was born, across county highway K on one of the two Lenz homesteads. His mother's name was Elizabeth [maiden name was Smitz], and his dad's name was Joseph M. Lenz. My dad had two brothers, Frank and William.

After my dad served in the armed forces during World War I, he married my mother , Dorothy Theresa Barbian, on September 24, 1919. Mother was born in the township of Wheatland on December 24, 1898. My mother's parents were Mary Althoff and Nicholas Barbian. Mom was from a large family, whose brothers were Frank, Jack, Ray, Leo, and Harry. She had two sisters, Helen, who died as an infant, and her other sister was my Aunt Florence.

I was one of three children in our Lenz family. I had an older brother, Robert, who is six years older than me, and a younger brother, Ardell, who was seven years younger than me. Unfortunately, I never had a sister.

My parents were the greatest people who ever lived. My mother was one of the most talented and creative women that ever was born. She was also a very caring, kindhearted, beautiful person who was the best mom that anyone in this whole wide world could ever have. I have to say the same for my dad. He was always there for us, the whole family, and was a very good provider, who worked very hard. I have to say that my dad was a very fun-loving person, and everyone who ever met him enjoyed his humor and good natured disposition who always had a witty remark or two. It seems to be that I have inherited my own fun-loving traits from my dad

My mother and dad bought the Lenz farm, which was very large and so they actually had rough going financially in their younger lives. Paying Grandpa Lenz for the farm was an enormous undertaking, so my mom for many years took the place of a hired hand so as to save money. This required much of her time and energy working on a farm, keeping a house, and raising a family, but never was any task too enormous for her, and nothing was ever left undone. Mother was a perfectionist in her own rite.

Mom's weekly chore was baking bread for the next week. She kept an immaculate house, we always had clean clothes, and always had balanced nutritional meals. Sometimes I look back in awe and wonder how she accomplished all the things that she did. And I can't forget how she also sewed clothes for us as children.

I remember when she would get out a dozen of eggs, separate them, and beat up the egg whites with a wire wisp for an angel food cake. Her arms must have at times felt like falling off, because it would take an extremely long time for the egg whites to form peaks, but those angel food cakes were surely good and would just melt in your mouth. My mom was known for being such a good cook and baker.

Mother was the only woman around the area who did her own wall papering of the walls and painted all the woodwork throughout the whole house. This was hard work, but as I have said before, mother was not afraid of work, no job was ever too big for her.

As a small child, I remember that every Sunday night the huge container called a wash boiler was brought up from the basement, put on the wood-burning stove and mom filled

2

it up with so many buckets of water until it was full. At that time, there was no such thing as a hot water heater, so all this had to be done manually.

Then the next morning, mom would get up early, again take the water by bucketful, only this time it was hot water and she put it into the wash machine. Her next step was to fill up two wash tubs each with cold water for two rinsings, get the first load of wash in, then hustle to the barn to help dad with the barn chores.

I often heard my mother tell that she always helped dad milk the cows until she was pregnant with me at which time she got kicked by a cow. That ended that! My dad went right out and bought a milking machine. But it was a few years later when dad decided that all this farm work was getting to be too much for my mother, so he hired a man to help with the farm work.

Actually life on a farm turned out to be that each family member had a job to do. My jobs were to carry in wood every day to fill the wood box that was kept on the back porch of our house. Of course this had to be done all year long including summer, because the stove was used for cooking and baking in addition to heating wash water. During the fall and winter months this stove helped keep the house warm.

My other daily job was to gather eggs from the chicken house. Oh, how I hated that job! First of all, the smell in there was enough to gag a maggot. Then to top it all off, the darn hens would sit on their nests, and peck at me because they didn't want to get off long enough for me to get their eggs from underneath them. I used to scream to the top of my lungs at those hens, telling them to get off their nests and let me have their eggs, because if I left any eggs in the nest, I'd get yelled at from my dad. After a few more pecks on the arms from the hens, they would finally get off, as if they understood what I was telling them!

One of my jobs in the house was to dust the furniture, the job that I detested the most. As a matter of fact, I did such a poor job of dusting that my mother would put pennies on the pedestal legs of the dining room table, in the corners of the window sills, under the doilies on end tables, under lamps, and any other inconspicuous place where she knew I would never even think of dusting. It took me a long time to catch on to it all, but after a fashion, I wised up. If I did a good job, I could end up with at least ten cents for the day.

3

Back then that was a lot of money for a kid to have.

In those days the stores in Burlington were open on Saturday nights instead of the usual Friday nights of today. If we were good all week, my brothers and I got to go along shopping with mom and dad. Then we could make our big purchases with the money we had earned during the week. Some weeks I only had two cents to spend, but that would buy a candy bar then. But when I'd have that dime I referred to, I could really splurge. That would buy a bag of bars.

As for jobs, my older brother, Bob, had to usually feed the pigs. That wasn't the greatest of jobs either. Sometimes he'd help my dad throw down hay out of the hay mow, and throw out silage from the silo, both of which were dusty jobs. There were other jobs, too, that he was responsible for doing, and you better well believe, that if you were assigned a job to do, you better do it....or else.

My younger brother was usually responsible to go to the water pump, fill the water buckets for use in the house. All the water that was used for drinking, cooking, and washing dishes, had to be carried in by the bucket method.

Ardell also had the job of seeing to it that all the outdated catalogs were taken to the 'out house'. Back then we had no bathrooms due to no indoor plumbing so we had to go outside . The outhouse had three holes: one small hole for the little butts, a middle sized one for - I assume - the ladies, and a large hole for the guys or anyone who had an outsized butt.

Toilet tissue was expensive, and there was only a roll of toilet paper to be found when we were to have company, or if someone had the misfortune of having diarrhea. When choosing a page from the catalog, one made sure never to get the colored slippery pages, as those pages didn't wipe the butt so well because they were harsh and didn't crinkle up, so all the black and white pages were torn out first. These pages were more conducive to doing a better job. Today I shutter to even think back of that whole situation.

By now, I suppose you are thinking, what a boring life! My parents provided much entertainment for us, and we never suffered for lack of anything we needed. We had more love shown to us than anyone can imagine. Sunday at our house was strictly a family day. Every Sunday we went to church, came home and had a delicious dinner, then piled in the Ford, and went someplace as a family.

In the summer when it was nice out, mom would pack

4

a picnic dinner, and after church, we'd go to Petrifying Springs, a park northwest of Kenosha, after playing on the playground equipment for a while, we went to a movie.

Our family was Catholic, as was through the past generations. Every Sunday we went to St. Alphonsus Church in New Munster. At that time, the pews in which one would sit went according to the amount of rental for each pew to sit in. The front section was the least expensive, the middle section was more in cost, and the last section of the church cost the most. My parents rented a pew about in the exact middle of the church. No one dare to sit in "your pew", because you rented that particular one. So every Sunday we sat in the very same pew because that was our pew. That system would never work out today, because the church could not hold all the existing parishioners.

Speaking of church, this is how little Miss Arlene acted every Sunday during Mass. I was about three years old, but I remember this so well. I was so mischievous and so misbehaved in church, that my mother would threaten me right in Church that if I was not a good girl, I'd really get it when I got home. She even tried to explain to me that Jesus was probably crying because I was so naughty in his house and I should at least be a good girl, sit still, and try to listen..

But at that point in time, how could a three year old relate to the Latin Mass? I believe I tested her a few times, so I ignored her warning. But 'sure a shootin', as soon as I got home from church, I got a good hard spanking. Mom would say, "Are you going to be naughty in church again?" And through the flowing tears, I would reply, "No, Mom, I promise I'll be good every Sunday".

But Sunday after Sunday, we went through the same ritual with no change. I can't believe to this day, how I had the heart to do this to my mom especially in church. This went on long enough until one Sunday, my dad took my brother Robert with him and I was left out. This cured me. It's amazing how some things work in disciplining children.

You just can't imagine what a daring little girl I really was. My mother always took me along shopping with her. We would go to downtown Kenosha on Sixth Avenue where all the larger stores were, including ladies' dress shops, gift shops, clothing stores, children's clothing stores, the famous Woolworth's, Kreske stores and other variety stores. We would go early in the morning and stay all day until almost supper time, when we'd return home.

One particular day, mom and I were in Wooworth's and mom was looking at stockings in the hosiery department. So being the curious little girl that I was, I meandered off away from mom and saw an African-American lady with a huge fabric shopping bag in her hand. Prior to this time, I had never seen an African-American before and I didn't even realize that they existed.

So bold little Arlene went right up to the lady and tapped her lightly on her butt. As she felt this movement, she turned and swung her shopping bag at me, and I ran like the dickens, yelling for my mother. All this while, mom had been watching me out of the corner of her eye and came to my rescue. My mother apologized to the lady, but she was so sweet and told my mother it was okay, and what a cute little girl she had.

Later mom asked me why I did that and I replied, "I just wanted to see what she felt like". In my mind I had an idea that she might feel different than mom and me because to me she looked a little different.

At the age of four, I used to follow the men around the farm. My Grandpa Lenz, who was retired from farming at that time, used to help my dad around the farm a bit and go out in the fields occasionally.

One day I followed him into a field that had just had the corn cut, and the field was full of what they called corn stubbles. I was running so fast that I fell. I had blood all over my face. A stubble pierced about a sixteenth of an inch below my left eye. Grandpa picked me up, pulled a big red handkerchief out of his pocket, and blotted the blood, as he carried me to the house.

Poor mom, all she could think of was that I may have injured my eye beyond repair. But after getting the bleeding stopped, everything was not as bad as they thought, just a bad scrape below the eye. For many years, I did have a scar. As I look back now, I get a little queasy thinking that grandpa may have blown his nose in that very handkerchief before wiping my eye with it. Yuk!

When I was five years old, I was tagging along after my brother Bob, and the neighbor girl, Georgiana Lois, who were walking in the pasture. Now I knew, that they liked each other and wanted to be alone, but I have always been nosy and my curiosity got the best of me, so I followed them. I fell and I broke my arm. Boy, did I cry!And were they upset! But they did take me back to our house. That meant a trip to the doctor to have a cast put on. I remember my brother asking mom, "Does she always have to be where I am?" But you realize, I was just a little girl! In fact a very nosy, inquisitive little girl!

That's part of the mischief part of my life that I can now remember, but I was a typical girl. I had many dolls, a little table and chairs, a cupboard, and an electric stove that really baked. These were all gifts from my Aunt Florence who lost her first husband and little girl. My parents were not rich, because they were paying for a farm.

Sometimes I think that I filled a void in my aunt's life after her dreadful loss of her two dearest ones due to Infantile Paralysis. She is the one who bought so many expensive things for us at Christmas.

I used to like to design hats as a five year old. I'd take a length of cardboard, tape it together and sew scraps of velvet around it, forming a pill box styled hat. If I do have to say so myself, they were pretty classy. I often played hat store and have always had a love for different styled hats. For many years hats were not fashionable, but now they seem to be coming back into style again.

Speaking of Christmas, my parents believed in the true sense of the meaning of Christmas. Oh, yes, we had gifts. We each got one present, mine usually was a doll. Under the tree was a huge basket filled with oranges. Next to it was a big bowl of popcorn balls, and boxes of chocolate fudge and divinity fudge which were made by my mother. The only time we ever had oranges was twice a year. St.Nicholas would leave oranges on the porch on St. Nicholas night, December 5, and at Christmas time.

It always amazed me how my mother did all the things she did without us ever knowing about it. Two days before Christmas, my dad would cut a pine tree out of the woods on our farm, fit it into the tree stand, and put it into the garage. Then on Christmas Eve, after dad and the boys came in from the barn after the evening milking and chores, they would all clean up, and together we would all go into the living room.

To my wonder and awe, there would be the Christmas tree all decorated, with the nativity set right underneath the tree, and the goodies and gifts there too. Now when in the world did mother do all that without my knowing when I was right in the house all the time! I don't know where I may have been in the house or what I may have been doing that she could pull such a fast one. Then we would open our gifts and all sing Christmas carols as my dad would play the accordion.

Many times a few days after Christmas, my doll would be gone away from under the Christmas tree. When I asked my mother where my doll was, mom would tell me that when little boys and girls were naughty, Santa comes back and takes the toys away until kids are good again. Year after year, I had my one gift taken away until I learned to behave again. It took years for me to catch on to this.

Another family custom was the manner in which our family observed the liturgical season of Lent. On the Sunday prior to Ash Wednesday, we all gathered together in the afternoon and Mom would explain the meaning of Lent, and we all had to decide how we could observe this season. Then we had to make a Lenten commitment as to what we planned to give up for the season.

After much pondering, we each were given a box. Undoubtedly, due to the fact that we never had many treats, our thoughts turned to giving up the eating of candy during that time. So, whenever we would get candy, we would put it away in that box. It's amazing how it all accumulated during the season, so on Easter, we had scads of candy. Consequently, our Easter baskets had mostly colored chicken eggs in it. I also remember so vividly that every year, each one of us had a chocolate cross in our baskets. My brothers and I always were so impressed that we had a cross made of chocolate rather than the usual chocolate bunny.

On Ash Wednesday we went to church as a family, to start the season out right. Every evening at home when the barn work was done and the men came into the house for the night, they would clean up and we would each kneel on the floor by a dining room chair to say the rosary. Mother would lead the rosary, and we would all answer the prayer responses. Later on when we were old enough, mom would have one of us lead the rosary.

As I sit here and contemplate on all the meaningful customs that my parents introduced to us and carried out throughout my early life, I wonder how did our society ever get so lax and corrupt, because I'm confident that most families of our era were adamant in their family customs also.

I guess this points out that when new ideas and concepts develop, much tradition is lost along with the ideals and morals, which can possibly account for some of the misgivings of society presently. To me this proves how progress can and does affect people's values and lives. I am most grateful that I had the bringing up that I did, my parents were very strict but that in itself helped me to become a better person. When I was five, I would go along with my mom when she took my brother Bob for violin lessons from Loretta Sherman in her home just up the street a little past Wheatland. There were about four or five boys all my brother's age that took violin lessons also, and they played together as an ensemble. Miss Sherman thought I had musical potential, so she started me out singing and she would accompany me on the piano. I sang solos at many of her musical recitals. It's amazing that I never became conceited by all the people telling mom how cute and precious I was. But I was just a plain little country girl, who was afforded many opportunities.

When I was six years old, I started taking piano lessons with Miss Sherman until she retired from giving lessons. A few years later, I started taking lessons from Miss Eunice Warren, who would come to our house weekly to give me training. I guess I wasn't all that hep on playing piano or to practice, but to please my mom, I did it.

Later in life, I thanked Mom over and over again for making me stick with it, because many opportunities were afforded to me, as well as personal enjoyment. But I sure did create a lot of static whenever I had to practice. I can also thank my two piano teachers who were always so patient and understanding and encouraged me to continue, both are deceased now, but I cherish the memories that I have for both of those talented ladies.

When I was about seven years old, I learned ballroom dancing at a dance hall in our neighborhood. At present, it is called Annie's Place, but back then it was called Fox River Winter Gardens. The place had several owners and while Harry Gordon owned it, a Kenosha County Recreation Board initiated a project in our immediate community for ballroom dancing. We had lots of fun and met so many other kids from the community whom we didn't go to school with. It's probably due to this training that I acquired such a love for dancing, because it has consumed a great part of my energy all throughout my life.

At this same hall, roller skating was also introduced through means of the same source as mentioned previously.

9

After Gordon sold the place of business my Uncle Frank bought the place, and specifically used the hall facilities for just the skating rink. Now our family had the advantage of skating whenever our parents would take us there.

But every weekend we went because my uncle served food, mainly chili and hot beef sandwiches. So mom would prepare the chili and roast beef for sandwiches in the afternoon, so we skated while mom was busy in the kitchen. Then when the rink would open up in the evening, we continued to skate. I was pretty good on skates, but my brother Bob was really good, as he could dance on skates, and do all the fancy stuff which really was graceful and fun to watch. I was happy to just be able occasionally to skate backwards, which for my age was quite a feat.

When I was ten years old, this same Recreation Board, offered the opportunity of learning to play a musical instrument, thus organizing a band. This was open to kids in Kenosha and the kids of the county. So I choose to play drum. My parents agreed, and I think perhaps that I was always bubbling over with energy and pep, they probably thought that I could burn up some of the excess via the drum. I really got to be pretty good at it, because I practiced a lot and I liked beating drums. My parents were very tolerant of the noise, but they also knew that I was sincere about playing this instrument.

I started to learn to play drum by beating out on a wooden block, which was the way that one could tell if that was really the instrument that was suitable for me. I had to learn how to hold the drum sticks, and how to read drum music which was very different from the piano music.

Actually drum music was easier to read because all it involved was the counting of the beats and to know explicitly the value of each beat.

My brother Bob and I were quite musically inclined because we were afforded a musical background. My younger brother was sickly with a heart condition so he couldn't have the opportunities that Bob and I had, but Ardell was a beautiful bass singer, and he sang in Barbershop Quartets. I have to credit him with his strong attributes, because we all loved him so dearly, and his deprivation was not by his choice, but by God's.

Soon after I had started taking lessons, my parents bought a snare drum for me, it was the most beautiful instrument and it was all mine. I was so happy! These individual lessons were offered to kids in the county and also for a few from the city of Kenosha. I am referring to the band director's daughter and some of her close friends from Kenosha. The band director was a middle aged man with snow white hair whose name was Mr. Duell, and he had the patience of a saint. Every Saturday, all the kids would get together for a whole day of band practice. Sometimes it was held at the Paddock Lake Pavilion, which is no longer in existence, and on rotating Saturdays, it was held at the Woodworth School, which for many years has not been operating as a school, but at present is an antique shop.

We would take our lunches along and had one hour off for eating and relaxing. Many times we'd take a stroll along the beach by the lake. Both places had a store within walking distance, so we always were allowed to buy goodies. We would arrive home about 4:00 P.M. after starting at 9:00 in the morning.

This band was not only a concert band but also a marching band. At that time, I only had a concert snare drum because one had to be at least 13 years old to be in the marching band, and I wasn't old enough, so I didn't get a street drum until I reached eighth grade. Then I had two drums, one for concert and the other for marching.

After a short while the band was ready to have uniforms. Now this is a hoot! You can never guess... this band was decked out in a Scottish Highland uniform which consisted of a kilt, which is a knee length tartan plaid skirt, a white shirt across which was draped a tartan plaid sash over one shoulder angled down the waist and hung gracefully as long as the skirt. This was accompanied with the little Scotch tartan plaid cap on the head, the little pouch worn at the waist, and all wore white knee socks. Under the kilt skirt everybody had to wear black bloomer tights. Can you believe that the guys actually wore these? But they did, and looked sharp in these uniforms.

I guess at age ten, I had some more opportunities. The Mangolds were close friends of our Lenz family, so their daughter, Helen, who was also an only girl was quite a bit older than me and was of dating age. She happened to date Marvin, who was as good looking as Helen was pretty. When they would go out on dates, many times they would take me along. Helen and I were very close even with the age span, but we were compatible in our likes and dislikes.

Many times they would take me along to the roller rink or to a movie with them. Then he would treat us to either a hamburger or an ice cream hot fudge sundae, which were both so popular in our days, after which they would drive me back to my house. I can't imagine anyone being so thoughtful of a kid, being me, at that time, to take me along on a date. It seems that ten had been a magical number in my early years of life due to the many favorable experiences that I had.

My Aunt Florence decided to marry a second time after the dreadful loss the first time around. My brother Bob was the best man and Georgiana was the bridesmaid. I, being quite tall at that time, was her flower girl. I was delighted to be a part of the wedding, but so disappointed that I couldn't have a long dress like Georgiana had. I had to wear a short dress, but it was very beautiful. Little girls always wanted to look older than they really were, and I fit so well into this category. No long dress at this time!

My Grandma Lenz was a petite woman who wore her hair in a bun at the top of her head. I recall so well how she would talk to her pet canaries and give them better care than some children of today. Grandma always had pet names for her birds, one of which was *Poop-i-kin.*

When I was very young, grandma always had a pet name for us grandchildren. Of all the names she could have selected, she called me *Poop-i-kin* . Yes, you read it correctly, that was my pet name from her. I must have fit in with her pet birds having her same pet name for me. Grandma always added a *kin* to anyone's names.

One thing that will always stick in my mind is the fact that mom always made a homemade angel food cake for each of our birthdays. As a child I never had a birthday party until later in life when I reached the age of twenty-nine, my mother had the only birthday party I ever had in my lifetime. Twenty-nine was my anniversary birthday as I was born on the 29th, so mom had a family party for me.

As I look back now at my early life, I can't help but think of how our present generations may have responded to the kind of life that I was accustomed to. By no means did we ever suffer for lack of anything. But all our activities were very wholesome, kept us busy and happy so we didn't look for anything outside that could cause us harm or deter our values. Gangs and drugs were unheard of . Our values were instilled in us by our parents and we had a good Christian upbringing.

House on the Lenz Farm

Mother Dorothy and Father Joseph in their youth

13

Big Brother Robert and Baby Arlene

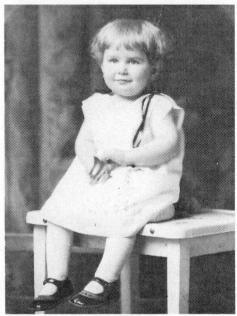

Little Miss Arlene

14

Chapter 2
Growing Up On A Farm

Farm life during my time was so much different then that of today. But the great out doors, fresh air, and freedom to be and move about still remain the same. Living in the country displayed God's goodness in the picturesque beauty of the earth in all its splendor. It was all right there before our eyes and we thoroughly appreciated and took advantage of what we had.

One of my memories of the farm was that I could go roaming around leisurely, singing, hopping, jumping, skipping, whatever struck my fancy. I was an over energetic child, so I treasured my freedom that farm life offered. Being brought up on a farm provided safety from ever being abducted and never to be bothered by any outside forces that could cause harm to us. I have always loved being there and I will treasure these special memories.

Being an only girl, anything that I did or said became momentous for my mother. She often told me in later life, how I always had expressed myself. Even back then I was very dramatic. One of these moments was when I was two years old and had been watching two of the chickens pecking at and jumping at each other. I ran into the house and called my mother to hurry to see these two little chickens. "Look, mother, they are so cute, they're jumping rope." Mom related this incident, of which to this day I really do not remember vividly, but years after it seemed to me that it somehow had been in the back of my mind at which time I could envision the whole thing.

There were many buildings on our farm, and in approaching the farm from Highway K, the driveway was very long and on a rather steep incline which curved when getting nearer to the main buildings.

Next to the house was the two-car garage. The barn was down an incline quite a distance from the house. Next to the barn was a tool shed, and across from the barn was the milk house where the tanks for cooling the milk were located. Right next to the milk house was the wind mill which pumped the water that went into this little building.

Off in another span of area was the granary where grain was stored. This building was built into a side of a hill which provided a lower level for storage of the machines needed to do farm work Near the granary was the corn crib and far behind that was the chicken house. Then continuing on was the huge apple orchard.

Behind the house was a wood shed which housed the wood for the wood burning stove in the kitchen as well as the larger chunks of wood for the wood burning furnace. Not far from that was a brick building called the smokehouse. It was there where the sausage was smoked after butchering and the making of sausage. Ham and bacon were also hung in this house to be smoked.

Last but not least was the "outhouse" that I described earlier. This is where one went to do a daily duty..... the necessity of life...... and it was located a considerable distance away from the house. I'm sure that whoever built it knew what they were doing when they located this little building. At times one needed to rush to get there.

In the barn was the area for milking the cows. This had two long alley-like rows where each cow was hooked up to a stanchion so as to be milked. Our barn had about thirty-five on each side. Between these rows was a strip about ten feet wide for walking and getting to the cows.

Behind the cows was a gutter in which the cows would relieve themselves at any time, and these gutters had to be cleaned out daily. This was probably one of the most repulsive jobs of farm work, but after a while your nose got used to smelling the odor. At the far end of the barn were two pens where the calves and young stock were housed.

At the extreme other end was the part of the barn for the horses. In these early years of farming, the horses were used to pull the farm equipment to do the field work. Many years later, my dad bought a tractor and sold the horses. One area of the horse barn was used for storing the food for the horses. This was usually in bags called gunny sacks made of burlap. The horse stalls were across from each other allowing a section for shoveling and scraping out the horse manure into the same yard as on the other end where the cow manure was scraped.

About once or twice a week during the winter months this was shoveled on to a wagon-type contraption called the manure spreader and then was taken and spread on the fields. This was the best fertilizer, and enhanced the growth of crops. During the warm months this was done daily or the job would become too enormous and too smelly.

The silo was adjacent to the cow barn, so this made it handy to throw down the silage for feeding the cows. It was a cylinder like structure protruding about sixty feet skyward that had an opening on the outside at the top where the shredded corn could be blown up by means of a shredder and blower until the silo was full. There was also an opening in the inside of the silo in the barn so the feed could be made available easily to distribute to the cows by the men.

I just referred to the horse barn, and this was located at the front end or entry to the barn. Just outside the huge double doors was an abandoned well pit about fifteen feet deep and about eight feet square. Dad always kept this covered with boards and this was to be our storm shelter in case of a tornado.

My Grandpa Lenz, after having retired from the farm who was now living in Burlington, used to drive out to the farm in his Model A Ford Coupe and wandered around the farm seeing what was going on in the different seasons, and occasionally helped my dad a little.

My grandpa was a very tall man with a broad build and liked to consume alcoholic beverages. Many times he would raid my dad's wine cellar, then meander around the farm. Well, this one particular day, my mother was outside cutting the grass on the lawn when she heard a muttered voice calling, "Dor..a, Dor..a, Dor..a, help me".

Mom looked all over and couldn't find where this mysterious voice was coming from. After searching and searching, she found grandpa down in this well pit. How he ever got there was always somewhat of a mystery. Mom couldn't help him out of there as he was twice her size, so she had to call my dad out of the field to help grandpa out. This really left an impression on me because I was very young and didn't understand what had really happened. Now I know that grandpa liked his alcohol and booze.

It was in the corn crib where my cousins, Ruth and Loraine Lenz, from the farm across the road, would spend many afternoons with Bob and me. One of our favorite past times was to play bakery.

Mother would save the lids off the mayonnaise and pickle jars, and we would make mud pies on these lids, and decorate the so-called pies and cakes with corn. When we had a supply of baked goods finished, we would play pretend buying and selling. We did this at a very young age, but this

17

proves that being brought up on a farm offered so many advantages that kids rarely were ever bored like kids of today.

Another interesting detail about our farm was that the railroad tracks of the Soo Line Railroad Company ran through the middle of the farm fields. They were located about a half mile west of the buildings. Being that it ran through the farm land, the cows had to be brought up to the barn from one of the pastures which meant crossing these railroad tracks. To avoid any accidents the railroad company installed a huge cement tunnel under the tracks for the cows to pass through.

Whenever we heard a train whistle in the distance, we would run as fast as we could to get inside this tunnel and let the train ride right over the top of us. We thought this was pretty cool. As each train car would pass over, there was the sound of hrump, hrump, hrump, hrump, and more hrumps. We would laugh so hard! My cousins, Ruth and Loraine, from the other farm would sometimes go running down to the tunnel with my brother Bob and me. We ran so fast that it's amazing that none of us ever fell and got hurt.

Then after this experience, we would still be so out of breath from running so fast, so on our way back we would stop at the side of a small hill where there was a spring. We would each take our turns, bend down and drink the cold fresh water from the spring right out of the ground. How refreshing to drink and to splash our faces with this cold water.

Being that the railroad ran through our farm, there were many stray men who would not work but would tramp along the tracks instead of walking down the highway. The railroad attracted them because in Wheatland was where the train cars were left as that was where they added or left odd extra cars for a journey. These extra cars provided a home or a place for these vagrants or hobos to stay so they would go to the neighboring farms, to beg for food to eat.

At my Uncle Bill's farm below the hill across the road, my Aunt Mayme would make a sandwich and my cousin, Ruth, who was preschool age, would take it out for the hobo to eat. Even the hobo was surprised that her parents would allow this little girl to give him his sandwich.

Whenever they would come to our house, mom always

made a sandwich for them, but I was too much of a fraidy cat to take it to them. They always had tattered, torn, filthy, dirty clothes on and were rarely shaven. They petrified me!

One day my dad had enough of these vagrants as the one who always came to our house was hobo Eskimo Pete. My dad told my mom that he would take the sandwich out to Pete. When he gave him the food and coffee, dad said to him, "Eskimo Pete, if you come and do a day's work around here, I'll invite you in to sit at our kitchen table and have a real meal". He replied, "Oh, yes, sir, yes, sir". But you know what? Eskimo Pete never returned again.

One of the benefits of having the tracks run through the farm was in the winter when we were 'snowed in' and my dad couldn't get down through the driveway to haul his milk to the milk factory located in Wheatland. So dad would put the milk on a farm wagon instead of the truck and would go through the fields to the railroad tracks and drive down the railroad tracks to Wheatland to get the milk there. This meant that he had to have the milk ready to go after the early train had gone through. This proves that where there is a will there is a way.

Our house was huge with three bedrooms downstairs, and three upstairs, with an extra room upstairs that was used for storage. On the main floor besides the bedrooms, were a big kitchen as well as a large pantry, a parlor which we now call the living room, a formal dining room, a laundry room that was later made into a bathroom, a back porch, a front porch. That's why there was so much dusting to be done in the house.

Some of the pastime on the farm was spent in listening to the radio. One could always find a radio in the dining room, in one of the upstairs bedrooms, and in the barn. The radio in the dining room was huge and my dad made a four-legged stool so one could sit right in front of the radio to listen.

One day this stool got me into trouble. It was that my grandpa smoked a pipe, and I thought that was pretty neat, so I stood on top of this stool and told my mom, "Look, mom, you have to be this big to smoke a pipe". And the words were no sooner out of my mouth when I had fallen and slit my lip open and had to have the doctor put four stitches in. Mom wasn't too happy about that little episode.

Getting back to the radio listening entertainment, some of the favorites in our house were the daily soaps: Guiding Light, Days of Our Lives, and Stella Dallas [whose theme song

19

was Memories]. Another favorite that aired on Sunday nights was Johnny Nesbitt's program called And So The Story Goes which were true happenings narrated with a musical background. Saturday nights included Lawrence Welk, Jimmy Dorsey's Band, Harry James' Band for good music listening.

Then there were the police/gangster dramas: Green Hornet, Jimmy Valentine, and Gangbusters. I wasn't allowed to listen to some of these because they had some crime and violence in.

There were very few kid programs on except some musical programs but I always enjoyed listening to the Fred Waring glee club and especially at Christmas time, the Christmas carols were sung so beautifully. I used to sing along with them every time I heard them.

Every Sunday, my brothers and I would hassle over who would get the comic strip section first. So that ended with taking turns who would get them first. Some of my favorite comics were: Bringing Up Father, Blondie and Dagwood, Flash Gordon, The Katzenjammer Kids, Tillie the Toiler, Mutt and Jeff, The Gumps and there was always a cartoon corner that I liked. My dad liked to keep the paper in tact so we couldn't pull the pages of the comic section apart, they had to stay together. Dad was very particular about this.

As for popular songs of my youth, there were names like: How Much Is That Doggie In The Window? or Mars-si-dotes [meaning Mares Eat Oats] - I'd say that was more corny than oatsy, wouldn't you? Another was Chat-a-noo-ga Choo Choo which actually was about a train. Others included: Bells of St. Mary's, To Each His Own, Moon River, I'll Be Seeing You, By The Light of The Silvery Moon, In The Shade of The Old Apple Tree, Beer Barrel Polka, Tennessee Waltz, and many others that I can't recall at present.

As for movies I always enjoyed Bing Crosby and Betty Grable in their musicals along with Fred Astair. But my favorite was Humphrey Bogart and Lauren Bacall in Casablanca. My truly favorite actor was Dennis Morgan in Desert Song. In later years I got to see Dennis Morgan and Irene Dunn at a theater in Burlington when they appeared there in person to promote a U.S. Savings Bond drive.

The telephone was a large box type that hung on the wall having a mouthpiece in which to speak and a cut-off cone shaped structure known as the receiver from which to hear the message. On the side of the phone was a crank with which you would so called ring to get whomever you wanted to speak to. We were on a party line which meant that there were about seven other people who had the same line. Each household had a different code for knowing that you had a call. The phone would ring in different sequences and our sequence was one long and two short rings. Our phone number was 8-W. Whenever anyone's phone would ring, everyone on the party line would hear and listen for the sequence, then you knew just who was getting the call.

If you so desired, you could take off the receiver and be real quiet and listen to someone else's conversation. Isn't that a hoot? In this way, I guess the housewives knew what was going on in the neighborhood. People referred to this listening as being a 'rubberneck'.

And speaking of gangsters; my father was engaged in a very illegal activity, allowing a still to run on his farm for bootlegging. My dad was paid well to allow this operation to function on his farm, so consequently dad got his farm paid for much sooner than he had anticipated. I was about four years old at the time, and I was so frightened every time the big shots would come into the house and pay mother to make sandwiches for them. They would be very happy to have fried egg sandwiches for which they paid my mother fifty cents a piece.

Then they would lay their big guns on the table which scared me to death, while they would eat. By the way, they would also pay mom a quarter for a homemade cookie . Back then a quarter or fifty cents was worth a lot and would buy a lot.

Then the head or leader of the gang was an Italian fellow with the dark eyes and dark hair, whose name was Jimmy. He thought I was the cutest little girl, and he always wanted me to sit on his lap and he'd say in his harsh gruff voice, "Arleena, give Jimmy a kussy", meaning a kiss. Being so frightened, I did it because I was deathly afraid of his gun that was laying on the table.

But the biggest scare of a lifetime was when the Feds would come, another group with guns. I can just recall the one night my dad had been tipped off that there would be a raid that night, so my Uncle Jack, who was the hired farm hand at the time was paid by the gang to be a lookout man and was to notify them at a minute's notice. He did his job well which

21

accounted for his nice cars and nice clothes.

He watched and helped the gang members break up the whole operation in short order. By the way, the pigs on our farm were fed well, as much of the molasses went to the hogs. The equipment was all buried under a straw stack, and when the feds came, they found nothing. There were many close calls like that. Many farmers in the area did the same thing my dad did, because times were rough for people and this was a way of paying off their farms sooner. The neighbors were also paid off by the gangsters just to keep their mouths shut.

My Grandpa Barbian also had a still on his farm, but poor grandpa got caught. The Feds took him to court and he lost the case. Everyone in our family was worried that grandpa would have to go to jail, but just before it was to be taken into appellate court, the gangsters came forth and bought off the judge, so grandpa was saved.

Some of this so-called moonshine was made into sort of a liqueur which was sweet and syrupy and was anise flavored. Well, whenever we kids had a stomach ache, mother would give us a sip of this drink called Kimmel. This was an old home remedy for kids' belly aches supposedly to settle their stomachs. We loved the taste of this stuff and so my brother Bob and I would fake more darn stomach aches just so we'd get another taste of this Kimmel. Perhaps our mother knew we were faking, but we'd complained so long so she'd give in to us and gave us a sip. It really warmed the tummy!

On our farm there was always a garden so we always had plenty of vegetables. Mom would can a hundred quarts of tomatoes each season, plus all the other vegetables that she canned. This would last the whole season until the next harvest.

Being that there were so many tomatoes grown, Mom would make catsup. I guess the two fascinating things were the putting of marbles in the bottom of the kettle so the catsup wouldn't burn while it was cooking; and the other was the bottling of catsup. After mom would sterilize the bottles, she'd fill them using a funnel so as not to waste any or burn herself, then she'd put the bottle under the capper and press down the cap. The capper would be used also in the bottling of home-made root beer.

During berry season, there was the awful job of picking the berries. On the farm we had black raspberries, red raspberries, and a variety of berries that were blue but not actual blueberries. In the heat of summer, one would have to wear long sleeved blouses when picking raspberries, because the branches had thorns that were very prickly. Then there were the strawberries. Mom would pick the small patch that was on the farm and in later years when there were freezers, she would go to a strawberry farm and pick berries. Kate Lois, a neighbor, would always go with us. One time I asked mom how much you had to pay for the berries that one would eat. She said you could eat as many as you wanted to at no cost. I decided that I would get my mom's money's worth, so I ate and ate and ate. Pretty soon I was so sick, I was vomiting so hard, I had to go to the car and wait for mom and Kate. I learned my lesson. I never went berry picking again. Needless to say, I didn't eat any strawberries for many years after that dreadful experience.

At one end of the huge garden plot was a big grape vineyard. This was where we had purple Concord grapes and green grapes. My dad used to make grape wine every year and then stored it in the basement wine cellar. There is where grandpa knew it was stored, and at the place where he indulged too much the day he fell in the abandoned well pit.

In the orchard many varieties of apples were grown: Snow apples, Greenings, Red and Green Delicious, and Jonathan apples. We also had one peach tree, one pear, and one cherry tree. Picking cherries was another story. Sometimes the birds got to them before my parents did.

One of the weekly jobs mom did was to make butter. Being that our farm was a dairy farm, there was always plenty of cream . Much was used for whipping cream on desserts, and much was used for the making of butter.

The butter churn was a monstrous looking thing made out of wood and looked like a big barrel that was slightly tipped to the side with a handle on the outside that was used for churning. The barrel would go round and round until the cream started to separate the butter chunks from the liquid. After the chunks were formed, she would remove them from the churn and put them into a big wooden bowl. With a very broad wooden like kind of spoon with a flat bottom, she would work out the rest of the milk that was left in the butter. The milk that was left in the churn was then called buttermilk and was used for drinking and/or baking. This buttermilk was excellent for use in making pancakes, donuts, biscuits, cakes, cookies, and even some desserts.

Then there was the butchering of animals for meat. One of the neighbors would always come and help, and so when the neighbor would butcher, my parents would help them. That was quite an undertaking. After a pig or a cow was butchered on the farm, the men would bring a quarter of an animal into the kitchen at a time, and the men would cut it and the ladies helped trim the meat. Nothing went to waste. After the meat was cut up, it was then canned.

In later years, after freezers came into being, then the meat was taken to a locker plant in Burlington, cut up there and put into a rented locker. Then each week, some one would go into the locker plant and bring the week's supply of meat home and put it into the freezer compartment of the refrigerator, or in a home freezer if one had one.

A couple points of interest in connection with butchering include the scraping of the animal's intestines with a table knife until they were very clean, then rinsed many times over. One had to be careful not to scrape holes in the casing or when stuffing for sausage the meat would ooze out. These were used for the casing on the outside of the sausage.

The liver was used in making liver sausage, and beef scraps were used in making summer sausage. The meat was ground, mixed with other ingredients, then put into a machine called a sausage stuffer. It was kind of like an overgrown crock pot with a funnel tube at one side near the bottom. Inside was a press and as one would turn the crank, the sausage would ooze out into the casing that was slipped over the funnel tube. If someone scraped a hole in the casing during the scraping, then when stuffing, the sausage would ooze out the side, and one had to start all over again. After the stuffing was done, then the ends of the sausage were tied with heavy string and they were hung out in the smokehouse if it was to be a smoked sausage, or if not, then they would be hung in the attic to dry.

The head of the pig was trimmed very closely and neatly, then cooked. When it was tender it was picked off the bones and made into Pon Haus. This is made with the meat, meat stock, white flour, buckwheat flour, water and spices. It is cooked until very thick. It is then put into bread pans and cooled and stored. To eat it, one slices it off into slices and

24

fries it until it gets golden brown. We all really liked this and this was an economical way to utilize all the parts of the pig.

The pig's hocks, the parts just above the toe area, were cleaned, cooked until tender, then pickled. I never acquired a taste for these, but the men in the family liked them.

The heart of the pig or the cow, was cleaned very well. Usually this was either sliced and fried, or it was cooked, then sliced, and pickled.

Another highlight of living on the farm was the harvesting of grain. The whole neighborhood of farmers who lived on Highway K, east of Highway W and west of Highway B, got together and did the threshing together. Mr. Brandes owned the threshing machine and went from farm to farm. Sometimes it would take a couple weeks depending on how the weather cooperated.

Now this meant that about fifteen men had to be fed at dinner time and if weather interfered and the season was running late, some families had to feed these men a supper also. Mom would prepare a twenty pound beef roast, potatoes and gravy, cole slaw, three kinds of vegetables, homemade bread, and two kinds of pies. These choices were necessary, because some of the men didn't always like the same thing.

Then there was the problem of having them wash up before eating. This situation was taken care of outside on the grassy lawn. The wash bench that held two wash tubs was put outside to hold them and two wash basins in which the men would wash. These tubs had to be filled with water, so that was the kids' job while my mother would prepare the food. Then we would have to pin big towels with clothespins to the clothesline for them to use for drying their hands and faces. I guess the worst of it all was cleaning up the whole mess after they were finished eating and went back to the fields.

I guess one of the memorable incidents of the past was due to Mom and Dad belonging to a card club, which included the families of Joe Lenz, Albert Vos, Phil Neuman, Gust Schulz, Joe Mangold, Fritz Getka, and the George Schulz family. They would all get together on a regular basis and play cards, and being that there were so many kids, you can imagine the fun we had being of all different ages. In the summer months they would all get together for outside picnics; some at the farms, some at different lakes and parks.

Living on a farm gave kids many opportunities that the now generation will never have the chance to experience.

Then there was the time when I was four years old, I thought I was really 'Big Stuff', so I pretended that I was driving the truck. I got into the truck which was on an incline, unknowingly pushed in the clutch, and I was rolling......faster, faster, and faster.....until I tried steering, but to no avail, so I steered the truck right into the windmill. Ooops!

I really didn't think too much about the whole situation, but was my dad upset! I'll never really know if this incident had anything to do with the procrastination of allowing me to drive later in life when I became of driving age or not.

But my dad never allowed me to drive until I was 18 years old, and had been in college for a year. I guess he had lost his faith in my ever driving.

As I grew older, the only farm work that I had to do was to still gather the wood for the wood burning furnace which was installed during my early teen years. I had to drive the tractor in the fields only when either of my brothers would take a vacation. Ardell had so many opportunities for many extended trips that were afforded him through being in 4-H Club. My brother Bob really wasn't gone that much, as he never was in 4-H.

Every time I had to drive the tractor, all I heard from my dad was, "Well, damn it, Arlene, don't cut the corners so damn short, you miss all the hay and the field stays a mess". I really was trying so hard, and a few times when he yelled at me, the tears would stream down my face, because I was trying to drive that darn tractor in the way that he expected me to. I didn't dare let him see that I was crying because I would have gotten yelled at more, for being so sensitive.

So after most of the corners, I had to stop and my dad had to get off the hay wagon and pitch the hay up with a fork onto the wagon. This was extra work and also took up a lot of time. I just wasn't meant for driving.

Many modern conveniences were installed in our house; plumbing facilitated inside, a bathroom was put in, also a hot water heater and a gas cook stove. This alleviated the boiler on the stove on Sunday evenings for the laundry the next day. It also eliminated the boiler on the stove for Saturday night baths, which we took by the kitchen stove in a wash tub, because now we had a real tub, a real stool and didn't have to go out to the 'outhouse' in the dead of winter. Things are beginning to change for the better.

As Georgiana , our neighbor girl [who we call Jan], was

26

old enough to get a driver's license, she took me along one Sunday afternoon and we went driving around. Well, lo and behold, didn't she hit a cow as a farmer was getting his cows in from pasture and crossing the road. If I remember correctly, we went straight home, promising that we'd never tell a soul.

And that we didn't until about 1992, when Jan and her sister-in-law and niece were here visiting and I let it slip. By now, we laughed and laughed and laughed. Then Jan went on to say how her dad inquired about a little dent in the car. But the ironic thing was, that she didn't seem to know anything about it. Even back then "Ignorance was bliss!" Note: I heard from Jan a few months ago, and she specifically asked me not to put this in my writings, because to this day, her own kids do not know about this. But I had to tell about it, as we had some good laughs over it together.

I can truly say that I am proud to have been raised on a farm, because this is something that no one can ever take away from me, those great memories. I realize that I have missed many other incidents of farm life but I'm lucky to have remembered what I did. I've always been a country girl, and to this day, I still consider myself a country girl.

Robert, Cousin Ruth, Arlene, Cousin Loraine
on Uncle Bill's farm in 1930

Arlene in later years on the farm

Chapter 3
My School Days

At age five, back in the year of 1931, I went into first grade at St. Alphonsus School. I loved school, especially the work. At that point in time, I knew that I wanted to be a teacher when I grew up. Because everything usually came quite easy to me, the nuns gave me many extra opportunities that other children were not as lucky to get. The eighth graders presented a play and needed a lead character, a little girl named Betty, and the nuns selected me for the part. I had many lines to learn. I loved the attention I was getting from the older kids. Wow! Now I thought I was really big stuff.

Being the little mischief that I was, you can probably guess that I was a high-flier. As much as the nuns really liked me, they were very determined to discipline me. And that they did! Their methods of discipline were very, shall we say crude. Whenever I would misbehave, I'd get wrapped on the knuckles with a ruler, or when the situation presented itself, the nun would pull my ears, so consequently to this day, I have big knuckles as well as I retained big ear lobes. As I think about that kind of treatment now, I realize how the gifted and talented programs of today are so vitally important to give kids, such as me, a challenge.

At that time, the seventh and eighth grades' classes were not as large as usual, so they started a program for ninth graders to continue their education at St. Alphonsus for an extra year. The only high schools in the area were Wilmot Union Free High located in Wilmot and St. Mary's High School located in Burlington. Many people could not afford to send their kids to St. Mary's because of the tuition and there was no transportation except to pool private rides in the neighborhood. This prevented higher learning for many kids, so they just stayed home or tried to find a job.

When the five girls graduated from ninth grade, each one picked a first grader to be her individual flower girl. Again I had an honor, I was selected to be one of the flower girls. I was flower girl for Bernetta Lohaus, who lived in New Munster right across from the school. My mom made me the most gorgeous dress for this occasion. It was of pink organdy fabric fashioned with a fitted bodice from which flowed layers and layers of ruffles. The bodice had puffy sleeves. I felt like a little queen in this dress.

My mother was the best seamstress in the country. All of my dresses that mother made were always so unique in style, because my mother was so creative, so through her creativity, she added the little feminine touches to a garment that one could never find in stores. My clothes always looked and in reality were very unique in design as well as exquisite. The nuns always remarked what beautiful clothes I wore, and so I think they thought that I was from a rich family, until mom told them that she designed and sewed all my clothes. Mom never used a pattern, she made her own patterns. As I look back now, it's a pity that mother didn't have the opportunity to become a designer. If given that opportunity, she wouldn't have had to work so hard helping with farm chores.

Riding to school was another experience. Sylvester Epping, the father of eleven kids, drove us to school each morning because he had the most kids. Then the other families whose last names were: May, Lohaus, Lois, and Lenz would change off getting the kids from school. We were packed in cars like sardines. No one ever wanted me to sit on their lap because I was so skinny and they said they could feel my bones.

And again, I got into trouble riding to school. One of the older boys smelled so bad of body odor because I think he never took a bath. My big mouth called him 'stinky' to his face and made quite an issue of it daily until he told his parents, and in turn, they came to see my parents.

Now I was in hot water, the hot water that he should have used to take a bath. After they left that evening, I got sent to bed without any supper and cried myself to sleep that night. I never called him stinky any more, I was cured of that! [But he still did smell, and everyone else knew it but was afraid to say anything.]

Speaking of the Epping family, Esther and I were very close friends. Every time Esther would ask me to spend a night at her house, I was delighted because they had so many kids and their mom, Leona, would just let us have more darn fun and never yelled at any of us. It was fun playing games because there were so many to play that we could play many different board and card games. Her two older sisters, Eleanor and Margie, were so kind and also so much fun. We also enjoyed running around their farm and playing outdoor games.

For a little girl, I surely did have a big mouth and my mouth got me into trouble when I was in second grade. The nuns used to sell penny candy at recess and noon time. I really liked it, the candy was little coconut squares with a glazed sugar coating. They were so good! I asked my mom for some pennies so I could buy some candy and my brother, Bob, told mom that candy was no darn good and it was so stale, that the nuns should be ashamed to sell it.

Who did you think picked up on that remark? You guessed it. Little Miss Arlene went right to school the next day and told the nun that her brother said that her candy was no good. So the nun approached him right in his classroom, and he was in eighth grade. How humiliating this incident must have been for him!

She asked him if he said that her candy was no good and that it was stale, and didn't he deny that he ever said it. So she called me into his classroom and asked him again, he denied it again, and I popped up and said, "Robert, you did too say that. You did so say that last night at the supper table". Bob turned every color of the rainbow, and if looks killed, I'd have been one dead little sister. So the nun made him eat a piece of candy right in front of everyone else.

When I got home that evening, I really got it. You can just guess, but I'll tell you one thing, I never told anything in school that was said at home again.

And then there were the lunches we ate at school. When I hear the kids complain today about school lunches, I think back of grape jam sandwiches every day, day in and day out. We had to bring our lunches along to school from home. We carried the lunch in a little bucket with a tight lid that Karo syrup had come in from the store. These buckets were washed up, and you had to have your name on it, because everyone at school had the same kind of carrier. My brothers' and my daily lunches consists of two grape jam sandwiches, an apple that was grown in the huge orchard on the farm, and a cookie that mother made.

In the fall, we were lucky to have a bunch of grapes that were grown in the vineyard on our farm. To this day, I hate Concord grapes, any kind of grape preservatives, any kind of grape flavored candy, or grape juice or grape soda. I had my fill of grapes as a child.

But we always had a big well balanced meal in the evening, plus our day was started off with an unbelievable daily breakfast which consisted of pancakes, sausage, apple sauce, fried potatoes, after a bowl of cereal, with plenty of farm milk to drink so we didn't suffer at all. No wonder I had all that energy in school to get into mischief.

Being that there were double grades in a classroom every other year one would be in the same classroom with the same group, except for those who would happen to move from the community, or if a child had to repeat a grade. This happened quite frequently. The nuns were good for making kids repeat a grade.

I really don't remember much as a third grader, perhaps I started to settle down by this time. But when I was in fourth grade, I remember of having many appendicitis attacks, consequently missing a lot of school.

We were having such severe snow storms that winter, and so Bob and I stayed up in Mew Munster with my Uncle Frank, who then owned the tavern where Marino's Restaurant is located. In this way we could walk to school, and my uncle would cook lunches for us, and we could leave school at lunch time and go his place to have a warm meal. We really liked that.

But as time went on my attacks of appendicitis were progressively getting worse, so my parents kept me home from school until I could have my appendix surgically removed.

In January of 1935, my Aunt Florence and I went to the hospital to have surgeries, my appendectomy and her hernia repaired. I was in the hospital for one full week after which time, I was confined to my home for an extended period of time. Back then, I feel that much unnecessary caution was taken, and actually too much time was allotted for recuperation. Prior to the surgery, I had missed much school, due to the dreadful appendix attacks.

Now I was out of school for one full quarter. How would I ever make up all that work? My parents went to see the nuns as to what to do about it, because mom and dad were sure that I would have to repeat my grade due to the extended absence from school. The nuns told them that if I passed all my exams at the end of school, I would pass on to fifth grade. And that I did!

When I was in the fifth grade, I had been diagnosed as suffering from rheumatism in my knees. I guess that was what one could expect when a child was as active as I was. It was also at this time that I had started wearing glasses as I had astigmatism in my eyes. I felt that at age nine everything was going bad for me, and I really looked like a dork in glasses. However, I was faithful about wearing the darn things, no matter how I looked. I realized myself that I needed them.

One of the most humorous incidents that happened while I was in sixth grade, was one day during art class. We were all painting so we needed water to wash out the brushes. Sister Mary Margaret was my teacher, who sent a fifth grader, Joe, down to the so-called kitchen to get a pail of water. When he returned, he politely asked, "Sister, what shall I do with this bucket of water?" Ask a stupid question, get a stupid answer.

Sister replied, "Pour it over your head". To the astonishment of everyone in the room, Joe poured the whole bucket of cold water over his head. We laughed until we almost cried, it was so funny! Absolutely hilarious! The distressing part of it all was, that we all had to help Joe clean it up. This lessened the humor immediately.

Sister Mary Margaret was the organist at our church. She also directed the children's choir, so every Friday afternoon, the girls would have choir practice and the boys would meet with the priest for servers' practice. One of the other sisters would help the priest by hearing the prayers of the servers. Remember at that time, the servers had to learn all the Mass prayers in Latin. This became very involved for the boys, as Latin pronunciation was very difficult, especially because they didn't know what half of the prayers meant.

Every Saturday, Sister had to go the Alverno Conservatory of Music in Milwaukee for organ lessons. Being that the nuns at that time did not drive, Mother and Mrs. Toelle would change off every other week to take her there. Due to this weekly job, the nun made arrangements for Mary Ann Toelle and me to take voice lessons while there. What a deal! Mary Ann and I really liked this, I don't know if it was the voice lessons or the fact that we both got out of doing chores at home every Saturday, and we also got to go shopping plus eat out. In those days, that was really a treat.

When I was in seventh and eighth grades, I guess that was the time when girls started having crushes on the boys. In our class, there were only four boys and eight girls. But it just so happened that four of us, including myself, rather put a monopoly on those four boys, not by their choice, but rather ours.

One of the boys, Don, later became a priest, and in later life, he reminded us how he and Gene would let themselves be talked into practicing for Christmas caroling around town by a couple of girls. Where did Mary Ann and I take them for prac-

33

tice? Down to the basement of the school where the coal bin was located. Yeah! Right! Little did one ever dream at that time that Don would ever become a priest. It was really quite innocent, just being with them was the extremity of our behavior.

Many times the students would gather round the foot-pumped organ in the classroom and I would play and they would sing. Classmate Bob would always round up everyone so we could sing our old standby which was 'The Bells of St. Mary's'. Thank God, we weren't from the Rock and Roll era! That may have turned out very disastrously.

This activity was done when the weather was inclement, and during the noon recess when all the nuns went across the playground to their house for lunch. Many times the students were left unsupervised, but they trusted us. Many times as older kids, we would go into the first and second grade room and play games with the little kids just to keep them quiet and safe, that they would stop running around in their classroom which was very dangerous.

Some of the recess games that were played included: Church Against School, Pom-Pom-Pull Away, Dodge Ball, Red Rover, Red Light-Green Light, Hide And Seek , Jump Rope, and many other games too numerous for me to remember.

We used to help the nuns with church work after school and on some Saturdays. The nuns would ask us to take servers' vestments home and have our mothers wash and iron them. We would also help clean out candle dispensers , and dust around the altar. To us, this was a special privilege, just to work around the altar in the sanctuary, and even in the sacristy.

As a graduating class, there were the twelve of us. Our teacher was Sister Marciana and the priest was Father Joseph Pierron. Graduation involved getting our diplomas at Mass, followed by picture taking at Warner Studio in Burlington. Then everyone had their individual family parties at their own respective homes.

A momentous memory that stayed with me was when the Kenosha merchants would come into the little towns in the county. They were known as the 'Boosters' and would drive in a caravan through the main street of New Munster. The nuns would allow us to line up along the street to catch the goods that these merchants would throw out for us to get. They gave away some neat stuff to advertise their products. Every year, on that day that they would come, we would all go home very delighted.

One of the memorables was the unsightly green curtains that divided the coal bin area and the kitchen area from the dining area in the school basement. Mass was said in the chapel during winter months in the school basement. All the scraping and shoving of kneelers and chairs was quite harsh to the ears. There was a humungous tree between the school and the church which presented many unforeseen accidents.

I have to express my feelings about my elementary school days at St. Alphonsus School. I have to admit that even though I was a high-flier and always didn't work beyond my capacity, which I should have, I have received the very best education that anyone could have ever gotten. To this day, I thank the Agnesian nuns for their patience with me, and the love that they gave to me as a student, and for the morals and values that they established within me. Many, I'm sure, of my teachers of the past are now deceased. I do remember them in my prayers. They were very dedicated women of their time.

In the fall of 1940, I started high school at what was known then as St. Mary's High [known now as Catholic Central High] in Burlington. What a change going into a school in which I had a different teacher for each class, and each class was held in a different room. I soon grew accustomed to the changing of classes. When the bell would ring, that meant the end of one class and hurry to the next class.

I was used to hearing a bell ring during elementary school days which occurred before and after the morning recess, before and after the noon recess, and at the close of the school day. Now I was hearing the bells every hour.

Another tremendous change was the time allotted during the school day for study or rather the study hall period. This was a place of quiet and if someone had any questions about an assignment, the study hall teacher in charge would try to help the students. This was one place where I would shut my mouth as I wanted to get my homework done so as not to take it home. I had better things to do there.

There was no bussing at that time, so I rode to school with a neighbor girl, who worked in Burlington. Each day I would have to wait for her at the Burlington Public Library which was located at that time across the street from the present library. This meant that I never would get home until 6:00 P.M. I did get much of my homework completed at the Burlington Public Library while waiting for Ruth. Her younger sister, Theresa, and another neighbor girl, Kathleen, would also do the same thing.

Many times while waiting in the library for our ride, I got into mischief as per usual. Some of my friends, knowing I was in the library, would come in to visit. We would go behind the book stacks and talk and giggle. This was an absolute no-no in a library, which at that time positively no whispering was permitted. Many times we got quite noisy and the librarian whose name was Eloise gave me many warnings to be quiet.

That lasted for a while, then we talked louder and louder and giggled louder and louder until dear Eloise had just enough of our foolishness and kicked us out of the library. My friends could go home, but I had to be in the library to wait for my ride, as in winter months it got pretty darn cold outside.

Then one day Eloise had enough and told me that I couldn't wait in the library anymore, and as brazen as I was, I said to her, "Well, I have to wait for my ride in here, so you can't kick me out for good". How that dear woman ever put up with me, I'll never know. Now I wish I could just make amends to her and apologize to her for all the trouble I caused her.

The next two years, Ruth's hours changed, Kathleen graduated from school, so Theresa and I lived in a private home in which we had one room to live in and sleep in. Our meals were taken in the evening at the Newell Boarding House where the present post office is located in Burlington. We didn't like this idea too much because Burlington High School and Elementary School teachers lived there and ate there also. I guess we felt inferior to them. We were both very quiet and shy, if you can believe that of me. I started to settle down by that time.

The Newells were a very English family and Edith prepared much lamb. She was a fantastic cook, but on our farms we were never accustomed to eating mutton. Theresa and I were both from dairy farms, and our parents raised beef and pork. Many nights when we knew that we would have leg o' lamb, we would skip going to the boarding house for that meal. Instead we would go the bakery and get a dozen of sweet rolls and each get a pint of ice cream. How unnutritious! But we enjoyed that kind of meal, kids are kids.

At noon time in high school, we had open campus as long as we would be back in time for the P.M. bell. Many students took advantage of this so-called freedom. One of the farm boys drove to school, so at noon a group of us would each pay Jim a nickel for gas and he would tool us around town.

He was not the most desirable kid as he was one who

neglected to take baths and he smelled, but he had a car and that was all we cared about. However, he bragged to all the other guys about how much the girls all liked him. Liked him???? No way, it was his car we liked, because that was the only means we had to get around. I look back now and think, how could we ever be such users!

As for friends in high school, I was still a close friend of Mary Ann from grade school and during my freshman and sophomore years we became a part of the conceited group including the rich kids from Burlington and the kids who were a clique from St. Mary's and St. Charles' grade schools.

After my second year of chumming around with this group, I realized that they were as flamboyant as could be. There were no real true friendships to be had in this clique, and I didn't like the way in which the other girls in our class were being treated. So I found real friendships in the other girls and a girl named Evelyn [whom was called Sue] and I remained close after graduation. Sometimes it takes a while to find out that people who have money abundantly lord it over someone who knows the value of friendship and the prudency of money-handling. That was a good lesson learned.

Being that there were two high schools in Burlington, I became friends with many of the girls from the public school. I got to know some of these through playing in the band, as both the high schools merged into one huge band.

Once a week all of us from St. Mary's had to go to B. H. S. for band practice which was on the other side of town. Many of us rode with Mary Ann's brother, Ray, and we were packed in his car like sardines, especially everyone having instruments, some of which were pretty large. Then Kathleen and I would walk to the library where we waited for our ride.

During the summer months, we had practice once a week at Cooper Elementary School on Conkey Street in Burlington, needless to say on the second floor with a double flight of stairs. It always seemed that my drum got heavier and heavier.

Speaking of band, everyone was always working so hard for first chair position in their instrument section, which meant that person was more deserving of and perhaps played a little better than the previous one in first chair. I played drum and had second chair, so I worked and worked to get first chair because I had a crush on the bass drummer, Jim, and I wanted to be next to him. He went to B. H. S., so I only saw him at practice. After some time passed Mary conceded, and let me have first chair position. I guess he was as thrilled as I was, because he told me that he had a crush on me also.

We became good friends, and many times he would invite me to his house after school and we'd play records. Occasionally we dated, but the extent of our relationship was our music and a frequent after school hot fudge sundae at Jackson's Drug Store where they served the best sundaes in town. In my senior year, Jim and I went to prom together. After graduation, we both went our separate ways as I went to college and he joined the working forces.

In my junior year as a student, I came to realize that there were many opportunities that I had missed in prior years. Sister Estelle, a Notre Dame sister, coached me in several dramatic renditions, and enrolled me in the Thespian Group. This was a real honor because you had to be pretty good in dramatics to even be considered to be a member of this group.

She saw potential in me and she brought out my talents with hard work and the desire to participate. I did many declamations in contests, and I made her as proud as I was myself. My favorite of all of them was the one titled, Antigone, because it was so very dramatic and I had the feeling of living the part.

Sister Estelle was also my Latin teacher for two years of Latin class. She was a beautiful woman and I always wondered how she ever escaped falling in love with some good looking guy and went off to become a nun. I am glad that she chose to be a sister teacher because I would never have had all those opportunities that I did otherwise.

She directed the spring plays and I came very close to getting the lead part as an Elizabethan Queen, but a girl named Vivian got it because she was a senior and I had a chance for another role when I became a senior. I did have to learn the whole part because I was her under study. This made me happy in spite of the fact that I didn't get to act in that play. To me this still was an honor. Practicing took up so much time, that I had to quit my job I had after school and on Saturdays.

Oh, yes, I had a job ! ! ! ! I worked in the Five and Dime Store on Pine Street in Burlington. My boss was far beyond his age to be operating a store and was so adamant about the help not taking any pieces of candy that was in a counter and sold in bulk. The other ladies and I used to laugh when one or the other of us would get caught snitching one tiny piece of candy. I think one could hear him yell all the way to the end of the block.

My wages were 21 cents per hour. It hardly paid for

my mom to bring me into Burlington, go back home, and come back later in the day to pick me up. I'm sure that the gas for the car took far more than the money I made, which was $1.05 for a five hour day on a Saturday. After school, I would get in one hour of work. I think back now, it seems to be a joke.

Being a Catholic high school, we had a Religious Sodality. It was an organized group in which we would promote prayer through various all-school activities. Every spring we would have a living rosary, which meant that the students were positioned into the form of the rosary, to the extent of even making up the cross. As each prayer on each rosary bead was said, the student would hold up a lighted candle so all people in the church could follow the rosary as the student body would lead the prayers. The lights in the church were dimmed so you can imagine how effective, and inspirational this was.

Then following the rosary there would be a May Crowning, which involved a girl dressed as a bride with two children attendants. One of them carried a fresh flower crown which this selected girl would place on the head of the statue of Mary. The other child would carry a rosary which was placed by the same girl over the folded hands of the Mary statue. I was selected for this honor two years in a row.

The officers of this sodality had the option to attend a national learning conference called, Summer School of Catholic Action. All of our officers including a classmate of mine named Rita went the summer of 1943 to represent our sodality. Our group was assigned to stay in the Morrison Hotel in Chicago. Rita, being from a small town, and my being a country girl, had never stayed in a plush hotel such as the Morrison before.

I guess neither of us even knew what a bell hop was. So the bell hop carried our luggage and escorted us to our room. Upon entering, he put down our luggage, opened the drapes, and told us to enjoy our stay in the hotel. Together we replied, "Thank you." He just stood there, and we were hoping that he would leave, but his reply was, "Thanks girls, I can't eat much on a thanks". We never knew what he meant until we got back to school and the nuns had to explain this to us that it was customary to tip for any services provided,that were not included in the hotel bill.

This conference lasted for five days, and it was wonderful. We got to interact with and share ideas with other kids from all over the nation. This in itself was a priceless learning experience. Then, of course, we got to meet so many nice kids from all over and some ended in lasting friendships. I had a crush on a fellow from Michigan, and he had a big crush on me. We corresponded for a couple of years. Later on Chuck came to see me at my home, but I was already in love with someone.

In my junior year of school, it was our year to sponsor the prom. Our theme was Little Miss Muffet, which sounds corny but it was really beautiful. In the center of the dance floor in the gymnasium, was a tree with a little girl [mannequin] dressed the part of Miss Muffet, and a huge spider in the grass. Around this was a little low white picket fence.

I went to the prom with Ed, who actually was a distant cousin of mine, but with his humor and my wit, we always enjoyed being together. This was not the case of a boy/girl date relationship as one would think, but we were good friends.

Most of the boys in my class were so stuffy and stuck up, that I didn't want to go with any of them. So Ed and I enjoyed the evening watching most of the snobs in their ploy to impress others with their snooty mannerisms. You can just imagine the fun we had watching them, as we danced, commenting with wit and humor over their show-off ways.

One teacher who stands out in my mind was Sister De-Padua, my junior homeroom teacher, who also was my Biology teacher. Well, the year started off really good and I highly respected her as she was pretty tough on the kids. I was doing a great job in her Biology class, including dissecting the little critters, until we had to do a project on Heredity.

I wanted to maintain my status in her class so I figured if I went all out and did a bang-up job on this project, I could pull an A+ in her class. I even went so far as to include pictures of some of my ancestry and how hereditary features could be accounted for. I turned in a superb project and when I got it back three weeks later I couldn't believe what I was reading on her comment sheet. You'll never guess what grade she gave me, a C-. I cried right out loud when I saw this grade.

Then after reading the comment she had written, I really wailed. It said, "It's too bad that you couldn't have done your own work and had to steal Robert's work that he did a few years back, it is a good project". I was upset because I remembered the project that Robert had done also, and he did a bare minimum just to pass her class.

I approached her and after much ado she did apologize, but also told me it was A quality work, but in redoing the grade she could only up it one letter grade, so I ended up with a

B in her class. I never liked her again and had as little to do with her from that time on, as I became bitter just because she accused me of cheating of which I was innocent.

In early May of 1944, graduation seemed to come closer and closer with more and more anticipation. During the last week of May was senior week which meant that on each day of that week, there was a particular activity. At graduation, being a solemn ceremony held in church, there could be no throwing of the mortarboards, but we were happy anyway.

Now all parted to go on to join the working force or on to college. I chose college because I knew I was going to become an elementary school teacher

As a closing thought of my high school days, I have always wondered why all the handsome men had to become priests ! During my days at St. Mary's, there were three young priests who respectively were: Father Niglis, Father Darneider, and Father Hanauska.

Then there was, as I referred to before, Monsignor Kersting, who was a little pudgy man who always reminded me of a character in the comic strips, 'The Little King'. He was a man in his middle age but a most knowledgeable clergyman. He was full of wit and humor, and we all loved him. God took him to his final rest at an early age.

All of these priests taught religion classes to the students and I am forever grateful for what I learned from each of them. I hope that God will especially bless each one of them for being such saints to put up with us in high school. I'll always have fond memories of them.

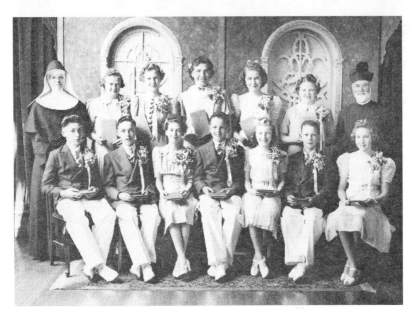

8th Grade Graduation St. Alphonsus School 1940
Back L-R: Sr. Marciana, Margaret Linneman,Theresa
Jochem, Agnes Lohaus, Arlene Lenz, Margaret Heiderman,
Rev. J. Pierron
Front L-R: Robert Vos, Donald Elverman, Anita Lois,
Kenneth Hunsbuscher, Mary Ann Toelle, Eugene Robers,
Esther Epping

Arlene - St. Mary's High School Prom 1943

Chapter 4
4-H Club Youth Organization

When I was eleven years old, I joined the youth organization - 4-H club. This is a club that is so prevalent today, that mostly everyone knows of or has had some affiliation with 4-H. Before explaining about all the learning, merits, opportunities, and character development that 4-H offers, it is important to know how this program ever came into existence, because 4-H goes back a very long time.

The 4-H movement began in United States during the early 1900's by a group of educators. The purpose at that time was to provide something outside of school for learning useful skills and was offered only to farm kids. Later, as these people saw the need, they opened the opportunities for learning these skills to the youth in rural areas, cities, and towns.

Membership was for young people from ten to twenty years of age with the objective of helping young people not only to learn useful skills, but how to serve their communities, and to have fun in developing their character to become productive, caring citizens of our community.

Land grant colleges such as the University of Wisconsin System along with the United States Agricultural Department sponsored the 4-H Club organization. In 1914 the Smith-Lever Act established Cooperative Extension Services which provided County Extension Agents who are responsible to 4-H Clubs on a county level. They were to assist the local clubs in any way a club needed their assistance.

During the 1920's the agricultural clubs throughout the United States adopted the 4-H emblem and the name 4-H Club. The emblem is a green four leaf clover with a white H on each leaf of the clover. The H's stand for head, heart, hands, and health. The motto of 4-H is: 'To Make The Best Better', and the slogan is: 'Learn To Do By Doing'. The 4-H pledge is: 'I pledge my head to clearer thinking, my heart to greater loyalty, my hands to larger service, and my health to better living for my home, my club, and my country'.

Local clubs were organized, and many parents served as general leaders of the local clubs. Sometimes someone from the area who had a special talent would volunteer to help lead a project. Leaders are strictly volunteers who enjoy working with kids and are willing to give of their time and talents. This is how all this wonderful training for young people got started.

My parents, not knowing that a club was in Wheatland area, had me join the Salem Livewires Club. A man by the name of Mr. Basinger was the general leader, and was a good one. But that club didn't have a sewing leader, and I wanted to learn how to sew. The project that I took was Foods and Nutritions which involved what the name implies, learning about the nutritional values of different kinds of foods. It also was a learning process in the planning of menus in order to include the daily food requirements, preparing of food, serving it attractively, and cleaning up the kitchen after all was done. I liked this project, but I still wanted to learn to sew.

Being that the Foods project started out by learning how to read a recipe and how to correctly measure the ingredients, it included doing simple baking. I wanted to learn more right off in the beginning so I did become a bit bored and the project meetings were few and far between.

My Grandma Barbian taught me how to read a recipe, measure and to bake cakes and cookies when I was six years old, so you can understand why this was not as much fun learning as I had anticipated it would be, so consequently I became bored with the whole project.

The general meetings were held in club members' homes, rotating from month to month. I didn't even know anyone as those kids went to Mound Center School, a one-room public school, and I went to a parochial school in New Munster. There weren't many girls in the club either. I was not very happy being a member in this club even though the games after the general meetings were fun and everyone was nice to me.

One of the boys in this club was especially considerate of my feelings and always looked out for me. His name was Arthur Besch, and I will never forget him as he was the one who made my presence feel welcome.

In the meantime it was brought to our attention that there was a club nearby that had an extremely talented, dedicated clothing leader, so the next year, at age 12, I joined the Wheatland Willing Workers 4-H Club. I knew some of the kids and this club held its meetings at the Wheatland Town Hall in New Munster.

In the Wheatland Club were kids from Wheatland, New Munster, Slades Corners, Powers Lake, High Street areas and an area southeast of Burlington. This was a large club so I met many new kids. Now I finally got to learn how to sew. Mrs. Schlax was a great clothing leader and a beautiful seamstress herself. By the way, the sewing project was known as clothing project.

After the first year in the Foods project, I also enrolled in Foods and Nutritions again, Food Preservation, Home Furnishings, Conservation, and Safety projects. I did very well in all these projects and won many blue ribbons at the Kenosha County Fair in Wilmot, and also the Wisconsin State Fair in West Allis. Year after year, everything about 4-H was getting better and better, and the opportunities afforded through being a member were endless.

Through the years, I participated in all county dress revues, and three times was chosen to represent our county at the state dress revues. By way of explanation, a dress revue was a showing of the clothes that a girl would sew for herself and then model it before a judge who would give a placing to win a prize. The prizes were a ribbon and money according to the placing one would get.

One year, after winning the county and state revues' placing, I was selected as an alternate for the national style show with a simple dress that I sewed. My mother who was very creative and also a good seamstress, helped me design my own dress. It was of green and white checked gingham and had a plain bodice with short set-in sleeves and a gathered skirt. At the neckline, sleeve hem, and skirt hem, were fifteen rows of white cross-stitch that were hand embroidered, forming a border and added to the beauty of the simplicity of the dress. At that time the little Dutch-styled soft hats were in style, so I made one which had the same cross-stitch design on as the dress. It was a complement to the whole attire. Many people including the judges commented on the originality of the outfit.

During my years as a member, the county agricultural agent, E.V. Ryall, would come out to our farm and he would take slides of me in the various outfits that I sewed. He also would take slides of some of the boys who had dairy animals. These he put together in a slide presentation for the county achievement awards night. This was the evening where many awards were given out.

A special recognition was awarded annually to the club that had 100% achievement for the year and was presented with a traveling trophy to be displayed in the club for a year. After a club got it for three consecutive years, the club automatically earned and owned it. Well, the Wheatland Willing Workers after a few years of one, two, then three consecutive wins finally won it for keeps in 1943.

Then the traveling trophy idea was disbanded, as too many clubs became frustrated with the whole deal because some thought a club had to work too hard to get everyone to achieve in their projects. Wheatland had a very thriving club and was always doing extra activities over and beyond what was required, and there were other clubs in the county that envied the Wheatland group.

At county achievement nights which occurred at the end of each club year in November, pins, for completing all your projects and filling out a record book for each project, were given out first. Then the special awards were given. These could include medals for doing outstanding work in a given project. I received the Clothing, Foods and Nutritions, Home Furnishings, Safety, Conservation, Dress Revue, and all-around club member awards several times.

I had so many medals, pins, ribbons,and even a silver tray that I had earned in my club work. But due to the fact that I had earned them, I really appreciated having them. Each time I'd wear or look at one it was a reminder that I had learned so much and had worked hard to achieve my goals and objectives.

Filling out a record book was very extensive and involved. One had to keep track of expenses for each project involved, and then had to estimate the market value of each item to see if one had a gain or a loss.

In the domestic arts projects, one always had a gain, but in the livestock projects, many times the boys had to show a loss. This would also happen if the crops did not yield as they should due to mainly bad weather or a less desirable growing season, and they had to purchase food for their animals. Invariably it would end up as a loss.

The purpose of record keeping was to be able to evaluate the project at the end of the year, and it also taught how to keep records in a bookkeeping system. This in itself was good training for young people. Many times there were about fifteen pages per project. Pictures to help describe your work in your project were recommended to help tell about you project, then one had to write a story about that year in club work and specifically tell what you had learned and tell all about club activities in which one participated.

Then these record books were sent to the county office to determine who was to receive recognition. A few books were sent on to the state to determine to whom the state awards were to be given for state recognition.

When I was fourteen years old, I could qualify to take Junior Leadership as a project, so I enrolled in that project. This was a project in which one could help the leaders of the club. I helped in the areas of fun and learning activities in planning, constructing, and supervising various club activities that were not projects. This project was set up to create an interest in leadership and preparing for adult leadership in the future.

In 1944, I was selected on a state level to attend National 4-H Club Congress in Chicago. The Wisconsin group represented by twenty-two counties of the state who were selected to attend, stayed at the Stevenson Hotel. [By the way, this time I knew that tipping was the customary thing to do.] Each state wore something to identify their state, so Wisconsin delegation wore red scarves.

This was a time of appreciation that all the hard work one did was now all the more worthwhile. We got royal treatment. We had three banquets a day. Can you imagine having a banquet for a breakfast meal? Well, we did. Many large corporations sponsored the meals, hired many world renown speakers and superb quality entertainments, paid for all the awards given, and picked up the hotel bills for the nation's one thousand young people and state leaders from each state who were in attendance. State leaders who attended from Wisconsin were Miss Agnes Hansen and Mr. Verne Varney. It was so neat having state leaders with us.

A gift from some company or other was given at every meal to each delegate. Some of these were books, cook books, fashion books, and youth novels for the girls, agriculture books and youth novels for the boys, and many gifts of jewelry. It was just an unbelievable experience of a lifetime! Thanks to 4-H that I had this trip made possible for me through my worthwhile efforts.

One year I was selected to model, demonstrate, sing in the state chorus, and judge at the Wisconsin State Fair. Because I was involved in so many activities at different times during the nine days of the fair, our county home agent, who was Irene Schulist at the time, made arrangements for me to stay at the youth dormitory at the fair.

Now this was something else! There were about six rows of cots with twenty five in a row in one huge room. You kept your luggage under the cot, and your nice clothes on hangers hung against one wall with hooks on. As I look back now, we were very trustworthy but no one ever took or messed up another girl's clothes, much of which were to be worn in a dress revue or were uniform clothes for band or chorus. The girls who stayed there were from all parts of Wisconsin. It always amazed me to find out how much one had in common with girls from different areas and different backgrounds.

As for food, we ate in a huge dining hall. The dishes were enamel coated metal compartment plates, cups with handles, and tarnished metal knives, forks, and spoons . As one entered the hall you picked up all your utensils for eating and formed a line along the serving tables, where the chef would put the food on your plate. There were no choices to be had, you just ate what was put on your plate and be happy that you got something to eat. None of the kids could afford to eat on the fairgrounds because even a simple hamburger there was expensive.

Next you would pick up your dessert, which was sometimes a cookie, or an apple, an orange, or a piece of dry cake. But it was food and we ate it and there were no seconds to be had either. We all survived.

I had to watch my times for chorus practice, as we would practice behind the Colosseum where there was no activity. When we performed we sang in Radio City Hall for the public. Our uniforms were white slacks, white shirts for guys and white blouses with a collar for girls. We all wore green ties and white socks and shoes. As a group we looked sharp and sang equally as well. That was a fun experience.

The judging contest involved knowing how to select proper wearing apparel. One had to judge four sets of items, having four articles in each set, and then one had to take notes, place the articles and tell why an article was good or not so good as wearing apparel for a girl your own age.

Shoes were the greatest item of importance for a girl in those days and a tie oxford with an arch support was best because of the added support given. A penny loafer would be the next choice, as it didn't give as much support as the tie shoe. Tennies would be the next because of their being a soft shoe even though they were tie shoes but not being leather, would be ranked third. Lastly would be a summer sandal which would be strictly taboo, due to no support. This was the way in which judging was done. The other items were under garments such as panties, slips, bras, and anklet socks.

After looking over these items, taking notes, then you

would have to talk to the judge and be rated on your answers and reasons verbally. This went on for two days, then you would get your ribbon and prize money in the mail after the fair was over. This was a good learning experience for girls in knowing how to purchase these items.

Another activity was demonstrating at the fair. This is not the kind of demonstrating that you are thinking of. This activity involved showing how to do something or how to make something and presenting it to the public. This went on in a large building called the Youth Center. Representatives here were from different organizations: 4-H Clubs, Boy Scouts, Girl Scouts, Future Farmers of America [FFA], and Future Home-makers of America [FHA]. All of these organizations had displays showing how to do something or for promoting their group.

My reason for being selected to be there was to show how to make soy bean muffins. During the war, flour was rationed out to families, and the Extension agents taught people how to supplement with another product and this, in many cases, was soy bean flour. This flour was made of the soy-beans, and farmers were encouraged to grow these on their farms, then the beans would be sent to a mill where they were ground and made into flour. This took the place of grain flour in many recipes and was very good.

My job at the fair was to promote this flour by making these muffins in the presence of the crowds of people and giving out samples. While I was preparing the batter and on through the baking process, I had to explain step by step what I was doing and also explain about the nutritional values of this product.

As for the other activity, Dress Revue, I have previously explained this activity. That particular year, I was selected to model my navy blue wool sailor dress that I sewed, and won a blue rating. Modeling the garment that I made was partly judged on the construction of the garment, how I walked, and how poised I was. This was all part of winning.

While at the state fair, we were responsible for being in the right place at the right time for the right activity and any other time when we were not involved in activities, we were free to do as we wished.

It seems that the scouts had their booth right next to our 4-H booth, and one of the boys named Frank and I got along really well. Whenever he had free time and I had free time, we would ride on the roller coaster and other rides together and see the other exhibits on the fairgrounds. We rode the roller coaster so much that the man running it told us that whenever there was no line waiting to ride and we were there, we could ride free. We took advantage of that and every evening when we were free, you can guess where one could find us. That's right, at the roller coaster. Staying at the fair was great!

During this year, I won the first Kenosha County Safety speaking contest, and was sent on to the state competition, where I also placed first. Then I was invited to give my speech at Radio Hall to be on a Milwaukee radio station. This brought back memories of the summer and seeing that Frank lived in Milwaukee, he came to Radio Hall to hear me and see me. That was the last I ever saw him, but he kept writing to me but I never answered him back, as I really was not interested in him. He was just okay to hang out with at the fair.

Just about every summer, I would go to camp at George Williams College Summer Camp Grounds in Williams Bay, Wisconsin. We would stay in either cabins or tents having six occupants in. There were no indoor facilities, so one had to go to the central facility to take showers, wash hair, brush teeth, and other necessities for personal grooming. This was the only part that I didn't care for, but one just had to learn to cope and then appreciate the comforts that were at home.

This was another learning and fun experience. There were separate meetings for club presidents, vice-presidents, secretaries, treasurers, reporters, and photographers. Then mock meetings were held so each person had a chance to role play their office. This was so helpful, and each member learned correct parliamentary procedure according to Roberts' Rules.

One of the state 4-H leaders, Wakelin McNeel, and assistant state leader, Verne Varney, were both at these camps. It was an honor and a pleasure meeting these people who were so dedicated to 4-H. It was rather ironic that Mr. McNeel's son was a medical doctor in Burlington at the clinic where we went for health services. In fact, Dr. McNeel did a major surgery for me in 1970. I guess this proves that people from all walks of life some how have much in common.

Back in 1943 there was no county fair, so the Wheatland Willing Workers had a round robin and went to everyone's house or farm to see projects of all the members. The girls enrolled in clothing had a clothes line exhibit in which all the garments that the girls made were hung on a clothesline for all to see. Then the girls modeled their other clothes in a mini dress revue. This was followed by a pot luck supper at the Toelle farm.

In 1946 I was chosen to be the first Kenosha County Dairy Queen. I have the privilege of reigning over many fair activities.

Following is the article that appeared in the Kenosha Evening News, dated Monday, August 12, 1946.

Arlene Lenz, 19
Chosen 'Dairy Queen' at Fair

Arlene Lenz, 19, pretty Wheatland 4-H Club member and daughter of Mr. and Mrs. Joseph Lenz. was selected as Kenosha County's Dairy Queen over a field of ten contestants Saturday afternoon at the county fair.

Miss Lenz was presented and crowned by County Board Chairman Peter J. Harris Saturday night at a special dance on the fairgrounds.

Included also in the ceremonies was the Dairy Queen's court of honor, Arlene Edquist, 17, Hillcrest 4-H club member and winner of second place; Esther Epping, 19, of Salem, winner of third place; and Marion Pringle, 17, of Bristol, winner of fourth place.

In State Contest

Judges for the queen contest were Mr. and Mrs. Lloyd Landgren, prominent dairy owners; Miss Marion Steinmetz, Kenosha Chamber of Commerce member, and Miss Isabel Wright, home agent from Janesville.

The queen will represent the county in state wide competition in the State Fair finals later this month. Winners in the county received cash prizes from local donators of $20, first place; $10. second place; and $5 for third and fourth places.

Fair officials reported that attendance at the fair was one of the largest in history. More than 10,000 persons visited the fair during three days. Good weather on all three days tended to counteract the polio epidemic and rain drought which has hampered the fair.

This, at the time, was the highlight of my life, and what a beautiful way to end my days as a Wheatland Willing Workers 4-H club member due to graduating from 4-H at this time, as I'd turn 20 years old in November. During my years as a member I learned many life skills, made many acquaintances, developed leadership skills, took on many responsibilities, and learned good citizenship through applying the ways and means of being a good citizen. Being in 4-H gave me the many opportunities that I otherwise would not have had.

4-H provided all these opportunities to help me to grow to become a better person because to this day in my tender age I strive to make the best even better.

I'd like to comment on the fact that my brother, Ardell, had equally as many opportunities as I did, and he, too, had many county, district, and state honors as being "first" to ever achieve in many areas of 4-H. Our family was truly a 4-H family in which we all got involved.

I was not about to stop here, I enjoyed being in 4-H and now my intent was to become a leader in the Wheatland Willing Workers 4-H Club.

Chapter 5
My College Days

As I have said before, I wanted to be a teacher ever since I was five years old. My mother was totally in favor of my getting an education, but my dad was dead set against it. His theory was that I would just get married and never teach school after completing my education.

At that time the best teachers came from the Rural Normal Schools, which were specifically teacher training colleges that had not only basic studies, but also methods courses that prepared one for the teaching of all subjects. That is where I wanted to go. It would only involve two years of training and I'd be ready to teach.

After much pleading on my mother's part, my dad finally gave in to the idea. So I enrolled in the Racine-Kenosha Rural Normal School for teacher training at Union Grove. Union Grove is only about ten to twelve miles from my home, so it was convenient being so close to home.

Now the next big decision was whether I would stay in the dorm or have someone drive me to and from school daily. You see my dad always felt that it was not important for girls to drive. This is a throw back of having boys in a family who could drive the farm tractor, with the only exception being if there were only girls in a family, then the girls would have to learn to drive. Due to the fact that I had two brothers, my dad wouldn't allow me to learn as he thought there was no purpose in the whole idea. Some times I wondered if it could have anything to do with my early childhood days when I tried driving the truck and hit the windmill. I'll never really know the reason why.

So my parents decided that I would stay at the dormitory as mom would take me there on Sunday nights and get me on every Friday after school to be home each weekend. Many weekends I was permitted to stay at the dorm when there were school functions or if we girls planned an activity. As girls who came from a distance had no other choice on many weekends, there were about four or five girls who would come home with me and spend the weekend at my home. My mother was always open to having our friends come and stay at our house. She always had enough food, room for sleeping, was the greatest hostess, and encouraged us to bring our friends home. And that we did!

This school, Racine-Kenosha Rural Normal School, was built in 1919 on the corner of Highway 45 and Highway 11 in Racine County.

The students' dormitory was completed in 1922. The principal of this teachers' institution was the renown Arthur J. Smith, a common name for an uncommon, intellectual, prestigious man. He was married and had three children of his own, of whom the middle child graduated from this college also. Mr. Smith, as we always addressed him, was a man ahead of his time, a mutation spurting from a long line of mediocrity.

His physical appearance deceived one to look at him, as he was not one to be judged like a book which is to say not to be fooled by the cover. He was of average height, rather slim, had a receding hair line emphasizing the silvery gray hair around the temples of his face, wore wire rimmed glasses perched on his nose, and was as spry as we teenagers were.

As a teacher, Mr. Smith encouraged discussion in an age when students were expected to sit still and listen. He understood perfectly that teaching was to encourage thinking and learning rather than to give out concrete facts. He never taught without thinking in units. The students learned that unless one saw the whole picture, there was little sense in learning little bits and pieces of this and that.

Consequently in every subject area, we had to prepare units for future teaching. So from him we learned that what's true in the classroom was also true in life, and this concept was exemplified through his own personal attributes.

He was one who could wither you in a glance, because he expected you to do your best and if you didn't live up to his expectations, you could sense the intensity of his displeasure. Somehow he could always find the good in all students and he had a way of bringing out the best in his students. Inside of him was the boy within the man, because when it was time for fun, he would engage in the student activities with the same intensity that we did. He could tell the most comical jokes with the straightest facial expression and after the punch line, he'd laugh as hard as we did. He enjoyed recreational activities as much as he did his teaching. He was the greatest man of all times, and I am very grateful for not only the privilege of having known him as a person, but also having had him as the best teacher in the world. His memory lives on in our hearts as we had a magnitude of respect for him as he did for us.

The school was small, the classes were small, and one

received an excellent education. Our curriculum consisted of psychology, methods courses, and every kind of sport. The methods courses were in the areas of Mathematics; Reading; Geography/History combination; Science; Language Arts which included Spelling, Phonics, Penmanship, Mechanics of Grammar, and Children's Literature; Art; Music; and Physical Education. These methods courses are just what the name implies, methods of learning how to effectively teach these subjects to children.

As for teachers, the principal of the school, Mr. A. J. Smith, taught Psychology, Science, and Geography/ History methods. Miss Sieverkropp taught Math, the Language Arts including Reading, Art, and Physical Education. Miss Carnahan taught Children's literature. Mrs. Beardsley taught Music methods. The Librarian was Miss Carnahan, and the school secretary was Mrs. Vyvyan.

We had first hand experiences with elementary school children, because in the college were two classrooms where children of school age living in the area would attend school. This was known as the model department, with the first three grades in one room and the remaining three grades in the other. Miss Roskilly taught the first, second and third grades. and Miss Buckley taught the fourth, fifth and sixth grades.

There were nineteen girls in my class. The first year one was enrolled there, you were considered a junior, and the second year a senior. Our classes went on all day long except for three hours out of a week when we had to observe in the model department, take notes and complete an observation report. On the other two remaining days, each one of us worked with a few students from the model department on a one-on-one basis. We kept the same students from this department for one quarter and then a different child was assigned to each one of us. After working individually with these pupils, each one of us had to compile another weekly report and give it to the classroom teacher in the model department, who graded us on these reports.

Every day was a full seven hour day of learning, studying, and doing the endless assignments, fortunately with a few study halls a week to do research in the library. There were many nights that we never even thought of going to bed. This became the usual procedure on the nights prior to another unit being due. One never turned any assignment or unit in late, as a due date meant just that, turning in the work on that day. Late work was not acceptable and we all knew it. I can see the merit in this ruling because we as students were being trained to expect the same from our students in the future when we would be the teachers.

The psychology course was quite difficult as we had to learn every theory that anyone had ever proposed, and the names of each psychologist and identify his theory of human behavior and how the brain functions. Even though it was very difficult, it was a most interesting subject and later in life I had put this knowledge to good use in my dealings with children. Thanks to A. J. Smith for his excellent teaching of this subject.

The history/geography course was a combination of the two, because what good would it do to just learn about the physical features of a region without knowing an account of what happened in the region and what the culture of the people living there was like. This is an example of the whole picture that A. J. firmly believed in.

Our science consisted of a combination of life science, natural science, physical science, earth science, and social sciences. Again one had to perceive the relationship of one to the other in a broader perspective. Most assignments were reading chapters from one day to the next, then making units of study on the various topics at the end of a book unit consisting of many chapters. Our study in the sciences was very intense and required many hours in the library. We were allowed to go to the library during some evenings, especially when another unit of work was due.

A unit of work included: objectives of the subject matter, behavioral objectives, materials needed, instructional procedures, predicted outcome, accompanying worksheets, tests, time frame for teaching the whole unit, an evaluation overall, a listing of resources for a student to use, and a bibliography of our own research.

Now you can understand the time involved in preparing these units. At times we wondered if it was worth all the effort, but as we got out into the teaching field we found that these prepared units were time savers when a teacher had so many subjects to prepare for.

It was at that time when I could realize that all the nights of working on a unit and never going to bed became all worth the while. Never before did I ever drink so much coffee and drink so much soda with caffeine in it just to keep awake to complete the last bits and pieces of the unit to be able to turn it in the next morning. Many times many of us went to morning classes looking frazzled, but our work was in by the deadline, and that was all that counted.

I have to tell you a bit about Miss Sieverkropp, who was an excellent teacher. She was in her thirties, not married, a very happy person, and most intelligible. She knew her subject matter and presented it to us in an expertise manner. Many times she would engage in various activities and outings with us and she knew how to have fun as well as we did. She felt that it was important to interact with the students socially as well as mentally. When it was time for fun she had fun right along with us, and when it was time to settle down and be earnest, she would do just that. This taught us that this would be the proper means to having good rapport with our students when we were teaching. She did have a boyfriend with whom she had been dating for quite some time, but it took many, many years before they ever married.

Another favorite person of mine was Mrs. Vyvyan, the school secretary. She had many tasks to perform: took our absence excuses, sorted our mail, run the school store, deliver messages, and do all the office work including the records and filing. She was a wonderful person and did her job well and was liked by all the students. She, too, was a former student at R. K. N. S. and taught school for ten years prior to becoming secretary at the school.

The school colors were royal blue and gold, and our emblem was 'The Wise Old Owl'. Often I heard that the class of 1921 adopted the owl as the emblem, which is very significant. Our first athletic letter to earn was the owl, and the second and last letter to earn was the big 'N'. There were no school jackets at that time, but rather a royal blue sweater on which to place the emblems.

OUR SCHOOL SONG
O, Normal School Days,
How dear to us you seem,
As we look backward
Just like a happy dream,
Here friends are gathered
In days that used to be,
In happy fellowship
Where comrades all agree.
Chorus:
The past needs no regretting,

But we're not forgetting
Our dear Normal School.
Nothing could be nearer
Than that Normal School
Which gave us our schooling,
Taught us how to rule in
Our own little school.
That's why you are hearing
Graduates are cheering
Their own Normal School.

The other favorite song that we always sang at school activities or school functions was the non other than the old fashioned favorite:'School Days'.

We also had a school newspaper called 'The Owlet' which was published by rotation of the students monthly. Sometimes it was very newsy and sometimes it would tell about who met whom of the young men in Union Grove. The word spread so fast. Even then the news media was idle gossip.

Our schooling consisted of earning one hundred twenty eight academic credits in two years without any summer school courses. Most colleges at that time required that amount of credits for teachers in a four-year span. So this gives you an idea of the work involved and the short time span. But the sad part of it all was that when we went to transfer credits at a state university, we lost over half of these credits, and had to transfer many years later when the state laws became strict and we needed to hold a degree from a university in order to retain our license.

We had all kinds of sports at R.K.N.S. because you need to keep in mind that we had to teach our own physical education when we went out to teach. We learned the skills and teaching methods in tennis, volleyball, baseball, basketball, archery, bowling, and skills of touch football. We also learned all safety rules of play on the playground equipment. Along with these skills of teaching went the skills of coaching, refereeing, and serving as an umpire at baseball, a referee in other sports. I was probably the best at being an umpire.

I became over zealous one day in archery. My aim somehow or other was always off in any direction except where I was aiming. One afternoon after school hours, I was practicing as our instructor had requested us to do on our own time, and so I did. Well, I took aim, pulled back the string on the bow and let that arrow fly. Guess where my arrow went that time. Right through a school window and pierced a huge hole right in the middle of the Biology flip charts in the biology lab. I immediately went into school and into the lab to check out the nature of the damage. Oh, Lordie, was I in trouble now! This set of charts was about twenty pages of heavy stock cardboard and it pierced all the way through. Dollars and cent signs danced through my mind, as I had no idea of how I would ever replace this. Many thoughts were abounding in my mind as to how I'd explain this to A.J. Smith. Should I just shut my mouth and act as though I knew nothing of how these charts got damaged? Or should I own up to it and shed a few tears of my sad feelings? I pondered these thoughts all night long.

The next morning I had decided what I would do. So I went to biology class with guilt expressed all over my face, and when A.J. asked what happened to the charts, I felt like the world had closed in on me and that all eyes were affixed on me. Slowly I raised my hand, and he called on me. I responded in a low toned whisper, "I did it". His reply was, "I'll see you in my office right after class". Oh, dear God, if I ever needed help from you, I need an abundance of it right now.

After class I went into his office back in his private room and he said to me. "Miss Lenz, please have a seat". Gosh, am I in for it now, I just hope that I don't get expelled from school. I sat down and he sat at his conference table and asked me how it happened. I very truthfully told him how I was practicing archery and with the poor aim that I had, I misjudged and the arrow was far from the target. Then I expressed how sorry I was that I had done this, but I felt that he really understood.

Then he said to me, "Miss Lenz, you are a very good student and you have all the potential to be one of the best of teachers and I realize that accidents do happen. I commend you for your honesty and we'll go on as if this had never happened. The charts will be still be usable and I never have to explain to any future classes why they are damaged."

He held out his hand to shake hands with me, and I almost wanted to kiss him, but it was not the proper thing to do. With the biggest sigh of relief I answered, " Thank you, Mr. Smith, for being so understanding. I wish more people in the world were like you, you're the greatest". At this time I meant every word I said and he knew it.

"You may go back to your work, Miss Lenz". He never even thought of reprimanding me due to my honesty, but this is really the way I was brought up by my parents. I was taught to always tell the truth, no matter how bad it sounds because there is always a solution to every problem. At that point I was happy that I chose to do the right thing, because the night before I had debated in my own mind as to what I would do, but honesty paid off.

Outside the office around the corner, were my closest friends waiting to hear what he had to say. I just told them he accepted the incident as an accident. I wasn't about to divulge the compliment that he had just given me. But after that incident, my respect for him grew even greater than before.

For physical education, we bowled every Monday or Tuesday night, whichever fit best into our schedule. The bowling alley was down town in Union Grove. We had the option to set up pins for each other, and we were paid ten cents a line. This reduced the cost of bowling for us. Besides it was fun if you knew enough to stay out of the line of fire when the pins flew. This was another experience for each of us.

Whenever we had a chance and the weather permitted after school hours, we would jog around the country block which was exactly one mile. We needed this form of exercise as we sat a lot in classes and doing our work and assignments. Sometimes after an exhausting day, it was quite fatiguing just to run the mile, but I guess we had a lot of stamina and endurance. After all, we were to become teachers!

Now I want to tell you about the dormitory. It was a huge building right next to the college. The name of the dorm was Storms Hall. It had two floors with the individual rooms in, and a basement in which were the cafeteria and kitchen, and down another hall was the laundry room for the students to use.

On the second level was one wing set aside for just the teachers of the school with the exception of A. J. Smith who lived in his home with his family about a block away from school. I believe there was a motive to have the faculty far from we students, because at times we got pretty noisy with our giggling and our shenanigans that we were involved in.

When we worked, we worked hard, when we played, we played hard, and when we were mischievous, we held nothing back.

On the main floor was a small wing of rooms for students, and a huge lounge for students to meet dates, or have parents or who ever came to visit. No one except parents were ever allowed in the student rooms. On the other side of the lounge was the living area for the matron of the dorm who was a middle aged heavy set woman whose name was Miss Richter. She was very kind, however she didn't know too much about girls our age, because we got away with a lot that she never realized. She had a strange religious belief and if anyone ever got sick, she would not allow a doctor to even enter Storms Hall.

Many times when someone was sick, we would call the local doctor, Dr. S., who lived across the street and a few doors down from the dorm. We would call him while someone would divert Miss Richter's attention, and then we'd tell him to come up the fire escape and someone would let him in. He was very obliging as some of us took turns baby sitting for his children.

One night we had to call him about ten o'clock, because one girl had too much pressure from the school work, and started to knock her head against the walls. Several of us tried to calm her down but there was no reasoning with her as she just kept knocking her head against the walls harder and harder. Her roommate couldn't even settle her down.

Dr. S. came by means of the fire escape and sedated her so she finally fell asleep. The next day we talked to A. J. and told him what had happened so he talked to her, and when she had expressed that all the hard assignments were getting to her, he suggested that she leave because she apparently wasn't meant to be a teacher. She was very relieved at this decision, so she left. To this day, the matron never knew why this girl left the school.

I used to get down the faculty wing, because I would set Miss Sieverkropp's hair. Then when her hair was dry, I could go back and comb it out for her. It really was a privilege to be able to be in that wing. They had a bathroom for each of their rooms. We had one bathroom with several stools, wash basins, and shower stalls. It was the only facility for students on each floor.

At times, one had to wait for quite a while to get in to take a shower. But we all somehow managed and everyone was very congenial and there were never any arguments.

If any students went home during the week, one had to have a legitimate excuse. I think my uncle died many times over and over, but Miss Richter never caught on. Either she didn't catch on or she thought that I had dozens of uncles, but she never stopped to even think about it. I felt that if she was gullible enough to think this, then I'd keep trying. After all, this was not done in any malicious intent, I just wanted to go home at times.

Curfew was at 8:00 o'clock to be in the dorm, and at 10:00 everyone had to be in their own room. Many times it was possible to get permission to come in late, but that was not to exceed 11:00 o'clock. There were times when there was a lot of sneaking in by coming up the fire escape, and you always made arrangements ahead of time with one of the other girls to let you in. We pulled so many tricks on the matron and she never caught on.

I was on the second floor and Sue Martin was my room-mate. We had gone to high school together so we knew each other very well. We had the biggest room of all and it was facing the main highway with two sets of windows rather than one set like all the other rooms had. We each had our own bed, our own dresser, our own desk and lamp on the desk, and one small sink. The closet we shared, but it was large enough for all our clothes. Sue's mom and her selected the drapes for our room. They were an allover floral print and were heavy enough to keep the sun out and also hindered anyone from looking in at night, being by the main highway.

Many people in town would call the dorm and Miss Richter would allow us to go baby sitting. I used to sit for the Hauper's children as Mr. Hauper was the local druggist and owned the drug store down town. He and his wife were quite the socialites so they went out often and paid very well. Many times I also baby sat for the doctor and his wife, as they also went out often. But the druggist and his wife paid better than the doctor, so I went there whenever they needed a sitter.

Miss Richter was a very good cook, but at times she had meals that were not appealing to our age group. Her specialty was chocolate cake with fluffy cooked frosting, it was so yum-my. She served well balanced meals in an attractive way. There were always flowers or some other centerpiece on each table. There were four place settings at each table. Few of the girls worked in the kitchen and helped serve meals to work off some of their room and board.

Our matron was a very dedicated woman, and tried to make special days eventful for us. The one that impressed me most was the pre-Christmas and Christmas season. All the girls would get together and put up the huge tree and all the other decorations in the lounge. Miss Richter would make cookies and hot chocolate for us. Everyone looked forward to this evening as we had so much fun.

Then on the twelfth night after Christmas, we would all get together, take down the decorations and we'd all have the opportunity to burn a branch of the tree in the fireplace at which time she told us to make a wish. I always wondered what all the other girls were wishing because each one was so intent. Then what was left of the tree was taken outside in back and the janitor, Jim Hembrook, would take care of the rest of it. Another holiday custom that she adopted was at Halloween time. She would set up a treasure hunt for us, some of which involved going to the local cemetery about a block from school on Highway 45 and a committee would sit out there dressed up as witches and ghosts to scare the girls as they entered. Sue and I always thought of this custom as ludicrous as we felt that this showed disrespect to those buried there. Later the matron would have apple cider and donuts for us.

All school functions were fun and wholesome activities. What seems to stand out in my mind are the school dances. Many of the girls' boyfriends were in service at that time, so soldiers serving as military police from the nearby army camp where they held prisoners of war in the area of Sturdevant, were invited to dances in the college gymnasium. It was a way of entertaining service men and then we had someone to dance with. Many times the sailors from the Great Lakes Naval Base in Waukegan were invited to dances. We girls were smart enough to just dance with them, but never get involved with any of them.

Spring prom was an eventful evening. The girls all wore long dresses as at that time the long styled dresses were in style. We would do each others' hair in fancy styles and I had long hair so the girls always did mine in an up sweep hairdo and I wore a fancy head band in my hair.

The first year when I was a junior, my boy friend was in the U. S. army, so not having a date, I played in the swing band that played for our prom. A few fellows from Bristol had gotten a band together and wanted me as the drummer, and we played around the area on weekends. A few times, they would have one of the fellows fill in for me and for one of the other guys from the band and we'd dance a few dances together. It was fun being in this band and we were known as 'The Jitterbugs'.

As a senior the next year, my boyfriend, Phil, was home on leave and so I felt like I was in heaven because I had my own fellow to dance with and I could show him off to the girls. He and I were very compatible and both liked a bit of mischief, so you'll never guess what we did!

Yes, we spiked the punch with vodka, and the funniest of all was that Miss Richter, A. J. Smith and his wife, including all the teachers raved about how good the punch was at this dance. Miss Richter was the one who always made the punch for the events. She had stated, "I made the punch like I always do, it's the same recipe". All of us were laughing up and down our sleeves. We pulled that one off very smoothly, but if I was ever caught, I have no idea what the consequences would be, as we were all underage for drinking. The legal drinking age was twenty-one, and we were all eighteen and nineteen. That was a most enjoyable night, and all the girls agreed to this fact.

Many times we would entertain the Military Police from Sturdevant in parties in the dormitory lounge, which were all planned and put on by Miss Richter. She would have organized games all ready for us and would always make our favorite cake and her famous punch [No spiking done at these parties though, it was too risky].

One night one of the soldiers said that he had the ability to hypnotize people if someone would be a willing subject. No one wanted to volunteer and his feelings were just crushed as I think he wanted to show off his talents. So guess who volunteered! You're right, it was Arlene.

But before hand I had asked a couple of the girls to look out for me and not to allow him to do anything that would be regretful to me later. So they promised they would and I trusted them as we got to be very close to each other and always looked out for each other.

He started by telling me to fully relax, which at times was difficult for me as I was a perfectionist and a high strung person. I tried to relax and as he went on to tell me to fully concentrate it wasn't long and I was under. I don't remember much of what went on, but the girls told me that he asked me to wave, stand up, walk, dance, and a few other simple movements and I responded well.

After a while, he had said to me, "When I count to three, I want you to wake up." I heard the three, and I was back in existence. It was quite an experience. He did not, however, ask me to say anything which was probably most fortunate for me. You never know what I might have told him, including the thought of telling him off.

Back at the dorm, my roommate Ev and I got into our

share of mischief also. We were fooling around one night and we had this thing about a couple of girls who always wanted to hang around in our room after hours. So Sue and I rigged up a bucket of water and attached it to the door of our room so that when it was opened, whoever was outside would really get it. We had moved one of our desks right inside the door and Sue got up on top of the desk. I was handing her the rope to attach and didn't she fall backward right into the closet. I shuddered as I just knew she was hurt badly. But even if we were employed in mischief, God was good to us, but poor Sue had a sore back for a long time.

Nearing the close of our senior year, Sue had become close friends with Shirley and Marge on the first floor, so she moved down on that floor. Now I had this big room all to myself. In the meantime I had become close to Ethel and Ellen on the second floor, so this move really didn't disturb me at all.

In preparation for teaching, we students had to go to schools in our home area and do practice teaching. This involved one week of observing our host teacher, and then he/she would assign the classes we would teach for the next two weeks. We had to have our lesson plans approved by the host teacher and then a college supervisor would come twice during this teaching period and observe our teaching. After the observation on the part of the supervisor, which was Miss Sieverkropp for the first time and A. J. the second time, they would sit right there and tell us how we did.

But you'll never know the anxiety of waiting until the end of the quarter to find out our grade. This is where our unit teaching was put to work, and we were glad that we knew how to construct units.

In my first practice teaching, I was assigned to the Twin Lakes State Graded School called Cottage School. My host teacher for the lower four grades was Erna Tandrup and for the upper four grades was Myrtle Hauerwas. They were great girls to work under, and being products of R.K.N.S., they really knew what they were doing. I learned so much from them, as they both possessed the ability of how to interact with the children. During inclement weather all the children who weren't playing card games, would gather around the piano in Myrt's room and she'd play and all would sing with her. The children highly respected these two teachers.

The second time for my practice teaching was in Somers at a one-room rural school called Burr Oak School. Here my host teacher was Florence O'Neal, who had been teaching for a long time, but she was an excellent teacher and the children learned from her. It was a joy working for her and I learned much from her also.

My third time out for practice teaching was in another one room rural school in the Randall School District called Randale Rural School. My host teacher there was Lester Grevenow, who in my estimation was of top notch quality. He knew how to maintain a classroom, interact with the students, play on the playground with them, and was a strict disciplinarian. The kids just loved him.

I always felt that A. J. Smith sent me there with a motive in mind; that perhaps this was the school for me for my first teaching job, as he knew that Mr. Grevenow was looking for a job in the city of Kenosha which was closer to his home and that would cut down on miles of commuting. It just so happens that I later did sign a contract for teaching there. So A. J.'s perception was so correct.

The one thing that I didn't like about all the country schools was the fact that there was no indoor plumbing, so that meant that one had to carry in buckets of water from the well for drinking, and had to go to the outhouse to relieve oneself. But this was common in the schools, as very few had indoor plumbing at this time. But remember if you really wanted to be a teacher, all these things didn't matter or interfere with your profession.

I know that I forgotten many interesting happenings affiliated with my days at R.K.N.S., but you can bet that I was a leader and an instigator of much of the mischief that went on at that school. I enjoyed my days there even with all the hard work that I did, because by now I was confident that I had chosen the right career and I was sure that I was meant to be a teacher.

R.K.N.S College Graduation - 1946

R.K.N.S. College Prom

Chapter 6
Searching For My True Love

So many times in a relationship, I would think that might be the real thing, only to find out that it was mere infatuation. So I asked my mom one day, "Mom, how will you know when you have found your true love?" My mom so graciously replied, "All I can say is that when you find genuine true love, you will know it, there's something very special about it and your heart will let you know". Knowing that my mother never lied to me I believed her and later found out how right she was.

Dating in my day was customary to go out twice a week, which was on Wednesday night and on Saturday night, known as date nights or one might do something on a Sunday afternoon and into early evening, but never be out late on Sunday nights unless there was a special occasion. The next day was school, or if one was out of school, it was work the next day.

My parents never allowed me to date until I was fifteen going on sixteen years old, while some other girls in our community were dating earlier than that. So this meant that it was almost the end of my sophomore year in high school.

During the course of my dating, I started out by dating some of the country farm boys in our area. How wholesome they were, but somehow not one of them ever struck my fancy.

In high school, most of my dating was attending school games, school dances, or other school functions with guys who were my classmates. A lot of this was more group dating than on an individual basis, so there were guys and girls and no one was with anyone in particular. This was fun because you got to know what many of them were like outside of the school classrooms. It's probably rude to say, but many who were so utterly brilliant in classes were so utterly stupid socially.

During my dating years, it was customary to get both parents' permission to go out on a date. How exasperating when a fellow would call me on the phone asking for a date, and I would have to ask him to hold while I got permission to go. This involved asking mother, who in turn would tell me to ask my dad who was usually in the barn in the evening.

So I would have to run to the barn and ask my dad if I could go [after describing the guy and telling dad all about him and where he lived,etc.] He would say to me, "What did mother say?" I had to tell him that mom said to ask him. So he'd reply, "If it's O.K. with your mom, it's O.K. with me."

Back to the house to tell mom what dad had said, and can you guess what her reply was? "If it's O.K. with your dad, it will be O.K. with me, but be sure that it is alright with your dad". Now another trip back to the barn to confirm that it truly was alright to go.

By this time I really didn't care if I got to go or not. During all this time, remember the person on the other end was waiting at the phone for a simple 'yes' or 'no'. All I can say is that even during those times, patience was a virtue.

Another stopping block during my dating was my older brother, Bob. If he knew the person I was inquiring about to date, he would always put his two cents in. Many times, he told my parents that particular person was not good enough for me. Can you imagine his thinking?

I guess being the only girl in our family, he became over protective and choosy as to whom his sister would date. At times, I felt like 'where in the world did I ever get so special because I'm just an ordinary country girl'. As I look back now, I believe that I misinterpreted the whole thing as he was just looking out for my well being. He was always very proud of me and my 4-H accomplishments, as I'd always be his 'little sister'.

I had many girl friends who lived in the Brighton area. Almost every Saturday night there would be a dance at one of the local dance halls. My best friend, Eleanor, would invite me to stay over at her house, and we'd go to the dances. By the way, Eleanor and I liked to sing together, she sang the melody and I'd harmonize. Actually we were pretty darn good [no bragging intended].

Back in those days it was customary for guys to ask girls if he could take a girl home after the dance. I guess in a way this was sort of like dating, at least one got to know lots of guys. This usually consisted of stopping off for a hamburger or an ice cream sundae. At that time pizza was unheard of. Many times this would lead to later dating.

There were also many dances at the Fox River Gardens right in my neighborhood. Then Eleanor would stay over at my house. Many times she and I would go home with other girls and guys as a group. Part of this group included another close friend, Kathleen. She lived with an old maid aunt who obviously never had children so she was always on the defensive as to where Kathleen was.

I remember one night, after a dance at the Gardens, we all went for hamburgers and then just drove around here and there

70

and it got to be pretty late. So Kathleen's Aunt Kate called my mother out of bed in the wee hours of the morning and insisted that my mother go with her looking for us. Mom assured her that we were both reliable girls who knew how to take care of ourselves and she didn't have anything to worry about, we would be alright. Too bad her Aunt Kate didn't trust her as my mom had trusted me.

But you probably can guess what that Aunt Kate did. Yep! She went out alone looking for us. Did she find us? No! By the time she got home, Kathleen was already in bed sleeping. We often laughed about that incident. Even my mom thought of it as a joke.

As for dancing, the jitterbug was the style of dancing during my younger life. It consisted of very fast steps, sometimes double steps, swinging out from your partner, doing a dip, and always at the end of a song, a very deep dip. It was a fun style of dancing. The music was either so fast or so slow.

Dancing slow gave one the chance to get nearer to your partner, in fact, very close. So when slow music was played, and someone asked me to dance, I was very picky as I didn't want to get so close to just anybody, so I'd just make up an excuse if I decided not to dance with that particular person.

And then there were times when I would sit and hope that a certain guy would ask me to dance. Luckily it worked out in my favor most of the time.

As you well know, that every dance hall either had a bar in the dance hall or right next door. Being in my late teens, I did the sociable thing at a dance, had a few drinks, but not to the point of getting plastered. The drinking age at that time was 21 years of age, but bartenders never checked an I D. There weren't any kids at a dance who ever got drunk though.

We always drank Sloe Gin and 7-Up. What a sickening sweet drink this was, but it looked pretty as it was a deep, dark red, almost a burgundy color. It was the most mild alcoholic beverage and I'm surprised that we never got sick from the stuff being so sweet.

The nice part of it all was that it was customary for the guys to pay for the drinks for themselves and the girls. In this way, we girls never needed to have money. Good thing, because my twenty-one cents an hour at the Five and Dime Store would never had bought much.

This group dating was the most fun, and that way one had the opportunity to find out what everyone was like. Some of the boys I liked better than others, but I didn't love any one of them.

At 4-H major functions, I met many young men who were outstanding in personality and looks, so I dated some of them for a time, but none were the Mr. Right. A country magazine called "The Prairie Farmer" did a news article on me being a 4-H Club member which included a picture of me in one of the dresses I had sewn in my clothing project. I received much fan mail from young men all over the country.

One that I answered became my pen pal from Logansport, Indiana. He came to see me a few times. Lloyd was spontaneously in love with me, but I could not share the same feelings for him. He was just okay in my estimation and I wanted no part of him in my life, so I dumped him. I disliked this guy so I told him to stay home and never to come to see me again.

But time after time, he would come to my house and wanted to see me, but my dear mother told him that I had no desire to ever see him again. Still he tried coming one more time and my dad told him to get lost. That finally was the end of it.

During my last year of high school I dated one of the kids from school. He was fun to be with and we did many things together still after high school graduation. When he wanted to become serious, I stopped going with him.

Being that our college classes were ninety-nine percent girls, there were no guys in class who I wanted to date. Soon after I enrolled in R.K.N.S., I met this really nice young man who ran a business in Union Grove. He asked me for dates often, so finally I went out with him. We dated for about the first month of college. He was handsome, classic, and spent a lot of time with me, also took me to many nice places. We went dancing many times as he was the greatest dancer and I feel that this was what attracted me to him.

Often times he wanted to become serious in our relationship. This became frightening to me as I knew that he was not my 'Mr. Right'. So I was cautious that I didn't spend too much time with him after that even though I enjoyed his company and he was a wholesome young gentleman.

It was late September of 1945, when my dear girl friend, Helen Mangold, whom I spoke of earlier, decided to get married to Marvin. She asked me to be a bridesmaid in her wedding, and I was thrilled at her request, and told her that I'd be honored to be in her wedding.

As with every wedding, there is always a rehearsal at the

church the night before the wedding. We were all to meet at the Mangold farm and go to the church together. This included the maid of honor, the three bridesmaids, the best man, and the ushers. She only had a male partner for the maid of honor and the bridesmaids walked alone.

On the night of the rehearsal, as we walked into the Mangold home, I saw a young man there whom I immediately became exceedingly interested in. He was the most handsome young man that I had ever laid eyes on. My heart was all aflutter, and I couldn't wait to meet him. Somehow or other I had the feeling that he felt the same about me.

Finally someone introduced us to each other. My gosh, it was Marv's younger brother, and I never knew that Marv had another brother except Ralph. After practice I went home again with my parents. I dreamed all night about Marv's younger brother, Phil. Would he ask me to dance at the wedding dance the next night, or was I just so hopeful that he might?

Well, the next morning was Marv and Helen's wedding, and all the girls met at the Mangold farm to put on our gowns and get ready for the wedding ceremony. I didn't see Phil until we got to church, which was a little country church in Lyons Township called St. Killian's Catholic Church. He was an usher.

Now this was in the days when everyone had to fast the night before, from midnight on, prior to receiving Holy Communion during the Mass the next day. I have always had a queasy stomach and was so hungry. During the ceremony, didn't I faint dead away at the altar!

Now the good part starts, who carried me out of church? Phil's dad and Phil. Honestly I really did not faint on purpose as I had no control over that. I was totally out, so they found a little brown jug in which was holy water in the vestibule of the church and they gave this to me to drink. When I finally came to, I thought I had died and went to heaven, there holding me was Phil. He and his dad both asked me how I was, and all I could think of was 'just heavenly to be in the arms of this young man', but I just answered with a reply "I'm fine now, thank you". This could not have been any more awesome than the way it turned out.

All through the breakfast at the Mangold farm, I kept staring at him from across the table. About the time that I got enough nerve to talk to him, Mrs. Mangold took him away to drive her to the bakery to pick up the wedding cake, and all I could think of was, "Kate, how can you do this to me?"

Next came the pictures at the Photography Studio. Even there I didn't get a break, the photographer didn't even have me stand next to Phil,

The dinner was at a restaurant in Delavan and again I didn't get near him as Kate had him running more errands with her after dinner. The rest of us all went back to the farm for the afternoon reception. It was almost supper time when we finally got to talk a little. But all afternoon we had been exchanging glances, and wouldn't you know that we never even got to stand next to each other for any pictures that were taken?

Later that evening everyone went to the Fox River Gardens Dance Hall for the dance. With a pounding heart, I gaped at him that evening in anticipation that he'd ask me to dance. At last he did ask me to dance and that we did the rest of the night. The song, 'It Had To Be You' became our song that very night, and had been ever since.

Then he asked me if he could take me home. By this time my heart was just melting away, my dream had come true. So he took me home. It was here where I finally got to know him a little better. But I'll tell you right now, it was love at first sight on my part, but now I wondered if he felt the same way about me.

I hate to admit this but we really made a night out of it. At last I felt as though I had met my 'Mr. Right'. Somehow or other we just couldn't or rather didn't want to part. He was so gentle, caressed so warmly and kissed so tenderly. He asked me if he could see me again, and said he'd give me a call. But all good things must come to an end, and at 4:00 A.M. in the morning I finally strolled into my house. Now my mother was waiting !!!!!

"And where have you been, young lady?" my mom inquired. I told her that we had both fallen asleep, which was the truth. Because she had always trusted me, she politely told me to go to bed, and I did. Did I sleep? Not really, my thoughts of him would not cease, I knew that I was in love with him, my true love I had found at last. My heart told me so.

When he arrived at his house in Burlington, the milk man was delivering milk. His real mother was deceased, and his step mother was so engrossed in her own kids, that she never said a word to Phil because she never gave a hoot for him anyway. His dad didn't say anything either because he trusted Phil.

From that night on, we dated quite steadily, and soon he was inducted into the army. This was a most sad thing for both of us, because we'd be parted for a long time. I was in my first year in teacher's college, stayed at the dorm, and wanted to say goodbye to him on the night when he left Burlington, but didn't know how I could manage this. Being that I thought about it all that day, I wasn't thinking too much about my classes, but just hoped that I'd find a way to get to Burlington. At supper that evening, the brain storm hit me. One of the girls from Lake Geneva had her car at the dorm for commuting back and forth on the weekends. Her name was Nancy, and so I asked her to take me to Burlington so I could see my love.

She really gave me a lot of static, because her boy friend was already in service, and I noted a tinge of jealousy. Finally I offered her five dollars to take me After a long discussion, Nancy finally agreed to take me there. Now the whole world started to look a little better, but he was still going to be gone for a long time.

So after the last kiss goodbye and a tender hug, Phil boarded the train and they were gone in a flash. Now when would I see him again? As soon as they got settled he sent me his address, so I'd write to him.

Now all this while, I still was not real sure how he felt about me, although I somehow knew that he really liked me, but I wanted it to be deeper than that. I would just have to wait and see.

I waited and waited and waited and I still heard nothing from him. Every day in the mail, I'd look and look in my mail box at school and no letter from Phil. Then on weekends when I was home, I would dash down our long drive way to the mail box at the end of the road and look into the mail box. Still no letter from Phil.

I became intensely sad and I began to think this must all be a one-sided love affair. I knew in my heart that I really loved him deeply and I was sure that he was my 'Mr. Right', the one person whom I wished to marry and spend the rest of my life with.

But my doubts prompted me to think, was this just an infatuation on his part? Did he have another girl friend? Did he find someone else in the meantime? Did he really love me? How would I ever know? So I did not plan to just sit around and become stagnant, even though I knew that I loved him.

So I started dating the fellow from Union Grove once again, just for the sake of going places only a night here and there. I knew that I did not want to have this relationship get

75

out of hand, as I had no intent to become serious with him.

Now I began to feel how a one-sided relationship could be and how it was, because I felt that what I was doing to the young man from the Grove could be what Phil was doing to me. Never the less, I would have to go on. As a matter of fact, I was guilty of using this young man, but he didn't seem to mind, as I know he knew it too.

Then one day when the mail came in at school, there were two letters for me from Phil. I was almost afraid to open them, for fear that it was a Dear John type of letter, telling me that it was all off between us.

Hurriedly I ripped open the letter while reading it as fast as I could. I was on cloud nine, everything he had written sounded like I might still have a chance with him.

I went to the library and quickly wrote a letter back to him and told him how happy I was that I finally got a letter from him. I was so cautious as to what I wrote back to him, because I wanted him to make the next move, as I didn't want him to think that I was chasing after him. I wanted to play the game in a cool fashion, but in my heart I knew all along that he was the one for me.

When he came home for furloughs, he would call me and we'd go out. He was my date for one of the college proms as I had explained earlier about spiking the punch.

One night when we dated, Phil had borrowed his dad's almost brand new Studebaker and this was not a common practice for Phil's dad to ever let his kids even drive his car, so we could never figure out how he ever allowed Phil to take it for the night.

So we were tooling along the road, when Phil said to me, "I wonder how fast this car can go, should we find out?" Well, of course, this would be great fun to open that Studebaker up and check out the speed. He kept his foot on the exhiliator and we were progressively going faster, faster, and faster, until the speedometer hit 100 miles per hour. Wow! This was great, I'm sure that after that, there was no carbon left in that engine. Of course, you need to know that the reading of 100 was as high as the speedometer could register on that car.

The next step was for him to go overseas to Italy. Again this meant that there would be another lull before I could possibly get a letter from him, so I was back to the waiting again.

In the meantime, I met up with a girl from the community, whose parents played cards with a card club that my parents belonged to and she came to my house with her parents one night when they all got together for their usual card playing, We were in my bedroom talking, and she noticed a picture of Phil on the mirror of my dressing table.

Her name was Betty. She told me that she had dated Phil and that he was writing to her also and she had the same picture that I had. Now I was mad, not just angry but absolutely mad! Oh, how I hated her guts from that moment on! I wanted to tell her to get out of our house, but I kept my feelings to myself and started to interrogate her.

She was so oblivious that she told me anything I wanted to know. It happened that he had dated her all the while he was dating me, and I never knew about it. She lived in Burlington, and it was more convenient to see her than me, due to my living in the dorm and having a curfew time. [Little did he know that I would have sneaked out and back into the dorm through means of the fire escape at anytime, because there were plenty of my friends to cover for me]. But you see, Phil didn't know all the mischief that I had gotten into during my life in the past, and how daring I was.

Now I definitely had doubts in my mind about him, but I wasn't going to stop here, because I knew that he was the love of my life, and I was confident that he would see it the same way as I did in due time. How did I know, maybe he did feel the same way about me, but he was quite shy and might not have had the courage to tell me yet.

My only worry now was that he'd fall in love with an Italian girl, as those girls could be quite persuasive at the service canteens where the soldiers could go for recreation. I never doubted for one minute about his being involved with one or several of those girls, as he was far from home and at the young age that he was, and I'm sure there were plenty of times that he felt homesick, but I had hoped that he would not forget me..

Then he got the shocking news that I had been stricken with the worst of worst, Poliomyelitis disease. What really ticked me off, was that his step mother had to write to him and make a big deal out of it. She tried to persuade him that he should drop me and continue to see Betty. His step mother's name was Liz, and she was a 'bitch'. She always had in her mind that Phil should some time in the future marry Betty.

After several months had passed, Phil came home on a lengthy furlough shortly after Christmas, soon to be discharged from the army, and he came right to see me. By this time I was

77

walking on my own power from the Polio without any aids. Now we dated many times, and I felt as though he had the same tender feelings for me that I had for him.

In January, I was invited to be a special guest at the March of Dimes auction. This was a non profit organization which raised money for research on Polio. It was an annual event, that always took place in January, and was held at Liggett's Royal Palm Night Club at Browns Lake. It was a night of dancing, and later in the evening was the auction. The local bakery in Burlington baked a huge decorated cake and slices of cake were auctioned off to the highest bidders. Some slices went for hundreds of dollars. Phil went as my date.

Before the announcement that the auction would begin, I was introduced as their special guest and they told my story of how I had been victimized by that awful disease. Then they announced that I would be dancing out on the dance floor. The orchestra played a very slow song, 'It Had To Be You', and Phil and I danced [if you can call it that] with no one else on the dance floor. He held me so close and so secure. The dance was very short as actually he was holding me up and I merely was moving my feet, but everyone applauded and applauded and I thought they would never stop cheering.

It was at that very moment that I knew more than ever before that I needed him and wanted him. He was my Prince Charming. To this day, I believe that this was the turning point in his life also, because the way he treated me was so special.

Later I had a job at a country school, so many Sunday afternoons Phil would help me put up bulletin boards, straighten out books and my office, and any other jobs that I had for him to do for me. Many times we'd find ourselves getting more involved in love making than the school tasks. Now I realized how compatible we were.

One day as we were driving home from working at the school, I was sitting close to him. He had his one arm around me while driving with the other, he made a comment to me. Included in the comment were the words... 'When we get married'..., and I knew this was not a proposal, but I knew exactly where I stood from that moment on.

I had found the love of my life, my Prince Charming, my Mr. Right. He was everything I ever wanted in a man and now he would be all mine.

The following November, was my twenty-first birthday on the 29th of the month. He showered me with gifts, and the final present was his proposal along with the most beautiful diamond engagement ring. We were both so excited that we couldn't even think beyond that momentarily, so we put our wedding plans on hold for that day. We both knew that we had now pledged our love for each other. We were so much in love and through the years that has never once changed.

As a young girl, I played the field, dated many young men, but my mom told me that my heart would tell me when the right young man would come along. Now I knew mother was so very right, my heart told me that Phil was my real and genuine love.

Phil in the U.S. Army

Phil in 4469 Quartermaster Trucking Co.

Phil, My Mr. Right - The Love Of My Life

Chapter 7
Contracting A Dreadful Disease

It was the day after the Kenosha County Fair had closed, the article of my being crowned queen of the fair had been published in the Kenosha Evening News paper and I was delighted but I didn't feel well at all. I thought all the excitement had worn me out, so I rested all day Monday and the next day, Tuesday.

On the third day, Wednesday, August 14, as evening approached, I retired early. My head felt like it was about to split with such pain, as I never before in my life had a headache as I had now. Mother gave me aspirin and a cold compress for my head and told me to try to get to sleep as she felt that I was exhausted from all the activity and excitement of the fair. So I did, mom always knew what was best when someone was hurting.

As the night went on, the pain started to not only grow worse, but it traveled into my neck and back. My pain was excruciating and I was at a loss as to how to cope with all this pain. I woke my parents and mom told me to take more aspirin and try to get some sleep, as they would take me to the doctor in the morning. I endured that awful night but as to how I'll never know. I just kept thinking that in a few hours I'd see a doctor and he could and would do something for me to alleviate this awful pain.

I've never been a morning person, but on this particular day I surely was happy to see daybreak because for me it meant that perhaps soon I'd get relief. Mom took me to the doctor at 8:30 and we waited for his office to open, and he saw me immediately. He examined me and walked off to the side of the room and shook his head. As he turned toward us, he said to mom and me, "I can't determine what it is, but go home and rest and take these pain relievers". Looking directly at mother, he said that if I was not better in a day or two to come back and see him. So we went back home and I was still hurting. I think he suspected what could have been wrong, but I think he still had hopes that it was not what he had thought it might be.

I went to bed when we got home and the pain pills helped me to get some sleep as I was exhausted from being up all night.

The next day, Thursday, I felt a little rested, however the pain still continued. But mom thought it was better if I stayed in bed and rested more. I did. In the meantime, my brother,

Ardell, who also wasn't feeling well, complained of a headache so mom gave him aspirin also. After one day of resting, he felt a little better, but I was still hurting as now my arms and legs started to ache so badly. All I could think of was what was left to hurt, my everything on my entire body was aching. This went on again all through that night.

On Friday morning, I got out of bed to go to the bathroom when I fell in a heap and could not get up by myself. My older brother carried me to the bathroom and then back to bed. Mom called the doctor and he came right to our house. All I had was pain in my limbs, but at this time, I could not move my legs. I still could move my arms, and I couldn't imagine what was happening to me. By now I could no longer even bend my back, I had started to become incapacitated, and I was frightened.

Doctor Bennett ordered a spinal tap and said he would come back after office hours and do this procedure. I had no idea what to expect and at this point with all the pain I had, I guess I didn't even care. He came back in early evening and tapped my spine, told me to keep my head down flat and not to move. That comment was kind of a joke, because I already couldn't move, and now my arms began to cease functioning.

At midnight, he called my parents and told them that the results of the spinal tap were back and it definitely was diagnosed as Poliomyelitis. To me this meant little as I was not in the least bit familiar with this disease, except I knew at this time that I was paralyzing at a fast pace. I always thought that with paralysis there was no feeling so there was no pain, but I soon learned that this was not true, as there was an over abundance of pain that never stopped or let up for even an instant.

Now the next discussion was where would they take me to an isolation hospital. Doctor Bennett would have to send me to Madison Hospital as Burlington had no such facilities for isolation for communicable diseased patients, and his affiliation was with Burlington Hospital. However, anyone could go to the University Hospital in Madison, as a doctor didn't need to be affiliated with that hospital due to it being a university hospital.

My mother cried and cried and told him that would be too far away, wasn't there any kind of arrangements that he could make nearer to home? His answer was to transfer the case to Doctor DeWitt in Silver Lake and then I'd be taken to Kenosha Hospital, which would be a good idea anyway because that was where all the patients were being admitted during this polio epidemic throughout Kenosha County. So he called Dr.

DeWitt and made arrangements for me to go there the next morning.

Again this night was horrible and I suffered pain beyond control, and now my temperature started to elevate to the point that at times I did not know what I was thinking or saying. All I knew was that my head and my body were hot, and I thought that I was burning up. Again I endured another night of pain and suffering and couldn't wait till morning.

It was early morning, my mom put slippers and a robe on me, and my dad carried me to the car and stretched me out on the back seat, trying to make me comfortable as if that could even be possible. Then my mother sat in the front seat and my dad drove. Mom cried all the way to the hospital. I felt so sorry for her and tried to show compassion for her by saying, "Mom, don't cry, I'll be alright, I'll just be gone for two weeks and when I'm out of isolation, I'll be home again." Boy, what a disillusion that statement was! Obviously I had no idea of what Polio was even like, and I just thought that in two weeks I'd be as good as ever.

On the way, I said things like, "Dad, will you have lots of cases of beer at home when I get back?" My dad answered, "Sure", as he was choking to hold back his grief so I wouldn't notice. I had never liked beer in my life and never even drank it. There were many other requests that I had made on the way to Kenosha, and my parents just pacified me with answers that they thought I wanted to hear. I don't even know what I all said, as my fever was getting worse right along. For the longest time, I couldn't figure out why my mother was crying so hard and why my dad was so upset, until at a much later time I realized that their thoughts went back to the time when Aunt Florence lost her husband and child through Infantile Paralysis as this very disease was called back then.

When we got to the hospital the attendants were waiting for me and came to the car and put me on a stretcher. My parents followed into the hospital and as they got to the front desk, a nurse told them that they could not go any farther. My mother bent over to kiss me and the nurse almost went into orbit with rage. "You can't touch her, she is very contaminated !" With that mom even gave me a big hug and told me how much she loved me, as the tears were streaming down her cheeks. Then my dad did the same, kissed and hugged me, and the nurse had a hissy fit, but my parents didn't care what her reaction was.

The attendants carried me up stairs and into a room. As I

looked around the room, I became so frightened wondering what kind of institution I was in. There was a bed and a night stand in the room, no curtains on the windows, and the cold looking floor was linoleum covered.

Then the attendants left and before I knew it, I was being measured for hot packs for the start of the treatment. Another nurse took my temperature and told the other one what a high fever I had, so she got some pills for me and a glass of water. I couldn't lift my head, so she spooned water into my mouth and told me to swallow. It was August and the weather was hot, but at this point I was cold and had the chills. I don't know what happened to my parents, but I didn't see them again for what I thought was a long time.

The next day was Sunday, and our parish priest had come in to visit me and to anoint me. It was Father Michels, and I was so happy to see him but I could hardly recognize him as he had on a long white gown, a white head piece that covered his entire head, white mitten-like coverings on his hands, and white foot pieces over his shoes. The only persons allowed into my room were the nurses, doctors, and the clergy. I almost felt like I was poison as all I heard was the fact that I was so contaminated and the disease I had was so contagious.

It was a drastic epidemic that struck the area in August of 1946 and there were hundreds of cases of Polio throughout the county and city of Kenosha. I had to be one of these less fortunate people who contracted this awful disease. A special kind of treatment was needed to help us survive the disease.

Trained Red Cross nurses were sent from all over United States to administer the Sister Kenny treatment. This was also called a hot-pack treatment. A machine would heat strips of gauze and strips of wool in hot mist and then spin them out almost dry but just a little damp. The nurses would put the wool next to the skin and then wrap tightly with the gauze and pin into place. They started at the neck, then the trunk and lower body, now the thighs, lower legs and feet. Next would be the upper arms, lower arms and the hands. This heat was very soothing and somewhat eased the pain. During the course of one day, I would get a total of ten treatments during the day and continuing all through the night.

My mother suffered right along with me, as she came to the isolation hospital every day to inquire if she could see me, and was always told a flat out 'no'. But still every day she came to see how I was doing even though she couldn't see me.

Then one day she asked the head nurse, Miss Randal, if she could show me the powder compact that was sent to me by the committee for the State Dairy Queen contest due to my having been selected county dairy queen and not being able to participate in the state contest. It was heart shaped with "1946 Dairy Queen-Kenosha County" engraved on it. Miss Randal said yes to her that day but also told her that the compact would have to be destroyed after I saw it because then it would then be contaminated. She also informed my mom that she may in no way touch me because of the risk of the disease being-spread.

All I can say is that she didn't know my lovable mom very well. I was the happiest to see mom that day and we both cried as we were so happy to just see each other, and of course, mom kissed me and hugged me, but Miss Randal never knew about that. Mom showed me the compact and I told her to take it home and keep it for me. I guess it kind of made up a little for all the fun activities that I missed out on by not being able to participate in the state queen contest. It was the day that mom and I were going to shop for my formal dress for the contest that my parents took me to the hospital. I'll never forget that Saturday, August 17 of 1946, at age nineteen.

After two weeks of being in this awful isolated place, I was to be taken to the general hospital as the quarantine period had ceased at that point. So two attendants from the general hospital came to get me. It happened to be two lads in their thirties who were black, and when they saw me, one said to the other, "Oh, Lordy, she's a big one". I was one of the few patients who was as old as I was, as most were younger children.

I didn't weigh much but I was tall, five feet and nine inches, and lying down on a stretcher seemed to make me look even taller. But they were very careful carrying me and got me into the general hospital safely. I thanked them and one of them said, "She even has manners too". I don't know what they had expected but I was always taught to say 'please' and 'thank you' as my parents raised us properly.

I was put on the first floor in a bed and was as helpless as a newborn baby. I couldn't feed myself, or bathe myself, or brush my teeth, or brush my long blond hair, or even turn myself into a different position in the bed. I was a poor helpless creature who at one time could do all these things and always took all these things for granted because that was the way of nature.

But somehow God had decided to take this all away from me. I made up my mind right then and there that I was going to fight this battle and that I would walk and do the things I had done before being stricken or I'd die trying.

I guess the situation that hurt me the most was the fact that I had signed a contract for my first teaching job back in January, and now I'd have to break it. I felt badly because how would the school board find a teacher at this late date in August when school started in September after Labor Day. This job was at the school in which I had done my last practice teaching at Randall one-room rural school and I liked the district and above all the children who were enrolled there. But this was something that God wanted me to put on hold, as that is the only explanation I could ever figure out.

The Sister Kenny treatment continued on along with heat lamp treatments and now they started physical therapy for me. This was a long slow process, but any iota of progress made me so happy and I fought harder. I wanted to teach school that bad. I also had the love of my life in the United States Army and I wanted to be ready for him when he returned from Italy.

When I reached the point of trying to learn how to walk, the physical therapy was done having three therapists working with me at one time. One on each side of me to help hold crutches. The third one would sit on a step stool with wheels in front of me and she'd pick up one of my feet at a time, telling me to concentrate and think of placing my foot and trying to step. Then she would rotate back and forth attempting four steps in a session. By that time I was exhausted, but I soon learned that the harder I concentrated, the better I could do. This was their method of educating dormant muscles in my limbs and training them to work in place of the muscles that had been destroyed with the polio disease. After a few days time, the therapists would increase the amount of steps. I could tell by this that it would take a long time for real progress to even be noted.

Then after about three weeks into my therapy, the orthopedic specialist came to the hospital and checked each patient to address the seriousness of the paralysis and what the expected outcome would be. Everyone's parents were to sit in on the evaluation for their son or daughter. The doctor's name was Doctor Montgomery from Milwaukee, who by the way was very young and so handsome.

After examining me, he looked up at my parents with a

distressed look and said, "Mother and dad, I hate to have to tell you but your daughter will never walk again". I thought at this point that my mother would pass right out as she started to cry. But I looked up at him and said, "Doctor, do you want to bet?" After a brief pause, he turned and looked right at me and replied with a smile on his face, "Well, with that kind of attitude you probably will, and I hope you prove me wrong".

He knew at this point and time that I was a fighter and I would fight this thing no matter what it took. He patted me on the arm and wished me good luck as he smiled at me, and I smiled a look of approval back to him. I was going to prove him wrong and he knew it. I would be seeing him again in another month, October, for another evaluation and consultation, and I wanted to have a surprise in store for him, so I worked all the harder, because I was old enough to know that the quicker recovery I made the best possibility I had of walking again.

I know that particular day when my parents left the hospital I had such deep feelings for my parents because I knew that they had a heavy weight on their hearts with the news that they had just heard. I also knew that my mother would go home and continue to pray to St. Jude, who is patron saint of hopeless and impossible cases, and I also knew that with her prayers and my strong will and stubbornness I would walk again. After all, I had the love of my life in service waiting to serve his term and to be discharged to come home, and this was a great incentive for me. Plus I wanted to teach school and was eager to start my career.

My therapy continued, and the therapists continued the stretching of the muscles and the attempt to get me to walk again. I hated the stretching because it hurt so much, but the therapists would tell me to just scream and let it out, as they didn't mind because they knew how much it hurt. They worked as hard as I did.

My right side was the last to paralyze, so it was left the weakest. My right hand paralyzed in a closed position and it became so difficult to stretch the muscles for them to administer therapy on it, but the one therapist worked so diligently with it and again I had to concentrate on the motions that she was telling me she was doing.

All the nurses and therapists wanted me to start doing things with my left hand, but my being stubborn and of pure German descent told them that I had always been right handed and I would still be right handed and in no way would I ever change that. So no one argued and they continued to help me. I struggled diligently with my right hand, but I was not about to give in. Underlying my thinking was that I would be teaching children how to print and how to write, and I would do it using my own right hand.

My room mate in the hospital was a girl who was in high school at the time, so we had something in common with her being a year younger than me, but we seemed to get along very well. We had a radio in our room and we listened to music during the day when we were in the room. The only visitors that we were allowed to have were our parents with very restricted hours. I was so homesick for home and I missed my two brothers as much as they missed me.

All this while, everyone at home was in quarantine for several weeks, which meant that they could not leave the premises to be in among people, and dad could not ship milk. This was a financial burden on my family as the monthly milk check was used to pay all the bills. Now with my disease and extended hospital stay would add to the financial difficulty for my parents. They did receive little aid from the Polio Foundation, and though they suffered a severe financial setback, I never once heard them complain. My family took this all in stride.

Mother and dad had to fumigate the house with potent disinfectants to kill the virus. Anything that I had been in contact with prior to the onset of the disease, had to be laundered in boiling hot water with strong soap as to rid the germs. Some of my possessions had to be completely destroyed. All these jobs that had to be done according to the rules of the health department, were all added tasks for my family.

At the same time during the quarantine, the nurses back at the hospital begged my mother to make homemade butter out of the milk that could not be shipped to market, and they paid her a sizable amount just to have butter that was home made. Still in no way did this replace the monthly milk check for shipping milk, but my parents made the best of the situation, as their only concern now was that I would be able to walk again and lead a reasonably near normal life.

I had the best nursing care and physical therapy that anyone could have asked for. Somehow or other, I was then used as a role model for other patients. When Dr. Montgomery came back the next month, he watched the therapists help me take steps. He was in awe! He then told them that my mom should bring street clothes, shorts and a tee, the nurses should dress me, and he was sending camera men out to the hospital for filming so other doctors and interns could study my steps of progress in hopes of helping other patients all over the states. I always felt in my mind, that he wanted to prove that a case that he had diagnosed as being completely hopeless could perhaps regain movement enough to partially function through extensive therapy and strong will on the part of the patient.

Up to now, we would each day wear what was called a loin cloth which we wore on the lower extremities, and a triangular breast cloth that tied around the neck and around the waist. This type of covering did in no way restrict any movement during therapy. I started to believe that I was losing all my modesty by wearing such scanty clothing day in and day out. But all the patients wore the same thing and each patient was treated privately.

On this visit, Dr. Montgomery held out his hand to me to shake hands as I extended my right hand, so curved and so crippled out of normal position, as he said to me, "Arlene, you knew what you were talking about, I don't know how you have made this much progress, but you are determined that you will walk again, and I can now see that you will. The first day that I saw you in that worst condition that you were in, I had no hopes for you ever to walk again. But here you are making such great progress and more power to you!"

Then he looked at mom and dad and said to them, "You parents must be very proud of your daughter, she's a fighter who has more determination and spunk than anyone I have ever seen, and in a year from now, I am confident that she will be teaching school". He recommended that I should go to Orthopedic School for treatment after I would leave the hospital.

Now I wouldn't be seeing Dr. Montgomery for a few months not until February. As the days went on, therapy became more difficult and extensive, but I could see small amounts of improvement and each move was another incentive to keep going on. Now more than ever I missed seeing my brothers. I was downright homesick.

My mom talked to one of the nicer nurses who was not so rigid about rules, and she told mom that if my brothers could come to the hospital at night about 9:00 P.M., she would let me see my brothers out of the window if they could be on the fire escape which was right outside the window of my room. She also told my mom that they could not stay there for very long, as she could not run the risk of getting caught disobeying orders.

91

I couldn't wait for nine o'clock to roll around that night, and right on the dot were my parents, my older brother, Bob, and my younger brother, Ardell. I cried and cried tears of joy, as I had missed them so much. They must have been so happy to see me, but both brothers had very sad expressions on their faces, as they had no prior knowledge of how helpless I really was. I looked at them through the open window and said, "Don't feel sorry for me, I'll lick this thing and I'll get better, and I will walk again. I'll be home eventually, I will teach school, and I am waiting for Phil to be discharged from the army. Just keep praying for me as you have been. I love you, guys". I only saw them for about five minutes, but it was worth a lifetime to me and to them.

After they left that night, I slept better than usual. I only had to be turned from one side to the other side four times during the night. I still couldn't move by myself, nor feed myself, nor do anything for myself. I was totally dependent on the aid of those wonderful nurses.

Being that I only weighed ninety pounds, the nurses encouraged my dad to bring beer to the hospital for me to drink, so as to put on weight. Dad did that, and brought it in a suitcase, and the nurses would put it in the refrigerator and give it to me in the evening, they always said that the beer helped me to sleep better. The nurses would put it in a glass, and I'd have to sip the beer through a straw. I never thought I'd see the day that I would get to the point of liking beer, but I developed a real taste for it.

Speaking of trying to gain weight, I never had so much ice cream in my life, trying to put on weight. I never seemed to have that problem since, as now I try to lose weight.

Two of my favorite nurses were Pat Bates and Audrey Gilson, both sent in from Michigan. They were so kind and understanding of my needs. In the evening when they would come on duty, they would come in my room and talk to Lynette and me. They would tell us about the young men in their lives they met while in Kenosha working, and about their dates and where they would go on their dates. When they got to telling about dancing, I felt the sudden urge that I really missed dancing now in my life.

With them knowing how much I had liked to dance, one night I begged them and begged them to help me dance. These girls would do anything to make me happy because they knew that I was trying so hard to get on my feet to walk. So they made a promise to me. They would come back in my room later that evening when everyone else was asleep, and help me with my request.

Later that evening, they both came into my room and asked me if this was really what I wanted to try, and I said "Yes". Pat then told me that I was not going to be able to dance, and wouldn't I just give up the whole idea. I replied that I wanted to try this and would they please help me.

So Audrey went into the hall and looked in one direction and Pat went down the other, and they also checked the nurses' station to see if the head nurse, Miss Cloak, was anywhere in sight. Luck was that she was probably in the break room having her coffee and donuts. So they both came back in my room and asked me if I was sure that I wanted to try dancing, because they knew that I would fall, and they were both afraid that I could hurt myself.

I went on begging, and finally Pat and Audrey both helped me out of bed and held me up to stand next to the bed. Pat took hold under one arm and Audrey under the other arm. As I tried to lift my one foot, I fell in a heap. Luckily they were both attentive, and so I didn't get hurt.

At that moment I felt that my whole world had crushed in upon me. I came to realize that I wasn't so darn smart after all, I couldn't even walk yet, what ever made me think that I could dance? So there were things I had to learn the hard way, and that was one of them.

The same procedure and activity went on day in and day out for three solid months in the Kenosha Hospital. During this time, I was progressing a little faster than I had before, so my parents were informed that I would have to be taken to a foster home in Kenosha so I could attend Orthopedic school in Kenosha on a daily basis. When I heard the news of staying in a foster home in Kenosha, again I was crushed, as I thought maybe I'd get to go home at this point, and be able to commute to that school for treatment. But no such luck! After all, I had been away for three months.

The next question was, where would I be taken? I knew Kate and Ed Lois [Jan's parents of whom I spoke of in an earlier chapter] who used to live on the other Lenz farm across the road, highway K, and had moved to Kenosha after retiring from the farm. I wanted to stay with them, but their health conditions and home had to be checked out by members of the physical therapy group affiliated with the Polio Foundation.

Upon checking, they found that Kate had a hernia and would be restricted from lifting me as I was totally helpless yet at this point. I could neither dress myself, nor undress myself, nor could I get on or off the hospital bed, that my parents had rented, which was later taken to their home. However, the committee did okay their home because Ed would be there to help Kate with me.

The day I left the hospital in late November, I asked my dad to drive down many streets of Kenosha so I could just see people. It was very difficult for me to even sit in the car, but my dad complied with my wishes, and drove miles and miles up one street and down the numerous others just so I could see people. My mother was so happy at this point because this was a step in the right direction, just being dismissed from the hospital.

When we arrived at the Lois home, my dad carried me into the house, and put me on the hospital bed that was already there waiting for me. Dear Mrs. Lois turned one of her sitting rooms into a bedroom just so I could have a window facing the street, so I could still see people as they walked by. At this point, I was happy to be in a house and out of the hospital. This would be my home away from home for the next seven months, actually for the remainder of the school year.

Being late November, school was already in session. The next Monday morning, I would start attending Orthopedic School. This was a school for academic classes and during the day, one would be taken to the clinical section for therapy and treatment. Now my thoughts turned to, "What in the world will I do at a school when I had already graduated from college and was ready to teach school?"

When the Monday morning came and Kate had me all dressed and ready for school at 7:00 o'clock. A taxi cab driver came into the house and took me from the bed and carried me into the cab. He was to pick me up daily for school and bring me back to my foster home daily after school was over for the day. He was a man about 45 years old whose name was Ray, and he was the nicest guy you ever wanted to meet. He handled me so very carefully and always was so friendly to everyone.

So we drove around the corner from my foster home and picked up Pat Griffen who also had been stricken with polio during the epidemic. Then several days later, Ray picked up a little five year boy, Jimmy, who was a spastic child. Jimmy couldn't sit by himself, so Ray would put Jimmy on my lap for me to hold. My heart went out to this child as I couldn't believe how helpless this little boy was.

Being that I have always liked children, I really got attached to Jimmy, but one day he pulled a boner on me. It seems as though he had a full bladder and couldn't tell anyone as this type of child could not speak clearly, just mumbled. So you can imagine little Jimmy 'peed' all over me and I was soaked. Ray took Pat and Jimmy to school, took me back to Kate, carried me back into the house and Kate had to wash me up and dress me all over again. Ray waited patiently during this time, and once again we were off to school.

Each morning when we arrived at the school, there were portable cots all lined up outside of the school. Those who could help themselves and could walk, walked into school and went right to their classrooms as many of them were not in the hospital as long as I was, so they were already oriented into this situation. Most kids came by school buses so only a few came by way of a taxi.

Each day as our cab driver stopped, a lady who was secretary of the school, came over and took little Jimmy off my lap, and carried him to a cot. Then Ray would carry me over to a cot, and many attendants helped roll all the cot patients into school. It just so happens that the secretary lady, Miss Betty, had been treated here at this school for a condition in her earlier life. She was one great lady, and she knew what handicaps were all about. She showed compassion for everyone, no matter how bad or not so bad anyone was handicapped, but she understood them all because of her own affliction.

Remember at this point, this is my first day out here at school, where children were educated by certified teachers and treated by certified therapists. Now I knew that I would also receive treatment, but what would I do throughout the day? All these thoughts raced through my mind and gave me a scary feeling because this place, as nice as it was, still had the markings of an institution.

When I got inside the school, all I could see were many classrooms on one end of the long hall and the therapy wing at the other end of the hall. So as I was wheeled into a classroom and put in the back of the room, everyone turned and stared at me, being that I was nineteen and they were all of junior high and high school age.

At this point, I already felt that I was not going to like it here at all, when the male teacher, who was young and very handsome, came back by me and tried to comfort me. My facial expressions showed how I felt about this place. He quietly told me that he would get his class started and he would come back and talk to me, because he had something for me to do to help him in his teaching. Now I smiled an expression of contentment as I felt my self-worth at last.

After everyone was doing their work, he introduced himself as Mr. Diedrich and asked me if I would like to teach the English course to four freshmen and sophomores who were also on cots. Immediately without any thought, I accepted the offer. Then he told me that I could help each day with attendance records, take lunch count, and help other students with any problems they might be having with their class work. Now everything didn't seem so bad after all, I was really going to teach, even though it wasn't what I had anticipated before the onset of the Polio, but this would suffice for now.

At 10:30 in the morning was the milk break, and milk was brought to the rooms for each student. Gosh, was I in for it now, I hated milk and besides I was used to drinking the raw milk from my parents' farm. This milk was pasteurized and homogenized and I never drank this kind of milk before. I had just wished for nothing at all to drink, or just a glass of some kind of juice, but this was not the case. I tried the milk, and it was warm, I gagged and almost puked, but struggled through it.

One of the kids noticed the problem I was having with the milk that morning, so at lunch time while he was sitting at a table that was assigned, he came over to my cot where I was eating, and told me he had a deal for me. His name was Burt Watring, and he had been going there for a couple years. I was all ears as I wanted to hear what he had to offer. He told me that the milk was delivered at 4:00 o'clock in the morning and being that there was no one there to take it in, the milk stood out in the sun until it was served at 10:30. He didn't mind drinking the warm milk as much as he hated eating the cabbage soup that was served about every three days. His deal was that he would drink my milk every day, if I would eat his cabbage soup every time it was served. I almost jumped at this deal, so we shook hands on the agreement.

Now with a deal like this, one did not dare run the risk of getting caught, because there would have been severe consequences for such an act, so being that he was on crutches and could walk and get around quite readily, each morning when the milk came in, he would hurry and drink his own carton of milk

96

then come to the back of the room where I was sitting, take my carton and give me the empty carton. His excuse was that he had to open my carton of milk for me every day because of losing the total use of my right hand, he had to open my carton for me. The teacher believed it and so we got away with this deal.

Mr. Diedrich was very kind to me and was happy for any help that I might be able to do for him. Each day in the morning he would wheel the four kids and me into the hall and this is where I taught the English course. I really enjoyed this, and those kids respected me very highly and were eager to learn.

During the rest of the day when I was not in the treatment center, I corrected students' papers for him, averaged daily grades for report cards, and at the end of a quarter, I helped him fill out the report cards for the students. .

At noon time everyone who was a patient was taken to the dining room where those who could sit went to a table that held six persons. Those of us who were on cots were wheeled in there and placed together in an area along the walls. All of us who were on cots had our food brought to us on trays. The rest of the students were served at their tables.

The food was very nutritious, but not always to the kids' liking. About three times a week we had cabbage soup so Burt would bring his bowl to me after he saw that my bowl was empty, and he'd exchange bowls. No one ever said anything about this exchange. As time went on and I was able to sit at the table when I was using crutches, I could sit at the table with the older kids who had become my friends.

After lunch was over, everyone in the school had to go to the sleeping hall on the second floor to nap. Those who could walk, walked up the ramp and those on cots were pushed up the ramp. Well, can you imagine what those who were ages fifteen to my age of nineteen would do during a nap time? The occupational therapist gave us permission to talk if we whispered and she also permitted us to play cards, but that meant that we had to be very quiet.

Treatment at the orthopedic school was very rigid. I had one morning treatment and one afternoon treatment. One of the lady attendants would come to the classroom to get me and roll me to the treatment room. There she would help me undress and put on these loin and breasts cloths, help me onto the treatment table and put heat lamps on me to limber up the muscles.

Next a therapist would come in and work with my hands, after which I was taken to a huge pool room where there was a

97

very large tank filled with warm water. The therapist would help me unto a hoist that would hold me as I was lying on my back, and slowly let the hoist place me into the water while remaining on the hoist. Then the therapist would exercise my limbs as I would concentrate with each movement. It felt so good as I could feel the movement of my limbs almost as if I was moving them by myself. What a wonderful feeling, thinking I was moving all on my own, but this movement helped to train muscles how they should move on their own.

After I was removed from the water and taken off the hoist, another therapist helped me to put my right leg into a whirlpool for a long period of time, then she would stretch my anterior tibia because I had a very bad dropped foot. She always felt that if she could strengthen the muscle enough, I could avoid a muscle transplant in the interior of my foot, which Dr. Montgomery had anticipated would have to be done. But only time would tell.

This was what the everyday sessions were like. As time progressed, the therapist helped me to learn how to climb a couple of steps. Now was the time that I could ambulate with underarm crutches. Back at my foster home, my parents came every night after my dad had the milking done, to spend time with me. My dad would always help me stretch and do more and more exercises which I had learned during the day. My parents were so supportive of me, and my dad never refused anything I wanted to try, he readily helped me.

Progress was going steadily now, and back at the Ortho school, the therapists were wondering how I could be making such good progress. I never divulged that my dad was helping me outside of their therapy, until one day I told Miss Fredrickson, the main therapist, that I could go up five steps and back down again. She was in awe! Her pet name for me was Peanut. So she replied, "No, Peanut, can you really?" I was so proud to reply, "Watch me". She did and she screamed and yelled, "Good for you, but how did you know that you could do that?"

I then told her that my dad had been helping me every night at my foster home. First he would stretch my limbs, then he'd help me try the things that I wanted to try. My dad was great, and Miss Fredrickson was amazed how he was giving me that extra stretching and exercising, to help me gain more and more strength each time I tried.

It was the spring of the year of 1947 now, and Dr. Montgomery was due to pay another visit for another evaluation of progress. At this time he told me that I would have to have that muscle taken from my leg and transplanted in my ankle. He would do this procedure in June at St. Catherine's Hospital in Kenosha.

Everything about the Ortho School really wasn't so bad, after a long period of adjustment. I say adjustment, because up to now, that seemed to be the story of my life. Adjustments, disappointments, adjustments, more disappointments, and more and more adjustments. I was getting used to that by now. My life centered around the goals that I had set for myself and no matter what happened along the way, I was going to accomplish those goals one way or another.

As you have probably guessed by now, having been a little mischievous during my lifetime, this awful disease wasn't going to get in the way of having a bit of fun.

So getting back to the noon napping time at Orthopedic School, one day after I could barely walk with crutches, instead of going to nap, the older kids and I sneaked out and went to the Washington Bowl behind the school. This was affiliated with the Washington Park where I believe that many band concerts were held during the summer evenings and on weekends. Well, we got down in the bowl and none of us could get back up and out so we were stranded, Needless to say, we broke the school rules.

After a bit, when the nap hour was over, the six of us were missed, and so the principal and the secretary of the school and two therapists came out looking for us. When they finally found us they were quite upset, but they did help us get out of there. Guess who got yelled at the most! Miss Arlene, who was nineteen years old and should have known better, was termed the leader of this mischief. In all reality, the kid, Burt, who drank my carton of milk for me every day was the instigator, but I graciously took the rap for it all. When they inquired as to why we did that, we simply told them that we were bored.

The next day, the principal make arrangements for me to take a college course at the Technical School in Kenosha. The only class I could get was Political Science. It wasn't my choice of courses but at least I was now happy because I liked school and now had something worthwhile to do.

So I went to the Orthopedic School all day until 3:00 P.M., at which time the cab driver would pick me up from the Ortho School and take me over to the Kenosha Technical School, which today by the way had become Gateway. Ray, the cab driver carried me into the building, placed me in a desk, and he took off, and I was on my own until an hour and a half later at which time Ray would return to take me back to my foster home.

I had a tough teacher who was very gruff looking, spoke in an extremely harsh manner, and looked upon me as a bother in his class. I had very hurt feelings about the whole situation, but I wanted to have this course, so I was out to get him as much as he was out to get me. I worked with all the gusto I had so I could prove to him that I would be one of his best students and not a bother as I felt which was how he had termed me.

The other students in the class were so kind and helpful to me, and it was those students who made me feel like I was a human being and not some freak like I felt the teacher of this course thought I was. I enjoyed being in this class. I was one of his better students, and later he had to admit it himself. But I graciously accepted his apology for his misgivings about me.

I still feel a little bitter about this whole deal, as when I went to have my credits transferred to the State University System, these three credits were not accepted because this was a technical school and not yet a part of the Wisconsin University System. But the knowledge that I had gained about politics could never be taken away from me, and it was a truly interesting course of study.

Later on in life, I had often thought about getting into local politics, but at that particular time, my idea of marriage and raising children of my own took top priority over becoming involved in the political aspects of the community.

At Orthopedic School, I came in contact with a young man who was just about to be discharged from the U. S. Marine Corps., whose name was Dick . He happened to be home on leave and had the misfortune of being stricken with Polio, but he only had a slight case and could still walk, but came to Orthopedic School for physical therapy. He would come late in the afternoons and it happened that Ray was his cab driver also. So one day Ray picked Dick up at school after his treatment and Ray also carried me into the same cab. Ray introduced Dick to me and we became friends.

After a few days, Dick and I both decided that we liked beer, so we talked Ray into taking us both to Maywood's in downtown Kenosha. This, being a restaurant and bar, was a very nice place where friends came to meet and have a few beers after work. Can you imagine how I felt, being carried into and out of a bar? However people never thought a thing about it.

Dick and I really enjoyed being together as he, being twenty-one , was closer in age than most of the kids at the Ortho School and we could engage in adult conversations rather than being with younger kids all the time. He had a girlfriend who was in the W.A.A.C.'s, and we often talked about the love of our lives as my boy friend was in the U. S. Army. The extent of our relationship was being a friend with whom we could talk and listen to.

I can never ever express my feelings about Ray, the cab driver, but only as to say that he was one of the most gentle, kindhearted, patient, and caring men whom I could ever come in contact with. I always felt that in his heart, he had great compassion and pity for me as he often spoke of my teaching career being put on hold because of my misfortune. I used to tell him, "Ray, don't ever have pity on me, I am a very strong willed person with determination, I am of German descent, and I will fight with all my might until I reach my goal in life. Now you remember that I said this to you."

Ray would always look back at me with a smile on his face, and I knew that he never believed a word of what I was saying. But I knew in my heart that I would walk, I would teach, and I would marry the love of my life and raise a beautiful family.

I, to this day, lost all contact with Ray, but wherever he is, I only hope that he has had as good a life as I have. Who knows, he may even be deceased by now, but once in a while I remember him in my prayers regardless of where he is. I will always cherish the part of how he had touched my life.

It was mid June now, and I was back home in the country. I was now past walking with underarm crutches, and also past walking with what at that time were known as army canes, presently known as forearm crutches. They were a type of canes with arm pieces to help hold yourself up, and were initiated during the war for veterans of service. After they first came out into the market, the Ortho school was the first to introduce them to their patients.

By now, I was able to ambulate under my own power without the help of any aides, but I still was not dismissed from any type of therapy. Every day of June, I had to go to Kenosha to the Y.M.C.A. for swimming lessons. It was great, being in water I could move my limbs on my own power, and I had just learned how to float, and was getting into swimming strokes, when Dr. Montgomery decided that I had to have the muscle transplant at that time, as I would be in a cast up to my knee on my right leg for two months.

After the surgery, he had hoped that the surgery would be successful because if I didn't have this done, lifting my right leg to walk would become more and more difficult in future years and it would bother me.

So in the heat of summer, I walked around with a walking cast on my leg. By this time he knew that I had signed a contract to teach, so he had wished me luck at my career. He told my parents that I would need someone I knew and who could handle me to be with me in school, as if I fell, I had no way of getting up by myself.

The next and last time that I had to see Dr. Montgomery was in November of 1947, at which time he told me that I would have to have my tonsils removed because I had a bad grating in my right knee. I thought the man was out of his mind, but I took off from teaching on the Wednesday before Thanksgiving, had my tonsils removed by my family doctor and returned back to teach school the following Monday. Can you imagine, the grating in my knee ceased. What a smart man!

I never heard again anything about this wonderful doctor, until many years later, when I started doctoring with a local orthopedist, and he knew this particular doctor as 'old Dr. Montgomery, the best teacher in the field', whose son had carried on his father's work, and was then considered the best in the field following his father's footsteps. I really owe my recovery of Polio to this man and I, too, remember him in my prayers.

My life was finally coming back into order, and I had learned how to handle myself in any which way that seemed to work for me. At times I almost felt like a normal human being, except that I had many limitations but I knew how to deal with any situation that I was confronted with. I was happy and that was what counted.

At that particular time, I had never dreamed that in the future I would start back into becoming incapacitated as a reversal of what I had gone through after the onset of the disease. I refer to Post Polio Syndrome. I always feel that it was good that I had no idea of what was in store for me as to what I would become many years down the road.

I would never wish this dreadful disease on to anyone. I accepted this cross graciously with the help of God, my mom's prayers, my dad's care, and lots of strong will .

102

Chapter 8
Starting My Teaching Career

I graduated from teacher's college in May of 1946. As I have explained, my career was on hold as I was stricken with that dreadful disease, Polio, which caused me to break my first contract. My first teaching contract was at the school where I had done my last practice teaching, Randale School. The teacher under whom I did my practice teaching was taking a job in Kenosha as he lived near Kenosha. Mr. Grevenow had recommended me to that particular school board. I applied, and they hired me immediately. I was so eagerly looking forward to this job as I liked that school district very much, and loved the children in the district. But I guess it was not meant to be as I look back on the whole situation now.

So one Saturday afternoon in April of 1947, a man came to my parents' home and asked if I could teach at the school where he was the school board clerk. It was a gentleman named Clyde Cates who was a board member from a one-room rural school in Randall township called Oak Knoll School.

He went on to explain that the school was one of the few in Kenosha County that had indoor plumbing so there was a bathroom inside the school. So he asked if I could come over and take a look at the school, as the school board wanted me to be the teacher.

Then he went on to say that he had gone to RKNS, where I had gone to teachers' college and asked the principal, Mr. A. J. Smith, for a recommendation for a good teacher. A. J. told him about me, because he said I was one of the best of teachers, but he wasn't sure if the orthopedic specialist would allow me to teach at that time due to my period of recuperating from Polio.

I told Mr. Cates that I was very interested in this job, and I would be seeing the specialist the first week of May, and would ask Dr. Montgomery if I could physically manage at this time. Now, I was really excited! In the meantime, Mr. Cates said that they would hold the position open with the hopes that my reply would be an affirmative yes.

After meeting with Dr. Montgomery, he stated that I could sign the contract providing that I had a guarantee that someone I knew could accompany me to school to be there to pick me up in case I'd fall, as I had not yet accomplished this feat. Being that my younger brother, Ardell, had one more year of elementary school to finish, he could go to school with me each day as a student in eighth grade.

Now my parents had to go to the priest of our parish and get permission for Ardell to leave the Catholic school and finish in a public school. Father Michels was very understanding and gave his consent after making the comment, "I certainly will grant consent for Ardell to finish school with his sister as teacher, because I was so sure that she would never live long enough through that crisis, to ever be up to teaching school. You know she was one very sick girl. I firmly believe this is a miracle."

The very next day, I called Mr. Cates, and he brought the contract right over to my house. At that particular time, salary hadn't even crossed my mind as I knew now that I was going to teach at last.

So my parents and my brother, Ardell, and I followed Mr. Cates to the school and looked it over. I was ecstatic, it was the most beautiful country school that I had ever seen. It had a huge classroom, an office in which there was a telephone, and an extra alcove in the back of the room that I could envision as a library.

The hall was very large with a girls' coat room on one side and a boys' coat room on the other. In one end of the hall on the same side as the girls' coat room was a girls' bathroom and on the other was one for boys. The entry way led from one short flight of steps into the halls or into the classroom.

Also off the entry way was a short flight of steps leading down into the basement where there was a furnace room, a kitchen, and a large hall for indoor play during inclement weather or for special activities. This school was awesome!

I knew in my heart that this was going to be the school in which I wanted to teach. I knew nothing about the children nor their parents, but to me it didn't matter as I could get along with anybody and I could manage any disciplinary situations that may have been existing. Then Mr. Cates began to tell me a little about the families in the district.

He spoke of a discipline problem that had been in the school and the last teacher didn't do anything about it, so he stated that he wanted good discipline. For me that was no problem, I learned the value of real discipline from the Mr. Grevenow of whom I spoke previously. I knew that all it would take was reasoning and being fair to kids, and above all not to be so harsh and so staunch as I had been treated by the nuns.

Salary was then discussed and they asked me what I had expected, and I told them that at the moment I hadn't even thought about salary, I just wanted to teach. [Actually I was so excited about teaching, money didn't even matter to me.] They offered me $195 per month. Now I was really ecstatic, as many of my friends took jobs for much smaller amounts than that. At that time, this was an amount of salary that experienced teachers were getting.

So I signed the contract. Next I met the other school board members, whom Mr. Cates had called to come to the school. So I met Fred Raasch, Wayne Tilton, and Floyd (everyone called him Jiggs) Zarnstorff. They really welcomed me and so I was off to a good beginning. They asked me how I liked the school and I told them I thought it was awesome.

Then I asked if I could have some type of drapes or curtains for the windows. They told me to pick out what I wanted and turn in the bill to them, so I agreed. My mom who was with me at the time, suggested that we could select fabric and she would sew them and the cost would be minimal. This the men liked to hear and so agreed.

One Saturday, my mom and I went over to the school and measured the windows. Shortly after, she and I went shopping for material and she sewed the nicest drapes in an all-over colorful geometric print so typical for a classroom, office, and hall windows in a school. After hanging them up, the whole school looked so cheerful and gave a feeling of contentment and comfort, and so conducive to learning.

The next time I saw Mr. Cates, I told him there was one thing missing that other schools had, and that was a flag pole outside. It was then that I expressed the importance of teaching the children that patriotism was significant to appreciate and revere the freedoms that our forefathers had established for us, and that I felt it necessary for the children to establish a pattern of reciting the pledge to the flag daily. He totally agreed and Phil [who was my boyfriend at the time] volunteered to get the materials and put a flag pole up. Clyde gave the okay and told him to turn in a bill for materials.

In the meantime, I contacted one of our state representatives and inquired about getting an American flag. In a matter of time, Assemblyman Mollinaro sent one to the school.

Phil and my dad, put the pole up by October of that same year, so in November on the eleventh day, Veterans Day, we dedicated the flag pole and held a solemn program for the school district honoring all veterans. My dad was a veteran of WWI, and Phil and one of the dads of a student were veterans of WWII, so they wore their caps from their respective uniforms and participated in the dedication on Veterans' Day.

From that day on, when the weather was nice outside, the students and I would start our day by reciting the pledge to the flag outside.

All that summer, I had worked on bulletin board themes, checked text books and started lesson plans. During any spare time, I organized books and made the neatest library for the children. It was a place of solitude, peace and quiet, where the student could go in any spare time and read. It had one study unit in each of the two corners where an individual could work on a unit, or project, or homework all alone. One table with four chairs was in the center for group work, or for a student helping another student with assigned or drill work without any disruptions of the on-going class being taught.

In the early years of education in Kenosha County, there was a superintendent of schools whose job was to coordinate curriculum, visit each school in the county and observe the performance of the teacher, and to work closely with the school boards of the county. She would just walk in and sit quietly in the back of the room and took notes about her overview of the teaching being done in that classroom. After about two and a half hours of observation, she would expect the teacher to assign work to keep the students occupied while she talked to the teacher she was observing in private.

During this time of her conference with the teacher, she would evaluate one's work, pointing out any weak areas , and elaborating on the strong areas of the person being evaluated. All during this time, she would also give suggestions as to how a specific teacher could improve. If a teacher had any concerns or questions, she would be open for helping the person.

Following these visits, the superintendent would send a report to each school board informing them of the quality of the teacher's work in their school. Each teacher wanted to do her best during a visit from the superintendent .

A few months into the school year, I had a visit from County Superintendent Margaret Diehl, who held the position at that time. Now let me tell you, as I saw her walk through the doorway, I shuttered in my shoes and the fear of God bolted through my entire body as if I had been struck by lightning.

She smiled at me, I smiled back to her, and she sat down

on a chair in the library. I went on teaching as I had before she walked in.

The little children peered at her in wonder. Softly I said aloud, "Children, we have a visitor and she's here to see how we all do our work, so let's just continue on as we were." The little ones smiled at me and they knew what it was that I expected of them, so they went right on where they had left off doing their work. Every child was busy at the task that had been assigned to them. I kept teaching, changing classes, and continued on according to my lesson plans.

Utilizing my good peripheral vision, I kept my glances routed in her direction. Her eyes seemed to me that somehow they were roaming all around my classroom. Her hand was writing furiously, and all I could think of was that I must be doing an unsatisfactory job of teaching. Nevertheless I continued on because this was the way I wanted to teach because I was getting results from the children and that was what counted. They were learning. Finally she got up from her seat, walked into the coat room, and on into the girls' bathroom as I heard that door close. How snoopy she is, I thought!

When she returned, she motioned for me to come back to the library by her. I looked at the students and said, "Please excuse me for a few minutes, so I can meet with this lady because she wants to talk to me. You keep on with your work. Thank you". I went back to the table in the library to sit.

She started off by saying, "Miss Lenz, you are teaching like a veteran teacher, it seems like you have been teaching for years. I am impressed that you use lesson plans, and therefore you know exactly what you accomplish with each class taught. I can't tell you what a change I see in this school from what it had been. I like the curtains on the windows, it adds a touch of beauty. This little library corner you have set up is so conducive to inviting the children to want to read. You discipline with a kind but firm approach. Your manners with the children are commendable. The coat rooms look so neat, and the bathrooms are very clean. You display the children's work so beautifully on all the bulletin boards. Your board work assignments are done so neatly. You are so knowledgeable of all the materials that you are teaching. I'm very impressed. Now do you have any questions?"

I replied, "That's the good word, now let's have the bad".

"I can't find one thing wrong with your teaching, so just keep up the good work. In the future I will have the college send a practice teacher to do cadet work. You are that capable of having one your very first year of teaching."

"Thank you so very kindly, Miss Diehl."

Following that she placed the report on my desk and she left the building. I was thrilled to death that this kind of report would be sent to my school board by her. It was now that I let out a sigh of relief as this visit was not at all what I had anticipated, it was absolutely great!

My brother Ardell, who was an eighth grade student of mine, couldn't wait to get home to tell our parents all about the lady that visited the school that day. Naturally they wanted to know what kind of a report I had gotten, so I showed it to them.

After reading it, my mother looked at my dad and said, "And this is our daughter who would go to teachers' college and never use her education because she would just get married and never use it, so we would just be wasting our money. How about that, Joe?"

Dad was in awe, and decided not to reply at all, but the look on his face told me that he was as proud of me as I was of myself.

Children had to bring their lunches from home which included the usual sandwiches, fruit, something for a dessert and a thermos of milk as most of the kids were from farms. During the winter months, I allowed the children to bring soup or a casserole type food in a jar with a lid on it. Each child had his or her name marked on the lid and at lunch time I'd put all these containers in a dish-pan of water and place it on a burner on the stove. In a short while the food was hot and so each child had something warm for their lunch. The kids really liked this idea. I usually took something to heat up by this means and the students thought that was really something, because the teacher heated her food to eat too.

Once a year in the spring we'd have a fund raiser which was in the form of a carnival. Bingo was played for small prizes which were donated by the teacher. The children would do many craft projects in our art classes through the year and these also were used as prizes for games of skill that the students devised and ran. I would make bar-be-cue for sandwiches and people would buy these with potato chips. Coffee and milk was also for sale. This was a great activity.

This was a nice get-together for the district and after a couple of years, they would bring their relatives to this fund raiser. We mostly bought library books with this money raised.

A few times we ventured to hold a spaghetti supper and this went over big too. My dear mother would prepare the food, and the kids would help make the salad and also helped serve. I always took the seventh and eighth graders on a field trip, usually to Chicago. We would go on a train from Kenosha or Richmond. Some of the places that we visited were: Museum of Natural History, Museum of Science and Industry, The Planetarium, Shedd Aquarium, Art Museum, and just to see the tall buildings of Chicago interested these rural students.

Every payday I would have to visit the Fred Raasch's to pick up my wages. I always looked forward to this, not only because of pay day, but Mrs. Raasch was a very good baker, and she always had fresh pie, or cake, or cookies and I had to sit down and eat a dessert with them while talking. They were great people, but both have long been deceased now

The Raasch's daughter-in-law, Charlotte, was very active in the community, so I approached her one day and asked her if she would be interested in starting a 4-H Club. She was skeptical about it at first, but when I told her that I would help her get it off the ground and guide her for a year, she accepted and liked the idea. This was the start of Randall Rustlers 4-H Club.

Christmas was a time that a school district expected that the teacher would have her students put on a program. All public schools had a program. Being my first year there, I wanted to produce something dramatically outstanding, so I wrote an operetta. Each child had a speaking part and all had singing parts with some of them having solo singing parts. The name was, 'The Miracle of Christmas'. This was a smashing success! But now the district expected such an extraordinary performance each year.

From then on, I'd order an operetta from a publishing company and the students would perform beautifully. The kids liked to perform as well as the parents liked to see and hear their children act and sing.

In the last semester of the school year of my first year of teaching I was approached to be a host teacher for a student teacher from a college. My first cadet teacher was Betty Neinhaus, who was the nicest girl. She had all the qualities of being a good teacher, and did a super job in her practice teaching. Being a host teacher created much extra work in planning and working out a special schedule for the learning teacher, but I enjoyed it.

In my third year of teaching, I had a second cadet. This

time it was a girl named Marilyn Kahn, and was from the R.K.N.S. Teachers College. She did a good job, too, and I enjoyed Marilyn a lot. At this point and time, I was honored to be a host teacher twice in three years time. Many teachers never get an opportunity like this in all their years of teaching.

At the end of my first year of teaching I had two eighth grade boys in the class and they both passed to graduate, my brother Ardell and a boy named Jim. It was customary in those days that all eighth graders in the county of Kenosha were required to participate in a county wide graduation. This was held at a high school in the city of Kenosha because of the larger seating capacity. The diplomas were awarded by the superintendent so to Kenosha we went for the eighth grade graduation.

Somehow this seemed so impersonal, so we held a small ceremony at the school following the one at Kenosha, and the whole district participated in this celebration. We used this format for graduation for two years after which time the county graduation was ceased because the classes were becoming too large. From that time on, we held our own graduation at our school in the district.

There were so many wonderful families in this Oak Knoll School District, and some of them stand out in my mind still today. The Cates family was just extraordinary in every respect. Jim, the oldest of the children, in the intermediate grades, was truly a down-to-earth country kid who always was so respectful and eager to learn and to help anyone who depended on him. Down the line were Judy, Ray, and Duane, all of whom I had the pleasure of having as students in my classroom during my five years in that school district. The youngest, June, was not old enough for school at that time so I missed the joys of knowing this sweet little girl as a student.

Clyde, of whom I spoke earlier, was the best boss that anyone could ever work for. Mrs. Cates, whose name was Rose, was the most delightful lady and having been a teacher herself, understood what the teaching profession was all about. She was fully aware of all the added tasks that accompanied teaching during those times in which the classroom teacher not only had to prepare for teaching all eight grades every subject, but also had to teach art and physical education. In addition there were still more tasks expected of teachers: to supervise playground and to serve as a custodian. [If there were furnace or plumbing problems, Clyde had to be notified, but he was always there].

110

As I look back today, it becomes quite ironic how in later life that same little Ray Cates with the little pudgy rosy cheeks, became my so-called boss as a school board member in the Parochial School many years later. During this time I had taught both of Ray's children, Lori and Tim. Ray served in the capacity of school board president equally as well as his dad, Clyde, had always done.

The Weiler family stands out in my mind and had an only child, Donna. She was in the intermediate grades and on into junior high level as a student. Her intelligence superseded her chronological age so it became necessary to allow her to skip one grade level. [In those days there was no gifted and talented programs to offer as a challenge for advanced students]. Mrs. Weiler would constantly volunteer for any parental help that was needed.

Others who were helpful were these families: Blair, Tilton, Raasch, Zarnstorff, Minnis, Nelson, Clausen, Pacey, Kautz, Keisler, and two different Ehlert families. All of these people were friendly, helpful, and grateful. [I hope I haven't forgotten anyone's name but my apologies to them in case I did].

During the time that I was teaching there, I had the scare of my lifetime. Phil and I were then married and he drove our one and only vehicle to his job. He took me to work daily, and after his job was finished at 5:30 in the early evening, he came to school to pick me up. After school was dismissed for the day, I was totally alone in the building. Being that I was never frightened, I never locked the doors to the school until I left in the evening.

It just so happened on this one autumn day shortly after school hours, a strange car with two men in, drove slowly past the school. I really didn't think too much about it, because this was a heavily traveled country road that led into and out of Twin Lakes. In a short while, this particular car drove up again, parked along side the road, and the two men got out. I quietly peered out the window, as I saw them heading for the little one car garage along side the school as I heard one of them say to the other, "We'll put our car in here for the night, and see of we can get into the building for a place to sleep tonight".

"Yeh, a good set-up to hide in. Nobody'd ever look for us in a school, let's check the building".

In the meantime I quickly tiptoed into the office where the telephone was and tried to call to the Cates family whose farm was just hidden beyond the little knoll on the other side. To no

111

avail! I kept ringing and ringing and ringing but no answer. I glanced out the window again and saw them walking towards the back of the school building, and by now my heart was pounding so hard that I feared that they could hear my heart beating outside, it was so loud.

I tried the phone again, ringing and ringing and no response from the Cates farm. I'm trapped, no one else can be reached, I'm running out of time, but............ [thank the dear Lord for the party lines in those days] in a split second I heard a woman's voice on the other end asking if I was in trouble.

Now the men are coming nearer around the corner of the building and they are getting closer and closer to the door. All I could whisper was, "Help, teacher in school, help!"

A lady's voice said, "I'm on my way". Was I dreaming this? No, this whole episode was actually happening. I hung up the phone and hid myself on the side of the steel storage cabinet close to the wall, but my heart was even beating louder and louder, and I prayed and prayed in a low whisper. I could hardly control tears streaming down my cheeks as I kept praying and praying.

Then I heard one of the men say to the other, "Look, there is an outside opening, there must be a basement Boy this is a perfect place to hide. Let's check it out". This thought led them to the side of the building to the entry way to the basement from the outside.

As they were checking this out, I knew I couldn't get to the door to lock it, so I just stayed between the cabinet and the wall. What do I hear? Oh, what do I hear? Can it really be true? I removed myself quietly from the cabinet and peered out the office window, and what I had heard was exactly what I was seeing......... the most beautiful sight of a life time. A little older model of a car which was in need of a muffler approaching over the hill coming toward the direction of the school.

I heard one of the men say, "Here comes a car, let's get the hell out of here, we can't risk a chance of getting caught now". With that they went to their car and started out away from the school.

The lady in the car was now here, she got out and through her thoughtfulness happened to take the license number of that other car as it was driving off. She came in, and by this time I had lost all control of myself. I was sobbing in a state of distress and praying aloud, as she entered the building and found me in the little office. She hugged me and told me she was Mrs.

Davis, who lived a few miles down the road. She tried to calm me down and asked what had happened.

After I finally got the words out of my mouth and tried to organize them to make sense in explaining the whole happening to her, she was so kind to me and assured me that I had worried needlessly. She helped ease the distress and I started to calm down, feeling a little skittish about the whole ordeal. I must have perceived the whole situation in a greater dimension than what it had been, so now I was at ease. We spoke for a few minutes and she left.

It wasn't long after when Phil had come to pick me up after his own day of work. He helped me lock up and recheck all the entries to the building before we left. It was a Friday and I was glad, because I don't think that I could have gone back to the school building the next day.

As we were riding home, Phil thought it would be a good idea to inform the Cates family what had happened just in case there was something erratic about the whole situation, and they should be aware of it. So when we got home, I called Cates' house, and Rose answered the phone. I explained what had happened and how I tried to call their house as I was in distress, and she apologetically told me that she had been at the grocery store during that time. But she thanked me for informing them of this incident.

The next day, Mrs. Cates called me at home and told me that she did not intend to frighten me, but the two men from the day before that were at the school had been found. It was through Mrs. Davis turning in the license number of the car and found out that it had been a stolen car. This in turn led to the detection of the two men who had taken it.

Then she went on to tell me that........ those men were convicts who had escaped from the prison in Joliet located in Illinois, and the authorities were searching for them. After interrogation, the two of them had planned to stay in the school until later hours of the night and then scram out of the area. The school was located near the border of Wisconsin and Illinois which explains why they were where they were.

I can honestly say that this is one of the most frightening times of my entire life, and at that time, I hoped I would never in the remainder of my life ever have to encounter such fear.

After five years had passed there was a family in the district who thought that my discipline was too strict and my rules were too rigid. Being that I had not planned to lighten up on discipline or rules because this is what I was asked to do when I was hired, nor did I even intend to change anything as this is how my objectives and goals were established in order to help children develop their own personal characteristics to be the best person that they could be. My interest was in their children and I wanted to help them grow and mature mentally, socially, physically, emotionally, morally, and responsibly.

With no intent to abolish all that I truly believed in as a teacher, I made my own decision that I would terminate my work here and with that I turned in my resignation. I was leaving a place that I had come to love and felt so comfortable there, but these fond memories of my first teaching job would always remain in my heart.

Many of the children felt sad that I was leaving, and it was difficult finishing out the last months of school knowing that I was not coming back the next fall.

When this word got out, I already had another school board president knocking at my door, Mr. Ellingson, of the Salem Mound Center School, which was only about four miles from my home. He said they were looking for a teacher who was a good disciplinarian and he heard about me, so I made an appointment with him to look at the school.

I knew the Ellingson family previously to this contact, because Phil and I as 4-H leaders, helped their children with their projects because they were members of our Wheatland Willing Workers 4-H Club.

Prior to this meeting many thoughts ran through my mind. This was another rural school and I had hoped that it would have indoor plumbing as yet at this time, many of the schools still had outhouses, and no running water for drinking nor for washing hands, except through means of a well pump and a bucket.

When I arrived at the school the first thing I noticed was that it did have indoor plumbing and the school wasn't bad at all. I did see a lot of tattered old books and junk lying around in the basement, but I knew that if I took this job I would soon see to it that all this rubbish would be removed. At that time, I told Mr. Ellingson that I would have to think about it, but I'd let him know soon.

In the meantime I shopped around and none of the other schools that I looked at appealed to me, so I decided to accept this position. In a couple of weeks, I called Mr. Ellingson back and told him I would take the job. He was delighted and wanted to know when I could meet with him and the rest of the board members to sign the contract, so we set up a date and time.

Again I met a group of board members who were most congenial, and made me feel sincerely welcome. Then was the question of wages. After five years of prior teaching, I started becoming money conscious, so after they offered a wage, I asked them if they couldn't do better than that. They excused themselves and huddled together and talked a bit after which time they proposed a second offer. I was astonished at this second offer because it was a substantial salary, many times greater than their initial offer, so I signed the contract.

The children here were great kids, and I loved each one of them as much as every kid in the last school. During inclement weather, I would play the piano during recess time and the kids, big boys and all, would all gather around the piano singing. They liked this and begged me to hurry and eat my lunch that we could sing.

One little student whose name was Tim, would sit next to me on the piano stool just as close as he could get to me. He had a speech impediment and he would look up at me with those brown eyes and say so softly, "Oh, 'Mit..is Roa..haus', I love you", as he laid his head against my upper arm.

In a country school a teacher and students developed a closeness that today this proximity cannot be found due to the schools being so large. During every recess that the weather was satisfactory to be outside, I was always on the playground with the kids organizing games, teaching them new ones, and playing with them. This was a community in which all the kids, little and big, liked to play baseball, so being that I could not run, I served as umpire for them and sometimes the catcher. The students thought this was great, the teacher playing right along with them, as often times they'd remark how none of their past teachers ever came out on the playground to see what they were even doing, much as less play with them.

Across the road on the same side that the school was on, was a little gas station. The man who ran it was an elderly man who was pleasingly plump, spoke quite harshly [occasionally using a bit of foul language], but liked the kids and was good to the kids. Often times after school, the children would purchase candy bars or a bottle of soda. His name was Ivan and everybody from near and far knew who Ivan was, as he treated everyone with respect and was liked by anyone who knew him.

Many times after recess during the warmer weather, I'd send two older boys over to Ivan's to bring back refreshments for the students. Ivan would always remind the boys to be sure to count correctly and to be absolutely certain not to forget their teacher because she was a peach. This is how Ivan always referred to me, as the teacher Peach.

At Christmas time, I used the same operetta which I had written and composed at the last school, and rewrote s few of the parts to adapt to these children. Some of the boys even played the parts of girls, but they loved to perform. Mrs. Ellingson accompanied on the piano and enjoyed every minute of it. She even helped my mom and me sew stage curtains for this event. Here was another group of people who took pride in their children's acting and singing.

Being a rural school having one teacher, there were many odd jobs to perform, teaching, cleaning, caring for the kids when they accidentally were hurt, and providing extra curricular activities for the children. In addition to teaching art, one was to act as a physical education instructor. I scheduled many baseball games with other schools in addition to being an umpire.

Occasionally on a Friday afternoon, we would schedule a game rotating back and forth from other schools followed by a home game. The whole school would go and the team was made up of all ages, anyone who liked to play baseball. Kids who were not interested in playing usually played on the playground equipment as many mothers went along to drive and they were always willing to watch kids.

A few humorous incidents happened along the way while I was teaching. But the funniest and most embarrassing one for me happened during a geography class one day. Two students were sitting at the recitation table with me and as I was explaining a concept to them, the bridge in my mouth that held three teeth happened to be very loose and it fell right out of my mouth onto the table. In excitement little Ray Ziebell shouted out as loud as he could, "Mrs. Roanhaus has false teeth". I guess that was a shock to Ray because he related false teeth to older people, and especially not to a young teacher.

Needless to say, the rest of the kids were shocked also, but none of them made a big deal out of it. I really didn't think too much of it either, but I graciously excused myself from the table and went into the lavatory and crammed the bridge back into my mouth, and returned. Following that, all went on as if nothing happened.

When I finally got to cleaning the rubbish out of the basement, the children would help me at every recess until we had it all cleared out. This is how they sacrificed their play time just to help me so I could get done and get back to playing with them at the recesses.

All the junk was put on a pile right next to a barrel for burning paper, and one of the farmers volunteered to pick it up after we had it all together. All the paper items were piled up by the trash barrel where the burnable stuff would be burned when the weather was nice and the wind was not blowing. This was a sort of make shift incinerator, the place where all the contents that were flammable could be ignited into ash refuse.

Being that it was a nice calm day, we loaded this barrel with the debris and started it ablaze to dispose of some of it. A few of the older boys helped me keep an eye on it and everything was going along smoothly during this hour long noon recess. The boys kept handing me objects and I kept feeding the incinerator.

Now here comes the disastrous part of burning rubbish. The wind switched and the rubble started to fly out of the burning barrel and made its way east. I really didn't worry too much about it as the field next to the school lot was very large. But more and more was blowing out and more and more was becoming ablaze. Ivan came running across the street and started fighting the fire with a broom, but the more he battled it, the more it started out of control.

He said to me, "Damn it Peachy, call the damn fire department, it is out of control".

"No, Ivan, I won't. I'll call Quentin, he'll know what to do".

After calling Quentin, he rushed right down and he called the fire department. All this while the fire had approached the neighbor's barn filled with hay. Now I started to worry! 'Dear God,' I started to pray, 'please don't let Berner's barn go up in flames.'

The Silver Lake Fire Department had arrived, and they saved Berner's barn. It was a meager sort of fire and the firemen joked about it. I didn't think it was so funny, I was almost certain that my job was on the line right then and there.

After all was said and done, I expressed to Quentin how sorry I was that this had happened. Shyly, I asked him if I still was employed, but he was shocked that I had even asked. "Heavens, yes, you're the best that ever happened to this place, it needed cleaning up badly".

117

What a relief! But he did tell me that on the next week end he and a group of men would come and finish burning the rest of the rubble, but he was grateful that I had cleaned the place like I did because as he stated how much better the whole school looked.

One of the saddest experiences of my life was the loss of a little first grade boy, who was hit by a Wanzer Milk Truck on highway 50 as he was walking home from school. There was no school bussing in those days, children either had to walk to school or the parents would form a car pool. There were no children in the district who had to walk as far as little David had.

I had great concern for this little boy and emphasized the importance of safety on the highway as an extra class incorporated into the curriculum, due to all the children who had to walk a distance. I always had an eighth grade girl named Shirley, walk with him beyond her house to the top of a steep incline in the road which impaired visibility for a driver until getting over this incline.

I always went outdoors to see the children off immediately after school was dismissed. On this one occasion as Shirley, along with her brother and sister, and also David left the school and were well on their way and out of my sight, I went back into school. I was busy correcting papers when I received the news that David had been hit by a milk truck just over the incline after Shirley had escorted him to the top.

The sun was bright and the truck driver didn't see this little body along the road, so he hit him. Later that evening I contacted Mrs. Huff and she told me that David had passed away. I went over to their house and tried to comfort this poor distraught mother, but this was difficult because I was as saddened as she. A teacher grows to love each of her students, and so it was with little David.

A day or so later she made arrangements to come to school and get David's belongings. As the two of us went through these things, our tears flowed like a stream upon this little boy's books and assignment work.

All of our school children accompanied by their mothers went as a corporate body in to the funeral home. It was so sad as each of the children stood at his coffin saying goodbye to David. What a deeply sorrowful episode this was to hear each child's farewell to him! School was called off on the day of the funeral and I attended along with many others of the district.

After all was at its end, the sadness never went away because the cemetery located right across the road from the school was a constant reminder of David being close to us, but no longer an active part of us. I had always hoped that I would never have to go through a crisis like this again.

I loved being at Mound Center School, and would have liked to have stayed there for many years, but I only had this pleasure for two years. My dear mother became ill and I was needed at home, so I put my teaching career on hold. In the meantime I was called many times to do substitute teaching within Kenosha County.

During the next years, I took a long term sub job at Wild Rose School in Randall township for several months. Then our second child, Dolly, was born.

I also subbed many times at Bristol State Graded School for Mrs. Ada Luke, several times was called to Riverview School in Silver Lake for Mrs. Etta Barry, several times at Wheatland Center School, and a day here and there at other schools, but this was my way of keeping in touch with my field of work.

In 1954, I accepted a long term sub job at Wheatland Center School for Marilyn Griffiths, who was going to have a baby. Following this sub job, the principal asked me to stay on full time, so I did. I stayed there until I became pregnant with our third child, and was so ill with the pregnancy, that I couldn't sign any more contracts, and had to leave during the school year.

Our family started growing and our third child was born. At this time I decided to stay home and raise our family, but in the meantime to take on substitute work here and there.

I have enjoyed my initial years of teaching, touched many lives of children in a positive way, and left good impressions wherever I had taught. I loved kids and I loved teaching.

As a point of interest, I found the rules for teachers from long ago, and every day that I taught school, I thought about the demands that were put on teachers in the 1800s. These are as follows:

-Teachers each day will fill lamps, clean chimneys.

-Each teacher will bring a bucket of water and a scuttle of coal for the day's session.

-Make your pens carefully. You may whittle nibs to the individual taste of the pupils.

-Men teachers may take one evening each week for courting purposes, or two evenings a week if they go to church regularly.

-After ten hours in school, the teachers may spend the remaining

119

time reading the Bible or other good books.

-Women teachers who marry or engage in unseemly conduct will be dismissed.

-Every teacher should lay aside from each pay a goodly sum of his earnings for his benefit during his declining years so that he will not become a burden on society.

-Any teacher who smokes, uses liquor in any form, frequents pool or public halls, or gets shaved in a barber shop will give good reason to suspect his worth, intention, integrity, and honesty.

-The teacher who performs his job faithfully and without fault for five years will be given an increase of twenty-five cents per week in his pay, providing the Board of Education approves.

I'm happy that I was from the 1900's and not the 1800's. These appear like some ridiculous demands put on teachers, who likewise are human beings.

Oak Knoll Students and Teacher

Back L-R: Jim Edwards, Herman Kiesler, Bill Kautz, Ardell Lenz, Ray and Catherine Nelson, Teacher Miss Arlene Lenz

Middle: Bob Tilton, Jim Cates, Donna Weiler, Donna Edwards, Audrey Ranker, Dolores Blair, Carolee Clausen

Front: Dick Tilton, Diane Ehlert, Donna Rae Tilton, Nancy Pacey, Wayne Blair

121

Oak Knoll School - 1947

Mound Center School Students and Teacher:

Back L - R: Loretta Wllingson, Wally Partenheimer, Thelma Berner, Ron Ziebell, Donna Mae Minnis, Jim Minnis
Middle: Irving Partenheimer, Shirley Berner, Jim Ellingson, Tim Hubbard, Tom Hubbard, Tom Brandes
Front: John Partenheimer, Larry Berner, Ray Ziebell, Linda Ziebell, Eddie Ellingson
Standing: Mrs. Arlene Roanhaus

My first year of teaching at Oak Knoll School
Graduation Class of 1947
Ardell Lenz and Jim Edwards with teacher Miss Arlene Lenz

124

Chapter 9
I Married The Love of My Life

It was after Christmas when Phil and I started to make wedding plans. He had given me a beautiful cedar chest, better known in those days as a hope chest, but I didn't have to hope any longer, I had my man! This was my Christmas present from Phil.

I was finally invited to his house for a dinner. Of course, all his step mother's Betzig kids were there and I really felt very much like an outsider because some of the Betzigs were quite rude and not very nice to me. However I put up with the whole situation as I was not marrying them, but rather Phil.

When you are in love, you can put up with almost anything, even his family. Phil's dad was a very sweet, kind gentleman and how he put up with all this is beyond me, but I think he married Liz for companionship but I will have to say she was an immaculate housekeeper and one hell of a good baker.

All afternoon, Liz kept saying that I should show the rest of the people what I had gotten from Phil for Christmas. I politely responded that it was too big to be carrying around. Of course. she meant my engagement ring, but that was a birthday gift which she didn't know about. You see, Phil did not choose the girl whom Liz picked out for him, nyah, nyah!

I still to this day think the only reason that she accepted me was the fact that I was a teacher, and to her, that was status quo. All the Betzig guys and women were factory workers or alcoholic drinkers who engaged in telling dirty jokes. This in itself was not to my liking, as I was never brought up in such atmos- phere. Thank God that Phil and his blood brothers and sister were not at all like the rest of them, I specifically mean that family. How Phil's wonderful dad ever put up with all of this baloney was always beyond me, but being the amiable man that he was, he would just shake his head and try to change the conversations.

I was never so glad in my life as to get out of their house in the early evening. When we left, big old tall Liz who towered at about six feet two, had to give me a hug.

Now I like a hug from people who really mean it, but this was such a fake hug, pressing her big boobs against my slender body. I felt as though she was pressing every bit of life out of me, because at this time, I only weighed about ninety-nine pounds.After leaving their house, I was alone with Phil at last. I expressed my feelings to him, that I thought his stepmother was as fake as anyone could get. But this is all that I said at the time, because after all, Phil did honor and respect her as a mother, seeing that his own mother died right after Phil's birth.

I need to tell you at this point just a little bit about Phil's background so you know what kind of an atmosphere he was raised in. After his mother was deceased, his Aunt Elizabeth Dauben, Phil's mother Barbara's sister, took care of baby Phil and his brother Ralph who was three years old at the time. She took care of them in their early childhood with tender loving care.

Several years later, Joseph Roanhaus, Phil's dad, met and married Liz Betzig, who had three children of her own. She had two boys and a daughter who was in a sanitarium with tuberculosis. Now the combined families started adding up as Phil's dad had a girl and a boy from his very first marriage before marrying Barbara. Liz's oldest son Cecil was married and out on his own, but this left four of the Roanhaus children and one Betzig child all living at the same farm in Lyons township a bit south west of Burlington.

Liz always favored her son over the Roanhaus children, but the oldest daughter of Joe's whose name was Lucille always looked out for the Roanhaus children until she moved to Sheboygan Falls and married at a young age. Then it was Marvin to look out for Ralph and Phil, but Marvin got fed up with Liz and so he left home and relocated. I have often heard the story that Liz wanted Marvin out of the house so badly that he finally got fed up with her B.S. and left of his own accord.

After Phil's dad retired from farming, they moved to Burlington, and his dad went into carpentry and worked for the Elmer Scherrer Construction Company.

I always think he worked away from the house just to get away from her evilness. Not long after that Ralph went into service, followed by Phil's entry into the army shortly after.

Now back to the wedding plans. We decided to get married in June, the traditional month of weddings. Then we met with Father Michels at St. Alphonsus Church and he okayed the date of June 26 in 1948. June was the best choice for me as school wasn't in session during summer, and it was good for Phil because he could take off easier from work as that was not the busiest season where he worked.

Plans started fast and furious, as we had just six months to get everything arranged before this great day in our lives. My parents were right there for us every step of the way, but mom and dad and my brothers all liked Phil from the very beginning that I met him, and they were eager to include him in our family.

Next we had to select attendants as we already knew that we wanted a big wedding, and my parents approved because they were paying the costs. I guess anything I wanted they would have agreed on because they still had remarked how close they came to losing their only daughter during my dreadful illness.

Being that I never had a sister, I asked my sister-in-law Sophie, Bob's wife, as my matron of honor. Phil chose his brother Ralph as his best man. My bridesmaids were my dearest friend and soon to be my sister-in-law Helen, Marvin's wife; my cousin Ruth Lenz; my college roommate Evelyn Martin; and a neighbor girl Marise May as my charm girl as they were called in those days, now referred to as a junior bridesmaid. My little five year old cousin Sharon Wilson was my flower girl.

Phil had decided to have as his groomsmen his half brother Marvin; my brother Bob; and Evelyn Martin's fiance Bob Vos, who by the way was in my grade school class at St. Al's. My younger brother Ardell was the junior groomsman. Ushers were Phil's cousin Harold Roanhaus and my cousin Ray Toelle.

Now the fun began! I had sent out for books and books of invitation samples from which to choose. Phil and I agreed from the start as we both liked the same invitation so it didn't take very long for us to decide. We filled out the order blank and sent it off. Included in this order were personalized printed napkins and matchbooks. We also ordered a special cake knife.

Probably one of the most important jobs was the selection of gowns so Mom and I went to Milwaukee to shop for a wedding gown for me. We looked at several and when the clerk brought this particular dress out, called the Dorothy Doll style, both mom and I knew that it was going to be my dress. It was so beautiful, and I tried it on. Mom remarked to the clerk, "Doesn't she look just like an angel?"

Well I'll tell you that I was far from being an angel, but if mom thought I looked like one, I had hoped that I really did. It was a colonial style dress of white ninon. Lace trimmed the long sleeves, the yolk and the front ruffle-over-ruffle skirt front, having a very long train of ruffled flounces. A three-quarter length veil of imported illusion was held in place by a crown of orange blossoms which was also edged in lace. This was my bridal gown. Mom paid for it and at that time the dress and veil cost one hundred sixty-eight dollars. Today that is comparable to about four thousand dollars, but cost was not a factor as mom wanted me to have the very best, and that I did.

The clerk went on to show us the matching dresses for the attendants. They were equally as gorgeous and they all came in the pastel colors that I wanted. For headpieces, she showed us backless hats with a matching bow flowing from the back. She also showed us gauntlets to wear on their arms in matching colors. This is what I wanted for my girl attendants.

Two weeks later, all the girls and mom and I went back and the girls fell in love with the dresses immediately, so we ordered them. Sophie had powder blue, Evelyn had pink, Helen had orchid, Ruth had mint green, and Marise had yellow. Little Sharon had powder blue to match the maid of honor. They were all so happy because they liked the outfits so much, and now they could hardly wait for the wedding to wear them.

The next step was to order the flowers. Mom and I went to the florist in Wilmot, Mrs. Charlotte Schnurr, who was very creative in wedding arrangements and she knew what would look just perfect with the kind of gowns everyone was wearing.

She suggested for me, the bride, to carry a moline heart-shaped flower bouquet centered with three orchids and flowing ribbons with stephanotis trailing from the bouquet. For the girls, she suggested a colonial styled bouquet of white carnations tipped with the colors of each one's dress. She would also take care of making up the baskets of flowers for the church, flowers for the relatives, the centerpiece for the tables, and the cake knife at the reception.

She would deliver the flowers to the church, and have the floor runner ready to be unrolled. She was one great efficient lady and who knew what she was doing. At this point and time mom paid her for the flowers.

Phil chose black tuxedos for all the guys wearing black formal bow ties and the groom had a white formal bow tie. Each fellow had a white carnation tipped the color of the dress that the girl he walked with had. Phil, the groom had a stephanotis boutonniere.

The next was the ordering of the wedding cake. Mom and I went to Vogelsangs Bakery in Burlington and looked at several pictures until we decided on a three tiered white cake with white icing and flowers in pastel colors using the same colors

128

that we have in the gowns. The top tier would have the traditional bride and groom on. Then mom paid for the cake as special cakes had to be paid for in advance.

Mom and dad went with Phil and me into the Hotel Burlington one evening and made arrangements for the wedding dinner. We all had a part in the planning which was so much fun. Then dad had to write a check as a down payment for the dinner.

Then we went to see the band leader to engage a band for the dance at Fox River Gardens in the evening. Again my dad wrote out a check for that. My parents were so wonderful about everything

Plans were being made right and left and Phil and I started planning where we would go on our honeymoon. Together we decided that we both wanted to go to Canada. How exciting this all was, as each day became more and more fun in the planning stages.

Time went on and the date of our wedding was getting nearer and nearer. Then came the evening of the rehearsal at the church. Father Michels was so gracious and so kind to all of us, and everyone cooperated so well. I think everyone was almost as excited as we were, because none of the attendants had ever been in such a big wedding, although Helen and Marvin had a big wedding also.

Phil and I kissed good night and we knew we would not see each other again until at the church the next morning.

I could hardly sleep that night, as the night couldn't go fast enough for me, I was excited beyond explanation. Every couple of hours, I'd look at the clock and time passed so slowly, until it was seven o'clock when I got up. After completing the morning grooming, we all started to get ready.

Back then one had to fast from midnight on in order to receive holy communion at the mass the next day. Usually I found this to be very difficult as I have always had a queasy stomach, but this morning I had gotten past that and didn't feel sickish as usually before. So this meant that I could get past the fainting feeling and would not do a repeat performance like I did at Marvin and Helen's wedding.

When we arrived at the church the organist Evelyn Uhen was playing beautiful music before the ceremony started. The ceremony was set for 9:00 o'clock in the morning. Soon the wedding march would start and we'd be on our way into the sacrament of Holy Matrimony. As soloist we had a cousin of mine, Mary Ann Toelle who took singing lessons along with me in our elementary school days. The wedding march started and as little Sharon walked down the aisle, the groom and the rest of the men proceeded out of the sacristy. She was followed by the charm girl Marise, then Helen, Ruth, Evelyn, and Sophie.

My father then escorted me down the aisle, and when he presented me to Phil, he gave my hand to Phil as though he felt like he was losing his only daughter. All I could think of at this point was that he was not losing a daughter, but rather gaining another son.

We started up to the altar. At this time everyone was to genuflect, but seeing that I could not genuflect due to my residual handicaps from polio, Father Michels had told us before hand that everyone could omit the genuflection so that I would not be too obvious. Father was so understanding of what I could or could not do and was just great about everything.

After the Mass had started, I could hardly wait for the marriage vows, but it wasn't long before I got to say, "I do", and the same for Phil. Just before the ceremony was over and before we processed out of church as Mr. & Mrs. Phil Roanhaus, Mary Ann sang my most favorite song, Schubert's Ave Maria. During this time I went over the blessed Mary statue and paid tribute to her as the greatest lady ever known. As I was standing there during the song I silently prayed to Mary for her help that I could become a good mother in the future as she was the greatest mother. I knew that in the future, I wanted lots of children because I had loved everyone else's kids and now I could start thinking about having our own, Phil's and mine. But that never happened until a year and a half later.

After the church service, we all went back to my parents' farm home and had as our breakfast, scrambled eggs, bacon, toast, rolls, juice and coffee.

Following breakfast we all went into the photography studio on Sixth Avenue in Kenosha to have pictures taken. By the time this was completed, it was time to go into Burlington to the Burlington Hotel for our dinner to be served at one o'clock. We had a delectable dinner there, which was enjoyed by our families, relatives and friends.

At last we got to go back to the farm for the afternoon reception, where we had about two hundred guests. Phil and I had to receive and greet all the guests, and later we opened gifts, as was customary to do back then. Hors d'oeuvres and beverages were served all afternoon. Some people played cards or just conversed, while others consumed cocktails. All this while, three lady friends of my mom's, Kate Mangold, Gertie Kerkhoff and Anne Siehoff, were in mom's kitchen preparing food for the evening buffet to be served at 6:00 p.m. This meal consisted of roast beef, ham, buns, German potato salad, American potato salad, cole slaw, baked beans, cucumber salad, veggie plate, and other relishes. Dessert was the wedding cake and ice cream. The ladies did a great job of preparing and serving the food.

At 7:30 p.m. everyone started getting ready for the dance at the Fox River Winter Gardens about a mile from the farm house. We danced and danced the night away, but Phil and I slipped away from the dance while people were engaged in dancing, drinking, and conversing, so no one even noticed that we were gone, except our parents whom we said goodbye to.

Before the wedding we had been threatened by some of the guys that they were going to steal the bride, fix our vehicle, and do other mischievous feats to stop us from getting away. So we hurried into Burlington to Phil's parents' house, changed from our bridal attire into street clothes. We already had our luggage in the back of Phil's Studebaker which we planned to take on our honeymoon. But prior to that time, Phil had told everyone that we were going to take his dad's car, so no one was the wiser. We left our bridal clothes at his house and we were off, and no one disturbed us at all.

It was then that we were off on our honeymoon to Canada. The total cost of our wedding trip was $217.57, which was very inexpensive, in comparison to today.

Today, fifty-one years later,we are still as much in love as we were then. We count our blessings every day because we are fortunate that God has been so good to us to allow us to still enjoy life together. And that we do in every aspect of the word love.

131

Phil and Arlene - June 26, 1948

Phil & Arlene's Wedding Party June 26, 1948

Standing L-R: Bob Lenz, Ralph Roanhaus, Marise May, Arlene, Phil, Ardell Lenz, Bob Vos, Marvin Roanhaus

Sitting L-R: Sue Martin, Sophie Lenz, Sharon Wilson, Helen Roanhaus, Ruth Lenz

Chapter 10
Building Our Home

Our house was started before we were married. Phil, his dad who had done carpenter work after retiring from the farm, my dad and my younger brother, Ardell, all worked laboriously on building our house.

My parents had given us the lot to build on located directly west of the farm buildings in a parcel that once had been a crop field. In fact it was that very field where I used to drive the tractor for my dad. It was that very field where dad cussed and yelled at me many times when I turned the corners too short and he had to get off the hay wagon to pick up the hay that I had missed. And to think, this is now where we were building our house.

My dad had this parcel of land surveyed into several lots with the intent that when my parents retired from the farm, one of these lots was where they would build their retirement home.

This, of course, meant sacrificing a portion of the field where my dad had grown crops. The first lot that was located about a quarter of a mile north of highway 50 was reserved for my parents. The next lot was the one dad and mom gave us to build on.

Across the road from where we were building was Fox River, so this put our property along highway W, which is presently called 328th Avenue. Having the river across from where our house was being built gave us a picturesque view of nature, truly a place of striking beauty in the country.

Being that Phil and I had both been born and raised on farms, we were definitely country folks and we liked it. We were never ones to enjoy the hustle and bustle of city life, we only went to the cities to shop and do our banking, but most of our friends also lived in the country.

Now where does one start when planning to build a house? We had to decide what style we wanted, so we sent out to many companies for blueprints of homes. In the forties, colonial styled homes were in style and became popular, so this is what we were looking at. We looked and looked and discussed and discussed until finally we had selected one, allowing for some minor changes.

Phil and I used to kind of get a charge out of my dad as we were looking at blueprints, he'd always say, "Don't forget, every room costs a thousand". All through the construction time, we always had to chuckle a bit and kept reminding each other of what dad had said. It became a standing family joke after a while. But you had to understand that dad was trying to impress on us the value of money. Of course, being that time one thousand dollars most likely at present time in the approaching year of 2000 would be worth about twenty thousand.

After selecting the house we wanted, we sent away for the blueprints. It wasn't long and the prints came, so we were ready to commence to build.

Then Phil, along with my dad and his dad, sat down to figure out the cost of materials. They figured that in all reality, they most likely could build our house for five thousand dollars. Wow! That sounded like a great amount of money, and at the time it was a great amount of money.

Now the real question was before us. How would we begin to finance this house? Back then banks weren't keen about financing a house, and most people had to depend on a private loan from someone within the community who had ample money to lend. Who in the world would back us up financially?

We thought and thought and in the meantime, the Dauben family estate had to be settled. This meant that Phil and his brother Ralph, being the only living descendants of Barbara, who had passed on to eternal rest after Phil's birth, would be the heirs to her part of the estate money. Wow! What timing.

So after the estate was completely settled, Phil and his brother each received one thousand dollars. What a great help, now we could start our basement. Phil went out to buy supplies for the basement.

Being so prudent about how to spend this money so as to get the most out of it, my dad suggested that he would help Phil dig the basement. Actually it was the crudest method ever. No excavator was hired, so dad brought down from his farm a slip scoop. So with the tractor and slip scoop, our basement was dug. Many laborious and back breaking hours went into the digging of the basement project. But at last, our house was started.

At this time they were ready for the cement blocks and the mortar compound. Now some of the family members helped lay blocks. Phil would work after his regular job was completed for the day. My dad would help after the farm work was done and before milking the cows. My brother Ardell, who was still in high school, would help as soon as he got home every day.

Phil's dad would help when the other guys were there because we didn't want him out there alone. On weekends, much progress was seen.

The basement was going well, and soon it would be ready to start with the framing. We still hadn't any more money, so my dad suggested that we contact two men in New Munster, who had never married, and were quite well to do as they lived a miserly life. We called them and made an appointment with them, and they invited us to come to their house. So mom and dad went with Phil and me to see George and Bill. They were delighted to help us and told us that we'd have to go to the lawyer with them, but we needed two people to co-sign for a loan for us. They would set up the appointment with their lawyer and get back to us informing us of date and time.

In the meantime we needed to find two co-signers, so I asked my dad and Phil asked his dad. My dad agreed that he would, but Phil's dad refused because Liz wouldn't let him co-sign for us. Now what do we do that we only have one to co-sign? My mom came to our rescue and said that she would co-sign with my dad so we accepted her offer.

In the meantime we got a phone call from these kind gentlemen, informing us of the date and the time to meet with their lawyer, and would we pick them up as they had no car and didn't know how to drive anyway. So mom, dad, Phil and I picked them up at their house and they were ready and so eager to help us because they liked us.

When we got to Burlington where their lawyer was located in a dingy upstairs office, the man was a gruff looking elderly man who spoke as gruffly as he appeared. I always felt that he had a chip on his shoulder because he wasn't married, and I had the feeling that he didn't care for anyone who was happily married. The two men introduced us to him, and even then he was unfriendly and motioned for us all to sit down. The chairs had inches of dust on them and his office was the most untidy I had ever seen.

He said that he wanted to get right down to business and immediately inquired who our co-signers would be. When the one man told him that my parents would be, he peered over the top of his small spectacles, and said, "Both from one family, I don't like that."

My dad who was quick witted replied, "You needn't worry, this house will be paid for in no time. My son-in-law is very ambitious and my daughter is a school teacher who has a good paying job, so there will be no problems. The interest to these men will be paid before the due date each month." I guess dad told him what was right and them some.

Again peering over his spectacles with a frown on his brow, he stated that he didn't like to help young people borrow money for a house, because more than likely they would only put up a little shack and not a real house. Then when they would lose it for non payment, no one else wants to buy a shack. By this time my dad was furious, and it showed by his facial expression and the look in his eyes. He assured this old fart lawyer that it would be paid for and if he didn't want to do the paper work, dad would find someone who would. I guess he took that remark as a threatening statement.

Quickly he got out the paper work, and asked how much we were asking for, and the gentleman who was lending us this money told him four thousand dollars. It didn't take very long now and after we put our signatures on all the papers, we thanked him and left.

He didn't trust us with the cash so he made the deposit directly himself in our account at the Silver Lake Bank by means of a phone call. We were so grateful that the whole deal was now behind us and all we had to do was save and pay off on the loan every month plus pay the interest directly to the men.

Each time a few days before the interest payment was due, I would bake a cake or sweets of some kind and Phil and I would take the interest payment to them in person. They lived a very lonely life and they looked forward to having us come and visit them. In fact it was hard to leave once we were there because they enjoyed company so much. They were such sweet old guys who lived a life as hermits.

Now we could have the first load of lumber delivered as the basement floor was settled by now and the progress could go on. We became more and more excited. As time went on progress was going very steadily.

In the meantime, I became pregnant with our first child. Being that we were living with my mom and dad almost a year now, until the house was completed, we wanted to be in our house before the first birth in September. The men kept working rapidly, but fastidiously. Everything was taking shape and I became more and more excited.

In the meantime mom and dad went to Chicago with us to a furniture store called Libbys. We got good deals that day. We bought an area carpet that was gray for the living room. We

138

selected a burgundy colored couch and chair to match, with two end tables, a coffee table, and three lamps. That for the time being, would complete our living room.

For the kitchen we selected a table and four chairs. The table top was done in white enamel with a black design on. The chairs were chrome with black padded vinyl seats. The ends of the table had an extension that could easily be pulled out for added room.

For the main bedroom, we bought a double bed, one dresser with a huge mirror, and one high boy dresser. This was of blond wood, as that was the style at that time.

They held the entire order in their warehouse until we moved into the house at which time we just had to phone them to let them know when someone was coming with a truck to pick up all these furnishings. We borrowed Ed Toelle's truck to go to Chicago for the pick up.

We still needed a stove and refrigerator for the kitchen, a washing machine for the laundry room, and a dining room set for the formal dining room.

An appliance store in Kenosha was selling out and held an auction so we went there in hopes to find the appliances that we still needed. My parents went with us and my dad, being used to going to farm auctions, promised to do our bidding in the event that we were interested in any of their items. We had looked at some of the items previously to the starting of the auction, so we knew what we wanted to bid on if the price was right.

A few stoves were sold, and the last stove which was electric, was up now. No one seemed to bid on it, I guess all the people who wanted a stove already got theirs. This was luck for us, because we got a tremendously good deal on the General Electric stove that we really wanted. We got it for $100.

Washing machines were up now so my dad bid on a couple of them, but they all went for too high a price. Later we went to the Triangle Store in Kenosha and after looking at several models we selected a Speed Queen. This machine had two compartments, one for the washing and rinsing, the other was for spinning the water out of the laundry. This was the latest form of an automatic washer made.

We still needed a refrigerator, so Phil heard of a second hand one for sale in Burlington, so he looked at it and bought it for $75. It was a Kelvinator and the darn thing wore and wore, so it was a very good deal.

We didn't have a dining room set, so my sister-in-law Soph heard of a set being sold in Powers Lake, so we looked at it and bought it. We spent hours and hours of sanding and refinishing but when we finished it looked like a new set. It included a large table with three extra leaves, four chairs plus two hostess chairs with arms, and a huge buffet. It had upholstery on the hostess chairs, so when we were through with the sanding, staining, and finishing, we reassembled the chairs back together again, and reupholstered then with new fabric.

At this time we still didn't have a furnace, so Phil heard of a fuel oil furnace for sale because the people who owned it, called Lubenos, were installing a new furnace so they sold it to us for one hundred dollars. It gave us good service for about five years until one wintry day, it blew up and we had excessive smoke damage from the back draft. This was such a mess to clean up, but with the help of my parents, we accomplished the job. Then we bought a new one from Sears, no more second hand furnace for us.

In the beginning of August we were ready to move into our own house that would become our home. It was so much fun settling everything and starting to keep house for just Phil and me.

We had lived here a month when our first baby was born on September 3 in 1949. It was to be my third year of teaching, so I had a friend of mine substitute for me for the first month of school until I was ready to go back. My mom came to the rescue and took care of Darlene in our home every day for me while I worked. During the day mom would do my housework so when I returned home each day, I prepared the suppers and my parents ate with us. I spent the remainder of the evening with my husband and our new baby, in addition to correcting papers.

Our house was a story and a half. Besides the huge basement, we had several rooms on the main floor. This included the living, dining, kitchen, bedroom, bathroom, front hall that extended all the way back to form a long hall. You see, we hadn't finished the upstairs at this time. There was also a laundry room.

About a year later, our open stairway was put in and then we had a front hall and a back hall, with a closet under the stairway. The original blueprint showed stairs under the stairway to enter the basement, but we had the basement entry off the laundry room with the back entry to the house.

The upstairs wasn't finished until we needed an extra

bedroom a few years later. There were two huge bedrooms and a full sized walk-in attic used for storage. In these upstairs bedrooms were large built-in drawers for added storage of bedding and blankets and in other drawers went the seasonal clothes. These drawers, four in each bedroom, came in mighty handy and were always full.

When Dolly was born, Phil and I moved our bedroom furniture upstairs in one of the bedrooms, and Darlene and Dolly had the other bedroom. By having us upstairs, the girls felt more secure, so what had been our bedroom downstairs was used as a toy and playroom for the girls. This saved having toys all over the house and they loved to spend hours playing in there.

In this toy room were all the playthings that my Aunt Florence had purchased for me when I was a little girl. This included a kitchen cabinet which was about four feet tall having two doors on the top, a workspace in the middle, and two doors at the bottom. The top held all the dishes and the bottom held all the pans used in play cooking. I still had my little electric stove which really baked mini cakes.

In the middle of the room was the table and chair set that we bought for the two girls one Christmas. Off in one corner was a doll bed, which was like a mini baby crib of today because it was large and the girls could put three dolls in at a time. It also had a baby bassinet that Mrs. Schlax, my former 4-H leader, had given to me from her daughter for our little girls who played with it so much in putting their dolls to sleep.

This toy room had many more of the playthings from my earlier life as well as what we had bought for the girls. It was a place of enchantment for Darlene and Dolly, a place of the make-believe world, a place of realistic learning and doing the things that they had seen mom do in her own domestic setting. It was education in disguise.

After Danny was born, we had to dismantle the playroom as Phil and I moved back downstairs into our original bedroom. The girls moved into the room upstairs that we had previously because it was the larger of the two upstairs bedrooms, and Danny had the other bedroom.

As time went on, the girls' bedroom became a girls' dormitory as all of them were in there at one time. For three years Darlene was in Fond du Lac, and a bit later, she moved in an apartment with girl friends, so we managed with the two bedrooms using bunk beds. The boys did very well as there were just the three of them, but all the children survived.

Our house stayed pretty much the same except for new carpeting in rooms now and then until 1959, we remodeled the kitchen. We had a sort of island coming out from one side of the room which took up more space than it was worth so we removed it and put in more upper cupboards giving much more storage room which we greatly needed.

Now that we didn't have a baby crib in our room any longer, in 1966 my dad constructed a built-in wardrobe in our bedroom which held our hanging clothes amply. Next to this wardrobe, he built six large drawers so we could eliminate the two dressers that we had in the bedroom. Next to the set of drawers, he made the most beautiful dresserette for me with a huge mirror behind it. He did this so I could sit and do my hair and put on my make-up. Above the dresserette, the set of drawers, and the wardrobe, he built huge cupboards for added storage. I liked this because we had much more room.

My dad did all this and refinished it while Phil was up north deer hunting. As he was nearing the completion of the sawing of wood for this project, he slipped and almost cut his thumb off. I was at school teaching, but Dolly was home so she rushed my dad to emergency. I felt so badly about this accident happening, but he did a super job on this project, and he made us both very happy even though he had the accident.

In 1989 we remodeled our bathroom as I could no longer get into or out of the bathtub, so we took it out completely and put in a shower stall. At that time the closet from the bedroom was taken out so as to enlarge the space in the bathroom. I only used that closet for storing things in anyway, because we had all this built-in structure.

Dell was instrumental for this project. He also saw the need for a grab bar next to the stool for me to pull myself up from the toilet stool so he put one in on an angle that was serviceable for me to help myself. He also put a short bar in a position that I could back into the shower by holding this bar as a guide to sit down on the shower stool and to pull myself out of the shower. I use a shower stool in the shower because I can't stand that long.

He also installed a dresserette with a marble top and three drawers next to the double doors undeneath for storage. Now I could help myself easier than before, and I felt as though these were luxuries.

In 1993, we remodeled the entire house outside. First of

all the electrical wiring throughout the house was redone. We purchased new windows and doors, siding, roofing, and finally put in an opening in the living room that really went someplace. In previous years there were two French doors that supposedly were to lead outside but there was never anything to go to outside, so we kept these doors nailed shut.

It was then that we began to see need for a ramp outside for me, as walking was getting more difficult, and provisions had to be made for use of a wheel chair in the future. Now was the time to do this when everything else was being redone. David and Dell built a deck adjoining the house and connected the ramp to it.

The two French doors were taken out and one door was put in its place. Now this opening really led to some place, to the deck. The finish on the posts of the deck railing couldn't be done until the wood cured, so to speak. During the fall of 1996, Phil started to apply stain in all the good weather of early autumn. I felt sorry for him being in that heat working all alone, so I helped him apply stain be means of sitting an a deck chair and moving along as needed to complete an area at a time.

Being that he took all the outside staining, I worked on the inside. We had the posts and railings done on the landing. so we started to work on the ramp. He, being on the outside could stand on the ground and stain, but I was doing the inside so I was the one on the slant of the ramp going down. Everything went smoothly and we were almost finished, when the one leg of the chair I was sitting on got caught between the boards of the ramp. The chair tipped and I rolled down the ramp landing flat on my face.

What a scare! Being that I hadn't been able to help myself get up for years, I had to wait for some one to pick me up literally. Upon landing and coming to a halt, our neighbors Chris and Marty were there immediately to come to my rescue to help me up. They are the best neighbors anyone could have.

Chris had been talking on the phone when she saw this happen. She dropped the phone and ran calling to Marty, "Come quick, Arlene fell". Phil picked up my eye glasses that had flown far from where I landed and they were all bent out of shape to the extent that I couldn't even put them back on. After they picked me up and got me back on the chair on level ground, I started to feel the soreness. To this day, I am sure that I cracked my cheek bone and I also had a bump on my forehead.

During this predicament, I joked with Phil saying, "Well

don't worry, I'm going to get another new hip anyway", as the doctor had told me in my last visit to him. But there really was no joke involved as I was hurting.

Two years passed after that incident, and still no paint was applied to the railings, so Danny and his hired hands from his painting business came over one day and painted everything. He came to my rescue. Now our deck was totally completed.

In the back section of the house where the kitchen entry way was, David figured out how to redo my laundry room so I could walk out of the kitchen at the same level and have my washer and drier right there outside the kitchen door. Before this time I had to go down three steps to get to where the washer and drier were, but being that I could no longer lift my legs to walk steps, David figured it all out and what an improvement.

The steps to the basement were rerouted behind the washer and drier and it really looks nice because these steps are hidden. We still have the three steps to get to the landing where the outer entry way is and where we keep our freezer. David is so talented and such an excellent carpenter. I always told Phil that the day would come that David's profession would be carpentry, because when he was a little boy, he could take a piece of wood and construct something out of it and never use a pattern and he had a thing of beauty that he made. I always said that he had a natural gift for working with woods.

Recently we needed new hinges on the kitchen cupboards and somehow we just couldn't get anyone to do it. Phil and I together, like the blind leading the blind, installed new knobs on all the doors and drawers.

A bit later, Danny volunteered to put up the new hinges, but when he looked at the doors, as he was going to paint them for us, he said that the doors were very worn out after 50 years of wear, so his carpenter friend made all new doors and drawers. I did not want them painted, so he finished them in natural oak finish. Prior to installing these new doors and drawers, he had two of his men who work for him, Chuck and Barry, come out and paint the framework of the cupboards. This beautiful job is my Mothers' Day present. I told him that could be my Mothers' Day, Birthday, and Christmas gifts until the end of time.

Now our house looks very nice again, and together we enjoy our home. This is the story of our house from beginning till now and we always refer to it as our 'Home Sweet Home'.

Starting our house

Our house finished in 1949

145

Front view of our house - 1993

Back view of our house- 1993

Chapter 11
Starting Our Precious Family

As I had expressed before we wanted many children, and the Lord blessed us with eight, five girls and three boys. But after the eighth was born, that was it. Remember the TV program, 'Eight Is Enough'? Well, that's what we thought too, but we have enjoyed our kids from the day they were born until they grew up and left our nest. Actually today we still enjoy them as well as their spouses and their children, our grandchildren.

The first born was Darlene Dorothy, the name Dorothy after her godmother, my mother and her grandmother. Darlene was born September 3, 1949, weighing in at 8 pounds 6 ounces. She was beautiful, but you'll find that I will be saying that about all of our babies, because they were just that, beauty in every aspect. She had lots of golden blond hair and was so perfect in every sense of the word.

The only problem she had was her right foot was twisted, because I didn't have enough room in my uterus for her so her foot was cramped until birth. A pediatrician specialist put her foot in a little cast for three weeks so her foot would straighten. It was successful and she never had any problems after that.

Our second child should have been born on our 5th wedding anniversary June 26, but she wasn't born until Independence Day, July 4, 1953. On the 3rd of July, I was in the doctor's office for a check-up because she was already eight days overdue. After the doctor finished examining me, he told me that if the baby wasn't born in two more days, I should come in and they would give me a starter.

While he was telling me this, his phone rang. He answered it and as he finished, he said to me, "Do you know Margaret S. from out your way"? I told him I knew her well as she had been in our 4-H Club. And then very bluntly, he told me that she had just shot herself with her policeman brother's gun and was dead. His parting words were, "There, maybe the shock of hearing this will start things rolling, I hope to see you in the morning".

He was right, I went in to the hospital at 6:00 A.M. on July 4th, and that was the day our baby girl was born. Her name was Dorothy Ann, whom we wanted to call Dolly, but in those days the priest would not baptize children unless they had a saints' name. To us she has always been and still is Dolly. She weighed in at 9 pounds and 2 1/2 ounces on a hottest day of the year. Another golden blond haired little girl was a raving beauty.

Next child was a boy, and Phil was so very happy, now we had a boy. Daniel Phillip weighed in at 10 pounds and 13 1/2 ounces on March 16, 1955. Danny and I almost together left the world with this birth.

During his birth he was coming face up with arms open and my doctor called for another doctor to assist him. When I heard the plea for the second doctor, I began to panic, thinking I'm sure they don't either one know what they are doing, and to this day I know they were puzzled as to how to get this baby out of me. Technology wasn't then what it is today or I'm sure that knowing beforehand what a big baby he was, they should have prepared for a C section.

All I could hear was, "Mrs. Roanhaus, keep your head down, keep pushing". Yeah, they had good talking, I was the one trying my darnedest to push this baby out, but polio destroyed my abdominal muscles and I had very little push left in me.

Next I heard one of them say, "Save the baby", while the other responded with, "Save the mother, she has two children at home who need her". By this time, what little push that I tried to have was exhausted as the other two babies that I had given birth to previously had to be pushed out of me by the help of the doctor. At this point I heard one of them say to the other, "We're losing her, all her organs are coming down with the baby."

Now I began to really panic, as I was most conscious of what was happening. Then again, I heard, "Save the baby". The other said, "No, save the mother". All I could think of was, "Dear God, save us both, can't these doctors agree on anything?"

At this time all I wanted was my husband to be at my side with me, but that was not allowed back then, the husband had to wait in the waiting room. I always wondered what Phil might have been thinking after so many hours of hearing nothing. Then they decided to make incisions for the baby to come out, and when he did come, he was blue with the umbilical cord around his neck.

Now I really began to go into a frenzy but one doctor told me the baby would be okay. Finally the baby cried, and that was absolutely music to my ears. The nurse rushed him out of the delivery room. The doctors worked laboriously over me until I was out of danger. I felt as though I had stitches all the way up my back, and I was so sore!

For the two weeks that I was in the hospital, I was not allowed to hold Danny because he was so heavy. I had hurt feelings because I couldn't even hold our first boy, who was so perfect in every respect, although oversized. The nurses would put him aside of me in my bed and I could admire and feed him that way. I never breast fed any of the children, but rather bottle fed them. This whole ordeal was one that I never wanted to go through again, but still I did want more children.

When we just had these three children, we entered all three in a baby through preschool contest in Kenosha, sponsored by the Sheriff's Auxiliary Police for Civilian Defense. For one whole month, pictures of the child contestants were displayed in the window of a union hall in Kenosha. Every time someone would make a purchase in one of the down town stores in Kenosha, a ticket was given out and this ticket in turn could be turned in at this hall as a vote of a person's choice.

Being that we were out of town, our three children had a slim chance, but we entered them anyway, Obviously these votes were gained mostly by having been known in Kenosha or if people thought the children were outstanding in their category. Actually it was advertised as a beauty and health show, but we knew popularity entered into these ratings.

The ceremony to announce the winners was held at Eagles Ballroom on June 22, 1955. We were so proud of our children as all three placed in a category which was real success as hundreds of children never even got any kind of a placing. We were very proud of our own special little people, our children.

Our baby Danny who was three months old won honorable mention in the Baby category and was awarded a certificate. Our Dolly won honorable mention in the Tiny Tots category and was also awarded a certificate. Darlene won top honors in the Senior group of 5 to 6 years and was crowned Queen along with the little boy being crowned King, whose name was Ricky Pazera. Darlene and her little male partner wore satin robes and silver glittery crowns, as each was presented with a trophy. Phil and I, as well as Grandma and Grandpa Lenz, were extremely proud of our little ones.

The year of 1957 was ending on the happiest note for Phil and me. Deborah Katherine was born on New Year's Eve on December 31, weighing in at 10 pounds 1 1/2 ounces. When I went to the hospital for her birth the doctor asked me if I wanted to hold off so she would be the first baby of the year. This was the same doctor who had delivered Dolly and Danny.

I replied, "Get the show on the road, I'd rather have a tax deduction". So she was born a few hours before midnight. Another baby pushed out of me. But this ordeal went exceedingly better, and I was thrilled with another beautiful blue eyed blond baby girl.

Everyone's pet name for Deb was 'Cookie Babe', and her cousin Reggie used to pick her up and carry her all around the house, because she was so delighted with this new cousin.

The next pregnancy was a difficult one, as my brother Ardell had passed away at age 25, while I was carrying this baby. All through this pregnancy I was really stressed from the trauma of my brother's death. So when our baby arrived, we named him Dell Patrick, the first name being after my brother. This was now our fifth child being pushed out of me, another big one weighing in at 10 pounds 9 1/2 ounces on February 19, 1959. This was our second boy and now our family totaled up to three girls and two boys.

I went through some melancholic hours and days while I was in the hospital following Dell's birth. The only joys that I could appreciate were seeing my baby and having Phil come to visit me. My mom came every day and spent as much time with me at the hospital because she knew I was depressed after losing my younger brother who had everything to live for in the future but left the earth at only age twenty-five It was difficult for me to comprehend why God chose him.

It took a long time for me to get over this, so the doctor kept me in the hospital for an extended period of time. In the meantime I started to become homesick for the other four children at home, and this is what brought me out of this state of depression.

I was so eager to be home and be with the children. Now everything seemed to be the usual hustle and bustle of our ordinary life style. This kept me occupied and my mind started to ease and the pain grew less and less at this loss but the pain never goes away completely.

Number six child was Diane Barbara born on August 10, 1960, and the only baby of ours who decided to come into the world at a fast pace, so she was the only one who didn't have to be pushed out.

My water broke at home as I was in our garage about to get into the car to go to the hospital and needless to say, I was soaking wet. Phil wanted to know if I wanted to go back into the house and change my clothing, I just replied, "No, just drive as fast as you can and get me to the hospital or you'll be delivering this baby right here in the car". It was the only time during any deliveries that I felt like pushing and it was effective, not at all like any of the previous times when the pushing didn't do anything. Phil drove fast and as we got to the hospital, there was no time for them to prep me, so they took me right into the delivery room, wet clothing and all.

The nurse called the doctor and told him I was there and he should rush right over, and he thought he had plenty of time because of the slow process with all the other births, so he took his time. All of a sudden the nurse told Phil to call the doctor, as she needed to be with me.

We always felt that she was the one who really delivered the baby as the doctor walked in when Diane was coming into the world. Was he shocked! But this beautiful little blond girl with big blue eyes weighed in at 9 pounds 3 1/2 ounces.

Number seven was Donna Ruth weighing in at 8 pounds 9 1/2 ounces on December 12, 1961. On the evening that she was born, we were getting ready to go to a 4-H club pot luck Christmas party, when suddenly I realized that I wasn't going to a Christmas party, but I was going to the hospital. The other children in our family were quite disappointed about the sudden cancellation, but still were so thrilled about a new baby coming into our lives.

As it turned out, my mom and dad [the children's Grandma and Grandpa Lenz] took the children to the party as their grandmother was a leader also. I had a casserole dish all prepared and ready to take out of the oven, so mom took my casserole and she had made a salad to take to the pot luck. At least the children didn't get cheated out of the party, as Santa always came and gave each of the children a gift.

When I got to the hospital the nurse started to literally yell at me for picking that particular time to have a baby as it was the night of the Burlington Memorial Hospital Staff Christmas party, and she didn't want to call the doctor away from the party. Well, excuse me! When its time for a baby, it doesn't wait, it wants to be born. As it was, my regular doctor was out of town for the holidays, so I had to have one of the other doctors from the clinic. After several hours, the nurse did call Dr. McNeil and so Donna appeared into the world. Another blond blue eyes!

Phil had just started at the Kenosha County Highway

Department about this time, and it was a year of falling snow and more snow. This meant that when Donna and I came home, he was home very little because his job required him to be out plowing snow at all hours of the day and night.

The last of our family was David Michael weighing in at 10 pounds 7 ounces. He was born on none other than Friday the thirteenth of March, 1964. He was the cutest baby, and smiled at such an early age, so Friday the thirteenth was not so bad after all. David has been very superstitious ever since about his birth date, though nothing in my estimation should ever cause fear because of the thirteenth, as I have never been superstitious.

It was a cold wintry day and he was the only one who was born during the day except for Darlene. This meant that I had to call Phil home from his work at the Kenosha County Highway Department, in hopes that he would not be out on the road for a call but luck was with us, he was working in the shop. By this time my body was wearing out, so this was the caboose in our family train.

Now we had our family complete: Darlene, Dolly, Danny, Debbie, Dell, Diane, Donna, and David. This added up to a family of ten, eight kids, and Phil and me, but we always had been so happy and a very close knit family.

Feeding this sized family was a chore at times, but I became the most creative cook you ever heard of. With my past training in Foods and Nutritious project in 4-H, I knew the importance of serving well balanced meals.

At that time, hamburger was cheap, so I used it in many creative casseroles to keep cost of food down. Poultry was also reasonable so we ate a lot of chicken and turkey. Beef roasts and stew meat were more expensive, so those were served for special meals.

The extent of pork in our house was the usual Sunday morning breakfasts of bacon, eggs, toast, cereal, juice and milk. We all liked ham so we had that quite often, in fact so often that to this day Phil has been turned off from eating ham so we have it seldom to this day. Pork chops and pork steaks were costlier than most cuts of meat, so they were not served very often.

We always had potatoes or sometimes substituted with rice, especially if the meat lent itself for a good gravy. All kinds of vegetables were eaten and the children learned to eat every kind of vegetable there was. If it wasn't their favorite they were instructed to at least try it and eat a little for nutritional purposes, so after a while they got to like many varieties. The one thing that the children could never acquire a taste for were the lima beans, but Phil continued to like them as his favorite vegetable.

Every meal included a salad of some kind, and the children looked forward to this. At times. a salad might be a leaf of lettuce topped with a canned peach half and a scoop of cottage cheese, or instead of fruit, it may be a tomato slice, or cucumber, or green pepper strips, or carrot or celery sticks along with a scoop of cottage cheese. The children learned to be versatile in their eating, so we had a minimum of waste following meals. We all liked cole slaw as an alternative salad, as well as liking fresh spinach salad.

Many times we had pasta in lieu of potatoes. Spaghetti was less expensive to make, so we had that a lot, and today Phil is turned off from eating spaghetti, but he will eat linguine. Macaroni and cheese became favorites for the Fridays and throughout the season of Lent. We all liked the macaroni and tuna fish salad which had the vegetables included in the salad. During the season of Lent, we would buy large quantities of pickled herring and herring in cream sauce. We also bought large quantities of oysters to be made into oyster stew or deep fried oysters with a coating on them. The children thought that these were real treats, and they really were.

Phil did go fishing whenever he had a chance and usually caught bluegills. The children all loved these fish, but by the time Phil and I took the bones out of the fish for the children during a meal, we hardly had an appetite left. But we didn't want the children to debone the fish for fear that they may miss some and choke on a bone. A few times this happened even after having us take the bones out, but eating a piece of bread without anything on it usually took care of the bone.

As much as I enjoyed baking goodies, we rarely had desserts following a meal, except on special occasions. For each one's birthday I always made a decorated cake and we had a special meal on a birthday which made each family member feel special in his/her own right. I baked lots of cookies, some of which were used for school lunches.

The extent of baking was the weekly chore of baking bread, rolls, and coffee cakes. Whenever I made raised doughnuts, the kids were so delighted. Many times I never even had the chance to dip them in a topping or frost them because they ate them as soon as they done.

There were times when Danny used to beg me to quit working so I could stay home and bake raised doughnuts every other day, because he liked them so much. But somehow staying home to do baking wouldn't help pay the bills. But I had always planned that someday when I retired, I could have time to bake all these goodies again.

Sleep patterns for the family were very rigid and strict. Preschoolers had to nap every afternoon starting at 1:00 p.m. until they awakened, usually about two hours later. This meant that this aged child had to be settled down in bed by 7:00 p.m. and they were quite ready to be up early in the mornings. (Unfortunately, I never have been a morning person, but I soon learned I had to be with so many small children who needed immediate attention).

The only children who went to kindergarten were Deb, Dell, Diane, Donna and David. There was no such thing when Darlene, Dolly, and Danny were of that age. There was no pre-school in the area either, so these three of our children had to start school as first graders. They all went to the Catholic School in New Munster where I had gone as a child. The school was completely staffed with nuns of the Community of St. Agnes whose mother house was in Fond du Lac.

When Darlene started school she had a very young nun who was her teacher. This was the sister's first year of teaching, and being that she had no experience, she missed out on teaching many of the first grade basic skills that kids should be taught at this level. This meant that I had to do much teaching at home so Darlene could progress the way she should have in first grade.

At this time Reggie came over every morning to our house and went to school with Darlene. Many times after school when she would come home with Darlene, they both would have a learning lesson.

Reggie lived with her parents who all lived with Soph's mother in Powers Lake so Soph could help take care of her invalid mother who was bed-ridden. Bob ran my parents' farm and commuted each morning and then took Reggie home in the evening after the milking and chores were done. So Reggie was almost like another family member of ours.

When Dolly started school four years later, the nun who first taught Darlene had been sent to another mission so Dolly had a teacher with experience. School was much easier for her due to having a nun teacher who knew what she was doing.

At times we found it very difficult to pay a fifteen dollar book bill for each of the children. Many times it took us the whole school year to get them all paid, but somehow we always managed. When we had more children in school, and the book bill fees kept rising in cost, it became more difficult, but we always had it paid before the end of the school year.

By the time Dolly was in seventh grade, Danny in fifth, Debbie in second and Dell in first, I had started teaching the third and fourth graders at St. Alphonsus School. This was a good place to start because I didn't have any of my own kids in my class.

Time went on and with Darlene being the first to graduate, she decided that she wanted to go to school at St. Mary's Springs Academy in Fond du Lac, staying at St. Agnes convent. It was her hope of becoming a nun in the St. Agnes Order.

Sending a girl of fourteen years old to a convent so far away from home, was perplexing for Phil and me. Knowing that she had never been away from home for any length of time, we were afraid that she would become very homesick. But she felt that she had a vocation, and we couldn't in all honesty hamper that calling. At least we had to give her the chance to find out.

She had a list a mile long of the special clothing she had to have. Mom went shopping with me and I bought fabric for black skirts and white long sleeved blouses. We had to get lighter weight material for the spring and summer wear, and heavier fabric for the fall and winter wear. Mom had promised to sew all these skirts and blouses because it was much more economical to sew your own than to buy ready-mades from the stores. So my dear mother had her work cut out for her, but she was always so willing to help out wherever and whenever she could.

Next was the purchase of all the rest of the garments that were required, the toiletries, bedding, a trunk type container plus one very plain suitcase. Much seasonal clothes were stored in this trunk, and the suitcase was used to bring clothes in for the home visits during the summers. What a chore getting this all together, but we had to give her an honest chance.

The only times these aspirants, as they were called, could come home for visits were for Thanksgiving, Christmas, and Easter. The only family visits there at the convent was at the close of each quarter of school. This made the visits very limited, and many girls got so homesick. Darlene was one of these homesick girls, but she made up her mind that she was going to stick it out and she did for three years

She was allowed to be home every summer, and the last summer before senior year, she was to go to Fond du Lac for her individual class portrait, that she kept stalling me off from phoning for setting up an appointment for the sitting. This started adding up in my mind as I was sure that she did not want to return in the fall.

I mentioned this to Phil one evening when we were in bed. This was the only private time we ever had away from the children to discuss anything we didn't wish the children to hear. We both decided that she should be free to make her own choice, that what ever she chose, we would go along with her own decision. Of all things, we did not want an unhappy child. The next day I approached her and asked her if she was happy being in the convent. She was astonished that I would even inquire about this. I told her that her dad and I wanted her just to be happy, that she had to make up her own mind as we would not influence her thinking in any way, but she should think it over a day or so. At that time, I could see a facial expression of relief come over her. She responded right then and there that she didn't want to return. I was much relieved myself. I had never been selfish about sacrificing a daughter for God's work.

Now we had to discuss where she would go her senior year of high school. At this point, my heart reached out to her, because she had been so sheltered for three years and now I felt it was time that she be introduced to the real world. Phil and I had talked about this when we thought that she would not return to the convent. We both felt that in the event we send her to a private Catholic school, she still would not be exposed to how the world is, so we had decided it would be best if she attended a public school.

A few days later, after giving her the opportunity to change her mind if she still wished to do so, she and I talked again. At this time I told her she would have to go to Central High School in Paddock Lake. She was more than willing after I had explained to her that it was time for her to find out what the real world is like. Darlene had always been so innocent all throughout her life, never got into any real mischief, and was always so honest and sincere.

We both knew this would be difficult for her, and it was. Being especially quiet and reserved along with being a senior in a new school posed the problem of making new friends. As you well know, by senior year there are cliques and rarely does a clique ever acknowledge anyone new. One girl in her class volunteered to take her under her wing and help Darlene become accustomed to the school, so after a while Sharon and Darlene became best friends.

During Darlene's senior year of high school, she worked at Marino's Restaurant in New Munster as a salad girl. After high school graduation, she got a job at Gander Mountain Sporting Goods Store and Mail Order House in Wilmot. She worked there until she had earned enough money to attend Racine School of Cosmetology. Following that time, she worked as a stylist at Irene's Beauty Salon in Burlington, a stylist at Super Cuts in Racine, a teacher at Geneva Academy of Cosmetology, a teacher at Kenosha School of Cosmetology, instructor at Lake County Technical School, and her last move was to Cost Cutters Family Hair Care in Lake Geneva where she is at present.

Her present position includes being salon manager at Lake Geneva, district manager for all the shops including those located in McHenry, Fox Lake, and Woodstock in Illinois. She is happily employed for Cost Cutters Family Hair Care and likes it. She has a boss who is a very gracious business lady named Karla Corrigill. Many times Darlene becomes stressed over her job due to dissatifaction of the girls employed, but I don't know of any job that is completely without stress or dissatisfaction

All through Dolly's high school days she worked at Marino's Restaurant. First she was a salad girl and at a later time, she became a waitress. After Dolly graduated from Salem Central High School, she attended Waiver Airline School in Kansas City, Kansas.This was a six week course of training in many areas in the airline field of work. After completion of this course, she had her certification complete. However, she never pursued any of the jobs affiliated with this line of work, as a boyfriend seemed to interfere more at that time than an airline job.

It seemed as though kids at this age were still searching for their niche in life, until their maturity reached a peak level in establishing a career. Many young people completed education and became certified in a particular area and never seemed to utilize their credentials due to change of heart or change of interest. This seemed to be the case with Dolly.

Dolly chose to work at Nestle's, the well known candy company which was located in Burlington, and was built new at that time. Being that she started there at an early age, she worked there for seventeen years after which time she dedicated much of her time to volunteer work for various organizations in the community and continues to do so today.

Together Dolly and Jim worked until they reached their goal of building a beautiful new home after having lived in the

Mobile Home Park for several years. Jim has his own tile business called Quality Home Ceramics and is doing well. His business originally started with he and our son David starting the business together. Two relatives in business together very rarely works out, as this was the case of David and Jim, so Jim bought out David's half and continued on with this business.

Danny worked in his Uncle Bob's Welding Shop immediately upon graduating from eighth grade. During high school he worked for Regal China in Antioch after school and on weekends. After high school graduation, he started to work for a company called Sellergren's Painting and Decorating, where he was employed as a painter.

In later years he started his own painting business known as Countryside Decorating. Many times, he'll bring one of his employees along with him and do painting jobs for us in our house. He is very successful in his business.

Danny bought an older home in Pleasant Prairie and fixed it up and now they have added on and torn out interior parts making rooms larger and to their liking. This older home has the most beautiful fireplace in it and is so homey. They have much land and so they have a few animals that the children have as 4-H projects, and several horses. Their swimming pool attracts their whole neighborhood during the summer months. Danny also does much volunteer work in his community.

Debbie worked part time at Sentry's in Twin Lakes during her high school years and a few years beyond. She wanted to go to college to become a social worker. I discouraged her in this endeavor because I had worked so closely with a social worker on a case involving a child in one of our school families. This woman was so dedicated to her job and took such a special interest in this case, that she had expressed to me many times as to all the worrying she did and how she couldn't devote any time to her own family any more due to her work.

This is what frightened me for Debby, as I knew how tender hearted she was and I also knew that she would bring all her worries about cases involving other children into her own private life. I couldn't see that kind of life for my daughter, as having a family of your own can create worries and stress enough, without a job contributing to personal worry and stress.

So, having no other interests momentarily, she joined the work force of the world. She did consider going to realty classes but she was too involved in her dating and staying out late with boy friend Al on Friday nights causing her to want to sleep in on

Saturday mornings at which time the classes were in session, so she scrapped that idea for such a flimsy reason. But that's love! Then she worked at Gander Mountain in Wilmot; Intermatic in Spring Grove; Snap-On in Kenosha; Continental in Burlington; back to Gander Mountain; then she was elected into a local Wheatland Township office as treasurer.

While she served as treasurer for the first two years she worked part time at Pleasant which manufactured American Girl Dolls and worked in the newly created Food Court at Pick N' Save in Burlington. Recently she decided that she is kept busy enough at the Town Treasurer job so her decision is not to work outside of that job

She and Al rented a house for several years, then bought a little house, sold that house and bought a spacious house with lots of land in New Munster. Their basement has many rooms of which one is a sewing or sitting room, a bedroom, and a huge recreation area with a built-in bar. There is a fireplace in the recreation area and it is really utilized during the winter months and gives added warmth to parties.

During Dell's grade school days he worked for my brother at his welding shop, then during his high school days, he worked at Honey Bear Farm at Powers Lake along with his buddy, Al. He also worked at the Wheatland Store after George Schlitz, sold the store to Art Peebles. For a number of years after that he worked for George Richter at Sentry's in Twin Lakes even after he graduated from Salem Central High School, and expressed no desire to further his education, so he worked for Sentry's for a while, then went to Tenneco Packaging Corporation of America located in Burlington. He worked there for many years, but found a job in which he could better himself.

He was then employed at Sellergren Painting Company after which time he started his own painting business. A neighbor of his, where he rented a house in Burlington, got Dell interested in Communications and Electrical so he worked for Stan's Associates climbing towers.

He liked this kind of work, so he went to work for D. B. Communications which is a division of Divane Brothers Electrical. He builds towers and stacks them as high as 610 feet into the air. As a mom, I often worry about his climbing such heights especially towers, but I believe that any job can be dangerous in it own right, but Dell seems to like this type of work and this is what is important.

Dell and Debbie once bought a house, but after the two

children were born, they outgrew the house and rented apartments from then on.

During Diane's high school days, she worked part time at Sentry's in Twin Lakes until she graduated from Westosha Central High School. Upon completion of her schooling, she went to work for Northlake Engineering in Antioch, Illinois. Diane worked there for years until she married and moved to Merrill, Wisconsin, where she and Rick built a beautiful log home.

Diane has worked at Fox Point for seventeen years. She was a supervisor and now is production control assistant and CAD maker. She sets up the cost of what the garments will sell for. Some of the companies that Fox Point produced garments for include: Polaris, Cabella, Land's End, Oshkosh B'Gosh, Amity, L.L.Bean, Yamaha, Lemans, Galt Sand, and Artisan. She used to be the liaison for the Arkansas plant but now she is liaison for the foreign plant in China.

Donna was a cashier for Cheker Oil Station on the I-94 and Hwy. 50 for many years. She, too, graduated from Westosha Central High School. Donna has worked at numerous jobs in various fields. After her marriage and had children, she worked at a day care center and enjoyed this kind of work, so she went to school and got her certification in this field

She is very good with children and had expertise in this field, but didn't seem to have any luck in finding a job in that field. She now works for a company in Elkhorn where they make steel pharmaceutical parts. She and Paul have lived in apartments until two years ago, they bought a house in Burlington.

David, being the natural gifted and talented carpenter that he is, had worked in this field for many years. He has worked for several companies, but I believe the one he stayed the longest with is Nicholas. He has worked his way up the ladder, and contractors like his ideas, because he is so creative. Not only is he creative, but he is particular and precise about his work.

He does many side jobs after regular work hours and on weekends. This he likes because he can utilize his own designing and has had much major publicity in architectural magazines and on TV, elaborating on his creative designing.

He and Monica live in an apartment with the hopes of soon purchasing land, and building their own house.

Phil and I feel that we have a good and wholesome family. We have put our 'all' into giving them the things that were necessary to sustain a good life, and with God's help we feel that we have honestly achieved our goal.

Our Roanhaus Family in 1966
Standing L-R: Darlene, Danny, Dolly
Sitting L-R: Debbie, Donna, Dad Phil, Diane, David, Mom Arlene, Dell

Our Roanhaus Family in 1982
Standing L-R: Diane, Darlene, Dolly, David, Danny, Dell, Debbie, Donna
Mother Arlene, Dad Phil

Chapter 12
Joys of Raising a Family

Let me tell you, raising a family of eight kids during the end of the 40's through the 80's was not an easy task. Phil and I had to keep our wits about us in order to perform our parental job in a God-given manner. God knew that we both loved kids and so he blest us with these children knowing that we would be the best parents that we could be. These kids were a joy to have. Oh, yes, we had our problems but there is never a problem that cannot be solved if one wants to face up to it and hit it head on, and that we did. Now don't be shocked when I explain how we delved into this tremendous job.

As young children, our children were extremely timid and shy. What a contrast from what I was as a little person! I guess the fact that we brought our children up in an atmosphere of strict discipline, obedience, and respect for themselves as well as others, probably accounted for their timidity. But we could go any place with all eight children and never once did they ever act out of line nor did they embarrass us, they knew how to conduct themselves in any situation under any kind of circumstances. This gave us a feeling of genuine pride.

At home they let their mischief be shown, but never were they ever devious about any of the mischief they got into. They were just normal children, curious and inquisitive and wanted to explore new horizons, and that they did. Should I say that due to so many restrictive disciplinary rules of our home, most likely that's the reason that at times when they were playing, they let all hell break loose

Family meals have held a priority of togetherness so when the children were very young, it was a time in which they learned table manners, and the importance of socializing. It was also a time to realize and appreciate the value of well-planned nutritious meals which attributes to their eating all kinds of vegetables with the exception of lima beans.

Many times after a meal in which I had served lima beans, I was stacking and rinsing the dishes to be washed, I'd find a few limas peeking beneath the napkins so modestly hiding there. Being that we insisted that the children at least try everything that was served, I decided to stop serving lima beans as the meal vegetable.

After all, they did eat a variety of vegetables: carrots, celery, broccoli, green and yellow string beans, beets, asparagus, peas, brussel sprouts, swiss chard, green and red cabbage, radishes, cucumbers, squash, zucchini, green peppers, tomatoes, kale, onions, cauliflower, sweet corn, potatoes, and all varieties of lettuce. They ate a variety of green and yellow vegetables so vital for good health. None of these mentioned vegetables were ever found hiding under the napkins after a meal.

Prayer was an intricate part of our family meals and was never forgotten at our table prior to eating. We all prayed together as a family unit. After eating, we said the grace after meals. Then the children had to individually ask to be excused from the table, after which they went about their assigned chores.

There was always a job chart hanging in the inside of one of the kitchen cupboard doors with the listing of the days of the week, name of job and child's name on it. The children had to start jobs when the older two reached the ages of learning responsibility. Darlene, being the oldest didn't have to start jobs until the next in line, who was Dolly, reached the age of seven. It was then that I started to need help as every two years I was pregnant with the next child. So Darlene was now eleven years old and Dolly had reached the seven mark as there was four years difference in their ages.

These jobs that I refer to started with setting the dining table, clearing the dishes off the table after the meal, wiping the table with a wet dish cloth, and straightening the chairs around the table.

Along with setting the table was practice in counting out the plates, glasses, and silverware, which afforded practice in adding and subtracting. When we had guests eating at our table for a meal, the number countings were higher.

After the remainder of the family turned seven they were each added to the job list and as more of the children were added obviously more jobs were put on the list. Jobs added included: sweeping the dining room and kitchen floors after meals, rinse dishes, wash them, dry them, put dishes including pots and pans into the cupboards, wash off counter tops and stove top, and clean sinks.

By the time all the children were old enough to be on the job list, David had turned seven, so then the jobs kept rotating from week to week. This meant that everyone got a sample of what all the jobs involved, but David was eased into the task force until he was old enough to take on full responsibility.

A weekly monetary allowance was paid to the children

for performing assigned tasks. It was amazing how nickels and dimes talked, but later the fee grew to quarters, halves, and dollar bills. But this was all worth it as mom went back to full time work after David was born. On weekends the children were rewarded by mom and dad with special treats, and often the kids would go shopping with us to spend their huge earnings. This trained them how to spend money wisely with prudence. Speaking of treats, the usual evening snacking was pop corn, but once in a while I'd buy whatever snacks were on sale at the time. When Bugles first came out they were neatly displayed in the store at the end of the cereal aisle. Being that they were by the cereal, I thought that this was a new kind of cereal so I bought it. The children were very excited because they would now get to try a new brand of cereal.

The next morning at breakfast, I served the Bugles, and the children put sugar and milk on them and started to eat. They tried and tried to chew these, but to no avail, the darn things were so tough with milk on them. The harder they chewed the tougher it was. Then they expressed how yucky the flavor was and how salty. The children ended up putting all these bowls of 'cereal' in the garbage, and I never bought Bugles again.

It was at a much later time, when I found out that Bugles was not a breakfast cereal, but rather a snack. You can imagine how embarrassed I was, even to my own kids! The kids still joke about that one, how could I ever have been so stupid?

It was now that the older kids thought that they were being ripped off by having to do the more difficult jobs, and were sure that they were being taken advantage of. So this brought about the following rule: 'Do your job yourself or pay the younger kids to do it for you, but you are the one responsible to see that it's done, but it will be done one way or another'.

Many times, as the older kids now had after school jobs outside the home, they would pay the kids with a can of soda, or a candy bar, or perhaps a bag of snacks. To me, I termed this a form of bribery, but as long as the jobs were done and the children all kept happy that was what counted.

Another rule of the house was: 'You must have permission from us, as parents, to use the telephone'. The kids were very good about accepting this rule and liked the rule because this kept the phoning of friends under control and was fair for each of them. Time allotted for each call was five to ten minutes per call, and they abided by this rule graciously.

When the children uttered bad words they had to kneel

down by me and say the Hail Mary prayer. When they used words of blasphemy, they had their mouths washed out with soap. In short order their speech habits improved and were in control.

At times when the children would antagonize each other with name calling or would physically quarrel, they were told to kiss each other in my presence. Oh, how they hated that! Can you imagine kissing your sister or brother because you couldn't agree on something? Not good, eh? But this solved the problem in no time at all, and so the fighting ceased.

We were a close knit family and each one of the children would defend a brother or sister in any situation that required loyalty. In turn they would help each other whenever need for help was cited.

Did we spank our kids? You betcha' we did. We were cautious never to strike them on their heads or any other part of their bodies except their butts. Their behinds had nothing vital that could be injured as all bones were well padded, so this is where the spankings were given. As a mom, I usually used a wooden spoon or the palm of my hand, but I always seemed to get the bad end of the deal. I broke many wooden spoons [they were made so cheaply] on their behinds, and suffered many bursted blood vessels in my hand, so I suffered more than them.

Today, the law prevents parents from disciplining their own children as all one hears about is abuse, but on the other hand look how some kids are turning out because of no discipline. By no means did we ever abuse our children, and they learned how to show respect. Consequently the spankings were few and far between, because they knew. We usually used the reasoning method of discipline, explaining to them why an action was not acceptable and in this way they learned how to from a right conscience.

Phil used his hands and did threaten them with an end of a narrow green garden hose. At that time, most parents disciplined with the dad's leather belt, but that seemed so harsh. This little hose did the speaking for him as they feared it with all their might and they often threw these dreaded enemies either into the river or they would hide them.

We later found out in November in the year of 1992 when we had our bathroom remodeled and the walls were torn out. What do you suppose was found behind those walls? Two ends of narrow green hoses! Immediately we knew that Dolly and Danny had to be responsible for this little feat. At first it was a mystery as to how they got there. Everyone was so puzzled and Phil and I also began to wonder, then Phil figured out that there had been a small puncture in the wall that he had to patch. So he assumed this was how they forced the hoses through this opening.

So that following Christmas Eve, Dolly and Danny each had a special gift to open. Danny didn't come that year so we didn't have the pleasure of seeing his astonished look, but Dolly's facial expression was priceless when she opened her gift. Mom had written a little free lance rhyme as a hint as to what was inside the box and Dolly had to read this aloud before opening the box, but Dolly didn't have a clue. We all laughed and enjoyed the joke together.

Somehow or other, Danny was always a bit more mischievous than the other children. We always felt that he had truly inherited the mischief gene from his Grandpa Lenz and actually to this day he lives up to it and carries on this Lenz trait in the best manner ever.

When he was about nineteen months old and was in the learning stages of speech development, he could not clearly and distinctly enunciate all the consonants yet. As a family, we went to the Miss Kenosha pageant at Simmons Park in Kenosha. After many of the contestants had been introduced and had concluded their talent portion of the pageant, all the contestants as a group came on stage dressed in their formal attire.

Little Danny, sitting right straight up in his stroller as he stared at the girls with a gleam in his eyes, kept mumbling something. When we listened closely to him he was saying, "Um-m- m-m girls". In his baby talk not pronouncing the 'r', came out as. "Um-m-m Gu-u-uls". We laughed and everyone around us enjoyed this comment as much as we did. Many people remarked, "Whom does he take after?" Needless to say, all his life he had a flare for girls.

We always went to Sunday morning mass as a family. Danny was now a little past two years old, and was fairly good all through the liturgy, listening attentively, perhaps not understanding a word spoken by the priest. We always tried to train the children at an early age that they needed to do what we did in church. They didn't always understand but we tried to guide them by our example. As we all know some children have a shorter attention span than others. This was typical of Danny on this particular day.

It was during the part of the mass when everyone was

to kneel, so we all knelt, but Danny decided to use the kneeler for sitting. I saw no harm in this so I allowed him to sit on the kneeler, at least he was quiet. All of a sudden, the lady in front of us turned around and smiled at us. I smiled back, and she turned back again to face the altar. A few minutes later, we were to stand up, so I stood and motioned for Danny to stand also, so he did right next to me. Now the lady turned around, smiled and whispered, "May I please have my shoes back". I looked at her strangely wondering why she would be asking me for her shoes back, I didn't have them in the first place. She pointed to Danny and smiled at him.

Now it all added up to me, when we were kneeling, he must have taken her shoes off. I looked down in shock when I spotted her black patent leather sling pumps on our kneeler. I picked them up, handed them to her apologizing for my son's behavior, but she was so understanding and even bothered to tell me how cute Danny was. So he stood smiling at her as a Mr. Charmer plus. Cute all right! Naughty, I say!

Speaking of church, back in those days it was customary for the feminine gender to wear hats in church as a sign of reverence and humility. This involved buying hats for myself as well as for our five daughters in accordance with the seasons of the year. In years after, this ruling was changed so it became acceptable to wear a mantilla or hanky type head covering. Then years later, it was okay not to have one's head covered.

David was a baby old enough to walk but always sat on my lap in church so he could see what was going on at the altar and all during the homily at mass. It never failed, every Sunday he would take my hat off, twirl it around in the air, tease me to try to take it away from him, and at times he even dropped my hat on the floor. He got away with doing these things because I would never think of spanking my child in the house of the Lord, and after arriving home, a spanking was ineffective because by that time he didn't remember or understand why he was being reprimanded. So he continued doing this until he was old enough to know better.

While I'm reminiscing about church happenings, I remember helping Danny and Dell both learn the mass prayers and responses in Latin because they were altar boys also known as mass servers. It was so difficult for the boys of the parish to learn the Latin because they didn't know the meanings of those words and phrases, but they learned them and knew them all by memory. They did a great job and enjoyed serving at mass.

When David was old enough to become an altar boy or server, the boys were then called acolytes. By this time the mass no longer was said in Latin. When the last ecumenical council took place in the 60's, called the Vatican II Council, it was decided that the Latin Language would not be used any longer and along with the many other changes came the change that all masses from then on, must be said in English. It was so much easier to help David learn these prayers by memory because he understood the meanings of these prayers now.

It was basically the same thing with our oldest daughters who sang in the children's choir and had to learn the choir hymns in Latin. The younger daughters were fortunate because they could learn the hymns in English.

As far as health was concerned, our children never had to take many vitamins. Their main sources of vitamins and minerals were obtained through their healthy eating of well balanced meals. Perhaps the only thing that was ever lacking was the mineral iron. As babies they all had an iron supplement called Fer-in-sol which was the nastiest tasting liquid but they all took it without any fuss.

Dell was the only one at age three, who used to be an anemic, and we never knew about it. He used to hold his breath whenever he'd cry. Many times we thought that he was just being stubborn. As time went on, this condition grew worse, and he would each time hold his breath a little longer. One day he held his breath so long that he started to turn blue, and my mother actually had to breath air into his mouth, and he came out of it. But at one point I thought we were losing him. To this day, I'm thankful for my mother's quick wit.

The next day we took him to the doctor and after a series of testing, the doctor decided that he was anemic. He had an injection that day and this was followed by us administering a prescription of iron to him daily until his condition improved and his blood count was again normal. I'm sure that he inherited this factor as anemia ran on my side of the family from generations past.

When the children were young, I'd play the piano and they liked this. The moment they'd hear me start a song on the piano, they'd all hustle to the kitchen and bring along a pan cover, stood right by the piano, and played the rhythm by striking the covers together. This was our quality music time together.

Darlene was always the vain one of the family. When she was little, she could be seen often times in front of a mirror while saying, "Mirror, mirror, on the wall, who's the prettiest of them all? Why, it's Darlene". Then she would kiss her image in the mirror. Time after time she could be found admiring herself in the mirror, wherever there was a mirror at the time.

Diane led quite an exciting life! When she was young she, as well as all the younger children, had to nap every afternoon. I had gone to visit my mother at the hospital one afternoon and my sister-in-law Soph stayed with our children while I was gone. When I left that afternoon, I told Soph that under no circumstances could the children get off without taking a nap,

Diane begged and begged but she was told to take that nap. It was apparent that she disagreed with this, so she tied bed sheets together and started out of the second story window. It was then she decided this wasn't going to work, she begged Donna to help her, but Donna refused because she did not want to get into trouble. By that time she couldn't hold on any longer so she jumped out of the window.

When I arrived home, Soph came running to my car in the garage saying, "I'm so sorry, I'm so sorry!" All I could think of was sorry for what? It was then she told me what had happened. It seemed that Diane was not seriously hurt, but we believe to this day that it showed up later in life in her knees.

During hot summer days, if the children helped in the mornings, I'd take them to Lily Lake swimming. One afternoon we were all in the Rambler station wagon ready to go to the beach, I was backing out of the garage when Diane decided that she forgot something and opened the car door without thinking.

Crash! One smashed door on the vehicle! Needless to say, we did not go to the beach. Were the rest of the children upset with her, and they yelled and yelled at her. The poor little girl felt bad enough that it happened, so she didn't need the rest of the kids to get on her too, after all it was an accident.

Then one day when the children were playing in the little pool that we had in the back yard, Dolly and Diane were there. Diane was sitting on the picnic table, and she must have upset Dolly for some unknown reason, so Dolly pushed her off the table and broke Diane's collar bone. This meant a trip to emergency. Dolly felt so remorseful after all was said and done, but these are accidents with children..

Thinking back about Dolly, when she was two years old, she would get into the liquor cupboard which was the bottom cupboard in the kitchen. She would open a bottle of booze before anyone could catch her, and here she was actually swigging from the bottles. It always amazed me that she never got sick. Today she doesn't even like that stuff anymore.

On the other hand, Debbie didn't drink liquor when she was little, but one day she drank some perfume called Lucien Lelong. It had so much alcohol content in it, but I gave her a glass of milk to counteract the aftermath of that awful taste. One good thing was she didn't get sick from it.

It was Dolly and Danny who frequently got into mischief together. When they were very young, they decided that they wanted to become rich. So they found some house paint and painted rocks thinking then that they had gold. But the sad part of it all was that the house was not gold in color, it was green. But those two thought they were then rich. This is how they got the name, 'Gold Dust Twins'.

Speaking of Danny, when he graduated from eighth grade, all the boys were wearing sport coats and nice trousers. We, at the time, were very low on funds, and found it very difficult to buy a sport coat which he most likely would never wear again. So we shopped at a bargain store which had discounted merchandise, but everything was new. We bought him a $29.95 coat for the price of $14.95. Then we bought him a nice pants to go with it, because the pants he would wear often later.

I'll never forget to this day, the sad story of it all. The class had to bring their good clothes to school before hand to have their graduation pictures taken as a group. Well, that morning, I asked Danny if he cut the tag off the coat, or did I have to still do it. He told me it was all taken care of, and I believed him.

But to find out later, he cut the size tag off, but not the price tag. When he got to school and took his clothes out of the garment bag, one of the smarties in his class saw the ticket and announced to everyone that Roanhaus had bought a cheap coat, so everyone laughed. When Danny came home and told me about it, I cried, I felt so bad that someone made fun of one of my kids. But kids can be very cruel to each other.

When the kids were little, Reggie and Lennie would come over in the evenings in the summer and on weekends, and they and our kids would have water fights. The kids loved that but I could never participate, but I would watch them, Their dad would play right along with them. The kids would all gang up on Phil and really douse him good. My, how the children loved those days!

When Donna was little, we had just gotten a new car,

and didn't she scratch her name in big letters across the whole trunk of the car? That was bad enough, but Debbie who was older stood there and watched her do it. Phil and I were upset!

Donna and David got into a few episodes of mischief together. After we'd finish Christmas shopping, and were completely done, we would wrap these gifts nights when the children were all in bed. Then we'd put them into our bedroom closet which was a long and narrow closet used for storage.

By the time Christmas came, there had been holes poked into Donna and David's gifts, and some of them had been rewrapped. Those nosy little stinkers got into them to find out what they were getting for Christmas. From them on, all gifts went to my mom and dad's house until Christmas Eve

Dell, being left handed, cut his left index tendon in his finger, and so had to see a specialist, Dr. Frackelton, in Milwaukee. He underwent surgery to repair the damaged nerves and they took a tendon from his arm and inserted it into his finger, so this involved intricate surgery. He had to actuate therapy for a year after, but only 80% usage of his finger was restored. Being that it happened when he was so young, he has learned to use it in the best means possible through the years.

When Dell and Al were in Central High School, they decided to skip school one day. So they went to MacDonalds in Antioch for breakfast. Then they decided they didn't really know what to do now that they skipped, but they thought it was going to be a big deal.

The ironic part of it all was the fact that their absence from school stirred up a lot of checking out where the two of them were. First Bernice, Al's mom got a call from the high school, then she called my mother who lived next door to us. In turn mom called me at school where I was teaching, and I called Debbie who was working at Sentry's and asked her if they happened to tell her of any plans they had for the day. She had no idea as they didn't tell her anything. This phoning went on for quite some time, and we all began to worry about the two boys.

My mother went next door to our house and there they wer just sitting there not knowing what to do. This really became a family joke, two kids skipping school and didn't know what to do with the day off. They never skipped school again!

Right after Dolly got her drivers license, she was going to the little store in Wheatland for something that I needed for supper. Danny decided to ride with her. It was winter and the ground had an accumulation of snow on it, so before they left,

172

Danny threw a snow ball at Dolly which upset her, but they were on their way and Dolly slid into the ditch by the creek.

Danny was in a frenzy and threatened Dolly that he was going to run away. She worried about him, but instead he ran home and told us. Boy, he prematurely put some gray hair on her head that evening!

The kids' driving at times seemed very inattentive, at least that was in Debbie's case. One morning she had sneaked some of her dad's cigarettes out of a cupboard at home, and took some with her to her job at Sentry's. On the way there, she dropped a cigarette, and stooped to pick it up while driving, and hit a sign at the side of the road a short distance from our house.

It was summer months and I was at our church directing a choir for a funeral service, when all of a sudden Debbie rushed up into the choir loft at church and told me she hit something. Being that there was music playing loudly, I couldn't quite understand her, and I didn't know what she hit, but I thought it was a person. In shock, I asked her, "Did you kill him?" Her reply was, "No, just take me to work, please".

So I left the church and took her to work. After explaining what had really happened, all the while on the way to work, she kept saying, "What's dad going to say, what's dad going to say?"

I dropped her off and went back to church just in time to join the choir enroute to the cemetery. I told Phil about the whole episode when he got home from work, and so we decided that he would go to pick her up from work when her shift was done, and so he did.

I'm sure that she would have rather had anyone in the world except her father come to pick her up that day, but he never said one word to her all the way home. What anxiety she must have gone through all the way home. When they were pulling into the driveway, he asked her, "Well, did you learn anything today?" Her reply was, "Yes, dad". Nothing more had to be said, because she felt sorry enough about the whole deal.

Another episode encountered by Debbie was the time she was turning around in the driveway and hit the side of the house with her car, where the chimney was.

Then there was the night of Danny's eighteenth birthday. He celebrated with all his might and had indulged in drinking because he had just turned of legal drinking age, so it was at that time. At midnight he strolled into the house and headed for the bathroom. As he had been stretched out on the floor, he yelled to me, "Mom, I'm home, Richard Petty drove my truck and me home". In my ignorance of not knowing at the time who Richard Petty was, inquired, "Does Richard need a ride home?" As inebriated as he was, he just had to laugh, and with that, Phil helped him to bed.

Speaking of snow, when we used to have those heavy snow storms, I recall the year of 1977, at which time we were having a blizzard, roads were closing all over, factories and other places of employment were shut down, and all schools were closed. People were reminded that this was a storm emergency and all should stay off the highways and stay at home.

Well, what did our older kids do, but hurried to our house so they could all be snowed in together. Dolly and Jim lived in the mobile home park in Wheatland and Jim was snowed in at American Motors in Kenosha, where he was employed at the time. Only the two older girls were married, but some of the other older kids started out to Wheatland to pick up Dolly and little Jason so they could be with us, as she didn't relish the idea of being home alone in such a storm in case the electricity went out and they had no heat. They had to walk into the entry of the park as the roads were snowed shut there, so they brought Dolly and Jason and blankets and pillows along out with them and started for our house.

Debbie and Al were dating at that time, so Al was here also. Now with all those older kids here, mom had extra cooking to do. For lunch at noon, they all wanted Reuben sandwiches to accompany the beers that they had been drinking during the playing of cards. They had a blast!

Phil, of course, was working and so we didn't see him even that night, because they never stopped plowing the roads Those were the breaks of working for the Highway Department. After supper, they played cards again, and later everyone sacked out wherever they could find a space in the house. This is a day I'll never forget.

Raising eight kids was challenging but enjoyable, at times stressful, but we survived it all. Today we enjoy the visits from our kids and their families. We thank God for this beautiful family of ours.

174

Chapter 13
Teachers' Conventions

In the fall of the year, all public school teachers went to the convention in Milwaukee. Our county superintendent of schools required each of us to produce an attendance certificate which was gotten at a special booth at the convention that lasted for two days. This attendance certificate had to be given to your school board clerk to prove you were there, or that month's pay check would be held until the end of the year.

The convention was always interesting because the speakers who were engaged spoke on what was new in the teaching field. After the morning speaking sessions concluded, teachers went to the exhibition hall in Milwaukee Auditorium.

Each of the educational book and supply companies were represented. Each company had their own booth and whether you stopped to look at what they had or not, a rep would stand in front of the booth handing out something of the nature of what they were selling. Many good books suitable for the school libraries were given as tokens of appreciation for business conducted during the past years, whether one had purchased anything from that particular company or not.

Many samples of work books in the different areas of learning were also given out in hopes that when one returned home, that company's books would be considered for purchase in your own teaching situation in your school. I always felt that this was the best form of business and advertisement that any company could sponsor.

More than one company gave an apple to each person present. At times we would come home with a half dozen apples. Still others gave out cups of hot chocolate. Many endowed us with book marks having their ad on them, but these were appreciated as we could use them in the many teacher manual books that we taught from, because at that time we were all teaching in one room rural schools having all eight grades so you can imagine the stacks of teacher manuals we had on our desks.

When I first started teaching and going to conventions I went with Ada Luke and Florence Schenning. We went to the convention faithfully for the first five years of my teaching career. It was about this time that the conventions were getting quite chintzy, stale, and became boring. The speakers who were engaged were getting stale and monotonous, interest on the part of the teachers was getting less and less, many companies stopped exhibiting and the convention was falling short of what the intent was.

Many teachers, including my friends and me, only attended long enough to get our certificates of attendance signed. Hardly any teachers were present to listen to speakers, so most teachers could be found in the exhibition hall during the morning sessions, then leaving for town for lunch.

After lunch we would go shopping in downtown Milwaukee. You just won't believe how many other teachers we saw in the restaurant and later in the stores shopping.

At that time the main stores where women liked to shop were: Gimbels, Three Sisters, Marshall Field, Boston Store, Schusters, J. C. Pennys, Goodblatts, Woolworths, Sears, and numerous dress shops, but I can't remember the names of the rest.

For a while I didn't go to conventions, until I went back into teaching full time. But this time round I now went to the Catholic School Teacher Conventions.

Even though this was under the auspices of a different entity, basically it was much the same as the public school conventions, even held at the same place. But now this place was changed to be called Milwaukee Arena and in later years changed names again to MECCA Convention Center.

During these first few years of teaching in the Catholic Schools, there was no stipulation that teachers had to have a signed certificate of attendance. But later on, due to the fact that many teachers were just going to the city during this time for shopping, it became mandatory again to produce a certificate of attendance to their local parishes or their jobs would be in jeopardy.

This became serious, so this spurred teachers on to really attend these conventions. This requirement lasted for only a few years and then it was eradicated, no need for attendance proof.

In the meantime, the committees researched to explore the reasons why teachers no longer had an interest in these assemblies. After their studies were complete they found that the format of conventions had to be changed so as to create interest again.

In the 70's, instead of speakers all morning, there was an opening assembly starting at 9:00 A.M. This opening consisted of a welcome by the Deputy Superintendent of Milwaukee

Archdiocesan Schools, Father Darneider.This was followed by a greeting from the Archbishop, and announcements by the Master of Ceremonies.Then the groups went to smaller conferences.

This became very popular with the teachers as now one could enter into discussions and obtain ideas from other teachers, and could ask questions and gain a wealth of information that directly related to each one's situation. There were many sessions to choose from so that left each person free to choose which ones they could benefit from the most.

At noon teachers were not expected to be back in attendance until one and a half hours had lapsed. This meant that everyone could have ample time to dine out and be back for the afternoon sessions.

Some of the most popular restaurants in which we'd eat were: Madars, Toys at which Chinese food was served, Watts Tea House was located on the second floor as the first floor was a store, and often times we'd eat in the coffee shop at Gimbels. Down town there was also a Cafeteria, but at the moment I can't recall the name, where the selection of food was astronomical. It was here that I was introduced to salmon croquettes, so we usually tried to eat there on Fridays.

During these first years of teaching in the private school, I would attend conventions with the nuns from our school as I was the only lay person on the faculty staff.

Sometimes the nuns would go on their own so I went with a teacher from St. Mary's, Mrs. Rachael Herda. Rachael was the most wonderful person with a sense of humor that was unbelievable, and was a reading teacher in her present position. She and I had much in common in the way that we perceived education.

Every time we went to the convention together, we both could endure only a minimal amount of walking, so we took many sit-down breaks while going through exhibition hall to view the displays and make our heavy purchases for our schools.

After we would leave the convention, we would go to Broadway Street to a place called Railroad Salvage. It was here that one could buy cases of canned and boxed food, all non perishable items, at a very reasonable price. She and I would spend a great deal of time in here and went home with a carload of food. Then on the way home we both, being so prudent with money, would figure up how much we saved by buying at this place versus a local grocery store.

One year I went to the National Convention with the nuns. It was the one year that the national was held close to home. It was at McCormick Place in Chicago. This was a two day convention where we heard notable speakers from all over the nation, who were well versed in their fields. I thought of this as a golden opportunity, as not many local teachers ever get to a national convention.

Obviously I went with the nuns from St. Alphonsus. This was a hoot! Sister Rose Clare had just learned to drive and needless to say she drove to Chicago immediately after getting her driver's license. I have to admit many prayers were said under my breath on my part wondering if and how we escaped so many dangers due to her inexperience. Quite inexperienced, she was tooling along the toll road highways and before we knew it we were entering Indiana. As she noticed the sign, she yelled "INDIANA!" "How did we get into Indiana?"

A meek, mild, tender voice from the back seat replied, "Simple, Rose Clare, you drove us there". It was the voice of the sister who was the cook at the nun's house in New Munster, Sister Vida.

As Sister Rose Clare snapped back, "Shut up, Vida, you don't know a darn thing about it, I must have just missed a turn."

Missed a turn, indeed she did, way back where! Out of due respect for sisters, I saw the turn but was afraid to say anything. Now there were two other sisters in the back seat, Sister Regina Ann and Sister Stephania, who was principal at our school. Now Sister Rose Clare was puzzled, so she and I looked at the map and I showed her where I thought we should have turned off.

In the meantime, a squad car with the nicest officer came along. He got out of his car and came over to the car we were in [a borrowed car from a parishioner at that], and asked, "Sister, are you in distress?"

"Well, yes, officer, I must have missed my turn", responded Sister Rose Clare.

"Where are you going?"

"McCormick Place".

"Well, you're a long ways from McCormick Place. There is no turn off this highway for miles on end. But I'll tell you what I'll do, I'll get in my car and drive off, and when I'm out of sight you make a U-turn and go back to the fourth exit and turn off. That should take you right along the convention center. In this way my back will be turned and I won't witness your violation.

Wow, what a relief!! We did what he instructed us to do and we arrived at the convention about an hour late, but better late was better than never.

This convention was like the state conventions, speakers in the mornings. In the afternoons, one could choose more of the individual sessions to attend or one was allowed to shop in the exhibition hall for purchasing.

It was a cinch to bargain with these company representatives on the last afternoon of the conventions both at state and national levels. They were eager to sell more products so they would not have to pack up all their wares and take them back to the warehouse. I always enjoyed the wheeling and dealing with the salesmen, and many times I started to walk away from their booth when they called me back, meaning that I got the item I wanted for the price I wanted to pay. [My mother had trained me well, it was from her that I learned how to wheel and deal, and many times I was thankful to her for that because she had taught me well.]

Being that the Catholic schools are on such a tight limited budget, it became necessary to get the most for the money. All too often I purchased so many things that were needed so badly in the school with my own personal money. At times, I believe that I may have spent more on the school than what my bimonthly paychecks totaled up to be, but when something was needed and there were no funds to buy with, I bought things as a donation to the school. I can honestly say that I have never regretted having done this because it all reality I am confident that God has twice blest me for it.

Being that the national convention was in Chicago, the nuns made arrangements for all of us to stay overnight. They stayed at a convent where their Agnesian order of sisters were stationed. They drove me to a private home where I was to stay.

It was a retired couple whose children were all married and gone from home. I watched a little TV with them and had a soda with them. This was the time when Fresca soda was first introduced to the public. We discussed what we liked about the soda, so refreshing, the flavor had much appeal, and we decided that it would be a real 'go' on the market.

We told each other about our families and our parishes, comparing and contrasting, and found that we had much in common. She had a profession as a nurse, and he was a food distributor.

The next morning I arose very early and was ready to go by 7:00 a.m. because Sister Rose Clare was going to pick me up at 7:30 and I was to have breakfast at the convent with the nuns. I had a 'thank you' card with me on which I wrote a note of gratitude to them for their hospitality. So I left it on the dresser in the bedroom in which I slept. When Sister came, I left and we both were off to the convent.

Now eating with so many nuns at their table made me very uneasy. I felt them glaring at me all the while only to find out this was just my imagination. After convincing myself that they were human beings like me, I felt more at ease and joined right into the conversation with them. Their greatest amazement was 'How could anyone have eight children and still teach school?'

Following breakfast, we went back to the convention for the second and last day. It was marvelous opportunity to have just gone to a national convention, so I have Sister Stephania to thank for that.

In the more recent years, the state convention held in Milwaukee has been held for the Thursdays only, and the Fridays have been scheduled for local district meetings. These were most beneficial as they directly related to the schools in our own area.

In about the last seven years of my teaching before retiring, I didn't even go to the convention in Milwaukee, as walking became more and more of a problem for me. I had attended them for so many years all throughout my teaching career that they had become stagnant and insignificant to me anyway.

I never took these two days off from work though, because I always spent these two days working back in my local setting at St. Alphonsus School. I accomplished many tasks during this time.

Conventions always lent themselves to learning, having fun, meeting many new people, and socializing.

Chapter 14
How We Spent The Holidays

Being that holidays are for families celebrating together, we held to that particular tradition and custom. I was raised with the beliefs that family was always first and foremost in my life no matter what, so when Phil and I had our family we held true to this belief also.

Christmas was the greatest and biggest holiday of the year for us. In preparation for this blessed holiday, Phil and I would have my mother babysit for us and we would take one whole day just for shopping. This, of course, had to be a Saturday. This is just the materialistic part of the holiday.

Our children sincerely believed in Santa Claus and we told them we spent the day putting in their orders to Santa. They believed us so this made it all worth while.

For quite a few years, our family and my brother Bob's family spent Christmas at my mom and dad's house, until some of the older kids didn't believe in Santa anymore. It was at this time that Soph suggested that we have our own Christmas Eve at our own houses. Being that Phil and I had several children who still believed, we always had Grandma and Grandpa Lenz celebrate with us at our house.

My mother's birthday was on Christmas Eve, so I always made a very special decorated and filled birthday cake for her, as she was cherished by our whole family. Mom always looked forward to that evening.

The year that Debbie was born, we had our Christmas festivities earlier in December so I would be home for the opening of gifts, after all what would a Christmas be without the children's mom present? As it worked out, Debbie was overdue, and I was home yet for Christmas anyway.

After Donna was born on December 12, and we brought her home and the kids saw her, they decided that she was the best Christmas present anyone could have, a baby sister. It was their decision that we take pictures of Donna propped up under the Christmas tree because she was the greatest gift of all.

Christmas Eve was the night that we always opened gifts, and when the children were old enough, we'd go to midnight Mass together as a family. When the kids were grown and had families of their own, we all got together at our house.When our immediate family would get together, we number 39.

For many years, my cousins Ruth and Loraine Lenz would spend Christmas Eve with us and go to the midnight Mass with us at St. Alphonsus Church. After our family started getting bigger with the older kids marrying, Ruth and Loraine no longer came here.

Another holiday celebration we observed was New's Year Day with a special dinner of usually turkey and all the goodies that went with it. This was the day that everyone decided what they were doing as to New Years' resolutions. Many times these resolutions were broken in short duration, but the intent was good, and then we'd start all over again.

Valentine's Day meant an exchange of valentines at home as well as school, and a favorite meal in the evening which ever the children wanted and we had special Valentine treats.

St. Patrick's Day, even though we were not of Irish descent, meant corned beef and cabbage dinner.Some form of green dessert, usually jello was served as tradition, but we only had this kind of meal once a year on St. Patrick's Day.

Two days later, March 19, we always honored the two grandpas, who both had the name of Joseph. This was their feast day, and they had supper with us and spent the evening with us.

Next holiday was Easter. How I hated coloring eggs, because there were so many to color, but our kids liked the cooked eggs in their Easter Baskets. It was always fun for Phil and me hiding their baskets, tricking the older kids into finding theirs hidden in a difficult spot. As the children grew older, they helped color eggs.

Next was Mothers' Day, and our kids always made something for me. How special, knowing that this all came from the heart. Usually along with the handmade gift was a spiritual bouquet which consisted of a listing of prayers that they wanted to offer for me. It was the graciousness that was so edifying.

Memorial Day weekend usually meant the first picnic of the season. Mom always had to use the whole weekend making out final exams for the close of school. The children enjoyed this first picnic just to eat outdoors.

Fathers' Day followed in June, and again the children made handmade gifts for Phil. He too, received a spiritual bouquet.

Independence Day, July 4, meant that we had a picnic and sometimes we went to the park to picnic. At night when it was dark, the children had sparklers and Phil would shoot off a few fireworks. Many times we'd go to the park in Burlington to see the fireworks.

August was not a holiday, but it was the month of the Kenosha County Fair. Being in 4-H, the children were kept busy with exhibiting and participating in all the 4-H events at the fair. This meant spending all four days at the fairgrounds in Wilmot.

On Labor Day in September, was always the last picnic of the season, and the children enjoyed this. This also meant that school would be in session for another year.

October brought Halloween, and this meant that mom would make caramel apples for the kids and for the trick or treaters. The children always went to the neighborhood homes to trick or treat. We always made costumes out of a little of nothing because what would Halloween be without a costume? Our children were satisfied with so little, but we always managed for their sake.

November was the month that Phil went deer hunting, and we usually were alone for Thanksgiving along with Grandma and Grandpa Lenz. We would always go to church for thanksgiving.

During the year when Darlene was in Fond du Lac in the convent, she came home for Thanksgiving. We sent her money to come on the train, which stopped in Kenosha, where we were going to pick her up. Dolly, Danny, and my dad went with me as Phil was deer hunting, and when they stopped in Kenosha, many people got off all except our fourteen year old daughter. Now I was in a frenzy!

When the train stopped, and everyone was off, I asked the conductor if he would just call her name as I knew that she was on that train, and he told me, "Lady, if I did that for everybody, we'd be here all night". With that they pulled out.

So we found out that the next stop was in Waukegan, Illinois, so we hurriedly drove there in the down pouring rain. When we got there we discovered that the train depot was located in what was termed a 'bad neighborhood'.

When we finally got into the depot, Darlene was bewildered. but some kind lady looked out for her. That year we were extremely thankful as we found our daughter back.

November was always a month of excitement, because Phil always went North deer hunting. One year there had been a bank robbery in the area. The Silver Lake Bank was robbed one day late in the afternoon. I hadn't heard about it until I returned home from school with a carload of girls, Debbie's friends, who were going to spend the night at our house. I guess I really wasn't that concerned until much later when one of the sheriff's deputies came to our door and told us that one of the robbers was seen running across the field behind our house. He instructed us to keep our shades drawn and lights kept low in our house all night. They figured he may try to get away wanting some one's vehicle.

When I heard this, I didn't want to be responsible for all the extra girls in our house, so I called their moms and took them all home, and took Darlene to work at Marino's Restaurant. I told her that someone would have to bring her home after work and I'd be waiting at the door for her to let her in after work.

It was also the night that Phil was going to call home from up North, so when he called, he said that we shouldn't worry that everything would be okay. Well, such words of wisdom coming from him as he was not here with eight kids to look out for, but I was.

In the meantime, the nuns from New Munster called and asked if the children and I were all right. They told me that they would be praying for us so nothing bad would happen to us. Those words were more consoling to me.

We did just as the deputy had directed us to do, kept the light low, the shades drawn, and kept the station wagon keys on top of the TV, because if anyone wanted a vehicle to get away, I was more than willing to give them the keys, just to let us alone.

When Darlene's shift was over, David Barbian, who also worked at Marino's brought her home. I met her at the door, and just as quickly closed the door after she was in the house.

It was a terrible night, the children and I slept in Phil's and my bedroom, cramped in the room like sardines in a can, but we managed. We prayed together for our safety, at least we were all together.The night had passed and the next day was Saturday, and we were all so tired because we didn't get much sleep the night before. Again God was good to us and kept all of us safe.

With a family of this size there was never a dull moment in our house. We always were a happy family and our togetherness made all the holidays special for us.

Chapter 15
Special Family Celebrations

There are many events in a family's life that are celebrated partly by tradition and any special occasion that deems worthy of celebrating

Being that our religion is Catholic, we have always celebrated the sacraments of our beliefs which are: Baptism, Holy Eucharist also called First Communion, Reconciliation, Confirmation, and Marriage. These are very sacred and are milestones in a person's life, and so it was in our own family. The first celebration in a child's life is when the child is baptized. This involves the parents to choose relatives or close friends to be sponsors for the child. Baptisms for our children were always held on a Sunday afternoon at St. Alphonsus Church.

The ceremony of Baptism is very impressive and beautiful in every aspect. The significance of this sacrament is the beginning of new life with God and membership among the people of God.

After the ceremony was over, the grandparents, sponsors, aunts, uncles, and cousins were invited to the house for a dinner. After the dinner meal, pictures were taken and gifts for the child were opened.

For the first Baptism in our family, my mother designed and sewed a long white ruffled dress for Darlene's Baptism. Each of the other four girls wore that same dress for their Baptisms. Then the most significant part of it all was that most of our granddaughters were also baptized in that same dress. To this day, it is as beautiful as the day mother made it, and is still pure white which never yellowed as some fabrics do.

As for the boys in our family, Danny, being the first boy, wore a little two-piece knit suit in white, and so Dell wore the same suit too. It always amazed me that the size of this little suit was an eighteen month and it fit the boys perfectly. Then when David was to wear this suit, it was quite yellow being of a knit fabric, so we bought him a little two piece suit in a white satin-like fabric.

As for sponsors for our children: Darlene had her grandmother, Dorothy Lenz and grandfather, Joseph Roanhaus; Dolly had her grandfather, Joseph Lenz and her aunt, Dorothy Roanhaus; Danny had his uncle, Bob Lenz and his

185

aunt, Helen Roanhaus; Deb had her uncle, Ardell Lenz and her cousin, Janet Guse [now Weinaug]; Dell had his aunt, Sophie Lenz and his uncle, Ralph Roanhaus; Diane had family friends, Dale and Nancy Spiegelhoff; Donna had her uncle, Marvin Roanhaus and her cousin, Ruth Lenz; and for David we were running out of relatives so he had his cousins, Reggie Lenz and Eric Roanhaus.

The next sacrament that the children received was Reconciliation. Through this sacrament, forgiveness of sins committed after Baptism were mercifully forgiven bringing consolation, peace and healing to the penitent.

Next the children received the Eucharist, and receiving it for the first time was called First Holy Communion. This was undoubtedly the most solemn ceremony in a child's young life at a very innocent age of seven years old.

For this special occasion, little girls always wear everything white including dresses, socks, shoes, and some had gloves. This was always topped off with a white frilly veil on their heads. Little boys usually wore navy blue pants with white shirts and white ties, and black shoes.

The only exception to the customary attire for First Communion for our children was in the case of Danny's class. The boys had to wear navy blue robes and the girls had to wear white robes which were all rented. Somehow or other, this seemed very different, but the meaning of the reception of this sacrament was as solemn as if the children wore other clothing.Even though the children wore rented robes, they still had their personal First Communion blessed articles from that very special day for their remembrance. It was customary that the children each had their cherished prayer book, rosary, scapular, candle, as well as their certificate.

My mother sewed an individual dress for each one of our girls. Each of our girls had a dress style fashioned to suit her own personality. Each of our daughters also had their own individual veil, because I remembered back to the days of my First Holy Communion when I had to wear a borrowed veil of Helen Mangold's. Being that I never had my very own, I made up my mind that whatever the cost, our girls would each have her own veil to wear and keep.

Following the Mass for each child's First Holy Communion, we had a breakfast at our house followed later with a dinner in each child's honor. The afternoon was spent in opening gifts and taking pictures. In attendance at these gatherings were the child's Baptismal sponsors, aunts, uncles, cousins, and grandparents.

When the children were a little older, between the school grades of five and eight, they could receive the sacrament of Confirmation.

Confirmation strengthens one's commitment to Christ made at Baptism, so that a person can maturely face challenges and problems in daily life as a Christian.

Darlene was confirmed in 1961 by Bishop Roman Atkelski, taking the new name of Helen with her Aunt Helen being her sponsor.

Dolly and Danny were confirmed in the same class of 1964 by Bishop Atkelski. Dolly's sponsor was Grandma Lenz, her new name was Mary. Danny's sponsor was Grandpa Lenz, and he choose Joseph as his new added name.

It is interesting to note that I was in the hospital having David during this time, but prior to this event I had made cakes for the celebration of Confirmation and Danny's birthday and had them both in the freezer, so my sister-in-law, Sophie, had the celebration at her house as Lennie was confirmed in that same class too.

Debbie and Dell were confirmed in the same class of 1968 by Bishop Leo Brust. Debbie's older sister, Darlene was her sponsor, and Dell's brother Danny was his. They chose Mary and Joseph as their added names.

In 1972, Diane and Donna both were confirmed by Bishop Leo Brust. Diane and Donna both chose Ann as their added name, and Dolly was Diane's sponsor, while Debbie was Donna's sponsor.

Last of our family to be confirmed was David in 1976 by Bishop Leo Brust. His sponsor was his brother Dell.

Celebrations for this sacrament were mainly a get together for confirmants and our family, sponsors, grandparents, and a few aunts and uncles. No huge meal was involved, just cake, punch, and coffee.

The next of the sacraments for the children to receive was that of Matrimony or marriage. This is the sacrament in which a man and woman selflessly share life, love and Christian faith with each other and with God. This is the one that the children received by their choice as adults.

Other family celebrations included everyone's

birthdays as their very own special day each year. Even after their marriages, we still tried to continue the celebrations by having special meals and a birthday cake. Recently, we couldn't keep up with that tradition any longer due to being so busy so we send them each a card with a monetary gift inside.

As time goes on there are always wedding anniversaries to celebrate so we give our kids a card again with a monetary gift. Now at present it has gotten to the point of a celebration on every fifth year, and on the remaining years, we just send them a card. Being so many involved, and being that we are retired and on a fixed income, there is no other way feasible.

Now most of our gift giving is to the grandchildren, and we have plenty of them, all twenty-four. Somehow or other, these kids are so special in our lives as most of them are young adults now.

Speaking of anniversaries, when we were married twenty-five years, Mom and Dad Lenz got together a surprise party for us. All the relatives were invited, and it was very nice. Our older kids helped with this celebration.

At thirty years of marriage, Phil and I took the whole family out to dinner at Coral Reef Restaurant in Rochester. This was a place with a Hawaiian motif and the food was always so tasty there.

When we were married forty years, we didn't have the motivation to celebrate as two of our sons were not speaking to each other due to a petty misunderstanding on their part from long ago, which ended up in not a very nice mode. Still today they are not speaking or even acknowledging each other. This episode has been and still is very heart breaking to Phil and me personally. One of them would like to let bygones be gone and make amends, but the other one is not willing to practice the virtue of forgiveness. This resulted in his not having anything to do with the rest of the family, except a very brief visit to Phil and me now and then.

So if we would have had an anniversary celebration, it would not have been complete anyway. This put a damper on any family celebrations that we would plan in the future.

This was very hurtful to Phil and me, as we had tried diligently to raise a good family, and somehow we can't determine where we went wrong, Phil and I have always been so forgiving to anyone who has ever hurt us or our personal feelings, but apparently this didn't rub off on each of our kids. The sad part of it is that the boys don't pay the price for this misunderstanding, but Phil and I do.

It took years before we could even think of going on with any kind of celebrations, until our daughters convinced us that we should no longer bear the brunt of the boys' misgivings, but that we needed to go on with or without David's presence at family gatherings. We heeded their advice, even though the whole deal left pain in our hearts, we decided that the girls were right.

So when we were married forty-five years, we decided to celebrate with family and friends. Again David and his family were not present, but we went on anyway. Being this time of our lives, we wanted to celebrate because one never knows how long God will grant us to be together. We had a special Mass at the church followed by a party at our home. We are glad that we had our friends celebrate with us, as since that time some of them are deceased. It was the best party anyone could ever have, and Phil and I enjoyed ourselves.

This past year, Phil and I were married fifty years, and a golden anniversary was so important and meaningful. Seven of our kids thought it was important enough to attend our special Mass in church as at this age, we need all the added prayers that we can get. Following the Church service, the kids all brought a dish to pass, and we had a buffet supper together and enjoyed the evening.

All, except one, of our family remain a family of tradition, and enjoy getting together for special events. Phil and I have come to realize that perhaps in the future, we may then mean something to our absent son and his family. But it's not going to happen that way, unless some undue miracle occurs, because he no longer wants to even recognize that we are his parents. He absolutely made it known to us that he has cut off all family ties for the remainder of our lives, even though we will always love him and his family. So Phil and I continue on with our lives with broken hearts. All I can say is that after a parent's death is hardly the time to wake up and smell the coffee.

Our Golden Anniversary
June 26, 1998

Chapter 16
In 4-H As A Leader

Having been a member of Wheatland Willing Workers 4-H Club, I will focus on how this outstanding club came into being including my affiliation with this club as time progressed on.

In the year of 1936, Mr. E. V. Ryall, Kenosha County Agricultural Agent, along with the help of a Junior Leader, Louise Lauer, organized a 4-H Club in Wheatland Township. The leader of this club was Margaret Kerkman, who led a group of eight members. These members met in homes and their project work consisted of sewing tea towels, and doing craft work of braiding watch chains and bracelets. The name officially adopted by this 4-H Club was Wheatland Willing Workers.

In 1937, the club functioned under the leadership of Margaret Kerkman and the projects remained the same. Public exhibits were made at the Pavilion Building in Paddock Lake.

In 1938, the leadership was changed and Mr. Ben Kaskin served as general leader of the club and also supervised the boys' projects, namely dairy. Mrs. Helen Schlax of Kenosha was assistant leader and was responsible for teaching girls' projects, mainly clothing. In this year, public exhibits were made at Wilmot where the Kenosha County Fair was held.

From 1938 to 1948, Mr. Kaskin and Mrs. Schlax continued as leaders of the club. During most of those years, club meetings were held in homes of the members. Project meetings were also held in the homes of members, rotating weekly.

In 1943, there was no county fair, so all exhibiting had to be done at a local club level. Our club had a club tour in which members, parents, and leaders visited each member's home and viewed individual exhibits of the projects of all the members.

In 1946, Ray Toelle helped with the boys' projects as a project leader. This was the year our club had its first float in the Kenosha County Fair parade entitled, "A Swell Job Well Done".

In 1947, I graduated as a member and helped out by being a project leader for foods and nutritions, and my mother assisted Mrs. Schlax as clothing project leader, which in later years my mother took over completely.

1948 brought about many changes in leadership. Mrs. Schlax moved out of the community, thus resigning her leadership. Ben Kaskin also resigned, due to ill health. Ray Toelle served as general leader with the help of my mother, Mrs. Dorothy Lenz, as assistant leader. Club enrollment increased to 55 members so project leaders who volunteered to help were: Otis Dyson and Mabel Kessler.

In 1949, Ray Toelle, who was general leader, was inducted into the armed forces, so I replaced him as general leader. At the time my new husband, Phil, also helped as a project leader in the electricity project, and with other new project leaders, Charles Toelle and Cyril Kerkman, who led the dairy and poultry projects.

I started to become more and more involved and initiated many new activities in the club. Demonstrations were being introduced at a county wide basis, so I helped members, regardless of what projects they were enrolled in, to put together a demonstration so they could enter the county contests.

Safety projects were introduced into our club as well as conservation activities. So I started a safety and conservation poster contest within the club and we had high school teachers, school administrators, and county extension agents judge the posters and we gave placings and awards to the members. This became a very successful activity. Some of our judges were: Earl Floeter, Vaughn and Eileen Sorenson, Red Lueder, Paul and Charlotte Jaeger. These people were helpful in pointing out the pros and cons of good poster making and how to present an idea. Then when the members made posters for the fair, they knew what quality was expected.

At this point and time, clubs could have club displays called booths at the county fair. Each club would have a section in a tent which was used as a means of telling a story about some phase of project work or a club activity. Our club did very well on these displays and it was a way of promoting working together and having fun together by participating in a worthwhile activity.

In 1961, our club was thriving so well and we had a banner year. At the time I was very interested in music, so the girls and I put together our first musical for the county contests, called, 'The Girls 4-H Story'. I directed this musical for them and Lucy Toelle accompanied our group on the piano. We won the first place in the county and went on to represent the county at the district level.

This was the year that our club had been in existence for 25 years, so we had an anniversary celebration with 200 people in attendance. At this event, a memorial plaque in honor of deceased leaders and members was presented to Earl Floeter, principal of the local school district, Wheatland Center School, by Wheatland Town Chairman, George Schlitz. This memorial was to be kept hanging in the hall of the school as this had become our meeting place for general meetings. Inscribed on this memorial were: Ben Kasken, general leader for 10 years; Otis Dyson, poultry and dairy leader for 1 year; Ardell Lenz, member for 11 years, electricity project leader for 4 years; general leader for 2 years; Margaret Schenning, member for 7 years; and Fern Wilson, member for 8 years.

At the present time, no one seems to know what ever happened to the plaque due to many changes of administration at the local district school and it seems that after I resigned my leadership, no one kept up the inscriptions on the plaque.

Through the years, I continued to write the script that went into the musical productions, and continued to direct all the musicals that our club put on and Mrs. Evelyn Uhen, who was our church organist, played the accompaniments for these musicals. Listing the names of musicals that we produced include: *Springtime, Indian Pow-Wow, South of the Border, Winter Wonderland, Charlie Brown, Wizard of Oz, Singing Around the Campfire, Lullaby and Good Night,* all of which were group musicals including singing and acting.

One year I directed a triple trio composed of a medley of classical songs. The girls who sang in this trio were: Dolly Roanhaus; Mary Razor; Kathy, Theresa, and Marie Vos; Blanche and Judy Schuerman; and Jane and Ruth Vos. These girls all wore black skirts and white blouses and looked so uniform and professional, and sang beautifully. They were rewarded by winning first place in the county and representing the county at the district contest where they again won first. District was the end of the line for winning.

Many clubs in our county had wished that the Whealand Willing Workers would stop entering the musical competition, because they felt that they never had a chance to win top honors because our club always took the top placings, much as to say that we would enter more than one musical sometimes and that cut their chances down some more. Many times over and over again our club was envied because we participated in every activity that was available. We definitely had an active club.

The nice part of my directing these productions, was

the fact that this gave our own kids the priority of having some of the leading parts. In *Wizard of Oz;* Dolly was Dorothy, Danny was the tin man. Other leading characters were Joe Vos as the lion, and Jimmy Lois as the scarecrow."

In the musical, *Springtime,* Ron Vos sang the solo to the music of Singing In The Rain, and he had the most beautiful male voice for his age that anyone could ever have.

In *Charlie Brown;* Danny was Charlie, and John Schenning was Snoopy. John was the best Snoopy anyone could have, who howled and howled all through the number. This added a little pizzaz to the whole number, and the audience went wild over his performance.

In the number *Indian Pow-Wow,* the kids were all made up as Indians, I went to the Five and Dime Store in Twin Lakes, and Mr. Cheramuga, the owner, helped me pick out loose face powder and a cream to mix it with to get the darker color of the skin tone. Many of the moms helped make customs, and Wally Harrison and Roni Runkel played tom-toms beating out the Indian chanted beats which was very effective. As a finale one of the girls in our club sang the *Indian Love Call* song. It was a most effective performance.

All of our performances were spectacular because we put our 'all' into each production, and we had so much fun working together.

We would take a bus to Milwaukee for the district contests. Mrs. Marie Wilson, who was a bus driver for the local public school system in our area and also a mom of 4-H members in our club, would drive us safely there and back again. This was one of the fun parts of being in 4-H.

In the year of 1962, the county agent Red Lueder asked me to do a pilot program for the state of Wisconsin. I agreed to take on this task and so started a 'Little Leader' program. The general idea was to give the young people who were not yet old enough to be junior leaders a head start on developing leadership qualities in these members. They learned how to assist the junior and senior leaders in various projects and activities. This helped a great deal because when they were old enough to become junior leaders, they were already trained which was a great asset to the whole club as the club enrollment was growing rapidly.

This was very successful, and I had to write an article as to how I had planned and developed this program and to evaluate the program with the possibility of other clubs in the nation starting the same program in their clubs. This article was published in the National 4-H magazine. I no longer have this magazine as I gave it to one of the girls, Lisa Merrill, whose picture was in it, as I thought she would like it as a keepsake.

My first group of little leaders included: David Richter, Donna Richter, Larry Wilson, Linda Schmidt, Joanne Kerkman, Linda Kerkman, and Dennis Jensen. They were well motivated to be the firsts' in this program. The next year the group included: Darlene Roanhaus, Regina Lenz, Linda Haag, Camille Kach, and June Schmidt. This was another group who were very successful. Now the Little Leader program was well off the ground and others counties and states began establishing this same type of program.

In 1963, our club took advantage of the free tree offer from the state, and planted seedlings as a windbreak along the Palmer Creek on the Earl Harrison farm. We also had many more conservation activities and so our club won a conservation award which was a trip to Upham Woods in Eagle River and on to Randolph and the Wisconsin Rapids, then back through the Dells, and toured the Wisconsin River. The Wisconsin River is known to be one of the hardest working rivers in the country. I accompanied Regina Lenz, Linda Haag, Wally Harrison, and Roni Runkel as their chaperone on this educational tour.

Another activity that I led was raising money for the club fund by holding a bake sale. The girls who were enrolled in Foods and Nutritions project would come to my house and they would bake varieties of bakery that we could sell the next day at the sale. In those years, we would hold the bake sales in Burlington.

Usually these were held in the Chevy dealership showroom in Burlington. Many people would come in to look because we had our baked goods displayed in front of the huge glass front. In this way people who were walking down the street would stop and look, come in and purchase many goodies. These bake sales were very successful.

In 1967, a new project was introduced into the club programs called Exploring, which was for nine year olds who were too young to carry out a project. This gave them a sampling of various projects to help them to decide which project they would enroll in as a ten year old and first year member. At that time there were so many younger brothers and sisters who could hardly wait to join 4-H. This is the reason that this was offered to youngsters aged nine.

195

In 1968, our club observed Rural Life Sunday by attending church services at St. Alphonsus Church as a corporate body, and having breakfast in the school cafeteria after the church ceremony. Many people in the community were impressed that our 4-H Club held observances of this nature.

On the Sunday preceding Memorial Day, our club would gather at St. Alphonsus Church and march to the beating of drums by Wally Harrison and Roni Runkel, in a procession through the cemetery.

We would all stop off at a veteran's grave and put a flag on as a tribute to the deceased veteran who served his country so well. Again the people of the community remarked what worthwhile activities our club conducted.

This was the year in which the girls' triple trio were honored guests at the dedication ceremony of the Wheatland Gardenaires Garden Club memorial at Lily Lake, at which they rendered their vocal selections of appropriate songs. Our club members helped with the upkeep of the flowers in the following years.

It seems as though this was a banner year for our club, as Mrs. Dorothy Lenz, general leader, was presented with a diamond pin for her 20 years of service to the club. She continued to render her services as clothing project leader as well as Clothing Superintendent at the Kenosha County Fair.

In 1973, two of our own kids held offices in the club. Debbie was president and Dell was Sergeant-at-arms.

Club work was getting more and more involved with having more and more of our children as members and needing parent help, so I decided that with having gone back to full time teaching and helping our own kids, I decided to resign my leadership so in 1974 after having served the club for 27 years of service, I did resign my leadership The club presented me with a beautiful heart rhinestone pin as a token of their appreciation.

In 1975 general leader Alex Haag resigned and Rosella Wilson and Phyllis Epping took over co-leadership. This was the year that our daughter, Debbie, was selected to represent the county in the State Fair Dress Revue.

The following year, 1976, was the bicentennial year of our great nation, America. Phil and I, who were still involved as parents, helped the kids construct a float for the parade in New Munster for the Wheatland Township bicentennial celebration and for the parade at the county fair. New project leaders included Rita Vos and Nancy Nienhaus.

Our daughter, Donna, designed the Wheatland Township Bicentennial Memorial of beautiful red granite, which still stands in the park in New Muntser. Her design theme was, 'The Spirit of '76' which depicted a drum design with olive branches surrounding it as a memorial of the men who fought for our country's freedom. She was awarded a U. S. Saving Bond. All through the years, our club always had several window displays to promote 4-H during 4-H Club Week, a week set aside to inform the public about project work and activities in 4-H. Our club for many years had displays in the Pieters Brothers Dry Goods Store in Burlington which in later years became Barton's Fashion Store. Every year we also had one at the Wheatland Store owned and operated by the George Schlitz's. In the later years, we started putting them in stores in New Munster.

Now I know what you are thinking, New Munster, known as Whiskey Hill, because of so many taverns there, is where 4-H had displays! Let me clarify this; we had displays in the grocery store and the garage and filling station, not the taverns. You need to keep in mind, there is also a Catholic Church and school in New Munster. This is also where the town hall for Wheatland township is located, in addition to a post office, and the township's fire station.

Some times I was asked to help judge these window displays. I guess because of my teacher background and being an officer of the Kenosha County Council, people felt confident that I was qualified for this judging.

Square dancing had become the fad during the time I was a leader, so the county set up evenings where the kids as well as the adults could learn square dancing. The kids became so interested that they also started to teach the young people ballroom dancing. Where else could kids get all these wholesome activities? In addition to the safety and conservation poster contests I had mentioned previously, the county rejuvenated safety and conservation speaking contests that were held when I was a member. Winners were sent on to the district contests. This helped develop speaking skills for many of the kids, especially the shy ones.

Speaking of shy ones, I always tried to delegate a job to some of the shy club members, so as to help them overcome this and to become more outgoing. One member who was so shy was Roy Wilson, so I made him a chairman of a committee, which he carried out in an expertise manner. His committee

197

worked with him and enjoyed him as their chairman, and this was a starting point for Roy to overcome his shyness. This is one of the things that 4-H does for kids, helps them develop personal traits and they learn how to become a part of a group and enjoy being that part.

I helped initiate many other community activities in our club. The club bought paint, and after sending out consent forms to people in the community, the kids painted mail boxes for them. This was a project that went over really big in the community, and people were amazed that 4-H kids would even do this free of charge for everyone in the community who signed a consent form. Many people wanted to pay the kids, but we would not allow the kids to take any money, as it was a community service.

Many of these activities created interest in other boys and girls of club age and so the enrollment escalated to 78 members. But many parents of kids already in club work and parents of those who were first joining in addition to other people of the community came forth and helped lead projects.

Extension home agents, agricultural agents, home economists, and youth leaders of Kenosha county who were experts in their fields and served Kenosha County were: E.V.Ryall, Irene Schulist, Glee Hemmingway Leet, Charlotte Trewartha Jaeger, Doris Eskstein Caldart, Marlowe Nelson, Dr. Shuart Waldo, Paul Jaeger, E. J. Lueder, Gerald Gast, Phyllis Garside Northway, and Mitch Mason. There have been more since that time, but these are the names of the people with whom I have had the pleasure of working, during the times that I was a 4-H member or leader.

Being that I went back to teaching for the second time around, I became very busy and gave less and less of my time even as a parent to the 4-H program, due to my taking on a duel position of teacher/administrator in the local Catholic school.

Then after retiring from my full time job, I helped my grandchildren with their Child Care and Development project work and their county fair exhibits. I also helped them with their dairy table top displays. So I figured as long as I was helping them, I might as well help other kids with their projects, so I volunteered as a project leader in 1995. To be perfectly honest, I had missed working with 4-H kids all those years, as I have always loved kids and enjoyed working with them.

Being that I had twenty-seven years in as a leader, I had always had a goal for being a leader for at least thirty years. Now I surpassed my goal with 32 years in 1999.

It was very interesting getting back into leadership, as now it involved taking a class called ROPES, so as to work with children. R.O.P.E.S. means Recruit Orientation Placement Educational System, which became a necessity for anyone being in contact and working with children. This was a class in which we were all trained in how to best deal with children, their needs and problems, and we learned what to do if we suspected any type of home neglect and/or abuse. The whole idea was that volunteer leaders fully understood their obligations toward other people's children so the members would gain the best knowledge and experience in learning, and to enhance their participation in various activities of each 4-H club that they were a member of. The training was geared to 4-H youth protection and skill development.

Three general categories of skill development were:

1.) Competency skills: which included creativity, problem solving, project and job skills.

2.) Coping skills: such as patience, confidence, efficiency, independence, empathy, responsibility, social skills, communication, speaking skills, and deal with stress by self-expression.

3.) Contributing skills: giving back to the community, have concern for public affairs, leadership, caring for others, and cooperation.

This class also educated the volunteer leader in reference to the workings of a club, and what the background of 4-H is all about. It familiarized them with the endless opportunities that 4-H had to offer to its members and were also given the resources for help in project work.

Families and other youth-serving programs place trust in the UW-Extension Service to provide quality leadership and care for participating youth. The opportunity to work with youth is a privileged position of trust that should be held only by those who are willing to demonstrate behaviors that fulfill that trust.

Guidelines for adult volunteer behavior were discussed as follows:

1.) Treat others in a courteous, respectful manner demonstrating model for youth.

2.) Obey the laws of the locality, state, and nation.

3.) Make all reasonable effort to assure that 4-H youth programs are accessible to youth without regard to race, color, national origin, sex, religion, or disability.

4.) Recognize that verbal, sexual, physical abuse and/or neglect of

youth is unacceptable in 4-H youth programs. Report suspected abuse.
5.) Do not participate in or condone neglect or abuse which happens outside the program to a child. Report suspected abuse.
6.) Treat animals humanely and teach 4-H youth to provide appropriate animal care.
7.) Operate motor vehicles (including machines or equipment) in a safe and reliable manner when working with 4-H youth, and only with a valid operator's license and the legally required insurance coverage.
8.) Do not consume alcohol or illegal substances while responsible for youth in 4-H activities nor allow 4-H youth participation under supervision to do so.
Failure to comply to any of these guidelines may be reason for termination of a volunteer.

Volunteers can help prevent situations where abuse can occur. For everyone's protection, volunteers should take the following precautions when working with youth in the 4-H program:
1.) Adults should work with young people in reasonably open places where others are welcome to enter - not behind closed or locked doors. Be aware that while spending time alone with a single youth can be positive and helpful, it can also be a reason for concern for everyone involved.
2.) Always welcome and encourage parents and guardians to attend meetings and events.
3.) Respect the privacy of youth when clothes are changed and showers taken. Adults should be involved only when there is a health or safety issue.
4) One unrelated adult should not room with one youth during an overnight stay, camping or an award trip.
5.) Never use physical punishment or deny basic necessities, such as; food, shelter, or medical care.
6.) Be alert to the physical and emotional health of the young
These precautions are designed to protect youth, adults, families, and the organization.

There are rules and regulations to follow in reporting suspected child abuse or neglect in Kenosha County. As far as 4-H volunteer leaders are concerned, this is the statement to follow for self protection. Non-mandated reporters include concerned family members, neighbors, and persons making self-referrals, therefore persons who report suspected child abuse or neglect in good faith are immune from civil or criminal liability. Reporting should be done through the county social services.

Don't let this scare you into not wanting to volunteer

as a 4-H volunteer leader. I can assure you that it is the most rewarding experience that any adult can ever encounter. I have enjoyed every minute of my 4-H leadership.

In November of the year, 1995, I was nominated for the alumni award, given to a former 4-H member who had done outstanding work to achieve a high level of success in the past, and who had become an outstanding volunteer throughout the community as an adult. I was informed that I had been nominated, but I had no idea of where it would go from there, because I felt as though I was just an average person in the community.

Being that my grandchildren had won many outstanding awards that year, they were to receive some of the county awards, so they talked me into going to the county achievement gathering which was also an ice cream social.

Phil and I went to see Tanya get so many awards, Missy get her numerous awards, and Josh, Ashley and Kelly also their many awards. We have always been so proud of our grand children's accomplishments and were equally proud of them that day. Next on the program were the presentation of the 'Friends of 4-H' and the 'Alumni' awards. I was so totally in awe when the mistress of ceremonies started reading the accomplishments of an alumni, and I got to thinking that I, too, had done these same things. Just then she called out my name. I was in shock! I had to pick up my crutches off the floor and go up and receive this award. I was so ecstatic and nervous at this point that I could hardly walk even with the aid of my crutches.

As I approached the front of the room, it was a former 4-H club member Donna Joerndt Ratzke, whom I had helped in our own Wheatland Willing Workers club in former years, who pinned the corsage on me and presented me with the award and a great big hug. I had to hold back the tears, as I was so happy. How exciting!

The couple, husband and wife team, received the friends of 4-H award. They were such deserving people, who put their whole heart and soul into 4-H. Their names were Alice and Paul Hrupka, and I had recognized them from years gone by.

Then there were pictures taken and news articles written for the local papers. The Kenosha county 4-H sponsors a monthly news letter called the 'Home Lite', which is sent out to all the 4-H families. Following is the article that appeared in the November issue of that newsletter.

201

HOME LITE

November 1998

Dear 4-H Families:

Sometimes, or so it appears, many people who give [or have given] of themselves to help Kenosha County 4-H are playing a game of Hide-and-Seek. You hear about them. You can see the results of their hard work. But when it comes to recognizing them, you might have to play games to get them to come out and take a bow.

At the Everyone in 4-H Ice Cream Social, these individuals renowned for their selflessness and dedication were brought into the much deserved limelight. Paul and Alice Hrupka were the recipients of the Friends of 4-H Award and Arlene Roanhaus was acknowledged as outstanding 4-H Alumni.

Between them, Paul and Alice have given 48 years as educators and volunteers to young people in the county. Together they were general leaders of the Paris Happy Workers and continue to be project leaders. Giving of their time and experiences, Paul and Alice are role models for today's 4-H'ers.

Arlene Roanhaus has been a one woman army in the 4-H program. Her contributions to 4-H range from general leader of the Wheatland Willing Workers to representing Kenosha County at National 4-H Club Congress in Chicago. Her years as a 4-H'er and volunteer prepared her to become a citizen who recognizes the need for every person to become involved in their community. Whether as a teacher, singer, clerk or committee woman, Arlene continues to "Make the Best Better".

How many current members have had the pleasure of visiting with the Hrupka's or Mrs. Roanhaus? You'd be surprised how many of your questions they could answer! So the next time you get the opportunity to speak with our current honorees, don't pass it up. And 4-H'ers remember this... if you want to know where to find a proven hero, now you know where to look.

Mitch Mason

4-H Youth Development Agent

      I cannot say enough about the training members receive through the 4-H program. My philosophy to the members has always been:

- select only the projects that you are really interested in or care to learn,
- complete each project entirely,
- if you are old enough, be sure to be a junior leader [called Youth Leadership],
- participate in as many activities as you can,

- get involved in your school,
- get involved in your community,
- get involved in your church,
- above all, take pride in your work.
Do the best that you can do, be the best that you can be.... this is how you can "Make The Best Better".

In the June 15, 1998 issue of the Western Kenosha County Bulletin appeared the following article in which my daughter's name, Dolly Thuemmler, former 4-H member appeared.

4-H Volunteers Take on Various Roles With the Group

When you think of 4-H, you think of state fairs, county fairs and maybe a yearly pizza sale. It's an organization that kids living in rural areas join.

All of this is true to a point, but 4-H is so much more, encompassing a larger number of people than those in rural areas. Between Kenosha County in Wisconsin and Lake County in Illinois, over 1,100 youth between ages nine and nineteen are 4-H members.

"When 4-H began, there was a great need for rural activity", explained Mitch Mason, Kenosha County U. W. Extension 4-H Youth Development Agent. "Now the average 4-H member is a suburban kid from an area of 50,000 or more".

4-H provides hands-on learning by taking action. It's the kind of learning both youth and adults can relate to. The four H's in 4-H stand for head, heart, hands, and health. The head is for building the life skills of making decisions and setting goals. The heart is for building team-work and learning to relate to others. The hands are for learning by doing, and the health is for taking care of yourself for a lifetime.

There are 11 community 4-H groups in Kenosha County, and 24 in Lake County. All of these groups are run by volunteers, who are extraordinary individuals that share their time, energy and knowledge with 4-H members. Many times these volunteers are parents of 4-H members.

"The volunteer's role can range from working a booth or giving rides to meetings, to leading the group's monthly meetings or teaching a certain skill to a group of kids," said Mason. "They can spend one or two hours a year or hours upon hours. It's their choice".

No parent should expect to not be involved when their child joins 4-H. Parental involvement is what makes the organization work. As a matter of fact, some 4-H clubs require parent participation.

"The first year a family is involved in 4-H, the parent should only take on one or two things that will get them acquainted with it", said

Mason. "Then once they know what 4-H is all about and the kinds of things we need help with, they'll be able to choose their role".

A 4-H volunteer can take on the role of general leader, project leader or activity leader. They can also be an assistant to any of these leaders helping out with various tasks.

The general or organizational 4-H leader runs the club. Activity leaders do a variety of organizational work including: sitting on committees, help with enrollment, do fund raising, make phone calls, do computer work and chaperone. Project leaders run the various projects.

"The general leader's job is to delegate jobs to other volunteers", said Mason.

Many times the general or organizational leader role is shared by one to three people. Married couples have been known to take on the task together.

"I share the general leader position with Mary Daniels," said Dolly Thuemmler, who is co-leader of the Wheatland Willing Workers club in Kenosha County. "It's easier for both of us because we each do the things we like."

The amount of projects a club has can be dictated by the number of volunteers they have to run projects.

"Right now we need help from volunteers for Cloverbuds, Exploring, camp planning, fishing, photography, roller blading, rocketry, small engines, tractors, and woodworking is desperate," said Mason of the 4-H groups in Kenosha County.

"Kids don't register with a group by the city they live in. They go to the club their parents went to, or to the club that has the projects they want to join", commented one leader.

This article proves the values of 4-H and how it helps children progress in the learning process through the efforts of people who volunteer to lead in any capacity in which they express an interest toward helping this development of our youth.

I can't say enough about the development of youth accredited to belonging to a 4-H Club. I have now completed my 32nd year as a leader, and from here on, I will be affiliated with the Child Development project in the capacity as an advisor, which means that I will help any members who need advice or help related to this project.

After all, I still maintain that anyone can work to 'Make The Best Better'.

Chapter 17
A Little Pizazz in My Life

During my adult life I did much volunteer work and spent many hours of enjoyment doing some of the things I liked to do besides working outside the home for pay.

I belonged to a ladies' card club. There were eight of us: my mother, my sister-in-law Sophie, Vera Lasco, Dorothy Banas, Stella Breski, Bobbie Kriofsky, and Lucy Harrison. We played the game called Five Hundred which was a game in which partners would bid for the tricks they thought they could get and in the suit that they wanted to make it. It was fun and challenging. We would serve punch, some kind of a snack including candies during the playing time. Then the hostess would serve cake or another kind of dessert for a lunch at the end of the evening with coffee, as we were all coffee drinkers. During lunch was a gab session.

We got together once a month in the evenings rotating at each other's homes. This lasted for about six years until Lucy had to move to another farm, so we found a replacement, Helen Sarmont, and went on playing for another three years, and at that time everyone became so busy with their own families that the group broke up. But we had fun in those nine years.

Phil and I belonged to a couple card club in which we played a game called Sheepshead formerly known in the older generation as Shoshkopp. This was a game in which diamonds were all trump and the queen of clubs was the high card, the queen of spades was second high, followed by the queen of hearts, queen of diamonds, jack of clubs, jack of spades, jack of hearts, jack of diamonds, ace of diamonds, ten of diamonds, king of diamonds. and the nine of diamonds.

When a player would pick up the blind, it was automatic that whoever held the jack of diamonds was the picker's partner. If the picker had the jack, then a partner had to be called by calling for the next jack. Sometimes calling a partner was near death, as he or she probably had very few trumps in his/her hands. This made the game challenging.

The aces counted eleven, the tens counted ten, kings were four, queens were three, and jacks were two. The picker had to have sixty-one to win the hand, which was called schneider. The opponent had to have thirty. If the partners who did the bidding didn't get sixty-one they lost. We usually played for nickels. If the picker and partner didn't get schneider, they had to pay the opponents, and if they got skunked, it costs double on the bump.

During the course of the evening we would serve one brandy cocktail, then we drank a few beers the rest of the evening. At the close of the evening, we would serve usually a sandwich and chips, followed with a slice of cake and coffee. This was simple so preparation didn't take much time.

Our group consisted of Marv and Helen Roanhaus, Chuck and Mary Schuerman, Ev and Fran Kerkman, and Phil and me. We met on the first Saturday evening of every month. We were all fun loving people so we had some good times together. Three of them are deceased so only five of us survive at present. With this card club we played until all of us became too busy to continue, so we disbanded. All our children were getting older and took up more of our time with their school activities.

I belonged to a homemaker group called 3-L. The name stood for 'Linking Learning with Laughter'. This was a local group that functioned through the County Cooperative Extension Service in Kenosha County. I can't remember all the ladies who were members because there were always members dropping out and new ones joining, but at one time we had eighteen ladies.

We would send two delegates to the county meetings at which they would be trained to bring the information back to the local clubs for the other members. There were many interesting classes, many about food selection and preparation of various foods, nutrition and meal planning, interior decorating in the home, political issues and current laws, raising children and knowing how to deal with their situations that arise, style in personal dressing, personal grooming, self-worth, horticultural knowledge of plants and flowers, crafts, holiday entertaining, refinishing and upholstering furniture, choosing the right schools for your children, and many other topics of interest to further educate women.

One of the classes which I attended was the making of pheasant feather hats. It involved getting a basic shape that you wanted to make up into a hat. Glee Hemingway taught this class to us.

Gathering of the feathers was the biggest job. Phil would skin the pheasant, then I would pluck the feathers which I thought had the variety of colors and then these feathers had to be dried for a day or so. Then I'd sort them according to size and color. Many times ladies would trade feathers in order to get the variety.

Next the design had to be preplanned before attaching the feathers to the hat with a special kind of glue. This was done through means of using special pins. When the design suited me, I'd start gluing them on to the hat form made of a stiff crinoline. Then the hat would have to be put on a head shape to thoroughly dry.

These hats were a thing of beauty and each of us who made hats were more than proud to wear them, especially when someone would ask you where you bought such an exquisite hat. What a pleasure to reply that I made my own!

Another series of classes that we took was upholstery taught by Charlotte Trewartha. We had to select a piece of furniture that needed to be reupholstered, take it to a lady's home who was a member of our 3-L Club. So I took a couch to this class and the classes were held in my mother's basement twice a week.

The first step was to tear the whole couch apart. Then we refastened all the springs back into position. It was amazing how, through time, springs came loose and when one would sit on this sofa, one could feel the springs out of their correct position.

The next step was to put on the patches of cotton padding and then the horsehair sheets for added durability. On top of this was more cotton padding. These had to be held in position by means of heavy upholstery cord. After the new fabric was attached, the finishing touches had to be done. Some pieces of furniture required decorative tacks over braid, and some required bias trim of the same fabric to be attached. Our sofa that I was redoing had to have the bias trim so this required added stitching on the heavy duty sewing machine.

This whole process required much arm and hand strength plus a bit of elbow grease. This was very hard work because stretching fabric and trying to hold it in place while stitching became quite a task. But the completed project was well worth the time and effort, because it looked as though it had been purchased in a store.

Another class that I participated in and enjoyed was the tailoring of suits class. This class was taught by Glee Hemngway Leet. We learned all the steps of tailoring from the laying on of the pattern to the finishing touches of bound buttonholes. After all the clubs in the county had completed their projects, we put on a style show at Honey Bear Farm in Powers Lake in the dining room with ample room to model clothes.

I made a suit with a loose fitting straight cut jacket and a straight skirt in pink tweed wool, and it turned out very professional looking. Mom made a coat for Darlene, and it too looked professional. Darlene and I modeled together in this style show.

This homemaker group was very educational and the County Extension Home Agents made the learning fun. It gave opportunity to socialize along with working with ladies of our own community as well as from the county and state. Kenosha County has always had the dynamic quality home agents who were the best teachers in the field.

Being a member of this group, I held positions in our own local group and was president of the county group for many years. This meant conducting county meetings. Our extension home agent at this time was Doris Eckstein who was a joy to work with as she had all the latest ideas and knew how to make learning fun.

Many opportunities were availed to me while holding these positions. I went to the state seminars usually held at Green Lake, which was a learning process and it also got me out of the house for two days and nights. I always enjoyed meeting so many nice ladies with whom I had much in common.

It was through the position of county presidency that I was afforded the opportunity for my first TV appearance. Along with the home agent and myself was the county secretary, Jewel Hilbert of Salem. We appeared on channel 4 in Milwaukee. What an experience this was in 1957 ! We were told to wear light colored clothing because of the contrast of the background. The lady in charge of make-up redid each of our own make-up that we had on, and somehow or other she over did it a little, and having been used to wearing my make-up very sparingly, I almost felt artificial. But when we got on stage for the presentation, the lights were so bright and so hot, that I felt like I was out in the hottest rays of sun at high noon.

Actually it was presented in the form of an interview. Doris would ask Jewel and me some questions about the homemaker group , and we would take over and expand on the information. It was great and one had to think so intensely quick about the topic so we didn't leave out anything of great importance. It was quite brief, lasting only about ten minutes, which to us seemed like hours when you are under pressure, but it was extremely interesting and lots of fun, marvelous opportunity for a 31 year old housewife homemaker.

Our 3-L Club would take a field trip every close of the season, which meant that the clubs in the county did not funtion during the summer months. Some times we would have picnics at which time we would invite our husbands. Other times we would go out to eat at a nice restaurant. We were a group of all mixed ages, but everyone seemed so compatible and had fun together. We younger women learned from the best, the generation before us, the ladies who were older and wiser, of which my mother was one.

Each year when our wedding anniversary rolled around on June 26th, Phil and I would go out for a dinner after saving up all year for this annual outing. My brother, Bob, and his wife, Sophie always accompanied us. This was a truly great treat, as it was the one night that we only had to cook for the children, who were very happy with the all time favorite, spaghetti and a salad.

I never got out much for many years of my life, as I was always pregnant. At one time, I felt as though I couldn't even speak intelligently any more, as the extent of my life was baby bottles and diapers, which does not make for the best in conversation. As much as I wanted and loved each child, I had many anxieties sometimes with such a limited life because I had always been a people person. I missed getting out among people. I also missed teaching so I accepted every substitute job that came along as long as my mother was willing to babysit for me, and that she always did.

I was always happy when our Wheatland Town Chairman George Schlitz and later replaced by Tom Grady, would call and ask me to clerk at town elections, because this got me out of the house and among people for two days a year for the spring and the autumn elections.

I really enjoyed this even though it took many hours to count the ballots. At that time all the ballots had to be counted by hand, double and triple checked so there were no errors.

One man of our community named Joe Pfeffer, was always the ballot chairman and he had the best method of counting. He would sort the ballots into stacks of twenty-five. Then each person who clerked was given a stack which that person counted, then passed that pile to the right and the next person counted, then the stack was passed to the right again and counted. This proved triple counting, so we never had even one

209

error.

I enjoyed this task of clerking at the town of Wheatland elections as one got to see and talk to many of the people of the community. In the early evening the town chairman would always order out and bring in hot sandwiches for us at supper time. I had clerked for many years until I went back into the teaching field full time once more

Another adventure that got me out of the house was when I was summoned for jury duty in Circuit Court in Kenosha County at the court house in Kenosha. It was the dead of winter as I was called for duty early January. At that time we had a yellow Ford that was most reliable, as I had to drive in every day because no one else from the immediate community was serving at the same time as I was.

Later on when there were more jurors needed and more names put on the list, a man from Fox River served too. But I still had to drive by myself, because if one would be drawn for a case and the other wasn't, then it meant waiting in Kenosha until the other was done with duty for the day. Anyhow I always was selected to serve on a case and he was only picked for one case, and he fell asleep during that whole testimony

Another juror who was later called was Charlotte Jaeger, the former Charlotte Trewartha, whom I knew from her work as an Cooperative Extension Home Economist in Kenosha County. It was most enjoyable having her serve on cases with the group. Most of the times she and I would go out to lunch together, and sometimes we would accompany her husband Paul, who would lunch with us. A few times we would go to their house for lunch.

Out of the numerous cases, my name was drawn every time, and the lawyer never scratched my name. I guess because I was young, this appealed to the lawyers on both sides, for the plaintiff and the defendant, so I always had to serve. It was a wonderful experience, as one finds out how the other half of society lives and where they place their values in contrast to the integrity of persons in society. I couldn't believe how people put so much emphasis on money they could collect and not on peoples' feelings or what this did to their emotions.

I was only excused one time for a land condemnation case, due to my husband being employed by the county. I never knew what bearing that had with the case, but it was okay because it gave me a day or two off from duty.

One time we had to go by bus out to the place that

was the scene of an accident, in which a lady fell and was suing the Kroger Store because she slipped on the carpeting and fell upon entering the store. Any darn fool could see what her aim was, to get rich overnight. The carpet at the entry had no holes or tears and it was quite visible that in no way could one possibly fall unless she was inebriated, tripped, or forced herself to do just that. However, we did not find that the store was negligent. You should have seen the expression on her face when we came back with the verdict. The jury awarded her zero dollars.

A very interesting case which was a bit comical but controversial was the case of a woman who was injured in an automobile accident. When her husband was on the witness stand to testify, he was asked why they were suing when his wife was at ninety per cent fault for the accident. He became so excited when he was asked this question, that he stood right up in the witness box and shouted out, "Why I'm suffering, I don't get any anymore." This was in the testimony in the cross examination by the defendants lawyer who said, "Don't get what?"

By this time everyone in the whole court room was laughing so hard and even the judge had to snicker as he politely tapped his gavel on the desk and called for order. It took a few minutes for everyone to compose themselves again, and the stupid jerk in his crisis replied at the top of his lungs, "Well, sex, a guy's got to have sex, and I don't get that anymore, my wife's no good, since the accident she's no good, as plain as that".

Again the whole courtroom of people burst out in laughter. As the testimony went on, the whole situation grew funnier and funnier, and the people in the courtroom could hardly contain themselves any longer because this guy stated in graphic detail what was on his mind.

All this while, I'm sure that the poor woman was totally humiliated by her husband's words and actions. Well, it ended up that the lady didn't get any money nor did he get any empathy from the jurors' verdict. It became a standing joke among the jurors as to whether the man got anything or not from that point on, as we didn't know what bearing money compensation would have on the problem he stated. This whole case was a waste of people's time and taxpayers' money. What a farse!

Another case I was picked to serve on was a skiing accident at the Wilmot Ski Hills, where a person had fallen off the ski lift and was severely injured. All the jurors had been selected and we were to go to the jurors' quarters to wait to be called for the case to open. We had just gotten in there and were drinking coffee when the bailiff came in to tell us that the case had been settled out of court, so we could all go home.

There were many other types of cases in which people were looking for large sums of money. Some of them deserved a settlement and so we gave it to them, but some of them didn't prove their case and lost. At times it was very difficult when a juror could only go on the testimony given that was heard when you knew right well that there was more to the case than what we heard. Lawyers have a way of making a witness say a 'yes' or a 'no', when there should be explanation given along with the yes or no. But we were instructed to take all that we heard for face value. I always felt that as long as I could live with my conscience after making a decision which I felt was the right choice, then I didn't have to think about these cases any more.

Nearing the end of my six month term of serving, my name was drawn for a murder trial. Now this is a different story. This means being sequestered in a motel room for as long as a trial could and would take. I had a very young baby at home. So I went privately to the judge in his chambers and asked to be excused from that case. When he asked what reason I had, I told him I had a small baby at home whom I couldn't leave. He responded that the judicial system would provide a baby sitter for me. Then I told him that a former girl friend of mine had a brother-in-law who was a relative of the defendant who murdered his wife and I had read about it in the paper so I had a preconceived notion in my mind. Therefore I was dismissed. Wow, what a relief!

Then a couple weeks later after that case had been over, didn't I get drawn for another murder trial. This was a case in which the girl friend of a police chief murdered the chief's wife. Again I went to the same judge and asked to be dismissed because I had to chaperone four 4-H Club members to a conservation trip to Northern Wisconsin which they had won. He told me absolutely no way, that was not a legitimate excuse for being dismissed from my civic duty as a juror.

Then I told him for religious reasons that I couldn't hear the case with an open mind because murder is murder and it is wrong for any reason. He smiled at me and told me that I was dismissed off that case. Incidentally, the jurors were sequestered for two months for that particular case.

That was the last of my jury duty for that time. In later years, I was summoned again for jury duty, and I just ignored it as I didn't intend to serve again.

I was back teaching again at St. Alphonsus School serving in the capacity of teacher/ administrator. I was teaching in my junior high classroom one day and one of the students raised her hand and asked if I had done something wrong because there was a police officer at my door. I then heard the knock, answered the door, and he told me he was to take me in because I was supposed to be at jury duty that day. Well, I had quite a task getting myself out of that one, after finally convincing him that I wasn't going to go with him no matter what. He knew I meant it and he suggested what I should do about the whole situation.

He told me to write a letter to Judge Michael Fischer in circuit court explaining why I didn't appear that day and why I planned not to come in at all. He also told me I'd have to write a pretty good convincing statement to convince the judge to let me off and to get myself out of that mess.

I immediately gave the students a study period, and I went straight to the typewriter, wrote a most convincing letter to his honor, the judge, stating the importance of my job and how it would be impossible to get competent help to take my place in this position, and that I did not intend to serve as a juror as I had served six months in years past and if every citizen did the same as I did, I felt that I had already done my civic duty. I addressed the envelope, stamped it and sent a student across the street to the post office to mail it for me.

All I can say is that you never saw so many frightened kids in your life as my students were. They were so afraid for me that I would end up in jail, but I calmly told them that would never happen to me. To this day, they can never believe how calm I was over the whole deal. (Secret! I was shaking in my shoes all the while but I never showed it at all!) I just told them I am pretty good with my choice of convincing words and that there was no need for them to worry, because I would be okay.

In my later life after I retired and have been in post-polio syndrome, I had been summoned for jury duty again, but this time I would like to have served but my handicap kept me from doing so, but such is life, you're dammed if you do, you're dammed if you don't.

When the first opportunity came along for getting back in my field of work, I expressed to my mother how much I would like to go back to work, as I had hoped that David would be the last child of the family. Having been in the past that I watched Bob and Sophie's two children, Reggie and Lenny, all these years so she could work, I inquired about her reciprocating and now watching my younger ones who were not in school. But to no avail, she, too, wanted to continue working outside the home for extra money and had to find a sitter for her children now that I decided to go back to teaching.

My mother, who was recuperating from a very serious illness, expressed her desire to watch our children for me so I could return back to the teaching field. The opening was at St. Alphonsus in New Munster where our children were still in school. I applied and got the job. I had begun to come back into the real world once again.

Phil and I used to go on fishing outings with our neighbors, Gene and Carol. They had a bigger boat than we had. Ours was nineteen feet long and theirs was twenty-one feet with a sleeping cabin under the deck. We both had porta-potties on our boats for quick relief of kidneys as we always drank a lot of beer while fishing. The name of our boat was the Big D, and Gene and Carol's boat was called 'Fun Two', being the second boat they owned.

The extent of our fishing was mostly on Lake Michigan off the port of Kenosha. It was so much fun catching big fish. I never cared that much for fishing, but this was the kind of fishing in which six poles were set up at the back of the boat in holders, and all the fisherman had to do was watch the pole. When the pole tipped down slightly, someone grabbed that pole and started reeling because there most likely was a fish on

I usually never took a pole to reel one in because I enjoyed watching the others reel them in. One day Phil said,"Arlene, you are going to reel in a big fish today, I'll help you". It wasn't long after he made that statement when a pole tipped, Phil grabbed it and helped me hold the pole as I reeled in. I reeled in so hard and so fast that my thumb and fore finger were actually bleeding from rubbing on the reel, but with Phil's help, I got it to the boat and someone netted it for me. Yes, it was a big fish, and I was so proud.

Most of our summer and early autumn Saturdays were spent on Lake Michigan when the weather permitted. We would be on the lake by five or six o'clock in the morning. Even though it was summer, the mornings on the lake were very chilly, and we usually started off by bundling up in winter jackets or snowmobile suits. After a while this apparel was shed and by afternoon we were wearing shorts and tee shirts.

Lake Trout and Coho Salmon were the kind of fish we caught. These were so good for eating, so every Friday night, Carol and I would make potato salad, cole slaw, have rye bread and fry fish. Gene and Carol would sometimes invite their relatives over and sometimes Phil and I would invite our parents and our married kids to enjoy these fish with us. It was like a Friday night ritual, fish fry at the Roanhauses.

Sometimes on weekends, we would take a whole fish, salt and pepper it, put butter, onions, and tomato wedges inside the cavity of the fish, then wrap it up securely in aluminum foil and bake it on the grill. This gave a variation of always having the fish fried, and was so tasty.

On one vacation with Gene and Carol, we took a Mississippi River excursion with Gene's boat. We drove to Onalaska, crossed the river on highway 90 and at the first lock and dam at LaCrescent, we launched the boat into the river. We went by boat up the river all the way to Winona, Minnesota.

This was exciting as we'd camp out along the river, and take off again the next morning. We would cook the fish that we caught. This was a different kind of fishing and luckily we trolled into a school of fish and we caught them so fast that the men were kept busy just baiting up our hooks. The fish were thrown down in the boat and at one point our feet were covered with these fish that were striped white bass, on up our legs that we couldn't move if we wanted to.

There were so many fish in the boat, and Carol's poodle, Gigi, who never had anything to do with me before, even jumped up on my lap in the boat to get away from the fish. We all had a good laugh out of that one.

During the course of this trip we went through two locks which were miles apart. The first was when we went into the lock and the water elevated. Along side of the cement wall were ropes and Phil and Carol each held onto a rope to steady the boat as we were being elevated. I had never seen a lock before, much as less to say be in one, so this was quite an experience for me.

Going through the second lock was equally as thrilling as the first, only this time we were going down so we were being descended. Again Phil and Carol had to hold the ropes and steady the boat.

After going a bit beyond Winona, we started down the river to get back to where Gene's truck and trailer were parked. This is an experience I'll never forget because we had such a

215

wonderful time. Gene and Carol were both fun people to be with even though they were so much younger than we were.

At another time, a trip down Lake Michigan was also so exciting. Again accompanying Gene and Carol, we took Gene's boat for a week long excursion. We took his truck and trailer with boat, and drove to Two Rivers, we fished and camped out in the truck and boat that night.

Our next stop was in Manitowoc where we fished again. We stayed in the Carlton Hotel there, had a dinner in the hotel where we engaged in a night of dancing and drinking cocktails. We actually slept in a real bed that night. We fished the next day and went on to Sheboygan.

Basically we did the same in Sheboygan as the other days, fished all day, stopped in restaurants for breakfasts and supper. Every time we stopped for breakfasts, we had the opportunity to brush our teeth and wash up which felt so refreshing. After the supper meal we camped out in the truck and boat again.

Our next stop was at Port Washington where we had real excitement. We were fishing all day long and all of a sudden a storm came up and we were far out on the lake. We decided to start in for shore when Phil and Gene noticed a very small fishing boat with two gentlemen in it. They were worried that these men, having such a small boat, would not make it in before the storm. Gene drove his boat slowly so we could keep the other boat in sight. The wind had picked up ferociously and I was scared. To myself I started praying my Hail Mary's fast and furious, petitioning for her help that we would all be safe.

Hopefully we are getting closer and closer, when all of a sudden shore was within sight, but we still had a long way to go. Everyone on the boat was in complete silence, so this told me that the men were even apprehensive about getting in safely. The men in the other boat are nearer to us now, it seems as though they sensed that we were waiting for them. Great, we can now see the piers.

Gene drove the boat up to one pier, the men drove their boat off to another pier. As those men got closer to the pier, a wave prompted by the wind pushed their boat right into the pier, smashing it to bits. Luckily the men were okay.

Now Gene can't get close enough to a pier because the waves are gushing and slapping the boat up and down against the pier. Carol and Phil tried to tie the rope up to the post of the pier, when the post snapped off. We are in distress! Phil and Carol stood on the pier holding the boat by the ropes, while Gene went to get the trailer. At this time I had no other choice but to remain in the boat and keep praying as the waves splashed and roared against the boat. When Gene backed the trailer down, I don't really know what all went wrong, but it ended up that Phil had to go into the roaring waves and hook something up that automatically wheeled the boat up onto the trailer. He was soaked up to his neck, and poor Carol could hardly hold the boat by herself.

On shore stood a multitude of people watching us in distress, but do you think anyone would help Carol hold that boat? I guess no one wanted to get involved, what did they care if anything happened to us, we were strangers to them. Finally a Coca Cola distributor helped her. There was a Pepsi distributor there taking pictures of it all.

All this while I'm in the boat, with the waves splashing over the top of the boat, and at times I couldn't even see Carol, or Phil, or Gene. Now Gene yelled to me and said, "Mother, we'll still leave you in the boat until we get in the parking lot, you'll be safer that way than if we try to get you out of the boat right now".

Of course, I agreed, because at this instant I thought I was about to meet my creator any moment anyway, but I continued to pray my Hail Mary's in hopes that I still may be saved.

Finally I felt the boat moving and I knew at last I was safe because Gene was driving away from the pier. "Thank you, God, you didn't want me yet."

That night we went on. We didn't stop in the Milwaukee harbor, but rather went right on to Racine. Again we fished and enjoyed because the weather was nice, no storm in sight, but that doesn't always mean anything because the last storm came up very quickly.

Our last stop was in Kenosha. We were back in familiar territory, so we fished again. We took home many fish with us. Later we pressure canned them and had them last through the winter. Many of the fish we froze.

We went out on Lake Michigan a few more times from the port of Kenosha, but this was the beginning of the end of my fishing episodes. Gene and Phil took our youngest son David out fishing many more times.

It seemed that Gene made another investment and bought a night club at Winthrop Harbor in Illinois. He became interested in that project fixing up the club that had been vacant for a while and he really modernized it and had many well known Country Music artists performing at his club. He called it the Harbor Inn. David spent many Saturdays helping Gene with the carpenter work as David was a natural with woods, and had many excellent ideas for enhancing this club. Carpentry was a gift of God to David, and he was creative with these skills.

When Gene had the formal opening of the club, I helped Carol make barbecue and her mother-in-law helped Carol make potato salad. The grand opening was well attended and we all had so much fun. Most of our family and their spouses or boy friends also went and all had a good time. Many times after that opening we went on Saturday nights until Gene was about to sell this club.

With Gene's time spent on this club, he became involved with another woman in that area. Sad to say but after a while Carol and Gene moved away from this area to Richmond. As time progressed, they decided to divorce and this kind of took them out of our lives except for Carol as we did keep in touch with her and periodically still do.

We met this couple when Gene and Carol had moved into the house next door after the Barbians moved out. They were not only good neighbors, but we became best of friends. We had many good outings together and after years of being neighbors, they wanted to buy that house but the owner wanted too much money for what the house was, so they moved on. We shall never forget how this younger couple had touched our lives.

Our boat hasn't been launched in years, and it was in our garage until last summer. We need to clean our garage so badly, so the boat now stands out in the back yard. Neither of us has any interest in fishing on Lake Michigan again. Those days have long gone by. Amazing what age does to a person and how our likes and dislikes change as now we enjoy life in a different perspective. It seems as though now, with so many grandchildren in our lives, we are back to being more family oriented again so that is how we spend most of our time.

But you must realize by now that in my younger life, there was a lot of pizazz in my life. Even though we raised a big family, we enjoyed life in our own right.

Chapter 18
Adventure And Excitement In My Life

It always seemed that there was something about cars that I felt had it in for me, and that automobiles would try some day to destroy me or someone else who was near and dear to me in my family. So it was that I had a fear of car accidents. Not long after I got my driver's license, my parents, my younger brother, Ardell, and I were in a car accident. We were going to Winthrop, Iowa, to visit my mother's brother, Uncle Ray and his wife, Margaret, and their family. The truth of the matter was that at that time this part of Iowa was a dry town, and no liquor could be purchased there. So my dad was transporting a case of liquor to their house in exchange for a case of butter as my uncle worked in a creamery and this was his way of paying my dad. Now in all reality, with my parents living on a dairy farm, little did they need butter, but they made a deal and my parents never went back on their word.

My dad, who was a very cautious and good driver, was driving. We had just gotten near Beloit when a tire blew out on a gravel road. The car completely rolled over and back again. Upon landing, my younger brother, Ardell, was under the back seat of the car that had given way and loosened, and I was on top of the seat. It was all a sight for sore eyes,whiskey was running down the wheels from the trunk as fast as it could run out of all the broken bottles. One whole case of whiskey running like a stream of water, and the smell was enough to knock your socks off, almost gave off a second hand inebriation.

Now we saw mother in the front passenger seat and honestly we thought she had left this world into her eternal rest. How scary this was! Dad and I pulled her out of the car, and prayed that someone, just anyone, would come along. Like it was divine providence, down the road came two elderly gentlemen in a four passenger old Model T Ford, as we motioned for them to stop. They stopped and helped us put mother in their car and I went with them and we were off to Beloit to the hospital. Ardell stayed back with dad.

When we arrived at the hospital these kind men went into the hospital with us and helped me with my mom. In the emergency room, the staff told me that she was badly bruised and banged up but there were no severe injuries, but she was undergoing extensive shock.

While at the hospital, I couldn't figure out why everyone was staring at my feet. After my nerves started to quiet down, I looked at my own feet and I only had one shoe on. The other foot was shoeless. No wonder my feet attracted so much attention. I never did find my other shoe.

In the meantime my dad had to stay with the car, due to all this booze running down the vehicle, and wanted to see if the car was still driveable. After we checked out of the hospital, these kind gentlemen took us back to the scene of the accident. Dad said that the car could be driven home. My dad offered these men money and they wouldn't take anything. We all thanked them for their kindness, and got into our own car and headed for home. Those men followed us for a long distance to be sure that we were okay and that the car was okay to drive. It was then that I realized that angels really do roam the earth, and we had just met them in these two men.

Upon our arrival back home, we helped mother to bed, as the poor woman was in dire pain. Then we phoned Uncle Ray and told him what had happened, that his liquor was all over the ground near Beloit. Everyone was still upset, but God helped us through this ordeal.

This next incident happened one night following my working in the 4-H building at the Kenosha County Fair in Wilmot. It was already late and my mother, who was superintendent of the Clothing exhibits, had to stay until the closing of the fair. I had been excused a bit earlier.

Going to my car, as I was walking to the exhibitor's parking lot, a familiar voice called out to me, "Hey, Arlene, wait a minute. Can I catch a ride home with you?" It was Chuck Toelle, another leader from our 4-H club, who lived about a mile from our house. So I said, "Sure". I was happy to have someone ride along with me so I didn't have to drive home all by myself.

I dropped Chuck off at his house and traveled on to my own house. When I stopped the car, I got out and started walking toward the house when I heard a strange noise, like someone was running after me. I couldn't run due to my past Polio, so I kept walking as fast as my legs would walk. The faster I walked, the faster the noise increased, faster, faster, faster, and yet even faster. Oh, dear God, someone's chasing me, please don't let him get me, I'd like to live longer. It seemed like a lifetime before I got to the house.

At last I was at the door! I hurried into the house and told my husband, Phil, that someone was after me. He immeiately went outside and found no one in sight. But there was no car in the driveway either where I had parked it.

Now he was puzzled, and as he looked around our premises noticed the car up against the utility pole on the corner of our lot. Across the road was a high bank of the Fox River and thank God that our car stopped before it got that far. All this while it was not someone chasing me, it was the car gaining momentum as it rolled backwards into a pole.

When all was said and done, Phil and I laughed together about my being so absent minded and forgetting to put the car in park. Being tired, I was not at all alert but I had the scare of my life. We still laugh about it today, but at the time it wasn't nearly as humorous as it was frightening.

Not long after the bank of the river was cut down, our neighbor lady's car did roll into the river. I was the fortunate one, my experience happened with the luck of a pole.

As to family adventures and excitement, we always tried to have outings together.

Phil and I didn't have much money, because it takes a lot when you are raising eight children. But every summer we would take our family to a resort in northern Wisconsin and spend one week there. We usually went into the Hayward area near where Phil went hunting with the Wheatland Trophy Deer Hunting Club. We would rent a cottage there and Phil would take the kids fishing. Usually we went either to Nelson Lake or to a flowage where the fishing was fairly good, as it was thrilling for the kids to catch fish.

The first few times we went we only had three kids: Darlene, Dolly and Danny. As time went on, we took four, then five, then six, seven, and before David was here, the older ones had jobs and so the number started to decline.

While we were there, we had numerous interesting incidents. One of the first times, we went to an Indian Pow-Wow at Hayward. Darlene and Dolly liked this so much, and so we sat in the front row due to Danny being in a stroller so he could see too. It happened that one of the younger Indian lads who was performing kept easing closer and closer to us, flirting with our two young girls. This frightened both Phil and me as well as the girls, so we left this performance early.

Another time when Debbie was about thirteen years old, she caught a good sized Bluegill while out fishing with her dad. Phil put it into the live box and they continued to fish. When they came back in toward evening, Phil went to the place at the resort where one could clean the fish and just as he was about to clean the good-sized fish that Debbie had caught, he looked up and there was a poster hanging on the wall telling about the local contest for big fish.

So that evening we all went to register her fish and Phil's fish that was just a little smaller than the one she caught. It ended up with Debbie winning the state record and her dad winning second placing for the year. She received many certificates and awards including rods and reels and other fishing equipment.

Phil had the two fish mounted and we had them hanging on our wall for years, and now that she and her husband Al have their own home, we gave these fish to them to hang in their spacious recreation room.

One time we tried a different resort, had reservations made ahead of time, and when we drove up to this resort, we saw a new Lincoln car full of Afro-Americans. This was rather shocking to us, as my husband has always been quite prejudiced. No matter what, we stayed because this was our family vacation and we were determined to enjoy it.

As the week progressed we became friendly with these people, who were very well bred and upstanding, and I used to sit out and sun with the ladies. One day their little boy got out into the water too far in a deep hole and couldn't swim, so Dell dove in and saved their little boy. You never saw such indebted people in your life, so they took Dell out for an ice cream treat. In these days this kind of treat was very special and anyway this little boy had a lot of neat water toys so after that incident, he allowed Dell to play with them too. Dell was so happy and proud of himself by saving another kid's life.

These vacations were always a good summer get away from the daily tasks of our jobs and household duties at home. But it always meant that when we got into the cottage, I always would take all the dishes out of the cupboard, wash and dry them, wash out the cupboard shelves and place the dishes back again into the cupboard.

I have always been a stickler for cleanliness, and who knows who had the cottage before we did. So this was always my big job as soon as we got settled there. But it was always worth the effort because I knew that my children as well as Phil and me were not susceptible to anyone else's germs.

We used to take the children occasionally to a movie at the theater, and this was something that the children looked forward to with anticipation. Sometimes this was used as a form of bribery to get them to do certain jobs, mainly to keep their rooms picked up, and not to throw their dirty underwear or dirty socks under the beds. This was just one of the tricks of the trade used by parents.

Some of them I can remember were: *Flubber, Shaggy Dog, Mary Poppins, Absent-Minded Professor.* Others included: *The Sound of Music, Cinderella, and Snow White and the Seven Dwarfs.* These were not seen by all our kids, but whoever was here at the time that the show was playing went with us to see the movie. I was quite irritated when we took all eight children to see *Sound of Music*, because we had to pay an admission for David, who was a baby, had to be held on my lap, but we still had to pay for him. He slept through the whole movie until the puppet show that was put on by the VonTrapp children, and then he woke up and watched that. When that was over, he fell asleep again. That turned out to quite an expensive nap.

Speaking of movies, one time while we were North, we took the children to an outdoor movie to see *What's New Pussycat?* So by the title, I thought it was a children's movie, but to my surprise it was not what I had anticipated it to be. I guess I should have known better. Wow ! Was I disillusioned when it started. I guess with my controlled cautious innocent upbringing by my parents, I hadn't realized what it would be about. So for our money's worth, the children got to see the cartoons before the movie started anyway.

We left and went back to our rented cottage and popped pop corn and had soda, so the kids were happy anyway. It took some tall explaining to the children why we left that movie, and they asked where the cats and kittens were. We were both very innocent parents who led quite sheltered lives but with raising kids we soon learned.

Something that caused excitement in my life was going to the dentist. Now this was not the usual excitement that someone would normally think of. Actually I can only describe these dental visits as the most irritating, provoking times of my life. I would think about these dental appointments days in advance before going, and by the time I had to go, I was a nervous wreck.

Even when I was a little girl, I hated the thought of going to the dentist. My legs would quiver so badly that I could hardly get into the dentist's chair. Then the moment he'd put the bib on me, I automatically had to go to the restroom to pee.

This always happened to me when I was excited, nervous, or upset, but Dr. Mower, the dentist always understood.

Now I think back of the old-fashioned equipment and surroundings in which I had to have my teeth worked on. First of all, the chair was a big old upright chair which had to be pumped up by means of the dentist's foot to elevate it to the dentist's working level. Aside of the chair was a movable tray with all the horrible looking instruments on, and the dentist would pull this tray that was attached to the chair right in front of my face. Now tell me if that wasn't enough to frighten any child.

Along side of the chair was another huge contraption that held a variety of drills with electrical cords going to a generator type tank. On the left side of the chair was a spit bowl that had running water in. Well, that running water was enough to induce anyone to have to urinate.

A visit always followed the same format. First, pick at my teeth, and I'd think, "Sure, pull out the fillings that I already have, you must not know what you are doing or are you wanting to pick out the old filling just so you can put a new one in and get more money?" Picking at my teeth was so frustrating to me, I just wanted him to look at my teeth so I could get the heck out of there. But no, it didn't work that way.

Then the procedure went on and on, and you can guess, by this time I had to pee again. I had to tell the dentist because I didn't want to wet my pants, that would have been embarrassing. So he'd take off the bib and allow me to use the restroom once again. My poor mom was so embarrassed to take me to the dentist, but she just took it all in her stride with the patience of Job.

Many years had passed before I went to any dentist, so right after I was married, I went to a different dentist, as my childhood dentist had long passed away.

I had toothaches that were almost unbearable, so I had to go to see a dentist to get some sort of relief from the pain. At this time x-rays were still unheard of for examining teeth. So he yanked out my three top front teeth and told me that would have to heal after which he would make a bridge for me.

Of course, this is just what I had always dreamed of, a bridge in my mouth. Up until this time my teeth were always in good healthy condition and had very few cavities or fillings. But the dentist now told me that the high fever I had when stricken with Polio damaged my teeth.

224

Six weeks later the dentist installed the bridge in my mouth. This was another ordeal. He hammered the thing into place with a mallet, then whittled it out to put cement on it and began again to hammer it back into place. Through the years I had much trouble with this bridge, and one day it started to bother me so much so I went to a different dentist.

Now this dentist had a reputation for being the best of the lot, so I felt fairly confident going to him. Well the tooth next to the bridge had been bad all along and should have been extracted along with the other three. It showed up on the x-ray

This doctor was tall, had a gruff voice, and his bedside manner, so to speak, was as gruff as his voice. As he injected the shot of novacaine waiting for it to take a hold, he said to me, "You had better start saying your Hail Marys because this is going to hurt like hell".

Well, about this time he had scared the hell out of me, and now I had to get to a restroom quickly because I had to pee again as it seemed every time I was nervous this is what I had to do. After I returned to the chair and tried to compose myself, he was ready for the extraction.

Now here he comes with the pliers, rather the extractor, and made a big issue over this tooth as he tries and tries to get it out. The darn tooth didn't want to come out, as he laboriously tried and tried again. Then he sensed how frightened I was. Thinking he would add a little humor to ease my tension, he said, "Well, maybe if I put my foot on the tooth and pulled a little harder, it might come out".

I failed to see any humor in his comment and by now I was almost saying my Hail Marys out loud. Finally I heard a crackling sound and sure enough the darn tooth came out in pieces. This meant he had to dig for the remains. By now I am completely petrified! I just wanted to be any place on earth except in that dentist's chair.

Several weeks and several hundred dollars later, I had a new bridge now having four teeth on. Again I went through the same procedure, hammering and gluing but I managed to survive through it all.

Our whole family became patients of this dentist, but the children didn't like him because of his abrupt mannerisms. He definitely lacked tact with children, but he was a very good dentist and did good work, so I had thought.

Three of our daughters had all sucked their thumbs as little children. Well, Dr. S. yelled at them at every visit they made to him. Each one of them; Darlene, Debbie, and Diane were so scared to even go to him because he threatened them by telling them that he was going to cut off their thumbs and add them to his collection of thumbs that he had cut off of other children. He told them, "I have a whole big bag of thumbs, and I'll put yours in there with all the rest". Now our children were as fearful of dentists as I was. I actually had to bribe them just to get them to go.

So a few years after the cracking off of my tooth episode and the passing on of that dentist, I went to the famous Dr. Rio, who was known as the best dentist in town. Now doesn't he discover another element that I had never anticipated. Years before the time when I had teeth extracted, the pain I was now feeling was caused by roots of teeth and bits of broken off teeth that were still in my gums and had now become infected. This meant that I had to go to an oral surgeon and surgically have all this removed. I was instructed to go to a clinic in Racine. My fear of dentists began all over again.

Now this is another experience! I was given what is known in layman terms as laughing gas. I was totally conscious all the while during this surgical procedure, but extremely light headed. I said some peculiar things, as the doctor and his nurse were laughing so hard, and I failed to see the humor in why they were laughing, because I was the one who was administered the laughing gas and I was sober and serious.

After the surgery was finished, I had to lie down for an hour until it wore off and then they gave me tablets to dull the pain from the surgery. Dolly took me and she had to wait all this while in the waiting room, how bored she must have been waiting to go home, but she never complained.

A few years later. Dr. Rio took impressions and had a denture plate made for my upper teeth. Now I had to go through having the remaining four teeth left on the top to be extracted. But at least now I thought my troubles were over, and they were for a while, until he decided that there was too much space left between the lower teeth in my mouth. So now I had to have a lower partial plate with three teeth on it in order to have a correct bite.

After having this partial made, I made appointments for further checkups and whenever the time came to go, I would find an excuse not to go and so this went on for years and years. I'd make appointments and at the last minute, I'd cancel them.

Then one day after six years had passed, his secretary

called me and told me that if I didn't come in for regular check-ups, the doctor was dropping me as a patient. This was music to my ears, now I didn't have a dentist at all.

After the eleventh year had passed and I had not even looked for a dentist, a new lady dentist came to Paddock Lake, Dr. Roucka. Dolly had gone to her and really liked her as Dolly had not been to a dentist in a long time, but Dr. Roucka was so understanding and never even thought of yelling at Dolly. So a month later, I made an appointment and went to her. Very apologetic to her, I had explained that I hadn't been to a dentist in eleven years, but she said nothing about it and carried on as usual with an exam.

At my first visit with her, I mentioned that my denture plate was very loose, so she took impressions and sent my plate out to the lab and had it relined. Now it fits very well.

At last after all these years, I no longer dread going to the dentist as she is so kind and understanding, so now I go regularly every six months for my teeth to be cleaned and for the exam. At last I have no apprehension like I used to have.

One of the other adventures in our life was at Halloween time when Phil and I would accompany other couples, including my mom and dad, and we went out trick and treating. This was when our older kids were capable of baby sitting for the younger children in our family.

There were about three carloads of couples of mixed ages and it was kind of a bar hopping venture. All we did was stop at a bar and trick or treat. If the establishment gave us a drink, then one of the guys would buy a round of drinks for every body, and we'd leave. At some places the establishments were reluctant to give a drink, so we politely left without buying anything and when we got outside we all soaped their windows, but good!

We would always make sure that at the end of the evening we were to a bar where they served food. After eating, we went back home. We did this for a few years until owners of the bars in the area all refused to give anything, so we thought it best to stop, but it was sure fun while it lasted.

After our daughter Diane got married, Phil and I went to visit her and her husband Rick once or twice a month. As time went on, they became busier and busier, but they always had time for us to come to visit them. We would usually leave early on Fridays immediately after work, so we'd get there by 7:30 or 8:00 o'clock in the evening. We'd stay until late Sunday afternoons and leave for home again.

We always went to a little store there that had anything in it from spices to laundry products, from small wearing apparel to lawn ornaments, so this can give you an idea of the variety of products. The price of every item they sold was unusually low, so it was fun to shop in there and get lots for your money. We always called it the 'junk store'.

The grandchildren always enjoyed shopping there because their sparse money, that they had saved for a time, would go far and so being that they also sold the old time penny candy there, the children had a hay day.

While we were visiting in Merrill, we usually took rides to see the beautiful country there, and we would often times go out to eat. They had a very good restaurant there called Club Modern, and in later years a good place for eating was called Three's Company. When we went for a lunch, we went to the Pine Ridge Family Restaurant, which was near Diane and Rick's log home.

Their log home was a place of sheer beauty, and was located in the proper setting to really show off its beauty, in the country set back off the road surrounded by beautiful trees. Many of those trees had to be sacrificed when they built their home, but it's so typical of Northern Wisconsin.

We don't get up there as much as we used to, because it is so difficult for me to travel those four hours with such a bad back. Now they come to visit us a little more frequently, but not as much as we'd like to see them and their two boys. We phone each other about once a week, so this is how we keep in touch.

The years went on and Phil's and my adventures and excitements started to change in activities, as we then became more and more involved with our kids and their families including our grandchildren.

We attend community functions with our married kids who usually take us along with them. Many Sunday mornings after church, some of our kids will invite us to go out for breakfast with them. We do this quite frequently. Sometimes during the day, Phil and I will go to a nice restaurant for a dinner. He doesn't care to drive during the evening hours anymore as night driving bothers his eyes.

Our community activities have extended our social horizons. We both cling to our memories of our past days of adventure and excitement.

Chapter 19
My Rare Driving Experiences

As you know, my dad didn't believe in girls' driving unless it was driving the farm tractor. However, my mom had taught me how to drive but I didn't have a driver's license. When I was eighteen years old and it was during summer between Junior and Senior years of college, I had the shock of my life.

One evening my mom and dad went out for the evening with their friends, Ed and Gladys, and at the end of the evening were at a bar about a mile from home. It happened that one of the Kenosha County Deputies had just gotten off duty and was headed for home, when he decided to stop in for a beer after work. The name of the place was Pine Oak Lodge which is now Luisa's Italian Bar where they also serve food.

Dad knew the man whose name was Harry from Silver Lake and in speaking with him inquired about what it would take for his daughter to get a driver's license. Harry addressed my dad, "Well, Joe, I have applications in the car, I'll bring one in". My dad is now thinking, "Is Arlene ever going to be happy that I'm bringing an application home for her."

So Harry brought an application and written test in, asked my dad all the information, filled it out, checked a couple answers on the test to be incorrect as he said no one ever gets a perfect score. He asked dad if I knew how to drive, and dad told him that I did. So he went back to his car and brought in my driver's license. In those days there was no behind the wheel tests to be done, as the deputies assumed that the people had prior experience in driving.

The next day, dad gave me my license. I was one happy girl! Now I could drive if dad would allow me to drive the 1945 dark green four-door Dodge.

Following that time, occasionally I was allowed to take the car by myself, that is: on short distances only. But this made me very happy, perhaps at last my dad saw the need for girls to drive.

One day I drove to teachers' college and drove all over in Racine. My friends and I went to the zoo, out for lunch, shopping, and down Lakeshore Drive. That drive along Lake Michigan is so pretty in the spring of the year. I drove as far as Kenosha, back to Racine, and back to school in Union Grove.

When I got home that night, my dad asked me since when was Union Grove 125 miles from home. I looked at him and replied, "Never".

"Well", he said, "it must be that far because that's what the mileage gauge shows". Oh, my gosh, didn't he check the mileage before I took the car! After that day, I never misused the privilege of driving again.

I hadn't been driving for long when I discovered that the car could and would accelerate quickly and without realizing it, I'd find myself speeding. Mom always drove like she was on a race track. She would tell everyone that she was always in a hurry. Not much of an excuse, was it? Mom drove fast and Arlene drove fast also, some people accused me of having a lead foot. Yes, I did and I believe that I had inherited that lead foot driving from my mom.

In fact my dad put a beeper on their car so mom wouldn't drive so fast. Dad would set this thing before mom would leave the premises, and while she was driving, the beeper would go off which alerted her that she was driving too fast. What did mom do? She just reached down and turned the thing up again.

When she'd return home, she'd set it just the way dad had set it before she left. The luckiest of all luck, she never was stopped by an officer nor did she ever get a speeding ticket.

Later my dad got wise to her tricks, so he put a governor on the car, which is a device that automaticallly controls the speed of the car. When mom discovered what he had done, she pleaded with him to take it off, but he left it on for a time until mom had promised that she would drive slower on her own, so he took it off. I often wonder when no one was with her, how often she went back to her fast driving.

When Danny was about two years old, I was driving to the doctor in Burlington one day to take him to the doctor. It was in November and the roads were very icy, but I had to keep that appointment. Mom, Darlene, Dolly, and Danny were all with me. As I was approaching Burlington, a dog ran out in front of me. I had to think quickly, it was either the dog or the ditch.

Thinking of my passengers, my mom, and my children, I decided it would have to be the dog. Being icy, I couldn't stop so I hit the dog and stopped. Two hunters were approaching the road. I told the man I couldn't help but hit the dog, because it was either the dog or the ditch which had quite an incline that was very icy, and I had to think of my children's welfare. I told him how sorry I was, and he apologized to me saying that the dog was uncontrollable, and it was not my fault in the least bit. My children were upset with me because mom killed an innocent dog, but they didn't really understand the logic behind it. As it was, I was pregnant and hardly fit behind the wheel anyway, but it was the ice that caused this incident.

Now my first crucial driving incident was really quite innocent [but then aren't they all] and if I hadn't had two of our children along with me, I may have gone right on speeding through Hales Corners just south of Milwaukee. Dolly, who was ten years old at the time, and Danny, who was at the age of eight, were accompanying me to Fond du Lac. We were to pick up our oldest daughter, Darlene, who at the time was an aspirant at St. Agnes Convent and attended the very cultural elite school of secondary learning - St. Mary's Springs Academy.

As the whole incident comes back to mind, the children were talking with each other, and suddenly Danny inquires, "Mom, if there is a car behind us with a red light flashing on top, what does that mean?" At this point, all that flashed through my mind was the fact that I'd probably have to pay a fine, and in my purse was next to zero dollars. Dear God, please help me!

I stopped...... an officer came over to my vehicle [the vehicle that could go, oh, so fast!], and said, "Are you in a hurry?" I replied, "Yes, sir, I'm on my way to Fond du Lac to bring my daughter home for the Easter season". About this time, I'm shaking in my shoes, my knees were knocking, my arms were trembling, my hands were perspiring, and my voice was crackling- what a sorry state I was in!

I believe to this day, the officer knew how upset I was, and the message he left me with was, "Please drive carefully for the sake of your children". I agreed that I would drive most carefully, and thanked him and he allowed me to go on without any citation or fine. Wow!

God was on my side that day. Being still upset, I wanted to turn right around and go home. Danny, who was always thinking and expressed himself very well, said, "But, Mom, Darlene will be waiting for us and we want to have her home for Easter, we have to go". And so I drove on at a much slower rate of speed than what I was accustomed to.

My second driving incident of being stopped, or caught was on an evening back on February 19, 1978.

At the time. I was a teaching principal at St. Alphonsus in New Munster, and that particular school board had a flare for wanting to interview teachers, but in reality the Archdiocese of Milwaukee under whose guidelines, regulations and policies we functioned, stated that the principal and pastor of the parish do the hiring and the firing. I guess that some people's ego becomes inflated if they think they have unauthorized authority. So I had set up a schedule for each teacher to meet individually with the board, as the educational board requested. I went to the school earlier to be sure that everyone was in attendance, and as the interviews were progressing well, I left to go home for a while because it was our son Dell's birthday. We had birthday cake and Phil and I had a few alcoholic cocktails.

When it was 8:57 P.M., I left to go back to school which was about 2 miles from our house. My appointment was for 9:00 to evaluate the teachers' performance so the board could compare notes. Actually I had a very good staff and I wanted to offer them all a contract for the next school year. I had three minutes to drive there, park the car, and be in the conference room. I was running a bit behind, so I pushed the pedal to the metal.

Now, wouldn't you know? I saw the red flashing light about a hundred yards just before turning into the school parking lot. About this time my heart was pounding so fast and hard it could have been a drummer in a rock band. Was I scared! I looked back in my rear view mirror and saw that it was .... a State Trooper. It seemed as if he came out of nowhere. All I could think of was, 'This is my premature death'. I pulled over, actually it was right next to the parish cemetery, and I felt very much a part of it right now.

The officer came over to my vehicle and asked to see my driver's license. My hands were trembling so hard, I couldn't control my hands to get my purse open, needless to say get a driver's license out of it. All this while the officer was watching me intently. After a bit, I finally succeeded getting my wallet out of my purse in which I had my driver's license. Trembling, I handed it to the officer, he looked at it and he replied, "Arlene, where are you going in such a hurry?"

Trying to speak, the words uttered from my mouth were, "Into the next parking lot to apply for a job". I knew that he would never have understood any kind of explanation, after all what would he know about hiring teachers and school boards? As he handed my license back to me, he told me that next time I should leave a little earlier in order to reach my destination without speeding, and that I was free to go now. I couldn't believe that a state trooper would let anyone off that easy, but when all was said and done, I believe he feared that I might have a heart attack right on the spot. I breathed a sigh of relief as he walked away from my vehicle as I was saying a quick prayer, "Thank you, Lord, you came to my rescue again, thank you, Lord".

As I was about to start out again, he turned back to me and came back to my car, as all I could think of was now he changed his mind and he's going to throw the book at me. Again I rolled my window down and he said, "By the way, Arlene, good luck on getting the job". All I could mutter was, "Thank you, officer". Whew!! I was one happy person to see him drive away, now it was over and done with.

Once I had to take Donna to finish her Christmas shopping at K Mart in Kenosha. It was after school hours and the weather was nasty out, but she had to go at that particular time, so I took her. I needed to be back home preparing supper for our family, but instead I was helping her shop.

After we left the store it was dark as pitch, and being in a hurry, wanted to get on the road to go home. As I was backing out of a space in the parking lot, some young broad wasn't watching where she was going as I was three quarters of the way out in road and she plowed into me with her brand new car. Now we had to wait for the police to come to report this, so I was detained some more.

I knew Phil would be worried at home so while we were waiting for the police to come, I went into the store and phoned him telling him of the incident and how we were detained. I was so upset with this broad for not looking where she was going and she came upon me so fast. Needless to say, she got a ticket for inattentive driving and her error made me later than it had been before.

What really ticked me off was the fact that she chewed me out for hitting her, until the officer explained to her that she was not looking where she was going and that she better shut her mouth. After all was said and done, we were able to leave for home.

Another time I was coming home from school on highway 50 and had my left turn signal on to turn onto highway W where I lived. There was not a vehicle in sight coming my way, so I started to make the turn when a man hit me in the side.

When I got out of the car to see what damage there was, there was little damage to my car. He stood there pleading with me that he was hurting because he had just come from the dentist and had a root canal done. He said that he wanted to hurry home, and would I please not call the police.

With a comment like this, I could have guessed that there was something funny about this whole deal, but I agreed not to report this accident. Later so many people told me that I should not have let my sympathy for him talk me out of reporting this accident, but I felt sorry for him being in pain.

But when I much later found out that he didn't have a valid driver's license and had no car insurance, I was really upset with myself for being so gullible. A police officer friend of mine checked out all the details but it was then too late to do anything about it. One more lesson learned the hard way!

In 1983, being that I had started into the postpolio syndrome, I had to use a cane for walking, so when I went to renew my driver's license at the Driving Examiner office, the old lady working there told me that before I could have my license renewed, I'd have to take a behind-the-wheel test.

Oh, Lordy, I was in for it now, as I had never taken a test before in my life. I asked her why I had to do this and she told me because I walked with a cane, In anger, I replied, "I don't drive with a cane, I only use it for walking".

She was so indignant about the whole situation, that she snapped back at me, "Well, you're going to have to take a test any way, so lady, get used to the idea. When do you want your appointment?" So she set up an appointment for the next week, the third week in November as my license expired on the 29th of that month.

I was teaching school, so that afternoon of the test, I had to get a substitute teacher to fill in for me while I was gone. By the time I got to Burlington, I was nervous, because we had just bought a new full sized van, and I had to take the test in that vehicle. This was what I drove daily to school, and it was the first van that I had ever driven, and now was about three months old and I was just getting used to a big vehicle.

I went into the place to register, and a middle aged man was to be my examiner for the test. He followed me out after which I got into the van, fastened my seat belt, and he checked the wipers, lights, and horn. Then he got into the van, and said to me, "Don't be nervous, as I am just another passenger sitting by you". I answered, "Correction, sir, you are the driving examiner, and it's up to you to determine if I can drive to work or not".

He smiled at me, and at that point, I felt that he would have compassion for me. He went on to tell me what a nice van we had, and asked if this was the vehicle that I drove to work every day. I told him most definitely this was my work vehicle, because my husband drove his truck to his job daily. He asked me if I would be taking students on field trips for school in this van, and when I answered that I would, he told me this was a pretty nice vehicle to be taking kids around in.

By this time the test was started and everything was going quite well as he kept engaged in conversation with me. Then he told me that he would be telling me to stop at a second's notice and I should stop as quickly as I could. I had imagined that this maneuver was to check my reflexes and actions if there was any emergency.

Now I was glad that he had prewarned me about this, because I had great difficulty lifting my right foot to step on the brake pedal. But I had the seat adjusted back as far as it would go, and having the seat in this position, if I concentrated very hard I could occasionally get my foot on the pedal without having to lift my leg with my arm as I usually did when driving a vehicle. So all this while I'm praying under my breath that I could successfully get my foot on the brake by having my leg and foot use their own power.

I was listening intently for his command and in a short while he said, "Stop". I stopped so sudden that he and I both almost took a leap right through the wind shield. To this day I'm not sure how I did this, but he didn't say a word, so my foot must have gone onto the brake automatically. When we were stopped, he said to me,"You could stop on a dime.That was done beautifully".

Then he instructed me as to what to do next, and it happened to be to make a turn left, and this involved changing lanes on the one-way streets heading east out of Burlington. Without thinking I asked him what I had to look for before changing lanes so I could turn left, and he said, "You know, so just do it".

Well at this point I really thought I blew the whole test merely through just not thinking. Remember, I was very nervous about this whole thing anyway. After making the left turn he told me that was good. So now we were headed back to the Division of Motor Vehicles-Drivers License Examiners Building from where we started.

On the way we had to cross a set of Soo Line Railroad Tracks, and I looked both ways, nothing was coming so I proceeded on. At that point he told me that I should have made a complete stop, then looked both ways and if all was clear to go on because a van is a truck. Now I was really sure that I blew it.

When we returned back to the building he informed me that I passed with flying colors, but to be sure to stop at all railroad crossings from then on whenever I was driving a van. So we went into the building and he made out my new license. I was so happy that I could have kissed this man. But, I didn't.

Many years later, I had another driving experience, however, this time I wasn't so fortunate because I did not just get a warning, but my first ticket in my lifetime.

I was on the way to the doctor's office one day as I had an early morning appointment which I had made previously because with an early appointment one usually did not have to wait the usual two hours to get to see the doctor. Being so early and my never having been a morning person, I was running a bit late. I took the back stretch down Market Street in Burlington and as I came around the bend in the road saw a squad car but it was too late to slow down then as he already had me clocked on radar.

He was an older gent who had been around a long time, and he didn't have one compassionate hair on his head. I will admit I was guilty as heck and I knew it, but again I was fearful. This time I got a sixty-five dollar fine and he took my license and told me to keep my appointment and to come to the police station after my doctor appointment was over. I went to the police station and they treated me as if I was a big time criminal. They insulted me, rather ridiculed me, took my money and gave me my license back after I had signed one of their official forms. I really was furious, and so I left in a huff and I made sure that I never even thanked anyone in that office.

Now here's the part that really made my blood boil! The elementary school class of 1940 from St. Alphonsus School was having its fiftieth reunion. So I bought a beautiful purple lace dress for the occasion and I intended to buy a pair of purple shoes to match my dress but I hadn't gotten around to buying them yet, as I had sufficient time for that shopping.

After this episode, the money I had saved for the shoes was gone, and I had nothing to show for it. I had to wear a pair of black shoes that I had for ages.

I never got another ticket after that ever, as I had learned my lesson this time, no more speeding.

I can't really hold a grudge against the law officials as they are only doing their job. From that day on, I was more than cautious about how fast I would drive.

Sometimes this is what it takes to make some people become aware while driving, and so it was with me.

Now I don't drive at all any more. This is of my own choice, because I feel that my incapabilities are hazardous, not only to myself but to everyone else on the highway. I do not want to jeopardize anyone else's life!

So with this decision there will be no more dangers of my putting the pedal to the metal!

Chapter 20
Our Kids Marry

There comes the time when our children had passed into the young adult stages of life, seeking for their own love of their lives just as Phil and I had done in our earlier stages of life. It was interesting to note how the times had changed from what we had known as the customary dating.

Girls would go out in groups to places where they thought had potential for meeting nice young men. These places usually were either bars or bowling allies. Many times after having seen a movie at the theater, they would go to a bar, play the juke box, dance, and have a few beers. This style of outings seemed to be the trend of that whole generation and so it became customary for that era.

Darlene, being the oldest, was quite reserved and more or less shy. These characteristics made it difficult for her to meet guys, and it probably stemmed back to her over protective background she had while she was in Fond du Lac under the close guidance and care of the Agnesian nuns.

Her closest girl friends were her cousin Reggie, Linda Haag, and Camille Kach who all were classmates in elementary school and all of them were 4-H Club members together.

Later on her other friends included Jean Childers, Georgiana Bauman, Brenda and Patti Betzig, Jean Katzman [now mayor of Burlington]. Some of these girls all rented an apartment together and got along very well. The first apartment they had was on Bohner's Lake so they spent many hours, apart from their jobs, at the beach.

Dolly and her friends from high school, Joy Delwich, Sandi Epping, Debbie Koldeway, and Maria Nauta mostly spent their time at the bars. They would shoot pool, dance, listen to music, drink beer, and mostly do boy watching.

It seems that both our older girls met young men at these bars also, basically doing the same things as all girls of that age did, and eventually some of the guys would ask the girls for dates. Time went on like this and so it was Dolly who fell in love first. Shortly after Darlene also fell into love.

Dolly's love of her life was Jim Thuemmler from the Brighton area. So it was that love got the best of them at a very young age and so they married on September 29, 1973. Because they were so young, many people including Jim's dad said that their marriage would never last, but Phil and I had every confidence in both of them and were willing to give them a fair chance.

When Dolly and I went to select a wedding dress for her, she had planned to borrow a dress from one of her close friends, but I wanted her to have her own dress. She looked just like an angel in the particular gown that she decided on. The style of simplicity in her gown of satin with few ruffles on, had a short flowing train and Dolly was a picture of pure beauty. Her veil headpiece was a simple netted veil held in place by a sort of floral tiara that gracefully nestled on her long, flowing, blond hair.

She had asked Darlene to be her attendant, maid of honor. My mother made the dress for Darlene of dark green satin fabric in another style of simplicity. Mom also designed and fashioned the headpiece to match the dress. Darlene, too, was an elegant sign of beauty.

Jim had chosen Steve Koldeway for his best man as they were the best of friends at the time. Ushers were Jim's brother Steve and Dolly's brother Danny. Jim's sister Lori and Dolly's brother David carried up the offertory gifts during the Mass. They were both in grade school at the time and being the little pee wees that they were, they were absolutely the cutest and so sincere.

Dolly and Jim's wedding reception following the church ceremony, was held at the home of my parents, Dolly's grandparents. We had it there because their house was larger and could accommodate more guests.

Jim's parents came to the church ceremony at St. Alphonsus Church in New Munster, over which Father Grabauskas officiated. But they refused to come to the reception after. Jim's dad objected highly to the kids getting married, because Jim was so young. As a matter of fact, Dolly was so young also, but we had no objections to their marriage as we looked at it as love conquers all.

All of Dolly's family and Jim's Grandma Daniels, his sisters and his brother came to the reception. Many of Jim and Dolly's friends were there also. Mom and I prepared all the food and Dede Dahl make a beautiful wedding cake for them. All in all, everyone really had a good time.

One of the funniest happenings of that day was the trick that some of the young men played on Dolly and Jim. Of course, our Danny, being the instigator of the shenanigans, filled Dolly and Jim's car with bits of wadded up newspaper. It must have taken them an abundance of time to get all that paper wadded up in order to get enough to fill the entire inside of the car. The younger kids in our family had a blast helping in this feat. When Dolly and Jim were ready to leave that night, they couldn't believe their eyes. To this day, I know that they thought it was a very clever thing to do, and I often wonder how many times they have played the same trick on someone else.

The old saying is 'Love is blind', and in this case, I truly believe there is truth in that saying. The two of them had their ups and downs several times, but their love always kept them together each time, and as time passed on, their love for each other intensified, which proved theirs was really true love.

Now the next wedding occurred nine months after the first of our kids to marry. It seems that Darlene had fallen in love with a young man named Norman, whom she had been dating at the same time that Dolly and Jim were dating. At the time when she met him, he was a bartender at what was formerly called Fox River Gardens, then known as Top Deck East. This was a place for the youth of her age to hang out.

And so the story goes on to say that Darlene and Norman were married on the 15th of June in the year 1974.

Planning for a daughter's wedding is quite different than preparing for a son's wedding, as we found out much later.

So we went shopping for her dress at Cloud Nine in Zion, Illinois. We looked at so many dresses and she selected one which was quite similar to my wedding dress. Then we looked at dresses for her attendants and selected two styles that were fashioned a little bit on the order of what the attendants wore for my wedding. At least the two styles we picked came in rainbow colors, but one of the styles was in a floral print design, but that was the closest we could find.

A few weeks later, the girls went along to select the style that they liked and all agreed on and then were fitted for their dresses. The maid of honor, Darlene's sister Dolly picked orchid, so the little flower girl who was Norman's niece, Karla Spence, was to wear orchid also. The other girls in the wedding were: Darlene's sister Debbie, her cousin Reggie Lenz, and her girl friends Patti Betzig, Jean Childers, and Gerogiana [Bauman] Shook. The other colors worn were: yellow, mint, pink, blue, and shrimp.

Being that Darlene wanted hats for the girls to wear, picture hats were no longer in style at that time, so she selected the big floppy hats that all came in white and only white. Now that presented a problem because white would cheapen the looks of the outfits and she had her heart set on the girls wearing hats. The lady at the bridal shop suggested that the hats be dyed in the pastel colors, but there was no guarantee as to how they would turn out. This was a chance that Darlene and I were willing to take. It so happened that the hats dyed beautifully and looked so picturesque.

After all was said and done, it did turn out to be an absolutely gorgeous wedding. Father Grabauskas officiated at their ceremony at St. Alphonsus Church.

After the church ceremony, pictures were taken, then everyone was invited to our home where we served cocktails and hors d'oerves until it was time to go to the dinner.

The wedding reception dinner was held at the Village Inn in Twin Lakes, then owned by Edward and Ruth Dicklin, who served the best food for miles and miles around. After the dinner, the band came in, set up, and then the people danced. All the traditional wedding customs were done also, the throwing of the bridal bouquet and then the garter and other special dances. It was a good time had by all.

Darlene and Norman went to Florida for their wedding trip, and upon their return, lived in a rented apartment on State Street in Burlington.

Their marriage only lasted for seven years, and their divorce devastated Darlene at the time because she really did love him and trusted him. There was no compatibility between them whatsoever. Norman would neglect to pay the bills that Darlene had worked so hard to get the money together for, and he spent this money for other purposes, all of which were not good. He could never keep a job, and there were times they had nothing in the house to even eat. When a spouse is not faithful to his wife and cheats on her, this breaks the marriage bond and gives reason for losing trust, so therefore it's not a true love anyway. So in 1981 after she found out what he really was like and was doing to her, the divorce became final.

The next one in our family to marry was Danny who married Luann Schenning on September 8, 1977, at United Lutheran Church in Wilmot.

Luann used to come to our house a lot because she and Deb worked together at Sentry's. Danny hunted and fished with Luann's dad and cousins, and so this is another reason that they knew each other. When they finally decided to marry, I always felt that Luann wanted to get out of her house and away to be on her own, and Danny always thought the grass was greener on the other side of the fence so I know he wanted to get out of our house as well.

They had a tremendously huge wedding. In the wedding, were: Patti Kerkman, Luann's girl friend; Nancy Schenning, Luann's sister-in-law; Barbara Schenning, Lu's cousin; Darlene, Debbie, Diane, and Donna, sisters of Danny's. Luann also wanted to have Dan's other sister, Dolly, but she was in the hospital having a baby on that very day. Luann's two nieces were also attendants, one was flower girl and the other was a mini bride.

Dan's attendants were: Dell Roanhaus, Dan's brother; Terry and Ken Schenning, Luann's brothers; LuAnn's cousin Bill Schenning; Dan's brother-in-law, Jim Thuemmler; Al Vos, Dan's sister Deb's finance. David Roanhaus and Tom Schenning were the ushers.

After the afternoon ceremony, all went over to Luann's parents' house for cocktails and snacks until it was time to go to the dinner and reception at the Wonder Bar in Twin Lakes. Phil and I commented about how different having a son get married, as the costs were so much lower than for a daughter's wedding. As the groom's parents, we were responsible for payment of the rehearsal dinner, and the cocktails served at the bride's home, plus the drinks at the Wonder Bar. All this didn't begin to compare the costs of a daughter's wedding.

Dan and Luann went on a wedding trip to Mt. Rushmore in South Dakota. Upon their arrival home, they rented an apartment in Lily Lake.

The next wedding in our family was Debbie who married Al Vos on May 23, 1981. They wanted to be married many months before that time, but Phil and I asked them to please wait until we had enough money saved to put on a wedding for them, so they complied with our request.

Debbie and Al knew each other since they were little children, but it so happens that Al and Dell were in the same class in elementary and high schools and were always the best of friends. If the two of them weren't at our house together, they were at Al's parents' house. They did most everything together as buddies, and neither one was ever really into sports, but rather enjoyed listening to music.

Al spent so much time at our house, and Debbie and Al became attracted to each other so they started dating. This went on for a number of years until they realized that they were not just the best of friends, but they were in love. It was then that they decided that they wanted to spend their lives together, so they became engaged to marry.

The night before the wedding was the rehearsal at the church and after the practice, all went over to Al's mom's house [his dad was deceased at that time] for the dinner. It was the first night that Al's mom Bernice had ever met the Weinaugs from Sheboygan, whose son Ken was in the bridal party. Bernice was a down to earth person whose hospitality was renowned, who served the best food and made the whole evening most enjoyable.

The funniest of all that evening was when Herb asked where the bathroom was and as he went in there, he couldn't find the light switch. He inquired, "Mrs. Vos, where's the light switch?" Being quick witted as she was, she said to him, "Just pull the string in the middle." Being that everyone had misinterpreted this statement, all began to laugh and laugh. Herb, who was never one to be embarrassed at anything, came out of the bathroom and laughed right along with us. Yes, this has become a standing joke.

On the next day, that lovely day in May, Debbie and Al were wed by Father Robert Gloudeman in St. Alphonsus Catholic Church in New Munster. Being that both Deb and Al were from large families, they had a huge wedding. The girl attendants were maid of honor Ellen Lighthiser, Deb's best friend; Deb's sisters, Dolly Thuemmler, Diane and Donna Roanhaus; Al's sisters, Doris Uhlenhake and Darlene Koldeway; Deb's cousin, Reggie Lenz; and Al's niece, Joanna Uhlenhake as flower girl. Their dresses were absolutely gorgeous with the maid of honor wearing a pretty shade of mint, and the other girls in a rich tone of apricot.

Al's attendants were best man Jim Thuemmler, now Al's brother-in-law; groomsmen being Al's brothers Jim and Denny; his brothers-in-law Tom Uhlenhake and Bob Koldeway; Deb's brother, Dell; and Deb's cousin, Ken Weinaug. Scott Vos, Al's nephew, was the ring bearer. Brothers David Roanhaus and Lee Vos were the ushers.

Debbie was a smashing sensation in her bridal gown of white satin. The outstanding feature of her attire was that her Grandma Lenz made her dress and her veil headpiece. Her grandma, my mother, was a beautiful seamstress and Debbie was as proud to wear this lovely gown, as proud as grandma was to sew it for her and to see her in it.

Deb used the heart that I used as a background for my flowers at my wedding as her floral bouquet with her selection of new fresh flowers on it. Grandma Lenz had removed the netting from the original heart and sewed new netting on the shape for Deb. Then Grandma made a smaller heart covered with the same kind of netting for the little flower girl. Many people commented on the fact that Deb had something old that happened to be new for her mother on her wedding day.

We held their wedding reception at Bristol Oaks Country Club which was known for its good food, and being able to have a good time. Bill Hassey's band played for the dance, and he always got the whole crowd to participate in many group styles of dance including the Bunny Hop, Hokey Pokey, and the old fashioned two step in which the caller instructed people to change partners and go on and change again and again in all directions sung to music.

At the end of the evening when the establishment made known that it was time to close, they meant it. But Phil wanted just one more drink and they refused him, so as we were on the way home in Jan and Herb Weinaug's van packed in like sardines, Phil grumbled, "I'll never have another dammed wedding reception at Bristol Oaks again". The humor of this statement is that seven years later, he had to eat those words.

Deb and Al went to LaCrosse for their wedding trip. This area is so beautiful along the Mississippi River, but when you are so in love as they were, scenery didn't matter much, just being together was all that counted.

Three days after the wedding, Phil, Bernice and I went to pay the tab at Bristol Oaks. Phil and I picked up the tab for the dinner, and Bernice picked up the tab for the cocktails served during the night. She was so sweet about offering to pay for this, and we were thrilled to have the monetary help.

Three months after Deb and Al's wedding, Dell and Debbie Lee decided to marry. The two of them met through being members of Jaycees and Jaycettes of Burlington.

Debbie was originally from Milwaukee and moved to Burlington after becoming bored working at Gimbels Store in Milwaukee. She, being an exceptional typist, took a job at Runzheimer Statistical Company. She had joined the Jaycette Group for women, as Dell joined the Jaycee Group for men. They both held offices in each of their organizations and worked very hard for the success of this worthwhile organization.

Debbie lived with Randy and Jean Conwell and family

in Burlington, as they were also in these organizations. Dell and Debbie started dating, and on the night he gave her the engagement ring, they both called us on the phone to announce it to us as parents. Likewise they called Debbie's parents, Merle and Noreen , to announce the news to them. Everyone was happy for both Dell and Debbie.

Being that this was the second son to marry, it seemed good that not as much pressure was put on as when a daughter marries. This just meant for us to again take care of the rehearsal dinner which we had here at our home as I prepared the food, and to pay the cost of the refreshments at the reception at Muskego Lakes Country Club

They were married on August 21, 1981, by Father Robert Wolf at St. Alphonsus Church in New Munster, with Debbie's parents Merle and Noreen giving her away. She had a beautiful gown and looked so nice in it. The wedding attendants were: maid of honor, Diane Roanhaus; best man was Randy Smits; ushers were David Roanhaus and Lennie Lenz. Renee Thuemmler was the flower girl and her brother Jason was the ring bearer.

I always thought the idea of both Debbie's parents giving her away was the neatest. Her mom and Dad were very distinguished looking people, Merle as a typical business man, and Noreen typical of a secretary. Noreen had such a pretty dress that she wore which accented and complemented her beautiful silvery hair.

Diane wore a soft pastel lemon colored floral patterned dress styled with simplicity. Grandma Lenz made Renee's white dress and she looked like a little angel in her long gown. Jason wore little tux just like the men and he looked like a little professor.

Being mid August, the church was stuffy and became warm as there was no air conditioning. The attendants were at the altar with the bride and groom, and it appeared to be even hotter there, and before long, didn't Diane faint dead away. Merle Lee jumped right up and went up there and took her back into the sacrisity. She revived in time for the recessional out of church. This added to the memory of Dell and Debbie's wedding.

Debbie and Dell decided to tour the state of Wisconsin for their wedding trip and they were gone for a week. They had been to numerous places within the state while attending Jaycee functions, and now they wanted to see more of our beautiful

Wisconsin, which truly is nature's wonder with scenic beauty. The next May, Diane and Rick decided to marry, so on May 29, 1982, they were married at 12:00 noon at St. Alphonsus Church in New Munster. We had to ask the kids if they would have an earlier ceremony because at 2:00 P.M. David graduated from high school. This was a rare situation, but in the end it all worked out. After the wedding ceremony, the photographer had to hurry to get the family pictures done, as David, Phil and I were off in haste to Central High School for his graduation.

Phil and I were constantly being eyed over and over again by people in the audience, because there we were in formal attire and some parents were there in jeans and a tee shirt. Sitting right in front of us was Mr. Schaubreck, whose kids I previously had in elementary school, and he was so understanding and so he conversed with us while waiting for the graduation ceremony to start, and others just kept staring at us.

During this while, all the guests from the wedding were back at our house for cocktails and hors d'oeurves, which Phil and I had all prepared and set up before we went any place that day. Being that we couldn't be there to serve our guests, Gene and Carol Nickel and Lennie and Annie Lenz acted as hosts and hostesses in our absence. They did a wonderful job for us and we always appreciated that they simply took over for us in our absence.

Diane had chosen for her maid of honor, Sue Robbins. Diane's sister Donna and Diane's friend Barb Bartlett were her bridesmaids. Rick's cousin, Kelly Bushar was the flower girl, and Diane's nephew Jason Thuemmler was the ring bearer.

Rick's best man was his very inseparable friend, Pat Neumeyer. Rick's other friend Mike Massa, and Diane's brother Dell were the groomsmen, while ushers were Diane's brother David and Rick's cousin Mark Arseneau.

Being that Debbie and Dell had their reception at Muskego Lakes Country Club, we liked it so we had Diane and Rick's reception there also. The food was so good and there was ample room for dancing.

People have often asked us why Diane moved away from here and settled in Merrill. Diane and Rick met in that area as Rick was from there. Diane had gone deer hunting with a girl friend Marion whose family had a place there where they stayed during deer hunting season. Rick and his friends knew Marion's dad as a hunter so this is how Diane met Rick and it seems as

247

though it must have been love at first sight.

Other than meeting Rick, Diane had ill luck that year she went hunting. First of all, she didn't get a deer, and then on her way home, she was involved in a car accident on the interstate highway. A car stopped abruptly on the highway and this caused several cars to collide into the back of the car in front of each other. She totaled her brand new El Camino truck near Madison.

Phil, Gene, Carol, David, and I were playing cards at home when the phone call came informing us of her accident. Wow, such distressing news! The call was from the hospital in Madison, but it seemed she was okay, but her truck could not be driven as it was totaled. Then Marion's parents came along after the crash, stayed with the girls at the hospital and then they brought the girls home.

Diane was so heartbroken as she just got her El Camino brand new, and now she had nothing to replace it. It took a while for her to get over this shock, but Diane had always been strong on the outside and so she never showed her emotions, but somehow I, as a mother, knew how much she was suffering inside.

Rick would phone her about an average of twice a week, and how her older sisters and brothers teased her while she was talking to him. They would make the smooching sounds and stand right over the phone into which Diane was trying to talk. Being younger in the family, she and Rick took much teasing from the rest of the kids, but they both survived.

Danny's first marriage ended up in divorce in 1983, and so he married a second time on February 15, 1986 at a Lutheran Church in Kenosha. This time he married Jonell Talbert, formerly Jonell Harrison, who also had been divorced.

For Dan and Jonell's wedding the attendants were: maid of honor Pam Welch, Jonell's friend; best man was Tom Schenning; bridesmaid was Dale Harrison; groomsman was Allen Weis; junior bridesmaids were Renee Thuemmler and Jessie Harrison; Chris and Jake Talbert, Jonell's sons, were mini groomsmen. Steven Roanhaus was the little ring bearer. Ushers were David Roanhaus and John Harrison.

Not long ago I asked Dan and Jonell how they met. I really had to chuckle a bit as Jonell was dramatizing while explaining to me, "I was jumping up and down on the bed, and eating potato chips, when Darlene snapped a picture of me".

I was a bit puzzled at this comment, but as she started

to explain the details, it all made sense. Jonell and Darlene were both in the same profession, Cosmetology. They attended a hair show in the Holidome in Stevens Point. While they were in their hotel room after sessions, was the time that they got to relax and talk. Jonell was unwinding from a stressful day so she let her tensions out by jumping up and down on the bed.

After this incident, Darlene showed this picture of Jonell to Dan, and he wanted to meet her. So Darlene set up a meeting for them. From that time on, they dated.

I recall that Dan was invited as Jonell's guest to a special party associated with the Kenosha School of Cosmetology where Darlene was employed and also Jonell. Prior to that party, Dan asked me to shop for a few items of clothing for him, and these were explicit instructions that were given to me by Dan. "Get me a new white shirt, a stylish new tie, and socks to go with my suit. This is special and I want to look good, because I got a special date with a special beautiful girl." So I went to Burlington to Bartons Ready-To-Wear and got these items for him, came home and pressed the new shirt.

From that time on, they continued to date until they fell in love, and decided to marry. I always had a feeling that their's was love at first sight for both of them. It's quite interesting that Dan and Jonell were both in the same class in Central High School but never got to know each other, because their class was so large.

Dan and Jonell had their wedding reception at the American Legion Hall in Kenosha. With the help of some of our family members, I prepared all the food for this reception. Just to give you an idea of the immensity of it all, one hundred-fifty pounds of potatoes were used in two kinds of potato salad, twenty pounds of macaroni and twenty pounds of shrimp were used in shrimp salad, sixty-five pounds of beef was roasted and sliced thin, and thirty-five pounds of ham was baked and sliced, plus twenty-five pounds of baked beans. This describes only the main food items, but there were many other foods on the menu. We cleaned fresh vegetables for one whole day for relish trays. All this food was prepared in my kitchen. It was a challenge but it was fun.

The two of them went on their wedding trip to Prairie de Chien, and being in February, they went ice fishing. Jonell still makes comments about this, because Dan had to get his fishing in no matter what or where. Needless to say, Jonell was none too happy with this choice of outing, especially a wedding trip.

Now Dan had no children from his previous marriage, but Jonell had two boys, Chris and Jake. Dan was willing to accept her two children and be a step dad to them, so he did. This was a little awkward and difficult at first because he was not used to being a dad, but as time went on things became better, and later Jake wanted to be adopted by Dan so he did and now Jake has the last name of Roanhaus.

Donna and Paul were married August 27, 1988, at Kemper Center in Kenosha with Judge Jerry Luke officiating. Bea Jacobsen, a music teacher from the area, accompanied soloist Al Vos, Donna's brother-in-law.

We had their wedding reception at..... the place where Phil had stated that he'd never again have another damned reception.....you guessed it .... at Bristol Oaks Country Club. Many people often expressed this statement back to Phil, but it is a nice place and the food was always good. This time we chose a sit-down dinner.

Donna's maid of honor was her sister Diane King. Paul's sister Valerie Dixon was the bridesmaid, and Donna's niece Missy Vos was the junior bridesmaid. Paul's best man was Art Steinhoff, groomsman was Mike Mangold, and junior groomsman was Paul's older son Jared. David Roanhaus and John Quast were the ushers.

Being the mother of the bride and having the pride that I always had, I wanted to be ushered down the aisle without the aid of my cane. David promised that he would safely help me to accomplish this and he did. To this day, I feel that he carried the whole weight of my body as I leaned so hard on him while hanging so tight with my arm locked into his arm. I'm sure that he had to take a long rest after this trip down the aisle.

Phil, of course, walked Donna down the aisle, of this old, but so beautiful, chapel. But, Phil and I were together as we walked out of the church. I felt bad for Mrs. Dixon as she was all alone at the wedding, because Paul's dad, Ron, didn't approve of the kids' marriage so he refused to come to witness their marriage vows. So as we left our pew, we invited Mrs. Dixon to walk out of the chapel with us.

To this day, I believe that Mr. Dixon, Paul's dad objected highly because we were Catholics, as he didn't believe in God of any religion. Be it as it may, his one and only son, Paul, is now a Catholic too, and is an extremely good father to his children which includes the training he gives his kids at home as well as sending them to St Charles Catholic School in Burlington where they are receiving the best in education.

Donna and Paul met through Donna's brother-in-law Al, who worked at American Roller in Union Grove. Being that Paul had been divorced and was looking for companionship, Al informed him that Debbie had two available sisters, Darlene and Donna. Paul decided that he wanted to meet Donna, so Al set up a blind date for them to meet. It seems that they hit it off well from the beginning so they continued to date, until they decided to marry.

Donna became an instant step-mother upon marrying Paul, as he had two boys by his previous marriage. Gerad was now seven years old, and Jesse was four. Paul had just gotten custody of Gerad and he was to live with Paul and Donna. Jesse was living with Paul's ex-wife, the children's mother.

These boys were totally accepted by our whole big family, and we invited Jesse to every event that we celebrated. Both boys referred to Phil and me as grandpa and grandma, and always addressed us as such. Being a mom instantly after marriage was difficult for Donna, as marriage is an adjustment in itself, and she had double adjustments to make.

As time went on, this living arrangement didn't work out so well because it caused so many problems between Donna and Paul and almost destroyed their relationship. Then Gerad moved to Madison with Paul's sister, Valerie, who home schooled Gerad as he lived with her and Paul's mother after Ron and Rose's divorce.

This proves that the kids took their marriage vows very seriously, and continued on as a family unit, for which Phil and I compliment them. They went through some trying times, but they managed to come through successfully.

Next and last of the family to marry was David who married a divorced lady with two children. David and Monica [Euler] Muller married on a very special date, September 24, 1988, which happened to be the month and day that my parents were married back in 1919.

They were married at the apartment where Monica lived downstairs and David lived upstairs. David had built an arch structure outdoors where they exchanged their vows and held the candle ceremony with the lighting of the two candles into one. Judge Jerry Luke officiated at their ceremony.

The procession started from the house into the garden setting on the large lawn. David and his best man named Jim , a carpenter friend from Illinois, were already at the arch, while

Dolly, Monica's matron of honor, started from the house to the music provided by Bea Jacobsen on a keyboard. Next to follow was little two year old Michael, David and Monica's little boy. Now the bride Monica, with her two children Erika and Marcus giving their mom away ,walked to the arch.

Chairs for all the guests to witness the ceremony were neatly arranged into semi circles on the lawn. After the ceremony concluded, cocktails and hors d'oeuvres were served inside a tent that had been set up on the spacious lawn with tables to accommodate all the guests.

In the early evening, a delicious buffet meal was served, which Monica and I prepared the day before the wedding. The later afternoon and in the evening, many guests played cards, as music continued all throughout the day and evening.

This is how our kids met their spouses and married them. Not all of them lasted, but today seven of the kids are happily married, and Darlene is still searching for that Mr. Right. She does very well without a spouse, but I am in hopes that she does meet a nice guy before I leave this earth, then I know she will be taken care of.

In citing our own kids, it has been proven that the bonds of love are strong and when they are meaningful they are not broken, just as Phil's and my vows and love are still as prominent and sacred as the very day we took our vows back in 1948.

Jim and Dolly Thuemmler Family
Jason, Josh, Renee, Tanya, Ashley

Darlene Roanhaus

Dan and Jonell Roanhaus
Family
Amanda, Jake, Grant

Al and Debbie Vos Family
Kelly, Jenny, Missy

Debbie and Dell Roanhaus
Family
Steven,Rachel

Rick and Diane King Family
Ben, Ryan

Donna and Paul Dixon
Family
Nicole,Paul Ryan

Chapter 21
Grandchildren Are a Blessing

Becoming a grandparent is a very special part of one's life. I became a grandmother at age forty-six. Now in my tender age, I have acquired twenty-four grandchildren; eighteen of kinship births, five as step grandchildren through our kids' marrying a spouse with children, and one as an adopted grandchild also through one of our son's second marriage. As a total of our two dozen grandchildren; eleven are girls and thirteen are boys. All of these children of which some are now young men and women have brought special joy to Phil's and my lives.

As we had always customarily had done, we give birthday and Christmas gifts to each one, and on special days like Valentine's Day, Easter, and Halloween we give them greeting cards and treats to let them know how special they are to us. We try to buy them treats or something special when some of them are with us shopping. Whenever they do a special favor for us, we reward them in some way, either monetarily or materially all wrapped up in love.

The greatest treat, reward, or gift is the love we and the children show for each other. As for affection, at all times of the year we express our sentiment as they have become a special part of our lives. We have always kissed and embraced whenever meeting, greeting, and leaving each other's homes. Now some of the older ones have grown out of that stage, but the younger ones still keep up the tradition of showing affection towards us.

At this time, I'd like to introduce these wonderful grandchildren to you. Jason, Jim and Dolly's oldest child, was born on January 25, 1973, and was our first grandchild. I was absolutely elated when he was born. He was so beautiful, a little bald gentleman with eyes of compassion and tenderness shining through, and those little tiny hands and feet, a gift of God's wondrous power and love. His parents gave him the name of Jason James, weighing in at 6 pounds and 12 ounces.

Being the first grandchild much special attention was afforded him, but by no means did we, as grandparents, ever spoil him. I made up my mind years before he was born that I would never spoil my grandchildren like my parents had done to their grandchildren, our kids.

It was great watching this little person through the years. His first few strands of hair, his first tooth, his first steps, and his first words, all of which added character in his early stages of development. Phil and I were so delighted every time we had the chance to baby sit for Jason. He was a little boy that listened and always wanted to do the right thing to make his parents proud of him.

Dolly was working at the Nestle' Candy Company and worked many hours, so one day being that I had a day off, she asked me to take Jason to the doctor for his immunizations. Now I was a proud grandma and this was an honor to take him for his shots. As we sat in the waiting room at the Clinic, so many people there told me what a cute little boy I had. I was so proud to thank them for the compliment in his behalf and let them know that he was my grandchild, not my son. This is not boasting, just a proud grandma.

The one thing about Jason that I shall never forget was the time I had to stop at the pharmacy, and there was quite a high step to get onto the sidewalk from the parking lot. Down the sidewalk a few feet farther the sidewalk gradually sloped downward and wasn't quite as steep as it was right in front of the store. Knowing that my equilibrium still wasn't so good, I asked Jason if I might take a hold of his arm to steady myself. In a very serious tone of voice as he peered up at me with his big brown eyes, he replied, "Grandma, I'd rather if you'd go to the end and help yourself".

I had to chuckle a bit under my breath because it came out so honest and sincere letting me know exactly how he felt about the whole situation. This had become a standing joke in the family ever since, but Jason barely remembers even saying that. After being reminded of it so often, he has come to know about it.

A few years later, Dolly and Jim had their second child Renee, who weighed in at 7 pounds and 4 ounces. Such a cute little baby girl she was! She didn't have much hair, but what she did have was blonde which complemented her large brown eyes. Being our first granddaughter, she became as special as Jason was.

Watching and sharing in her developmental stages was as exciting as it was when we had our own children as babies. Renee was always so loving and an affectionate gesture from her was not just a formality, her whole heart was in her hugs and kisses.

Renee and Jason had a close relationship all through their childhood, even though at times they would snarl at each other. But kids are kids, and Jason was very protective of his little sister.

One example is the time when Dolly and Jim had been over to visit us and after leaving at the end of the evening were driving home back to the mobile home park where they had lived. Immediately after crossing the railroad tracks in Wheatland, they turned onto the road that led them home when all of a sudden, Jason said to his parents, "Mom and dad, Renee just fell out of the car".

In bewilderment, Jim and Dolly looked around and sure enough Renee was not there. So they went back and there she was out in the road anxiously wondering if they were going to come back for her. This incident Renee remembers quite vividly and often jokes about it now.

Another time their family was at our house on a Sunday afternoon when Dolly, Jim, Debbie and Al decided to go to the bar down at the corner, Top Deck East. After their sneaking out of the house, it was a while before Jason and Renee missed their mom and dad. Upon discovering that their parents had gone from our house, Renee started to wail as loud as her lungs could, "Where are mom and dad?"

As the two children stood in front of the picture window peering out, little Jason put his arm around Renee trying to comfort her, saying, "It's okay, 'Nee', Grandma Roanhaus is right here, she'll take good care of us, don't worry, we'll be okay, grandma is here".

The more he tried to comfort her, the more and louder she cried, so I picked her up and held her in my arms telling her that her mom and dad would soon be back. In the meantime, I diverted her attention by reading both of them a story, and finally she calmed down.

One day as Darlene and I were discussing various nationalities in Jason's presence, out of the clear blue he pops up with a comment, "My dad is a Jew".

"Oh, no, honey, your dad is not Jewish, he is of other nationalities", stated Darlene.

"No, Aunt Dar, everybody says, 'Jim, the Jew' so my dad is a Jew".

What a misconstrued conception! Jim is always looking for a deal and at times way back when, this may have been linked to a scrap iron collector, who was of Jewish descent, as Jim is always collecting someone else's discards. It is cynical how children draw their own conclusions.

Jason always did show compassion for people and is a tender hearted person. He has the kind of personality in which he likes to have fun, enjoys helping people, and treats older people with respect and dignity. Not many young people in this day and age can have these qualities attributed to them. Although Jason has been and still is special in my life, our relationship has been impaired when he was of elementary school age.

To this day in my life, I know in my heart that he still has resentment towards me and perhaps even a bit of hate, and this wall of resentment can never be torn down. He has too much character to ever admit to or display these feelings but somehow a grandma knows what her heart tells her, and I regret now that I didn't at the time leave St. Al's School and apply for a different job at another Catholic School. These feelings could have been avoided. I made up my mind that when Renee was ready to enter seventh grade, I was sure to be retired, as I didn't want an impaired relationship with another grandchild, because grandchildren are a precious commodity.

To further explain this situation, I was principal of the school all during Jason's eight years that he attended grade school. Apparently I seemed to expect more from Jason than from other kids, in the way of doing everything right, just as I had always expected from my own kids during their school days. I was a very strict disciplinarian and expected Jason to be the shining example for other students.

I'll never forget the day as a first grader when he ran down one flight of steps at school enroute to the cafeteria, and I happened to be in range of seeing this, so I made him walk up and down that same flight of stairs ten times. Then I asked him, "Did you learn anything?" Meek and mildly he answered, "Yes, Mrs. Roanhaus". When I inquired as to what he learned, he said, "Never to run up and down steps again, always walk".

When Jason was in seventh and eighth grades, I was his teacher. Jason was intelligent, a good student and was an absolute joy to have in my class. In this situation many times I know in my heart that he resented and hated me. Even though I knew that, I always tried to push him ahead and offer every available opportunity to him. I sent his name in for the Washington, D.C. trip through the county sheriff's department that sponsored the Safety Patrol and he was selected to attend.

One of the other special advantages was submitting his name for the high school gifted and talented program. There were many other incidents in which I offered special opportunities to him.

He was a good kid but like all kids, he had a bit of mischief in him too. As the old saying goes, 'All work and no play makes a dull boy'. Jason wasn't about to live up to that statement. Prior to his last eighth grade basketball team game, we had a big pep rally in the gym. The team wanted to know if they could put on a skit, so I consented. They practiced in the school's small auditorium during recess time and after school.

The day of the pep rally, the team performed like professionals. They used a recorded cassette and acted out the playing of the instruments, as they all went on to lip sync. One of the boys was taking drum lessons at the time, so Chris really played drums to the music of the tape. Jason portrayed a guitarist and he acted this out so dramatically that he had the whole school in stitches, it was so funny! At the last measures of the music, he jumped off the stage platform and onto the main floor. The whole school clapped and clapped and cheered and cheered for him. He had become the star of the day.

On one other occasion, the very last day of school, I can't recall all the details anymore, but anyhow it was said that Jason had mooned to the kids on the Randall bus. I often feel that it was a dare because Jason's friend, Brian Minnis rode that bus, and when there was mischief to be found, you can be sure that Jason and Brian would find it together.

Often Jason would ride to and from school with me. When we had our first van that was silver in color, Jason used to refer to it as the Silver Streak and when I asked him why he called it that, he said, "Because now you'd see it and then you wouldn't". This was his way of describing my lead foot driving. After we got the gray van, he referred to that one as Grandma's Hot Wheels.

On the lighter side of Renee's personality, she was one who would spread herself out on the floor under the coffee table in our living room singing the commercial 'Stove Top Stuffing'. In her version, because she was so young and couldn't fully pronounce her s's yet, sounded like this, 'Tove Top Tuffing' as she went on to sing the whole commercial. Now this was one of the cutest actions from a child, and this was typically Renee.

I truly believe that Renee was meant to be a cosmetologist, because another time as a little girl, she would sing another TV commercial , 'Gotta' wash that gray right out of my hair' as she went through the proper motions of scrubbing and poofing

259

her hair. She could be heard and seen repeating this commercial many times throughout a day, a born beautician.

When she was in elementary school, she wore her hair long and always took much pride in how her hair looked. One day she came out of her room at home and her hair style was short. Dolly asked her how she got a short hair cut, and she replied, "I cut it last night". Dolly was amazed because it looked like a professional cut that had been done by a stylist in a hair salon. She started cutting her siblings hair when she was in high school and did a professional looking job.

While I was employed at St. Alphonsus School as principal just before I retired, she would always visit me in my office before school and at recess time. Each time she would bring me a server of coffee from the cafeteria. Often when I did eat, she would bring a tray of food from the cafeteria for me at lunch.

Renee and I have always had a good relationship from little girl on and even today, she is my private hair dresser. She gives me a perm on her days off at the Lake Geneva Cost Cutters Salon, where she is apprenticing at present. A week after she perms my hair, she comes to my house and colors it.

Six years after Renee was born, Tanya Marie was welcomed into the Thuemmler family on July 29, 1982. She was like a doll without much hair, had big blue eyes, with a half smile on her face as a newborn infant. Tanya was now their first blue eyed child.

Times had changed considerably and hospital rules changed to the extent that when a new baby was born into a family, the other siblings were allowed to come to see their mom and the new baby. So one early evening, Jim took Jason and Renee to see their mom and their new baby sister, Tanya, at the hospital. Phil and I were coming in later at which time we would take the two children home with us.

Now this is another story! It wasn't all that easy as it seemingly should have been. As we were leaving the hospital, Jim walked with the children and us to the elevator, and Renee clung to Jim as if we were the worst grandparents in the world. Finally Jim convinced her that the elevator was there and she should go with us. Now it appeared that all was well Until.......... we got to the car, when she realized that she was going home without mom .... and her loud sobbing began right in the parking lot of the hospital.

Phil and I helped the two children into the car as much as Renee objected to this whole idea. None of us had eaten supper as yet, so we stopped at Kentucky Fried Chicken and took a meal home for our own kids at home, mom and dad [who stayed with our kids], and the two children and Phil and me.

All the way home Renee cried louder and louder, "I want my mom". There was no stopping or consoling her, as every time we'd said a kind word to her or try to explain, she'd cry all the louder. Finally as we approached the railroad tracks on the country line road, JB, Jason said, "Grandma, can't you shut this kid up? She's getting on my nerves. She's giving me a headache". At this point I realized that Jason was just as tired of hearing her wailing as we were.

When we got to our house and took the children and the food in, poor little Jason was so uptight, he went to a big chair and just collapsed. Needless to say; neither Jason, Renee, Phil, nor I even ate one bite as all our nerves had been shattered. Then I held Renee and rocked her to sleep in the rocking chair. At last, her carrying on had stopped! What an evening!

Renee had a close relationship with my mother, her great grandma, and often times when she was old enough to play games, she and great grandma played many card games. My mom was a great influence on Renee as she taught her so many childhood skills.

Often times now we look back at the photos of Renee and great grandma and one can tell just by looking at them how much they admired and loved each other. On every picture, Renee always had her little arm around my mom when she wasn't even tall enough to hardly even reach mom while she was sitting.

All in all, we have had so much extra pleasure from Jason and Renee, as they were the first two grandchildren born, and were the only two for many years before any more grandchildren were born.

The next grandchild to be born was Melissa Vos, daughter of Debbie and Al. She, too, was a most beautiful baby with her blonde hair, blue eyes, and rosy little cheeks, an absolute bundle of joy. Now I became the happiest grandma in the area, I had another grandchild.

I'll never forget the night that she was born. Al was working at American Roller in Union Grove and was at work so Debbie was at our house with us as it was nearing her due date for Missy's birth. She hadn't been feeling very well all that day, and as time went on she started into the hard labor pains. I felt so much compassion for her, because I could relate to her pains that she was having, and as time went on she asked me, "How much worse can these pains get?"

At that particular moment I didn't have the heart to tell her that the pains get more and more severe as the contractions progressed on, but she was slowly finding that out. She was walking the floor, getting down to the floor on her knees and almost curled up in a ball at times, kind of moaning and groaning. This had gone on for quite a while and her contractions were getting more steady, so I called Al home from work and told him that I thought it soon was time for her to go to the hospital.

Many hours and more pains later, little Melissa, who everyone called Missy, came into the world. Debbie and Al had become parents.

It was so interesting watching her develop as the years went by. She was a very quiet child and rarely ever caused any confusion or distress to her parents. There were rare times though that she did display her feelings through verbal use. The one time that stands out in my mind was the evening that Al and Phil were helping David's friend, Peggy, move. Debbie was at work, so Missy stayed with me at my house.

It was shortly after supper and I had everything put away in the kitchen, but little 'Missy Nosy' started snooping in the refrigerator and found leftover sweet corn in there from our supper. She brought the bowl of corn into the living room, set it down on the coffee table, and started eating it with her fingers. Well, this was all well and good, I didn't mind one bit, but I offered if she would like it heated up, I would heat it for her. She shook her head no saying "Me help me-self", and about this time she had corn all over the living room carpeting.

Very patiently, I knelt down on the floor to pick up all the kernels that she had spilled. I no sooner was down on my knees, when little Missy climbed up on my back and wanted to ride horse-back. Well, I've been a lot of things in my life before, but never a horse. So I left her there until I had all the corn picked up and wanted to throw it away, so I had to remove her from my back.

A while later, I went back to the kitchen to get a glass of lemonade and a sipper cup of lemonade for her. I brought them back into the living room, set both of them on the table next to the big chair, as she crawled up on my lap. I reached for her lemonade and she drank some. Then I put her cup down and took a drink of lemonade out of the big glass. Now at this time she was very little and her speech development was just starting for her in the way of few words and syllables.

So she had another drink from her cup, then I had a drink from my glass and while I was drinking she accidentally bumped me and so the lemonade was spilled all over me and I was soaked. In a bit of disgust before I realized it, out of my mouth came the words, "G-- damn it, Missy".

Not a split second had passed and out of Missy's mouth came these words, "G-- damn it, Gamma". As furious and upset as I was, I had to chuckle a bit. It was then that my anger had quickly passed as I came to realize the humor of it all. It was naughty, but so cute! I didn't want her to think that I was still angry, so I let her know as I hugged and kissed her. Then I had to get out of that sticky clothes, completely change into dry clothing after washing up. I also washed her sticky hands.

It was at that time I realized that Missy's speech was rapidly developing, and from that time on I'd have to be more cautious of my own language around my grandchildren.

We had a two shelf bookcase in our living room that had sliding glass doors on. When Missy and Tanya were little, I came into this room one day and there they both were, one lying on one shelf and the other lying on the other shelf, each one covered with a little blanket When I inquired as to what they were doing, they answered, "We're playing bunk beds, grandma". Now how creative can children be?

Rachel, being Dell and Debbie's daughter weighed in at 6 pounds 11 ounces, on September 14, 1981. It was the Sunday afternoon that the family had a baby shower for Debbie, and she went to the hospital in the evening. Rachel was born at 1:00 A.M. She was such a special little bundle of joy, and thinking back, I remember that she had quite a bit of hair along with her blue eyes. She had a petite bone structure and resembled a living doll

Rachel's infancy began in a stressful manner as she cried so many times which puzzled everyone. This unhappy baby suffered from colic and it took some time before anything would comfort her. A friend of Rachel's Grandma Lee suggested giving the baby what was called 'green drops'. Debbie and Dell got this and gave some to Baby Rachel. Wow! It was a wonder drug! These green drops alleviated this darling little baby's discomfort, and she became a happy, contented baby along with her now happy and contented parents.

When Rachel was five years old, she took ballet

lessons. She was so limber and light on her toes, and did a wonderful job of dancing. We went to one of her dance recitals one evening, and really enjoyed seeing all of these little tots perform.

The year after Rachel was born, her brother Steven was born weighing in at 8 pounds 7 ounces, bigger than what his sister had been. He was one who really didn't seem to be in a hurry about coming into this world, as we anxiously awaited his birth. He came into the world at 10:30 A.M. on December 5, 1982, on his Uncle Al's birthday.

When Steven was born, my dad, Stevie's Great Grandpa Lenz, called him the Mayor of Lenzville, as this area in which we live was named by my dad. Steven was also the first male Roanhaus born in our immediate family, so now with Steven's Great Grandpa Joseph Roanhaus, Grandpa Phil Roanhaus, his Dad Dell Roanhaus, and now Steven Roanhaus, together made up four generations of Roanhauses.

The list of grandchildren's births goes on and on. Following in order down the line came Kelly Vos [Deb and Al's], born on February 19, 1984; Josh [Dolly and Jim's] born July 23, 1985; Jennifer [Deb and Al's] born on September 4, 1986; Michael [David and Monica's] born September 13, 1986; Grant]Dan and Jonell's] born September 24, 1986; Ryan [Diane and Rick's] born December 1, 1986; Ashley [Dolly and Jim's] born November 15, 1987; Amanda [Danny and Jonell's] born February 27, 1989; Lindsey [David and Monica's] born May 24, 1990; Benjamin [Diane and Rick's] born August 15, 1991; Paul Ryan [Donna and Paul's] born May 15, 1992; Nicole [Donna and Paul's] born May 7, 1994.

Our step-grandchildren who are just as near and dear to Phil and me as those of kin births. The oldest is Chris Talbert [Jonell and Dan] born on June 30, 1972; Jared Dixon [Paul and Donna] born June 1 about one year after Renee was born; Erika Mueller [Monica and David] born November 27, 1978; Marcus Mueller [Monica and David] born March 2, 1981; Jake who is legally adopted by Danny as his dad was born July 21, 1981; and Jesse Dixon [Paul and Donna] born December 16, 1983. This totals up to 24 grandchildren. Phil and I are the proudest and happiest grandparents that ever could be! There are three of them whom we rarely get to see.

Chris Talbert, who actually is the oldest of all the grandchildren, is busy at his job in Kenosha, and also goes to school. He is a very handsome young man, who has great mannerisms, shows much respect towards Phil and me whenever we see him. Being the age that he is, at holiday times and times of family gatherings, he hardly shows up at many of these parties, as I often feel that he thinks he has nothing in common with all the younger grandchildren. As of late he has been to my brother's funeral and to a Roanhaus family reunion, so I think that he realizes that we do love him and care to see him more often.

Jared and Jesse used to come to family gatherings when they were little, but we haven't really seen them in years. They, too, were always respectful towards Phil and me. Often times we would like to see them as we are getting older and the times to be with them may be shorter than anyone can anticipate. But this is the way it is and we accept it as such. It is not up to us to dictate their lives, so we don't attempt to interfere.

Erika and Marcus are such nice kids. They both refer to us as grandma and grandpa, and I truly believe that they feel as close to us as we do to them. Both of them are very talented. Erika excels in her communications field, is truly a great writer and writes children's books. She is very skilled with the modern technology and has done much of this type of work in her high school classes. She has always been a very intelligible student and works hard. She has gone to college in Montana by relatives of her dad's. She was very unhappy in Montana so after one and a half years of college, she moved back to Wisconsin.

Marcus, on the other hand, is not like most boys his age in the way of his lack of interest in sports. He prefers drawing and creating and is so proficient at it. He attends the same high school that Missy and Tanya attend, Westosha Central High. They are all in the same class soon to become seniors in 1999-2000 school year.

My hopes for him are to get a break with his artistic ability, and that he can locate a school of the arts that he will be able to attend. He would be a good illustrator for Erika's books that she writes. Only time and money will tell what his future holds for him in the way of opportunities.

Jake is the most amiable kid and who will also become a senior in the 1999-2000 school year. He doesn't particularly like the academic courses but he does so well in the fine arts. His specialty is drama, whether it be acting, prop man, or stage hand in general, he is competent in the entire field. I hope that he can go on in this field in the future and become successful. He is also very musically talented and plays the guitar. Jake will succeed in the fine arts industry if he can only get the right break.

Speaking of Jake, I have to relate an incident that just cracked me up when his mom told about it. Last Christmas he wanted to buy a girl, his so-called girl friend, a Christmas gift. She wanted something nice but useful. So this rather shy boy and a boy friend of his went into the Fredericks of Hollywood Store to buy a gift for his girl friend. I can just about imagine how embarrassed they must have been with all the scanty undies shown in there. To make a long story short, I believe that he bought her red silk pajamas. Now how's that for a teenage guy to give a girl!

Some of the other things that come to mind about the grandchildren are humorous and silly, while others are quite preposterous!

Kelly did some bizarre mischievous things during her childhood. She was playing with a lighter, which she shouldn't have gotten in to in the first place, and started the trash can on fire in the bathroom at their home.

Kelly, along with Missy and Tanya, at the Voses put shave cream all over their faces. They were grounded for two months and Tanya was not allowed to come over to their house during that time.

When Kelly used to get paste on her slacks in school, she didn't want her mom to know, so she took a scissors and cut those spots out leaving a hole in her slacks. I used to mend more slacks for this girl due to her paste cut-outs.

When Voses lived in Lily Lake, Missy accidentally locked herself in the bathroom by opening a drawer in the vanity and her mom couldn't get in to help her. This is when Grandpa Roanhaus came to the rescue.

When Kelly and Jenny lived in Burlington, they went sledding down the hill and couldn't stop so they slid right into the creek. Then they were so wet and cold, that ended the sledding for that time.

When Jenny was a little girl, she was told to jump in the tub, meaning to take a bath. Without any adieu she did just that. She jumped into the tub of water with her clothes on. Her excuse was, "I didn't know what you meant".

Tanya and Missy used to sing the commercial, "Oh, oh, better get Maaco". after which they would laugh hysterically. There must have been something about that ad that struck their fancy, but I'll never know what.

Josh wanted to drive at a very early age, like five years old. Phil would pick up Thuemmler's garbage and take it along

266

to the dump. This one day as Phil went in the house to find out what they had, he left the truck motor running. Lo and behold! Didn't Josh get in it and push on the gas pedal, and started going toward the river. Phil and Dolly saw him and they both ran for dear life to get it stopped just in the nick of time before crossing the road.

Another time when Dolly and Jim's family were visiting at Barb and Ted's house, Josh got into their van, pushed in the clutch and was rolling almost into Thuemmler's garage, but got stopped in time. All I can say is that Josh had a good guardian angel, and Grandpa Ted never said a word nor even got upset about it.

Jenny tells of the time when she was in third grade and was having gym class, as her pants split right in the butt. So embarrassing! On the serious side of school, she plays clarinet in the school band.

Then there were times when the kids would be at my house and do some baking. It was the time of Dell's birthday and Stevie wanted to make a cake for his dad, so he made a delicious chocolate cake for Dell. He was quite young when he did this, but he could read the recipe. He made a good cake and made his dad very happy.

Another time, Tanya and Missy were making cupcakes at my house, and they took turns beating. All went well until Missy's fingers got caught in the beaters, and she was really stuck. To this day I still don't know how they ever got her fingers out.

The children's Uncle Dan always wanted to endow pets on his Godchild Stevie, so when Stevie was four years old, Dan gave him a live rabbit for Easter. Now Dell's family lived in town so they had no room for any animal cages, so they had no other choice but to keep it in the house. Needless to say, the rabbit didn't last long.

Dan was quite adamant about giving pets for gifts. When Stevie and Rachel were seven and eight years old, he gave them each a bird. Now the problem comes in when the children form the attachment and then something happens. This was the case of the birds. The first bird died the first day off school, and the second bird died on the second day off. The children were heart broken, so it would have been better not to have had them at all, because it was too hard on the children.

Speaking of pets, Dan gave a rabbit to his Godchild Renee and it was cold outside, and she didn't have the proper hutch for it. One morning the rabbit lay stiff and cold. Being upset, Dolly called me on the phone. I knew how upset Dan would be knowing that two gift rabbits were gone in such a short time. So without thinking and with every hope, I told her to wrap it in a blanket and put it near the heater. Now wasn't that ever simple-minded? Quite the advice from mother to daughter!

Then there is Ashley, who just didn't want to give up her pacifier, and everyone bargained with her to give it up. I took her to town and let her pick out a short outfit to give up the pacifier, but this was not successful. The only thing that broke her of that pacifier was that Dolly promised her if she gave it up, she could go to preschool. She really wanted to go to pre-school desperately and this is what it took to break that awful pacifier habit.

Ashley was always such a good little girl and very often she helped me with many little tasks. One day I asked her to get something out of the closet but I happened to be in her way. So jokingly she shouted out, "Well, if you'd move...." Now when she is over many times just to be funny she repeats that phrase.

Darlene took Dolly and Jim's kids to the beach one sunny afternoon when Ashley was just a little pee wee. Well, she was afraid to go into the water, and didn't want any part of that, but she didn't want Tanya and Josh to be in the water either, so she put her little hands on her hips and very demandingly announced in a scream to the top of her voice, "Kids, come out of the water". This must have been a sight

Another incident occurred when Ashley was so young and was just to the point of her speech development We were on our way home from our summer Shawano vacation. The guys were riding in a van with Jim, and the rest of us rode with Dolly in her van. On the way home, little Ashley was sitting on my lap and was getting upset with her older sister, Renee, who was sitting in the back seat complaining.

After a short while, Ashley had enough of her grumbling and turned to Renee saying, "Shut up, Nee!" Following this comment, I said to Ashley, "Oh, honey, we only tell dogs to shut up, we tell people to be quiet".

Quickly her next response to Renee was, "Be ky-et, Nee", in her language, meaning to be quiet.

Ashley and I have always had such good rapport and she's always more than willing to do favors for me. Many times for gifts, she gives me a coupon book having each coupon worth

268

a helpful task. Some were: running something back from our house to their house, a house vacuuming, sweeping the outside walks, or any job I may need help with.

At times Ashley would always help me without being told or asked, so often I would reward her with a quarter here and there, sometimes even a dollar, so one day Ashley told me, "Grandma, you spoil me". Well, I look at it that she was worthy of being rewarded.

Speaking of speech development, Jenny, as a little girl used to call Renee, Hernee. It seems as though the younger cousins always uttered Renee's name in a shorter or distorted version.

Kelly is and has always been the family jokester. She treats happenings in the most humorous fashion. She and her sisters used to smash lightning bugs on the ceiling in their kitchen and then watch them glow.

Kelly often relates the time when the Vos family returned home from their vacation and everybody was helping to carry everything into the house except Kelly. After a while, Al was disgusted with her not helping and yelled at her, "G--damn it, Kelly, you can carry stuff in too". As he said this, his tooth fell out of his mouth to the ground- so..... he picked it up, put it back in his mouth and during this time he continued yelling at her. Even now Kelly reminds her dad of this incident.

Grant was born the same year as Jenny, Michael, and Ryan and is a true fisherman along with his dad. He takes the fishing project in 4-H and really enjoys it.

Grant's greatest feat is breaking mules for riding and jumping. A man in his neighborhood named Frank Ingram, has two mules which Grant named 'Stormy' and 'Pershing Gold Digger'. During the time Grant was working with these mules, owner Frank would become so excited that he would hee-haw at the mules and it got to the point of the mule responding back to Frank.

When a kid starts in the pony club, he is unrated, then the ratings start at D 1 and in due time keeps progressing. Grant, through his tedious work, has now been classified in the D 2 rating, as he is now striving for the D 3 rating. He has reached this objective in just the span of one year.

His experiences with the mules include the time when he was training Digger to canter and the mule tried to throw Grant. We all know that mules have a mind of their own and have always been known to be stubborn, so this interferes with the training process that Grant is engaged in. Now Stormy on the other hand is more agile and cooperative and can now jump seven feet from the stall. So he has been trained well. When Grant is not training in riding mules, he drives the tractor for Frank, or he can be seen riding the three wheelers. Grant is a boy who has learned how to appreciate having fun in his own back yard.

Grant's older brother, Jake, deals with situations with a cool head, and often times as he refers to himself in reminding his mom, "Mom, remember I'm the good kid!"

Ryan King was born at Good Samaritan Hospital in Merrill, Wisconsin, on December 1, weighing in at 9 pounds 5 ounces at 11:40 in the morning. After a few years, Ryan always begged his parents for a baby in the family.

A few years after, Ryan's wish came true, and Benjamin Phillip was born on August 15 at 4:20 in the afternoon at Wausau Hospital. Ryan was now a most delighted kid, as he has his brother whom he refers to as a good little brother.

When Ben was a baby, he relied on his pacifier so much that this continued on until he was four years old. Whenever he'd drop his pacifier, and someone would put it back into his mouth the right way, he'd turn it so it would be upside down. This was the way he liked to suck on it.

When Ben turned four, Diane wanted to break him of his pacifier habit, so she cut the end of it off. When Ben discovered this [not knowing that it was cut off intentionally], he told his mom that his 'nootchie' was broke and she should buy a new one. When she informed him that Walmart didn't sell them any more, he was contented and accepted this as truth from his mom, so no more pacifier after that time. Aren't parents tricky?

As the years went on for Ben, he became a clipper of a child! Could he have possibly inherited some of his Grandma Roanhaus' naughty childhood traits?

When Diane worked, Ben stayed at a Day Care that was run by a lady named Theresa, who was an excellent day care provider. She was a patient and trained professional, but had problems in dealing with Ben's behavior. In speaking with Ben's parents, they decided that they would take the situation in hand.

After discussing many options, they decided on one that they felt would work for Ben. They had always told the children that people who do bad things go to jail, and that kids that do bad things go to a baby jail. So they told him that in order to be prepared for this he needed to pack a bag because the jail would provide the clothing all except underwear and socks. So with that he packed three pair of underwear and three pairs of socks and put them into a gift bag. So as not to humiliate him at Theresa's in front of the other children at the Day Care, Diane and Rick taped it shut. Then he was told that he would have to take his 'Baby Jail Bag' along to Theresa's and to every place he went just to remind him to be a good boy.

So one afternoon Theresa took all the kids of the Day Care to McDonalds for a treat. Being within walking distance they were already outside the house ready to go when Ben discovered that he didn't have his Baby Jail Bag, so he told Theresa that he had to get his bag because his parents told him that he had to take it wherever he went. This is how serious this child took this threat, and it wasn't long after that Ben's behavior was improved so this whole method of discipline was successful.

Amanda has always been so shy until of recent years, and now she has such a pleasant disposition and enjoys being with people, signs of growing up at age 10. When she was a baby of 10 months of age, she knew what the reins on a horse was for, so while she could ride a horse she could actually control the horse herself.

At age three, she went on Trail Rides in the Kettle Moraine area and people were amazed at how she had control of the horse she was riding. She had a difficult time in pronouncing the hard sounds of 'c' and 'g'. When she wanted to ride, she'd say. "Tive me my trop so I tan tanter". It's a good thing that the rest of the family knew what she meant.

She enters and rides in competition where she has won several championships in hunter and jumping categories. In any of the pony, horse, or age group competitions she is at the top in ratings. Her latest fancy is raising a goat for a 4-H project, plus her interest in the 4-H fishing project.

Michael is a most studious boy and always is on the top honor roll at Wheatland Center School. Michael and Jenny have been in the same classroom in school for several years and so Jenny has the advantage of knowing Michael better than any of the other cousins, who never get to see Michael.

Michael engages in playing soccer on a community team and is a very good player. He is also a Green Bay Packer football fan and keeps up with the games and the players' achievements.

When Michael was younger he and his sister Lindsey

would come over occasionally and draw and play games on my computer.

In September he will turn thirteen, soon to become a teeny bopper. Time passes on so quickly and the grandchildren are all growing up too rapidly.

Ryan will soon become a teeny bopper also, as he will turn thirteen December 1, 1999. Ryan is an avid collector of collectible sports cards. So far he has 133 Michael Jordan cards and a total of 10,000 cards including all the sports. He proudly shows off his Mickey Mantle cards from the years that he played with the Braves and then the New York Yankees.

Ryan has been trained by the best fisherman, by his Grandma King. She started teaching him at age two when she took him along in the boat with her.

He also likes to be in the woods with his dad and Grandpa King, helping them cut wood. Rick takes Ryan hunting with him but this year could be the first time for Ryan to go deer hunting because he took the Hunter Safety Course.

Ryan plays basketball in school and for a community team. He is enrolled in 13 projects in 4-H and enjoys playing his clarinet in the school band.

When Lindsey was a little girl, she liked playing with Thumbkin dolls as well as her Barbie dolls. She could often be seen coloring and looking through books.

She liked the Richard Scary videos and also the learning games on the computer. When her mother used to work at Bouquets Store in Lake Geneva, she stayed with us. Every afternoon she and I would play Yahtzee, and she enjoyed other games that we played together.

The youngest of the grandchildren are Paul Ryan and his sister Nicole. Up to this time, Nicole went to Noah's Ark preschool and Paul Ryan went to St. Charles Catholic School in Burlington. This year Nicole will be in Kindergarten at St. Charles also.

The two children together have a pet ferret named Star and a dog named Pork Chop.

Activities and groups that Paul Ryan is involved in are: T-Ball, Karate, and Tiger Cubs. Considering the one year that he took Karate, he has learned many disciplines associated with character building. His favorites in Tiger Cubs are the learning skills in Archery, Swimming, Singing, Arts and Crafts, and safe practice using BB guns.

When he was four years old, he took an art course at

the Burlington Public Library after which he won a 'Little Rembrandt' award.

Nicole's favorite activity is to visit Grandma and Grandpa Roanhaus. When she's with us we enjoy her so much because with the things she does, knows, and says, she's six year old going on thirty six. One day as she and I were snacking on carrots, she said to me, "We have to eat carrots, Grandma, because our bodies need a lot of vitamins". I agreed with her statement as she went on to say, "You know we need to take care of our bodies, don't we, Grandma?" All I could think of was, what other six year old would think about a healthy body?

On the childlike side of Nicole, she enjoys playing with her Barbie dolls as well as her Little Tyke doll house. Being inquisitive and eager to learn new concepts, when she's with me it's a case of where I step out, she steps in. Many times I have to be cautious of not running over her little toes with the wheels of my chair because she is always so close at hand.

Being the youngest grandchild, I find myself giving her undue attention, but most of the other kids are growing up all too quickly and I want to enjoy her childlike stages of development for as long as possible.

I have come to realize how fast these kids are showing their pre-adulthood because they are now in the stages of driving and dating.

Not long ago at a party at Thuemmler's home, Josh so sweetly stated to the guests as he looked at Dolly, "Isn't my mother lovely?" Everyone in the room was in awe at this remark in admiration for his mother.

In Josh's school class one day, the students were required to write a selection about someone they knew who could possibly become a saint. Dear sweet Josh wrote about his Grandma Roanhaus because he said that she helps people and teaches people about God and the Church. Don't I wish I could become a saint?

Two years ago when I had to go to the Sacred Heart Rehab Unit in the hospital in Elkhorn following surgery, Josh had to come to check out this place to see if it was good enough for his grandma to stay there. When he came to visit the first time, he checked out every nook and cranny of the place and after a while, he decided that it was an okay place for me. Josh has always held much compassion in his heart for people and does yet today. By the same token his feelings are easily hurt.

273

The oldest three of the grandchildren, Jason, Renee, and Chris are all well established now and mature. Chris presently has a girl friend named Heidi, the sweetest girl, so I hope he thinks of her seriously. Jason has moved out of the family residence and into an apartment with his friend, Bart. Renee has played the field with guys and it seemed as though she may have found the right one, Chris, but only time and commitment will tell.

Then we consider the innocent Josh who suddenly developed a flare for girls. His latest is Kelly's best friend, Jackie, after terminating involvement for girls whom he went to school with. Yes, Josh has actually started into the dating of girls at age 14.

The first of this aged group to become interested in the opposite sex was Jake. I recall at Jake's eighth grade graduation pool party at his home, how all the girls claimed to be Jake's girl friend. It appeared to be Jake's harem. When he paid attention to his cousins, Rachel and Tanya, most of the girls left the party. What they didn't know was that these girls were his cousins. Now Jake's latest fling is with a girl named Amanda, but only time will tell if she is his real love.

Rachel has had several boy friends during her high school days, but the past year she has been dating a boy named Brian, the nicest kid who is a couple years older than Rachel, as he in college in the local area. He plans to become a lawyer. The two of them are very compatible and have mutual interests.

When Phil and I first met Brian, some time back, the two of them came to our house to visit. We ordered out for pizza while they were here and we sat through the whole evening talking. What impressed me most was that they took several hours out of their young lives to visit with a couple of older people. One doesn't find many young people of today spend time with older people.

Then there is Steven, who is playing the field and has several girl friends who all hang out in groups of guys and girls. Stevie has many friends and has been voted as president of his junior class. He works part time at Culver's Food Service, and he is liked by all the employees there. He is a special kid because he is always there for us when we need a helping hand.

Missy and Tanya both have boy friends who are and have been friends for quite some time. Both of these couples spend a lot of time visiting with Phil and me often. Many times it's just for an hour or so, just to say hello and check how we are doing. This is another example of younger people caring for older people.

Missy's friend is Dan, and Tanya's friend is Angelo, but his friends refer to him as Vern. They are both nice kids and are friendly to us. On the night of their junior prom they came over to show us how they looked in their formal attire. It was so amazing how different kids look when they're so dressed up.

It doesn't seem like too long ago that these kids were doing some clumsy actions. I refer to the time when Missy went to Nashville with the Thuemmlers and during a shopping spree at the mall, she had an embarrassing experience. She was trying to catch up to the group as she was lagging behind, so in haste she walked right smack into a plate glass window. She tells how clean and spotless this window was, so she didn't realize it was there.

Then at Great America, Tanya witnessed what a bump on the head feels like. Part of her group headed in one direction while the other part of the group headed in another. She walked straight into a utility pole. To this day, she still is reminded of that episode.

When Rachel was thirteen, she had the opportunity to go to Australia and New Zealand, with the group called People to People. This was an educational experience that she'll never forget. The first few days, she became homesick, but after a while she got accustomed to being there and enjoyed it. This is something that will always remain with her, and no one can ever take this experience away from her.

Now there's the driving incidents of the grandchildren who are all of driving age. The driving licenses were issued to Rachel, Missy, Jake, Tanya and Stevie, all in that order. It won't be long and Kelly will be eligible for driving, then Josh.

Rachel had a car that Dell bought for her, but she no longer likes it, so Stevie drives it now. Al bought a car for Missy, but it wasn't working properly for a while until the right person found out what was wrong with it, so now she is back on the road. Tanya is on her second car that her dad, Jim, bought for her. She had the misfortune of totaling her first car. However she doesn't like the hubs on the wheels on this car, but kids now days like what strikes their fancy, as long as their dads are paying for it. Danny is looking for a car for Jake, too.

This week Missy had her senior picture taken, and the photographer told her that if she got bored in college, she should become a model. He told her that she had a beautiful smile and most expressive eyes and she knew how to turn on the charm. This gave Missy the confidence that she sometimes lacks.

All of the older grandchildren have their goals and objectives for their future planned and this makes me very happy, because it demonstrates to us that our children and their spouses have done an outstanding job of raising their own children, our grandchildren. I can't help but think that all the sacrificing that Phil and I have done in the past is now manifesting its worth through the future generations, of whom we are so proud. A special tribute to our own kids for their own patience, understanding, loyalty, guidance and support all encompassed with love in bringing up wholesome families. Now you know why I say that grandchildren are a blessing.

Back Row4 L-R: Jake Roanhaus, Missy and Kelly Vos
Back Row 3 L-R: Steven Roanhaus, Jason and Tanya
Thuemmler, Grant and Rachel Roanhaus, Jenny Vos,
Josh Thuemmler
Back Row 2: Ashley Thuemmler, Amanda Roanhaus
Front Row L-R: Ben King, Grandpa, Grandma, Nicole Dixon
Renee Thuemmler, Paul Ryan Dixon, Ryan King

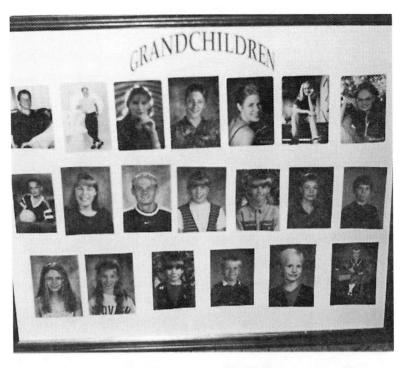

20 of Our Grandchildren
Top L-R: Chris Talbert, Jason Thuemmler, Renee Thuemmler, Jake Roanhaus, Missy Vos, Rachel Roanhaus, Tnya Thuemmler
Middle: Steven Roanhaus, Kelly Vos, Josh Thuemmler, Jenny Vos, Michael Roanhaus, Grant Roanhaus, Ryan King
Bottom: Ashley Thuemmler, Amanda Roanhaus, Lindsey Roanhaus, Ben King, Raul Ryan Dixon, Nicole Dixon

Mark Vos, Our Adoptive Grandson

Chapter 22
Teaching a Second Time Round

Back in the early sixties I had hoped for an opportunity to knock at my door for a second round of teaching. I prayed so reverently and devotedly that something would be available and so I trusted in God to answer my prayers. It wasn't long after when there was an opening at St. Alphonsus School for a lay teacher in grades three and four. When I heard about this, I was so interested but now there was a problem of a baby sitter for my three younger children who were not of school age as yet, plus the fact that the youngest was a small baby.

The whole truth of the matter is not only did I miss teaching so much, but also we were in need of an extra income. I asked my sister-in-law Sophie, if she would now watch my children as I watched hers in the past. To my disappointment, she didn't want to do it for me because she wanted to work too.

Now the thoughts of my not being able to apply for this job rather distressed me, and I was sure that the whole idea was hopeless, so I would have to stay home until all my children were in school. I had just begun to accept the fact that this couldn't possibly materialize, when my mother said to me one day, "Haven't I always taken good care of your children before, why can't I do it now?"

This statement really shocked me as mom, at the time, was recuperating from a serious surgery. Then I told her that she had given the best care in the past that anyone could, but I felt that she needed more time to recuperate herself and didn't want to put an added burden on her. Her feelings were hurt because she felt that getting her mind on something other than herself would help to improve in gaining her strength back.

As we discussed the pros and cons, and the effects it could have on her, she absolutely would not take no for an answer, so I discussed this with my dad, and the more we talked about this, the more convincing she was about wanting to watch our children. So we accepted her gracious offer with the understanding that if this became too much for her, I would discontinue the job [that is if I got the job].

That next week, I set up an appointment with the parish priest, Father Grabauskas, for an inteview. He was very interested in my background, he liked the idea that I had gone to school there and was a member of the parish. So without any further adieu, he hired me on the spot and didn't even want to consider any other applicants.

Next discussion was the salary. Well at this point, I just wanted to go back to teaching, so salary didn't become an important issue, because before I even went there to apply, I knew that the salary would be very low. He offered me $1,250 for the year. The surprising part of it all was that I had made more wages than that when I started my teaching career seventeen years prior to this time. I asked to sign a contract and he said, "There is no written contract, my word is good". So it was just a verbal agreement and a hand shake between the priest and me, so I had the job and would start in the fall. He told me that I would be teaching third and fourth grades in a self-contained classroom in which there were double grades. This I already knew as I went all of my eight grades there.

Now I was really excited, because this could and would be an entirely new experience for me to teach in a parochial school. I had always taught in the public schools before this time. However, there were several times I did substitute teaching at St. Alphonsus to fill in for an ill nun or for a nun who had a death in her family.

I was the second lay teacher to be employed here. The first and only lay teacher at our parish school was leaving and accepted a part-time teaching job at St. Mary's School in Burlington.

During the summer I went to the school and started making out my lesson plans. In those days there were many teachers who I knew that taught daily off the cuff, but not me. I wanted a projected plan of what I would accomplish in each subject. Remember I was a by-product of A. J. Smith from teachers' college who believed that teaching should be done through employing units, and having sets of objectives to evaluate the student's progression of knowledge learned.

When I started at St. Alphonsus, I started teaching the third and fourth graders which was a good place to start because I didn't have any of my own children in my classroom.

My first class of third graders included: Susan Breski, Pam Herda, Dan Kerkman, Michael Koldeway, Larry Lois, Carol McCarthy, Reggie Richter, Dan Robers, Diane Rossmiller, Don Scherrer, Carol Sheahan, Mary Wermeling, and Dan Zeiger.

As for my first class of fourth graders at St. Alphonsus, there were 19 students in that class which made a total of thirty-two students in the one classroom. Being double grades in one classroom had many merits as the fourth grade class learned so well. They were: Christine Banas, Dorothy Breski, Janet Butler, Larry Colewinski, Chuck Grasser, Lynn Joerndt, Patti Kerkman, Fritz Lois, James Martin, Jimmy Richter, Steve Robers, Barbara Schenning, June Scherrer, Diane Schmidt, Betsy Sheahan, Jimmy Schulz, Darlene Vos, Sandra Wagner, and Kay Weis. This was a great group of kids, and they developed excellent study habits. So my first year back teaching again was most enjoyable.

Time went on at St. Alphonsus, and each year a meager raise was offered until it got as high as $3,250 annually with no benefits offered. This went on for several years without a written contract. When 1969 rolled around I was offered a written contract with a salary of $4,000, and I refused. In the meantime I had an offer from a public school south of here and I was seriously anticipating leaving. When they finally realized that I meant it, Father Grabauskas offered me $6,000 but they locked me in for two years at that price, so being that I really loved teaching there, I accepted it. Still there were no benefits.

When the next contract was due, I was locked in again for two years for $6,360. In 1973, I was granted the principal job in the dual position of teaching also, for a sum of $7,490, because of the added work of principal. The next raise $7,900 was again for the dual job. Then the salary went by increments, $8,400, to $8,700, to $9,300 which was the first one signed by Father Safiejko, then $10,000. All this while there still were no benefits. Father signed my next contract in 1981 for $10,700 and this was the last year for a while that I served as principal due to a health condition.

Now Father Wolf was offering contracts and the first by him was for $11,200, followed by $11,700, $13,000, $14,500, $15,500, $16,750, then $18,000. Father Massey offered my next contract for a principal's job only . This job was granted to me to straighten out the school that was left in such a mess by the former principal. He offered me $12,000 for this part time job. But the whole thing ended up in a full time job with part time pay. I have always been under paid , but I was happy in my work, and that was what counted for me. I'm sure that the reward in my eternal life will be worth much more than money.

After teaching the third and fourth graders for eight years, I taught fifth and sixth for two years. It was then that I had to be disciplining the Junior High students, so I switched and taught seventh and eighth grades for fifteen years. I spent eight years in the dual position of teacher/principal full time, finished terms for Harriet Kaluva, Carol Degen, and Carolyn Chambers as they resigned during the school years, and spent my last year as a part time position.

My 26 years at St. Alphonsus have been delightful and rewarding due to the fact that the people of the parish always backed up the school in every manner possible.

When I first worked with the nuns, I had to take playground duty every morning and noon recess, because the nuns went home to relieve themselves, have coffee, and noon lunch. Many times I never got to eat lunch because I had to be on the playground, but I never complained because I enjoyed being with the children and also liked working with the nuns.

During the years, I've had ups and downs with one school board member who thought our school did not have to live up to Archdiocesan rules and regulations, but we functioned under the auspices of this entity and we lived up to their guidelines. We had the leave way of establishing our own policies for our school according to the school's needs and concerns.

Some of the many school board members who always backed up my ideas in initiating new concepts in accordance with the needs and concerns of the students and the school in general were: Rita Dunkin, Stan Lois, Joe Riesselmann, Sheila Siegler, Glen Kerkman, Jerry Alby, Ray Cates, Maggie Oberhofer, Dale Ketterhagen, Mary Kay Warren, Pat Vos, Dave Richter, and many others who do not come back to mind but they were as important in the decision making policy as those whom I have mentioned.

Sheila was always looking for ways and means to raise money to provide equipment and supplies for the school to make teaching more gratifying and effective. It was through her efforts that prompted Bob and Sue Riley and Clayton and Mary Lou Kretschmer to organize a Booster Club to raise money for support of the school.

This beginning of this Booster Club led to the brainstorm of Dennis and Gerry Lois along with Dick Elverman to sponsor a Baseball Tournament held on Memorial Day weekend. They worked most diligently to get it rolling and now it has became a smashing success.

Thanks to Dory Weis who was instrumental in introducing the activity known as the Smoker, which is another excellent source of money for the school.

This Booster Club in later years now, has been renamed to Home and School Association, but the original functions are still held annually only under a different title.

After having taught for so many years in the public school system and having ample supplies to work with, I soon became accustomed to conserving and utilizing any source of supplies that may become available. Many businesses donated paper to the school and we did student worksheets and parent letters on the backs of insurance forms and direction sheets for putting together certain products.

Many times when we teachers had special art projects for the children, I'd go out and buy the materials myself and never submitted a bill to the school. Later the school board allocated a petty cash fund that I was responsible for distributing to the four teachers. I never had the heart to refuse any teacher money out of this fund so when the fund was depleted again I supplied money of my own so the teachers could teach the art skills that they wanted to teach, opening many avenues to developing children's creativity.

When the Quaker Company sent the clay coated slippery sheets in the stack of donated papers, the primary teachers used them for finger painting, while others of us used them for cutting patterns, cuttings and tracings, positive and negative design patterns, and many abstract forms of skill development.

Jim Otto, an agent for Valley School Supply in Appleton, would take trade-in machines from schools that could afford to purchase new ones periodically. Then Jim would ask me if we could use any of them. He gave us duplicators; filmstrip, opaque, overhead and movie projectors; phonographs; and cassette tape players. Every time another school would update, he'd keep us updated with trade-ins.

Many times when Valley discontinued items, Jim would invite me to come and pick out these items from his garage, but the only stipulation was that we use them and not to take anything just to have it. That was no problem for us as we had a limited budget, and these items really helped out and were free for the taking.

One of the tasks that went with the principal's job was to clean up any messes that occurred during the day due to having a part-time janitor, who came in to clean in after school was dismissed. Sometimes this got to be a little repulsive, especially when a child vomited. A teacher would call me and one of my older students would help me get out the chemically treated saw dust product, while the teacher would take her students to another part of the building and call the sick child's parents. After applying the dust, we'd sweep this mess onto a dust pan and dispose of this properly followed by disinfecting the brush and dust pan. Then we would get out a scrub bucket and mop the floor temporarily, spray disinfectant so as not to spread the germs, so the teacher could come back with her students and resume classes.

Some of the major changes that I saw need for in our school were handbooks for teachers, parents, school boards, and Safety Patrol members, so I worked on them with the help of a committee composed of parents, school board members, and priest.

One of the greatest changes were the scheduling of field trips, some of which were all-school trips. One that the children all liked was the boat tour of the Milwaukee Harbor. We ate lunch on the boat and enjoyed the cool breezes while gaping at the Russian ship in the harbor with female sailors on it. Later we toured St Josephat's Basilica, which was a spectacular church.

On another all-school field trip, we went to Madison: first to the Capitol where we toured and had lunch, the State Historical Society, and then to a Madison TV Studio.

Other field trips included: Mitchell International Airport, Milwaukee Post Office, Kenosha County Court House and Jail, Burlington Newspaper, Memorial Hospital, Burlington Post Office, Milwaukee Zoo, Milwaukee Horticultural Domes, Johnson Wax Rondell Theater in Racine, Nestle Candy Company, and the movie called the *Life of Jesus* at Kenosha, and *Sound of Music* at the Plaza Theater in Burlington, and many places of interest.

Any place we ever took our students, the establishment always complimented on the excellent behavior of our students. This speaks well for our teachers on staff as to what they expected of their students and how the children responded.

During my course of teaching at St. Alphonsus, there was one class of students that I taught for five years in a row; fourth, fifth, sixth, seventh, and eighth grades.I liked this group of students as they were good kids, and worked well, with a few exceptions here and there, but for the most part they were studious and did develop good work and study habits.

Included in this grade were: Jim Benes, Jerry

284

Czarnowski, Brian Dunkin, Jackie Elverman, Jeff Epping, Bill Joerndt, Patti Johnson, Randy Kerkman, Sue Koldeway, Tim Lennon, LuAnn Lois, Janet Martin, Jeff Poepping, Renee Riesselmann, Kelly Riley, Mary Robers, Tom Rossmiller, Ray Vos, Tony Vos, Mary Ann Wawro, Ruth Wermeling. This class graduated in 1977.

When Joe Riesselmann was president of the school board, he thought of a new idea and presented it to the rest of the board. He felt that if the school children would not be required to attend Mass daily in the church, the Mass would become more meaningful to the children so they would participate better. All the board members agreed, but I was a little dubious as to how the priest and other parents would react, so we decided to give it a try with the priest's approval. The first, second, third, and fourth graders would attend on Wednesdays; the intermediate and upper grades would attend on Mondays, and the whole student body would attend on Fridays. After a fair trial, everyone liked this, especially the teachers as this gave them more teaching time.

Every Friday after Mass, we had singing practice in church so the children could learn new hymns. Mrs. Ev Uhen was so faithful about accompanying all our Masses and practices and all other school functions that were held in church. When the nuns were here, they had a children's choir, so I continued on with the choir. On Friday afternoon, we had choir practice in the classroom, while the servers briefly met with the priest, Father Grabauskas, after which time they would join us for practice.

After the nuns left our parish and I took over, the people wanted to know if we could have a Christmas program like the public schools did. I felt that December is such a busy month, so I used my bargaining power and promised if we didn't have to use precious time for program practices, we would have a Living Rosary and May Crowning during May in honor of our Blessed Mother. They liked the idea so that's what we did.

When Carol Degen took over, the priest suggested having a late afternoon children's Christmas Mass. This became a parish tradition until the Archbishop proclaimed that this was too much pageantry detracting from the solemnity of the Mass, so he put a ban on this.

Another activity that Carol introduced was the Science Fair. This was an extraordinary means for the children to show

285

what they had learned throughout the year in their science classes, utilizing the concept of scientific problem solving. This fair was carried out for many years until a new administrator changed it from Science to a Social Studies Fair, and is no longer competitive.

In 1990, we introduced a spring concert in April, which was an all-school activity displaying the children's lovely singing voices.

Our school students always exhibited school projects at the Kenosha County Fair in Wilmot. When the nuns were here, I used to help them put up our school booth.

After the nuns left, Mrs. Rachael Herda and I put it up together. I'll never forget the year that she and I started early in the morning at the fair grounds all through the hot day, and when evening came, we still were working at it. Being that we both were so darn fussy, we'd put something up, then not like where it was and take it down. At 8:30 at night, Phil and her husband, Martin, came to the fair grounds looking for us. By this time we were so exhausted and fatigued, so they helped us and we finished in no time because at that point and time we had given up on our meticulous way of putting up these exhibits. After that time, a committee was always appointed to help.

The first class trip at the end of the school year for the eighth grade graduating class was started in 1989. This was my last graduating class before I retired, so they begged me to go to Great America with them and all stay overnight at the new Days Inn, so we could spend two days and really have fun together. So I agreed, because their class had raised money and their trip was paid for out of class money. As chaperones who went with us were: Carol Lois, Mary Lois, Dolly Thuemmler and little Josh. We all had a blast, so much fun! This was always my favorite class, even though I termed every graduating class as favorites, but somehow or other this class was so special to me.

This class was composed of great kids: Robin Alby, Robert Bastrup, Bill Dale, Marie Dembowski, Brian Kerkman, Ryan Kerkman, Barbie Lois, Brad Lois, Sarah Lois, and Mae-Mae Oberhofer. Their graduating theme was, *May the Lord Guide You Always*.

At their Mass and graduation ceremony, each one gave a special tribute to me as they individually presented me with a red rose as this afforded me the opportunity to give each one of them a kiss that came from my heart. This was so impressive that many people in attendance in church were wiping tears.

The last presentation was a class gift to me, an electronic typewriter. They knew that they were my last graduating class, as I was retiring from teaching and the next year, I'd be the principal of the school, but they would be in high school. Such wonderful kids, I will never forget them.

Back in 1985, my severnth and eighth graders were given an assignment as part of the creative writing in their American Literature class. The topic to write on was, "Tell in your own words how a person whom you know has left a lasting impression on your life". In response to this assignment, Tim Cates who was a seventh grader at the time wrote the following.

A person who has made a lasting impression on me in my life is Mrs. Roanhaus. She is my teacher. She has taught me respect. Coming into 7th grade, I was thinking how hard the work was going to be! I thought I would never get it done. I was hoping to do good. The first few weeks or months of school were pretty tough. I was getting all my work done, but having lots of homework.

Mrs. Roanhaus knew just when to laugh, to make you feel good. She knew just when to yell at you to settle down [still does]. It got a little easier as time went on. I had a very fun year!

But I learned more about school work and life than I had ever learned before. She would listen to us boys rant and rave about our basketball, football, or baseball games. It must have been hard for her to listen to us. She had work to do, but she always finds time to talk with us.

This year is already in the 3rd quarter of school. Mrs. Roanhaus has had hard times in her "home"life, but she doesn't let that stop her from being there for us and helping us kids out.

When we boys went to the funeral home for her mother, we went to console her and her family members. We also went because we have a lot of respect for Mrs. Roanhaus. We knew that it would make her proud of us to go there. We knew it may help her out a little bit. So we went and she told us, we made her proud. I don't know about anyone else, but this made me feel really good inside. I sure hope that it helped her out a little bit, because I am proud to be one of her students.

I believe that this says it all! I have always been a strict disciplinarian and set high standards for my students to live by, I worked hard and I expected the students to work hard also. When students from our school entered the high schools, counselors always reported back to us as to the outstanding study habits that kids from our school had. This made all the hours of work, poor wages, and other sacrifices all worth while.

It's very rewarding now in my tender age, to have former students who are now adults, come back to me and thank me for the disciplinary measures and teaching methods that I used being their teacher, because this helped them to become better persons.

The memories that I have of all the students I have ever taught are pleasant and sometimes I wonder what each and every one of them are like today. My fondest visions are that each one is a unique individual, and my love for each one will always remain in my heart.

St. Alphonus School

Arlene Roanhaus
In school office

Class trip to Great America 1989
Back L-R: Ryan, Robin, Mae-Mae, Robert, Brian
Front L-R: Marie, Bill, Sarah, Barbie, Brad, Mrs. Roanhaus

Graduation Class - 1989

Back L-R: Father Robert Wolf, Robert Bastrup, Brad Lois, Father Robert Massey, Bill Dale, Arlene Roanhaus
Front L-R:Ryan Kerkman, Marie Dembowski, Mae-Mae Oberhofer, Robin Alby, Barbie Lois, Sarah Lois, Brian Kerkman

Chapter 23
Mom At Home - Teacher At School

One of the most difficult circumstances for our children was the fact that I was their mother at home, and was a part of the faculty at the school which they attended. It was their choice to call me Mrs. Roanhaus at school out of due respect to me as a staff member. Consideration in this matter stems from the expected discipline and respect that was taught to them in our home from us as their parents.

Often times they would have a slip of the tongue and call me mom, but that was not unusual at all because many of the children would accidentally in haste and excitement call me mom. I never corrected any child, including my own, because I had been a mom for many years.

When I taught at St. Alphonsus School, I had some of my own children in my classroom. The first of our family whom I taught was Debbie in third and fourth grades. I also had Dell and Diane in third and fourth grades. Donna was a student of mine when she was in fifth and sixth grades, and again in her eighth grade. David was in my classroom when he was in seventh and eighth grades.

I found that it was very difficult for my own children being in my classroom as I always demanded more from them than anyone else, and I also expected them to be the shining example for other students. This was very hard on our own children, but they never complained.

To put this in proper perspective I need to relate what poor Debbie went through having me for a teacher. When she was in fourth grade, she got the only F she ever got all through her twelve years of schooling. I, her mother, gave her this grade in Penmanship, but her writing has improved a little over the years. She will never foget that either. I point this out as this proves that I was a fair teacher.

When I had Al in my classes in the third and fourth grades, I never dreamed that some day in the future, he would become my son-in-law, but he is. What a small world!

Many times I would serve in the capacity as a mom for children at school in the absence of their own moms. I refer to times when the children would get hurt or become ill at school, at times when they just needed someone to listen to them and their problems, while other times they needed to know that someone really cared for them.

During times like that, children appreciated a hug from their teacher. In this way they knew that the teacher really cared for their well being and was there for them in time of need. At the present time a teacher wouldn't dare even think of giving a child a hug or the teacher may be prosecuted or even end up in jail. In our present society these gestures of caring are not acceptable due to so many warped minds that perceive a friendly gesture as an act of sexism even when that was never the intent.

However, there are so many kids out there today who hardly ever even see their parents on a day-to-day basis. Too many parents are caught up in their own social lives, their kids become a bother to them, and they can't have anything stand in the way of, or impair their social status. I sincerely maintain that couples should consider these outcomes before they even think of bringing children into this world.

Children do not have the option of being born or not, so couples need to take on the responsibility before acting, being that the consequences cannot be dissolved once they occur.

Actually I was a very proud mother because our children knew how to respect themselves, show respect for their peers, and give utmost respect to those in authority over them including teachers, leaders of local youth organizations, and people who were older than they were. We always taught the children that it is proper etiquette for a younger person to be the first to greet a person who is older than them. Our children were also trained to acknowledge people as Mr. or Mrs. and never to call people by their first name.

So many people in our community with whom our children have come in contact, have complimented us on knowing how to train our children in the proper procedures of etiquette. All the training and correcting that we did in their formative years paid off because they utilized their training by putting it into practice no matter if we were present or not. They knew how to act respectfully.

So I was Mrs. Roanhaus at school, and Mom at home. I was a very proud mother because my children knew the proper form of acknowledging anyone in authority over them and to anyone who was older and deemed respect. Our home training paid off and the kids knew how to utilize that training to make us both proud parents.

Chapter 24
Back to College at Age 46

I went back to college at this time because I hadn't had the degree that I needed as yet, being that I had my certification from teachers' college back in 1946. I had been teaching all those years taking courses here and there during summers whenever it was convenient due to raising a family.

First of all, I had to have a babysitter so I could even consider going back to college, but my dear mother came through for me again. She volunteered that she would come over every morning and get the kids off to school and be there for them as they came home again. This meant for her to prepare supper for my family in my absence.

The nun at St. Alphonsus, Sister Mary Ellen Johnson, urged me to take one year leave of absence and go back to college. Now in transferring my credits from teachers' college I lost so many credits that I had worked so hard for in the past. The University of Wisconsin system was very strict and reluctant about accepting credits from another institution, so I sat down and planned and planned how I could get the credits all in that I needed so as to complete this in one school year and the following summer.

After contemplating on what I needed in each category so I could be accepted into the school of education, I registered and was assigned a counselor, Professor Field. The day that I made an appointment and went to see him, I had shown him my plan and how I would accomplish this in the time allotted. He complimented me on how well I knew what I was doing, and okayed the whole course of action.

Although he was a little questionable about my taking a five credit course in Science, he had recommended that I take two courses in Science, a three credit and a two credit. As I explained to him that I was short of time and I'd have to take the five credit, he asked me if I knew how stiff a five credit course can be. I replied, "Yes, I do, but I don't have much choice, time is running out for me and I want to go back teaching at the end of the summer following the school year, and I need to have my licenses renewed."

Then he asked which science I was taking and I told him the five credit Biology and the three credit Physics. He went on to tell me about all the lab work that went with the Biology and I informed him, " I can do it and I will do it". He answered, "Then I will okay your plan".

Before I left his office, he asked me why I needed to come to him because I knew what I had to take and had a good plan, with a minor in library science. My reply was, I was told at the registrar's office that I had to meet with a counselor or I couldn't get a permit for an overload of credits. He shook my hand and wished me luck. To this day, I think that he thought I couldn't do it, but I made up my mind that I would be successful and after all was said and done, I did it.

The time element was not the only factor that entered into my plan, but the problem of money to pay for this had become an issue. But again, my dad came to the rescue and lent us the money that I could go back to school, with the verbal agreement that Phil and I would pay it back when I got back teaching again. So in all reality I knew that I wanted to be successful for a variety of reasons.

Everything was going on schedule, and finally I came to realize what the motive was for Sr. Mary Ellen pushing me so hard to go back. For a while during the past year of teaching, I had been wondering why she was piling so much extra work on me, work which I felt was her job as principal. She had trained me how to fill out national and Archdiocesan forms, but I did it out of the goodness of my heart because I thought that perhaps she may have been in ill health.

Then on the day that she and Father Grabauskas approached me and asked me to be the principal when I came back, it all started to make sense to me. They had told me that Sister Mary Ellen was being transferred to another place, and that our school was only to have a nun principal for the year in which I would be gone. I did consent only on the basis of my dedication to Catholic education and this offered another challenge for me personally.

The next thing I did was to apply to the Burlington Business and Professional Women's Organization of which Ruth Lenz was president. They had granted me a fifty dollar scholarship, which would help defray textbook costs.

Now I had to find a ride to Whitewater or else I'd have to drive daily by myself. I dreaded the thought of winter weather coming up so I was fortunate to find a lady who lived in Wind Lake who would drive and I'd pay her for the ride. Her name was Margie Graetz, a real cute little lady who, being a music major, sang beautifully. So each morning, I'd meet Margie in Burlington at the Burlington Library at 6:00 a.m. So this meant that I'd only have to drive to Burlington and back daily.

Margie had an early evening class so on certain days of the week, this meant that I wouldn't get back home until 8:00 P.M. But by the time I got home, mom had our kids fed and the children had their homework mostly done. A few times one or the other of the kids would wait for mom's help, but mom had much homework of her own to do.

Many nights I sat up all night studying Algebra, Physics, Biology, and did my multitude of assignments for library science.

These were the courses that had so much homework involved. In my Adolescent Literature course, I had to read three novels a week, report and index them according to the required categories. In the process I had to construct a library manual of methods and procedures which involved so much time in order to do a good job. The bibliography and cataloging classes were not quite so involved, but we had a quiz every day in both of these courses, not to mention the quiz every day in Algebra and Physics.

All was going well, I had the permit for overload for each semester and I worked hard. The provoking thing about any of the courses was the fact that I was assigned a young man as partner for Biology lab, and he never showed up except when our notes from lab work were due. Then he'd show up and want to copy my notes. I let him have my notes a few times, but then I got to thinking, I do all the work and he gets half of the credit, so one day I told him off and informed him to do his own lab work. It wasn't long after that time when he dropped the whole course.

After a while there were kids in my biology class who realized that I knew how to study, so all of a sudden I became very popular with the young students. I caught on to that before it got out of hand, but I did take one little African girl named Mavis from Rhodesia under my wing and studied with her every day in the study carrels in the library. She was ever so black but ever so sweet and ever so grateful for my studying with her. We got to be friends around campus and she had many friends who were nice kids.

One day I went to the Student Commons just to relax and get a cup of coffee while reviewing my notes before going to my next class to take an Algebra exam. A lady, who was quite a bit younger than me, came over with a cup of coffee and asked if she could join me. I delightedly told her yes, I'd be happy to have her join me. We both introduced ourselves and her name was Arla Ertl from Franksville. After conversing for a while, we found that we had much in common.

She was a teacher who already had been teaching, then stayed home to have her children, and now wanted to go back into teaching. She was taking a refresher course in Language Arts, actually the mechanics of grammar. She asked why I was there at my age, and I told her that I took a leave of absence to further my education. I had never minored in any field of education, as back in those days, everything was strictly education courses and more education courses. Now I wanted a minor in addition to more education courses, so I was taking Library Science as my minor.

My main purpose for being there was to extend my education in preparation for taking on the Administrator/Principal position back at St. Alphonsus to get my certification in administration. This had added to my study load also.

There were three ladies in my library science classes who were from Burlington: Sue Rausch, Mary Ann Bulgrin, and Jean Mayer from Honey Creek. These ladies were not teachers, but rather taking library science courses in hopes to acquire jobs either in public libraries or school libraries.

Another girl whose name was Linda Kmetz from Burlington, was finishing her college, getting ready to graduate then to teach, and so she was minoring in library science. Linda also rode to Whitewtaer with Margie, so I got to know her quite well.

Then we come to find out something that was rather a coincidence. Sister Joan Fisher who was principal for the remaining year of having nuns at St. Alphonsus, had hired Linda for the 3rd and 4th grades teacher when I would be back at St. Al's the next school year as dual principal/teacher. So after Linda signed her contract in February, we started to talk over St. Al's School,.

We were both to receive our respective degrees at the graduation ceremony, but I became ill and couldn't attend the ceremony. I received lifetime certification for teaching from the state of Wisconsin, and my certification in administration. I really enjoyed my days back to colleges.

Chapter 25
Twenty-five Years of Teaching School

I had been teaching at St. Alphonsus School for eighteen years and this was the year of 1982, which commemorated my twenty-fifth year of teaching school totally. The school board prepared a parish party for me which included our whole family. The 10:00 o'clock mass was for me, and this was followed by coffee and goodies in the school cafeteria. Many of the parishioners came to this celebration, which pleased me tremendously.

The pastor of the parish was Father Robert Wolf, and the teaching staff included Carol Degen as principal and fifth and sixth grades' classroom teacher. Betty Justman taught first and second grades, Sarah Peroutky taught third and fourth grades, and I taught junior high, seventh and eighth grades. Mrs. Treasure Besch was the school cook at the time and her assistant was Esther Scherrer. Henry Kretschmer was the custodian for the school. This constituted an excellent staff who were all friendly to work with and everyone was in unison with each other's feelings and the needs of the children.

The teaching staff had the children make banners that were hung in the church and they prepared a special celebration of the liturgy in my honor. It was so solemn and well prepared. The staff gave me an aurora borealis rosary as a gift, and I still have it today and still use it almost daily. Each time I use it to pray on, these people come to mind, so this was a gift which will always keep these special people within my heart.

I received so many lovely gifts. The Ladies' Guild gave me a gold necklace with a medallion having my initials inscribed on it, and the date inscribed on the back. This, too, became such a lovely remembrance. Mom and dad gave me a necklace and a monetary gift. Other monetary gifts were from our own kids, and the families of Erv & Sheila Siegler, Ray & Lois Cates, Norm & Judy Robers, Earl & Joan Johnson, Bill & Carol Wermeling, Bert & Lil Robers, Dale & Nancy Ketterhagen, Chuck & Pat Elverman, Jim & Tommy Haas, Don & Rose Vos, Dean & Jayne Luke, Larry & Sandy Smith, Ev & Marilyn Uhen, Lyle & Rosella Wilson, Stan & Dorothy Kerkman, Bill & Gen Uhen, Bernie & Mrs. Menheer, George & Dorothy Schlitz, Charlotte Schmalfeldt, Dolly Smith, and Gert Lois. Greetings were extended by Rich & Carol Kerkman, the Edward Gehring family, my niece Reggie, Denny & Judy Lois family, and the John Lois family.

It was edifying how people responded in gratitude for my work with their children as well as children outside the parish. What a sense of accomplishment when parents showed appreciation and how they felt about my work!

Maggie Oberhoffer, school board secretary, presented a program of "This Is Your Life". Thank heaven that she got the information from my mother, because she didn't know a lot of the in's and out's of my life. I certainly would not have wanted to endure any embarrassing moments or certain specific details of some of my past incidents.

Ray Cates, as school board president, presented me with an engraved plaque as a memoir of the occasion. As he expressed gratitude in behalf of all present, I saw a few tears of gratitude from some of the audience.

After the program was over, many people spoke to me and congratulated me personally but Phil and I had to hurry off as we were then on our way to Monroe. Our seventeen year old son was scheduled for surgery there the next morning and we had to have him at the hospital that afternoon.

Phil and I rarely had a dull moment in our younger lives, as there was always something that we had to do and it had to be done in a certain time frame. However this will always be a memorable day in my life having 25 years of teaching accomplished and many more to go in the future.

Chapter 26
Getting Into Amway Business

Back in 1988, I was riding with Dolly to go shopping one day and as we were talking away, she happened to mention something about the best vacuum cleaner on the market. I said to her, "Whose got a vacuum like that, I'd like to hear about it?"

She began to tell me that she had just bought one through Amway. Naturally I was curious and so we went on talking and talking and finally she told me that she and Jim had seen a plan for making money, lots of money.

Well, you can imagine that my ears perked up like a mule's and so I listened to more and more. After a while I became very excited and asked her how her dad and I could get involved in something like this, so she said that she would invite us over the next week because she and Jim were going to take another look at this money making plan.

I told Phil all about it when I got home stating that this was like music to my ears. Now we both were excited to hear and learn all the details of this money making plan.

Being that this meeting was held during the middle of the week, I saw no need to dress up so Phil and I went in clothes that we wore after we returned home from our jobs in the evening. which was fatigue clothes in which to relax. This is how we went to Jim and Dolly's. When we got over there and walked into the house, I was shocked to see that they were dressed up, Jim in a suit and Dolly in a dress. Dave and Lisa Hansen, who were giving the presentation, were also dressed like that, Dave in a suit and Lisa in a dress.

It was about this time that I wanted to crawl into the nearest crack or cranny in the woodwork that I could have found, that's how embarrassed I was! After apologizing to them, they continued on with the presentation. I still was embarrassed and wanted to crawl in a hole yet, but I listened attentively because we were direly interested in how to make extra money, any amount of extra money, even lots of extra money, if that could be true.

This was a networking marketing plan, and it

sounded like something that would be feasible and would work for a person if one just put a little effort into the whole idea. There were so many numbers tossed about and references made to PV's and BV's that although I was in a state of confusion, I could see where this could and would be very successful. But it was made very clear to us that night that we couldn't sign up the first time we saw the plan, because we had to fully understand the whole concept before signing up.

This was the type of ways and means to prosperity which could not be equaled by any other means of a business that could be done right in your own home. Following that might, we attended many open meetings which was by invitation only. Jim and Dolly invited us to be their guests to several open meetings. Each time we dressed up, Phil in a suit, and I in a dress. This was the Amway way because everyone had to look professional after getting into Amway as it is a business.

At the first open session that we attended, we were told to make a list of anyone we knew as friends, relatives, neighbors, or acquaintances. This list had to be done on the spur of the moment so everyone there wrote fast and furious. Then we were instructed to contact these people and set up meetings either in our own homes or at their respective houses. We went home and both were so excited that it was difficult to get to sleep, due to numbers rolling around in our heads.

But each time that we went to another open meeting, we would invite people to attend with us. The excitement grew more and more intense as the motivation compelled us to set up meetings and see what we could do.

This we did and we held many meetings at our house to start with. There were many people to conduct these meetings for us, and as time went on, Phil and I decided that we wanted to get into this Amway business.

It was a business that sold goods and services for many major companies and other businesses and these could be ordered through a catalog sales. The extent of the line of products and the many services was unbelievably endless.

The part about buying that we liked was to buy at wholesale price and in selling to charge retail price which netted a profit for a distributor.

In addition to this wholesale buying from yourself, added bonus money per month could be earned on a PV, point value at different percentage rates known as BV, bonus volume. This meant receiving a check from the Amway Corporation in Ada, Michigan, every month..

Time went on and we invited several people to our house to have this business introduced to them. Being a networking business, we had to show this plan to many people and sponsor them in so as to get a leg started. All during this time, we were using some of the Amway products which we liked a lot.

Finally we officially were accepted into Amway on November 19, 1988. Everyone was instructed to think of a name for their business, have business cards printed, and open a checking account just strictly for use in this business only.

We were so excited and couldn't wait to get rolling. Phil and I chose the name 'Philar Ventures', identifying us by part of his name and part of mine attached to it. Being that it was an enterprise, we wanted a name that seemed more original, so we chose ventures. It appeared that so many other people were already using the term enterprise.

Then we sat down and designed our business cards and had them printed at the Bulletin Office and Supply in Burlington. The owner of this company was in a leg which was part of our down line.

Our up line started with Dexter and Birdie Yaeger, who sponsored Jerry and Cherrie Meadows, and this went on down the line with the following sponsors: Greg and Jenny Wilson, Michael and Kathleen Cook, Gerry Ditzenberger, Mrs. Essman.

There is need to stop here before going on and relate to you that this lady, Mrs. Essman called John Rayniak to come to the meeting at her house and 'save' her from getting into a scam. So John attended the meeting at her house and could see the potential in this business, so he advised her that it was a going thing to get into, so she listened and got in it herself and consequently sponsored John and Mary Rayniak.

The Rayniaks sponsored on down the line including Mr. Tereski, Bob and Lois Hansen, Lisa and Dave

Hansen, Dolly and Jim Thuemmler who sponsored us into the network.

We continued on sponsoring many more people in order to build our business. We sponsored Deb and Al Vos, Barbie Vodak, David and Monica Roanhaus, Donna and Paul Dixon, Darlene Roanhaus, and Charles and Joanne Toelle. They in turn sponsored other people to form what was termed a 'leg'.

To anyone we sponsored, we become their up line and continued to help them progress with their business, so they too could become successful and earn this extra money.

Having a down line enhanced our own business, as the total number of point values that they earn are added to the up line person's point values. These added points contributes to the up line's monthly totals and automatically helps them into a higher bonus volume increasing the bonus money earned monthly.

The main idea is to help someone else get to where they'd like to be in the business and in turn that person is helping someone else. It is a phenomenal business set-up.

Goal setting is a major function of this business concept. Being Amway distributors has helped many people get their own lives on track through employing goals. I speak from experience as this goal setting has helped Phil and me in our own personal lives as well as in business.

One of the concepts that impressed me was the fact that this Amway business is moral, ethical, and legal. There are so many other network marketing systems out today, of which many have already folded, but Amway has been around for years and years and will be around for many years to come.

This corporation is so enormous and has thousands of goods and services to retail. It is a link to famous stores by means of catalog sales.

Every single product and/or service is guaranteed to satisfy each consumer. If a customer is not completely satisfied, the product may be returned, but through the years, we have had only one return which was a box of pop corn because the person claimed that it did not pop. The ironic part of it all is that out of twelve bags, he returned only one bag, but we gave him his full refund. Three weeks later he ordered the same box of micro-wave popcorn. To me this proves that he didn't have trouble with it popping but rather wanted to test if the guarantee was valid, and he found out it was. Every Thursday is order night through our sponsor, and the following Tuesday, the orders are in to be picked up from the sponsor. So we have weekly orders and therefore never run out of any products. Some of the products are so highly concentrated, that many last a long time, due to the necessary diluting process.

In order to progress after sponsoring and accomplishing one's set goals, the levels continue on from sponsor to Silver Producer, Gold Producer, Direct, Ruby, Sapphire, Emerald, Diamond. Beyond the Diamond are higher levels but I'm not sure of the progression of these levels. Double Diamond, Crown Diamond, Diamond Ambassadors and I can't keep up with the status. More and more Diamond levels had to be created as Up Lines progress with more and more sponsoring. These are the people with the six digit monthly incomes.

Phil and I acquired the status of Quick Silver when we first were in this business, which meant that we had the potential for becoming Silver Producers through building a down line within a given period of time. At many functions we were afforded special privileges and honors by reaching this status.

Phil and I attended so many functions out of state and entered many states where we had never been before. These larger group functions were called rallies, where the speakers were great, and learning more and more about Amway was so enlightening to help us progress in our own business.

People who had achieved the status of the Rubies, Sapphires, Emeralds, and Diamonds and beyond were all so down to earth and many times we were honored to have our photograph taken with them. These were the speakers at functions which was the greatest incentive anyone could have, because they told how they got to be where they are today.

This in itself was a motive for us to build a bigger business and endeavor to earn the status that they had.

There was always so much encouragement and support that it became difficult to fail with such wonderful backing of the up lines.

Now one can order direct from the corporation through means of the Internet, and orders then come directly to your home. There are strict rules for how one uses the Amway name. The copyright laws are very strict, and this keeps the Amway name from being used by any scam artists, keeping it legal and ethical.

Amway is a thriving business and the rewards of developing socially, learning business techniques, helping others succeed, and earning money are beyond compare. The main objective of it all is to use your own products, which means buy from yourself at a wholesale price. Building your business by giving others the same opportunity that was introduced to you is the key to success, but gaining customers also enhances the growth process of the business.

Today, Phil and I are still distributors, and we welcome that bonus check every month and that is satisfactory for us even though our down line has dwindled down, we're still reaping the benefits of being Amway Distributors.

Chapter 27
Times of Worry And Stress

Tension, worry, and stress have always been major factors in my life. First of all, I'm a perfectionist and consequently a worrier. Causes of my worry and stress have been from concern for my family and my job. When I say 'job', I mean from working outside my home for a wage to working from within my home.

In explaining this further, whenever a family member was ill or troubled with a problem, it automatically caused stress to me through worry. At times I worried about money matters, because family always came first, and sometimes it got to the point of: "Where is the next pair of shoes coming from? How will we ever get the fuel bill paid in the winter? Dear God, please don't let my husband or my kids get sick. Will we have enough money saved to pay the property taxes at the end of the year? How will I ever get the kids' book bills paid? Don't let other school kids have a bad influence on my children. Don't let anyone try to harm my children or hurt their feelings. When will I return back to teaching to help the family income? Can Phil endure holding down a regular job plus two moonlighting jobs just to keep our family going before it gets to him physically and mentally? How can I keep up this pace and still maintain my sanity? Will I ever get to a point in life at which time I won't have anything to worry me anymore?"

These were just a few of my worries that caused tension and stress, and believe me there were many more and as the children grew older, the worries and stress grew more intense also. But I always kept my faith and beliefs in God that He would help me in any situation, and to this day I know that He was always there for me or I never could have survived some of the situations that I was confronted with.

Much of the tension, worry and stress was due to raising a family. Illness can cause a tremendous amount of worry, and the outside forces of the world interacting with our children at times caused a great deal of tension, both of which caused us, as parents, excessive stress. Phil and I have both battled with stomach ulcers at various times of our lives due to this stress.

When Darlene was just a few months old, she caught a terrible cold, and I was scared that something would happen to her. In a frenzy, I called the young Dr. Jack Bennett out to our house and he gave her a shot and some oral medication. New mothers have a tendency to become very alarmed when something just isn't or doesn't seem to be normal.

Besides the normal winter sniffles and runny noses from colds, we were quite fortunate with not many doctor visits or bills. We did have a few instances in which we both suffered with stress with the more serious physical problems and illnesses.

When Danny was about fifteen months old, he had an umbilical hernia which had been caused through his inexplicable difficult birth. He had to have surgery to repair this.

On the day of surgery we took him into the hospital very early in the morning as his surgery was scheduled for later that morning. When he was in surgery we were two worried parents, as one never knows how a child can come out of an operation having been administered an anesthetic and how this little body will withstand the shock. All went well and we could take him home that evening. As we left the hospital that night, we were instructed to keep a close watch all night in case the incision would start bleeding. We were also instructed that he should not engage in any strenuous play and should stay very quiet.

Well that's quite an order for a fifteen month old boy, who had just recently learned to walk as was the case with Danny. This was a tremendously outrageous directive, as he was always so active and always into mischief. He was truly all boy; the active, curious, into all kinds of mischief, learn by doing, Danny.

Phil carried him into the house, put him down, and as I was taking off his snowsuit, he ran away from me and flopped on his belly onto the hassock. We were so frightened, immediately checked for bleeding, but everything turned out okay. We had Danny sleep with us that night but no major problems occurred. Phil and I both slept with one eye open that night, so consequently we didn't get much sleep either, following such a tense day of worry and anxiety.

At about age four, Danny's hearing was bad and the sound of his voice was very nasal, so the doctor advised having his tonsils and adenoids out. Another ordeal to go through with such an active kid! This surgery went equally as well as the first one had done. Fortunately in the same hospital room was a little girl who had her tonsils out the same day as Danny did. As Phil and I stayed with Danny all day, so this little girl's mom stayed with her. I knew her mother a little and her name was

Mary, who was a nurse. She took as much care of our child as she did her own. How nice this was for us, as we were not well informed about surgery for children. That evening Danny was allowed to return home, and this time everything went well and he was glad to relax and rest.

At one time during influenza season, Diane and Donna were so sick with flu and couldn't keep any liquids down and had diarrhea so bad that I thought they were almost at the point of dehydration. Needless to say I was pregnant with David and was ill with the same thing that the two little girls had. They cried and sobbed because their tummies hurt, so I had each one on my lap and tried to rock them in the rocking chair to quiet and pacify them. Finally Phil and I decided that they should both be seen by a doctor. I, being almost as sick as they were, was in no shape to help take the little girls in, so mom helped Phil take both of them to emergency at the hospital because it was a Sunday.

When Phil and mom were back home and drove in the driveway, I saw that one of the girls was missing, and I went into a frenzy. Diane had been administered a shot, but Donna was admitted into the hospital as she was near dehydration as I had expected. As sick as I was, I got dressed, mom stayed with the other kids, and Phil and I went right into the hospital to check on Donna's condition. It was so pathetic to see her in a crib with a netting over the top so she wouldn't fall out, but to me it was like being penned up. Phil took her out and held her in his arms and she clung to him so tight not wanting to let go of him. She was in the hospital for five days, and all the while when we would go to see her, she would not utter one word, even after our trying to talk with her. She was so full of fear, had no idea of what was going on as she was only eighteen months old. All that while, she spoke nothing and I became apprehensive as to whether the high fever had done something to her brain that she couldn't speak, such worry!

On the fifth day after she was released from the hospital, Donna never said one word all the way home. I held her on my lap, and when we stopped at the Wheatland store to get some 7-Up for her, the dog from across the street came running, and Donna said, "Doggie". Thank God, now I knew that there was nothing wrong with her speech, she had just been so frightened all along. After a few days of being home, she was back to normal.

During another flu season, six of the children, in addi-

307

tion to Phil and me, were all sick with the flu. We were too sick to function for ourselves, so Dolly and Danny at an elementary school age did a good job of caring for the eight ill people in our home. They made broth for us, jello for us, did the housework and even did the laundry. Mrs. Dorothy Schlitz, the Wheatland Store owner's wife made chicken soup and jello and brought it to our house. Those two young children carried on beautifully. It's amazing what two kids can do to carry on when the family is in a crisis.

Major causes of stress and worry were the minor ups and downs that occur when raising kids. I refer to when the children were older, the staying out late or not even returning home at all until the next day or even sometimes not returning after an entire weekend.

Many nights, I could be seen sitting in front of the dining room window looking at each car's lights coming down the road, hoping that one of them would be my child coming home. Often to no avail, so I continued to pray rosary after rosary petitioning the blessed Mary, mother of Jesus, to hear my prayers and intercede for me to God, to let my children get home safely. After all, she was a mother too. So many nights of my life were spent in prayer and hope with a watchful eye.

When David was a senior in high school, we had arranged for nose surgery for him at the Monroe Clinic that was noted for the best doctors comparable to Mayo Clinic. This surgery was to be done by an ear, nose, and throat specialist named Dr. Braedan. On a Sunday afternoon in spring of 1982, David and Phil and I went to Monroe to check David into St. Clair's hospital because he was to have surgery the next day early in the morning. Phil and I had already rented a motel room for our stay for a few days so we could be with David.

That evening while we were in the hospital room with David, the anesthetist came in to talk to us about the results of the blood testing that had been completed earlier in the afternoon. He had discovered through these tests that there was a factor that could cause David to be a high risk for surgery due to being put under by means of an anesthetic. He also stated that everything might proceed without any danger, but there was a high risk factor. In his explanations he stated that David was thought to have what is called maligna-hyperthermia. As he explained it in layman terms, it was the elevation of the body's temperature rising so high that it becomes fatal.

Wow! What distressing news this was. David, being a

minor, laid in that hospital bed with such fear expressed throughout his countenance, in anticipation as to what our decision would be. As we talked further with the anesthetist as to what could be done about this strange situation he did say that there was an antidote to counteract the anesthetic but the doctors would have to have it there as a standby. He also told us that the study about this condition was under extensive research at that present time as not much was known about this factor as yet.

Well, that pretty much made up our minds, why take a chance and ask for trouble when it may have been avoided. Then we asked David as to what he wanted to do because at this point we were not in favor of going on with this whole ordeal. He looked at us with a sigh of relief and verbally gave a response of no, indicating to us that he did not want to take this chance either.

Then we discussed the fact that he would continue to have the difficulties he had before with breathing, and all the problems that accompany a severe sinus condition. His rationale was that it is better to be alive than take the chance of death. We felt that the surgery could materialize at a later time after which more research had been done in regard to carrying this factor.

We were advised that at a later date, our entire family including Phil and me should go to Madison and all be tested, as this condition could be in the genes of either Phil or me. He advised that in the meantime if and when anyone needed surgery, that we make the anesthetist aware of this before any surgery began so the antidote could be ready for stand by.

Several years later David was injured on the job. As a carpenter by trade, a sheet of plywood slid away from the fellow that David was taking it from and the corner hit Dave in his eye and injured it severely. This required emergency surgery and now David's wife was as worried as we were. When we were notified, I left my job at school, Phil left his job at the highway department, we picked up Monica and we were off to the hospital in Barrington, Illinois.

When we got there, he had advised the staff about this maligna-hyperthermia condition and they were puzzled. They conferred with the clinic at Monroe where this discovery was made, and inquired what the antidote was. This hospital had what it took and proceeded with the surgery. What worrisome hours until he was in the recovery room. At least he was alive

309

even though he lost ninety percent of his vision in his eye, he was alive and that was worth a million.

Many other times in my life, much stress was caused by car accidents be it ever so minor or major. Many of these accidents I refer to were minor and involved some of our kids being in cars with their friends, but at the time I was prone to worry about later outcomes from their having whiplash. We always urged the kids not to sign off on anything with the insurance companies until they were reasonably sure that there would be no repercussions in the future.

Mostly our daughters were involved with someone else driving, but nothing really serious ever happened. In the middle of the night, it wasn't unusual for Phil and me to get a phone call from any one of the kids.

One night Danny had been side-swiped by a vehicle on highway 50 while turning off the bridge to highway W enroute home. One of the neighborhood resident owners called me. Phil was deer hunting, so Debbie got dressed and went with me. As we got there, Danny was like a wild man, because his car was ablaze and burning up with one of his friends in it. All he wanted to do was go by his car to try to save his friend, Jan. Deb and I had all we could do to hold him back. The fire department saw that it was a goner, so they let it burn completely, after releasing Jan from the car.

Then we had a problem of trying to convince Danny to go to the hospital and be checked out, but it was no use, he definitely was not going. His friend Jan went in the rescue squad to the hospital, but was released immediately. What a night of worry this was!

One early evening, Danny went to the local store using Debbie's Maverick Grabber to get some soda for mom. As he was leaving the parking lot, another car in which the driver wasn't paying attention slammed into the driver's side of the Maverick. Quite a bit of damage was done to Deb's vehicle, but this was another scene causing tension and worry.

One morning Danny was late for work at Regal China in Antioch and in his haste on this foggy morning he hit another car south of Highway C and the man in the other car had head injuries mostly in the face which included a broken jaw. He and Danny were both taken by rescue squad to the Kenosha Hospital.

In the meantime, someone in the nearby area called us by phone and told us that they had just heard on their scanner that Danny was in a bad car accident. Well, this was quite a blunt method of hearing that your son had just been in an accident, so we waited by the phone for an official call as to know where Danny was. Finally the call came and we were informed that he was in Kenosha Hospital.

Something was not working on our car, so we had to borrow my niece Reggie's car who lived two doors down from us, and Phil and I were on our way. When we arrived at the hospital , we were directed to the room where Danny was, there was another man in the room with him. As we were talking to Danny, the other man was being seen by a doctor, so the drape that divided the two beds was pulled shut.

Danny pulled us closer to him as he lay in bed and whispered to us that the man in the next bed was the one from the other car that he hit. Danny was in a frenzy and we couldn't calm him down. He insisted that he had to find his clothes and he was going home with us. We knew he couldn't because a nurse had already informed us that the doctor was keeping him over night for observation because his body had sustained a hard blow from the impact.

Later on after the doctors had gone from the room and the drape was again opened, the wife of the man in the next bed started ragging to us how some young kid had hit her husband's car, and it was an old car that he was restoring. She went on and on ranting and raving about this awful young kid who did this to her husband, and how no young kid should be able to even get a drivers' license. All this talk was really getting to Danny and also to us, after all what had been done was done and couldn't be undone. Danny was feeling such remorse for the man in the next bed as it was.

Phil and I could never understand why on earth they would put these same two men in the same room. It was a good thing that neither the other man nor his wife knew that Danny was that awful kid as she stated. Can you imagine the stress that was put on us during that time?

As we left that evening for home, we took Danny's clothes with us for we feared that he would leave the hospital during the night, and if we hadn't taken his clothes, he would have done just that. We told him that his clothes smelled like gas and was nauseating the staff, so we were instructed to take it home, and we really were, because the nurses feared his leaving also.

The next day we took him home from the hospital.

Then when all was said and done, our insurance company informed us that the other man did not even have a valid driver's license, nor a permit for that car to be on the road, so he was at fault too. We were glad when that whole case was settled.

The worst of accidents happened in 1983 in October, as a matter of fact, it was the eighth day of October. That was a terrible day in our lives as well as the days, weeks, and years to follow as a result of this accident. Donna was the victim of this one, and will feel the repercussions from it for the rest of her life.

She had been one of the kids who I always worried about coming home. This one night, I laid my head down on the pillow, and thought to myself, 'I can't stay up and keep that watchful eye tonight, as these pressures are getting to me. After all, she always does come home eventually'. So I went to bed. This was the one and only night that I didn't worry.

Now wouldn't you know, this is the one night that she doesn't come home. Very early the next morning Danny stopped in at our house and asked if Donna was home. Naturally I answered, "No". Well he went on to say that he saw her car smashed up against a tree near Silver Lake. Phil got out of bed and went with him looking for her. They searched and searched and found no one. They decided that the best move to make would be to go home and wait for an official word.

Debbie's husband Al came over to help Phil do something in the garage that day. Phil told Al about what they had found, but no Donna. In a short while a phone call came and I answered it. On the other end was a shaky, thin voice that said, "Mom, I'm at the County Garage, help me!" All I could reply was, "Stay there, daddy will be right over".

After I hung up the phone, I hurried out to the garage and Phil and Al were in the truck and out of here in a flash. When they got there, what they saw was not a pretty sight. Her face was so cut up, and she was still bleeding. Phil whisked her up, put her in the seat of the truck, Al jumped in the back of the truck and they were off to Westosha Medical Center in Silver Lake.

At this Medical Center, the staff worked over her until they got her vitals stable. Then they got her ready and Medix took her to Kenosha Memorial Hospital in Kenosha.

In the meantime, Phil rode in the ambulance with her, and Al brought the truck home. Phil had phoned me before leaving the Medical Center and told me to meet them at the hospital in the Emergency, as all did not look good. Al called Debbie and told her that he was going to drive me in to the hospital as he didn't think that I would be able to drive in all this stress. All the way to the hospital, neither Al nor I spoke a word to each other, as I think he was praying just as much as I was.

When we arrived there, the ambulance wasn't there as yet, so he and I waited anxiously for that ambulance to come in.

After they arrived, I got to talk to Phil but as yet had not seen Donna, as Doctor Cook was working over her stitching her badly cut up face. After a while, they allowed me to see her in emergency. I told her to hang in there, as we were all praying for her, and that she should fight hard. I know she heard me, because at that point she squeezed my hand as I was holding hers. I then knew that she had the incentive to fight for her life.

Phil and I told Al to go home and we would call someone that night to come in with a vehicle. What a stressful day! The Neurologist, Dr. G. ordered many scans of her brain, and much later he called us in for conference. At this time, he stressed that her life was in God's hands, and only a sheer miracle would pull her through. Her brain was bruised from the impact, and as he stated that if her brain didn't shift during the next forty-eight hours, there was a chance for her.

Phil and I went to the hospital chapel and spent the rest of the day there praying for her. In the evening we were allowed to see her in the Intensive Care Unit for only ten minutes at a time every hour. These were the ICU rules. After the ten minutes every hour that we spent with her, we could be found in the chapel. Neither of us could eat anything, and occasionally we'd stop in the cafeteria for a cup of coffee to keep going.

It was during these first few days that we were informed that her one side was partially paralyzed. I knew the extent of being paralyzed, and now this became an added worry. At this point, we wondered what else could they possibly tell us was wrong.

The rest of our family were just as concerned and worried as we were. All the while that Donna was in the hospital, I begged everyone to never let her have a mirror so she could see her face. She would have been bewildered at the sight of the hundreds of stitches in her face. After they were removed, it wasn't quite so frightening to look at, and today her face looks fine and she has a special knack for applying her make up.

After a long siege of battling on her part, she was to start therapy on her left hand and arm. Her left leg was affected but when all was said and done, it functions fairly well with no residual weaknesses. Her hand still gives her a problem at times.

Phil had just had back surgery shortly before this time and he was on medical leave from work, so he took her in to Kenosha every day for therapy. But due to the fact that she had no medical insurance, the neurologist dismissed her from any extended therapy which she really needed at that time. But this is the workings of the system.

To this day, we are happy that she came through this whole ordeal as well as she did, and we have her alive. She is now married and has a wonderful caring husband and two beautiful children, so we count our blessings every day, God has been good to her as well as us.

Phil and I have always come through so many times of worry and stress together. Our closeness helped us through many rough times, with the help of God.

As I have stated before, tension, worry, and stress can be caused due to a number of reasons. Throughout our lives, Phil and I have caused stress to our parents either by the simple little incidents of life or by the contracting of diseases. As children ourselves, we had the childhood diseases which are most common: chicken pox, mumps, and both kinds of measles, German and Red. Beyond diseases, as a child I had a broken arm at age five, and an appendectomy at age nine.

The year before I was married to Phil, I had a muscle transplant in my right lower leg in the area of the inside of my foot. This muscle was taken from a different part of my leg. Two years later, I had a tonsillectomy, but these were minor and didn't cause any major stress for me, just a bit of apprehension.

Through the years, I have come to realize that most causes of stress are either health or accident related, as we concluded in raising a family of eight children. Not only was stress caused by worrying about the children's health or accidents, but a spouse's health problems and surgeries of which Phil and I have both had more than the normal average person. When either of us had to undergo any prescribed tests or procedures, we were always confident that everything would always turn out favorable even though some times a surgery was required to correct a health condition. During these times the confidence was accompanied by a magnitude of reverent prayers and a zealous supply of anxieties.

I have always been so active in my earlier years that some of my joints, particularly my knees, seemed to be over worked, so in 1968 I started getting cortisone injections for arthritis in my knees. These treatments continued on for two years until the doctor told me that was the limit of shots that one could have without doing permanent damage. This helped for a few years after which time I had to endure the pain caused by this condition. Later the doctor started me on an anti-inflammatory drug, which at the time I knew wasn't good for the liver, but one does whatever it takes just to relieve pain to be able to function again.

In February of 1970, I had so many problems and when I went to see the doctor, he told me that I'd have to have a complete hysterectomy and very soon. I told him that the surgery would have to wait until summer when school was not in session, and Dr. McNeil replied, "By that time you won't have to have surgery, because you won't be here". Twelve days later, I had the surgery.

I was off work from teaching school for five weeks, and it was great getting a pay check because I had that much time accumulated for sick leave because prior to that time, I had not missed even one day of school all those years.

For the next seven years, Phil and I didn't have any major health problems and so it was a time where our worries about each other were alleviated, but these were the times that the children caused the worries for us. It was fortunate at the time that neither of us knew what the future held in store for us.

In 1976, Phil and I went to the famous Monroe Clinic and each had a complete physical. This proved to be worthwhile, because one of the doctors there discovered that Phil had a nasal obstruction which could and should be corrected through surgery. Arrangements were made and the next spring, Phil had the cartilage in his nose removed and a cavity was constructed to allow for sinus drainage to relieve pressure for him. The surgery was successful even though he was told before hand that his nose may collapse due to this kind of surgery. I guess Phil was lucky because his nose hasn't collapsed to this day.

For years Phil had always had such back pains caused from jumping off his construction equipment and this condition was getting progressively worse. He started having problems walking for a distance and also when standing in one position for even a short time. So two years after the nose surgery, he went back to Monroe and had vertebrae fused in his back. The bone for this fusion was taken from his hip bone. This surgery was successful to a certain extent, but I have always maintained once back pain, always back pain.

The next upcoming years started a whole new scenario for Phil. One evening in 1981, Phil had a difficult time breathing, had pressure in his chest, was dizzy to the extent that he couldn't envision how to walk without bumping into the furniture in the room, so consequently he started to panic. I called for David who was living with us, and he helped me get Phil into his vehicle and off to emergency we went. When we arrived, the nursing staff in ER called for Dr. Krismer. Dr. called this a TSA-transient skemic attack, so they admitted Phil that night for observation. The next day he was discharged but the doctor said he had a minor stroke. I was so saddened to hear this, and wondered what the future may bring.

Through the year he suffered from time to time having these TSA episodes. Once when Phil was home recuperating, Debbie called him daily to check on him while I was at work. It seemed that little Missy, Deb and Al's daughter, was in the bathroom in their apartment and opened a vanity drawer to put her tooth brush back, and not knowing that the drawer had to be shut before one could open the big door to get out of the bathroom, she assumed that she was locked in. Debbie at the other side of the door tried to explain to her what to do, but to no avail, Debbie would somehow have to crawl through the window and being in distress, she called her dad.

When she called Phil, he couldn't seem to understand which Debbie was calling. He thought it was Dell's wife Debbie from Burlington and just couldn't comprehend that it was Debbie from Lily Lake. Finally she got through to him and he went over there. He did help her get Missy out, but Debbie was very worried about him as he was so mixed up and confused.

While he was on his way home, Debbie called me at school and told me I'd better get home that dad was acting funny and was all mixed up. One of the other teachers at school told me she would take care of my kids in my classroom that I should just go due to this being an emergency.

I got home just immediately after Phil had gotten into the house and he was sitting on the couch looking so forlorn in the most pitiful state. I sat next to him, held his hand and said to him, "Honey, what's wrong, you're not feeling so well?"

He answered, "I'm so mixed up, I...I.. I don't know what's wrong, I can't talk right".

I said to him, "Perhaps you're having one of those attacks again. I'll take you into emergency".

His only apprehensive reply was, "Please don't let them admit me again." At this point I could make no promises, even though I wanted to assure him that he would not be admitted. So off to the hospital we went.

When we got there the staff called Dr. Krismer and this time he told me that Phil had another attack and this could continue on due to Arrhythmia which is an alteration in rhythm of the heartbeat either in time or force. This news was very distressing as our lives from this day on would mean living in suspense, not knowing when or where the next attack would be. But we would get through this like we had always done before, after all we had our bond of love to keep us going.

In 1983, I started having problems again, this time with my left hip which kept me in constant pain, so I started once again seeing an orthopedist, Dr. Hackbarth. He ordered a bone scan for me within the next two weeks, so his nurse set it up for June. At this visit he prescribed two options for me. The first was for pain relievers, and the second was for a cane.

When he handed me these prescription sheets to be filled, I laughed at him saying, "I'll have the pain relievers filled, but if you think I'm going to be fitted for a cane to walk with, forget it, I wouldn't be seen in public walking with a cane. Besides what would my students think of me walking with a stupid cane?"

Shaking his head, he looked at me and said, "Keep this prescription and when you change your mind, go to the hospital and they will fit you with a cane and instruct you how to walk with it". Again I laughed and said goodbye to him.

When I told Phil about this, he didn't think it was humorous at all, he thought it would help me take the strain off my hip and relieve some of the pain. Even now I was not yet convinced. After all, I did have my pride!

The excruciating pain continued on as usual. Just three days later, I told Phil I was going to the hospital to be fitted for that cane, who knows it might just be the answer to relieve some of the pain at last. As I look back now, I can't imagine how stubborn I was at that age.

After the bone scan, I had to see the doctor for results. When he saw me walk in with a cane, he was not at all surprised, and he asked me how long it took for me to make up my mind, and I told him. He said he thought it would take about three days for me because I had a determined disposition.

Then he said that I would have to have that hip replaced in the future but at this time he didn't recommend it because I was too young. Too young, for crying out loud, I was 59 years old! But he refused to do it yet, so I continued to live with the pain.

Many mornings before I'd go to school, I would have to psych myself up so I would not take out my pain on my students. After all, they couldn't help that I was in pain, so I was extremely cautious never to divulge to them that I had any kind of discomfort.

1983 was full of detriment for us. It was from that time on that our lives were like a calendar of chronological health tests, surgeries, stress, and worry. At times, I thought of all these episodes as something out of a fiction book, but it wasn't like that at all, it was real!

By now, one can determine why Phil and I have had so much worry and stress just worrying about each other. Many times we had to wonder what the outcomes would be, and at any given moment how our lives could drastically change.

At times, while Phil was recuperating in the Intensive Care Units, I could be found down on my knees scrubbing the kitchen floor with tears from my eyes streaming into the bucket of water. While these tears were flowing, my voice could be heard praying aloud to God in anticipation that my dearest husband would just live through it all. Phil had been confronted with so many dangers that held his life in jeopardy, but we always had God on our side.

In the last couple of years, his doctor keeps close watch on him and continues to order tests to keep abreast of Phil's heart and artery condition, and through consultations with his cardiologist.

Both Phil and I have gone through much apprehension in recent years, and as age marches on, the worries become more massive. When I found out I needed a hip reconstruction due to the glue loosening from the first one, I was so paranoid about undergoing another surgery. As I made my feelings known to Phil, I told him we needed to get our lives in order.

He agreed so we went to a lawyer and had new wills drawn up, made out a living will so our personal desire in regard to health status was made known to the doctor as well as the hospital, and appointed two of our children as personal representatives of our estate, Dolly and Danny. At this time we also got all our finances in order because I had always taken care of our bills and finances with Phil as my personal consultant. We always discussed everything about finances together.

Being that I was so certain that I was not coming out of this surgery, I made it a point of seeing all of our children and grandchildren before I went to the hospital.

I checked into the hospital at 7:00 A.M. on a Friday morning, February 21, 1997. I was happy to have this surgery, because if I did come through it, I knew that my pain would be lessened and it was worth that chance. I had misgivings about the whole situation, but I truly placed my trust in God's hands, if he wanted me, I was ready even though this would not have been my choice.

After the nursing staff did the preliminary prepping for

319

this surgery, I was ready to be taken to the holding room where all the so-called hook-ups were done. When Darlene and Phil each gave me that kiss before being wheeled away, I was so sure that these were my last and final kisses of my life.

Seven hours later, I had a vision of lots of people at my bedside, and through the blurred vision, I half recognized them. Was that really Phil or was I seeing a visage? I heard voices, familiar voices. Could it really be my daughters Darlene, Dolly, daughters-in-law Monica and Debbie? Or was I imagining this? Was I alive or did my family accompany me to the next life?' Off in slumber land I went, but much later, I found out that they really were there in person as I was trying to come out of the anesthetic. My beloved husband and dedicated family members!

Eight days later, I was told that I would be going to a rehab unit at Lakeland Hospital in Elkhorn, as this is where Dr. Dussault sent all his surgery patients. Then I was told that I would have to be accepted before they would take me. Accepted? Don't they just automatically take those patients who need it? Now I was puzzled, and started to worry.

What were the qualifications for acceptance? I was not just an ordinary person who needed the therapy following the surgery, but I had all my previous afflictions and handicaps due to the past polio to contend with. My only thoughts were that in no way would they accept a case such as mine, but again I prayed and prayed for my acceptance because I knew it was what I needed in spite of my being so homesick.

Later that day a young man by the name of Randi from the Sacred Heart Unit at Lakeland came to talk to me. He introduced himself to me explaining that he was the therapist in charge of acceptance. Now I really cringed, but he was so nice to me. His first question to me was, "What do you hope to gain from this therapy?" I answered, "I just want to get back to my normal style of life and do the things that are important to me, especially being there for my husband and to continue tutoring students. I just want to become as active as before the surgery in my own way in which I did before".

His next question was, "Are you willing to work hard for your goal?" I replied, "You bet I am, I have courage and stamina, and I can do it". He smiled at me, shook hands with me, and said goodbye.

Later towards evening, the nurse came into my room and told me that the Medix would be picking me up the next morning enroute to Sacred Heart. I had been accepted! Now everything was looking rosier and rosier for me and I was delighted.

The next morning, the nurses packed up my belongings and Dr. Dussault came in to see me. He told me how much I would like the therapy at Sacred Heart Rehab, and that it was the best place to get back to what I had been before the surgery. At this point, I didn't tell him how homesick I was, because I was too proud to admit this to anyone, but in my heart I missed the comforts of my own home and especially being with Phil and daughter Darlene, who lives with us.

In a short while, the attendants from Medix were there to pick me up. It was the gloomiest day outside and the fog was so heavy that the visibility was almost totally absent. Doctor Dussault told them, "You drive carefully now, I don't want this lady to be in any accident, so you had better get her out there safely." So the driver told the doctor that he planned to take the back roads.

Now it took two nurses and one of the attendants to slide me onto the cart. I was clothed in my slacks and knit shirt, but no jacket on. Now they strapped me down to the cart, like I had a ghost of a chance to get off it by myself, I couldn't even walk yet again. That was part of my therapy that I would be getting, was to learn to walk again.

Now we're off down the hall to the elevator, down to the parking garage. Now what bothered me most was the fact that all I could view were the ceilings wherever we went as I was flat on my back. Next they're sliding the cart with me on it into the Medix Ambulance. The driver got into the driver's seat, and the other attendant closed the door and sat right at my side. The driver is revving up the motor, and it sounds like a tractor taking off.

On the way, I felt every corner that he took, even at this slow speed. At the time I did realize that he was planning on taking the back roads to avoid a lot of traffic, but what I didn't know was what poor condition the back roads were in. At times with every bump in this road with all the potholes in, I felt like I was going to roll right off the cart even though I was strapped on.

The road was so bumpy and we hadn't gone very far, when I felt like barfing, so I asked the attendant if he had something that I could vomit in, so he got a container for me. This was honestly the worst ride of my life, and I felt like someone was punishing me.

321

After a long cumbersome ride we finally arrived. As we approached the next parking garage, we had to wait for the automatic door opener to decide to finally open. After this vehicle was parked, I was taken up to the fourth floor at Lakeland where the Sacred Heart Rehab Unit was located. A nurse was waiting for me and so I was taken to a newly remodeled room that was private, all to myself.

After being settled in, the Doctor, whose name was Dr. Origines, was accompanied by a nurse when they came into the room. All this while another nurse was with me, and helped me to lie down on the bed. The doctor wanted to evaluate my needs and status of my physical strength. As he approached the room, I was lying, stretched out on my back and his first words were, "Oh, my God, your right leg is so much shorter than your left". Well, I already knew that because I had been wearing a built up shoe for a long time.

Then he apologized to me for his statement, but he said he had no idea of this and it was rather shocking for him to discover it. Then he introduced himself to me and told me what to expect during my stay there. My first question to him was, "How long will I be here?" He answered with the reply that as long as it took for me to heal and to be able to motivate enough that he was confident that I could handle being home, I could go.

In the back of my mind were the thoughts that it sure sounded like my stay was going to be a lengthy duration, and I was homesick already, but I knew that I would work hard to show him what I could accomplish.

After this conversation, he checked my incision because I had been draining profusely up to now and still had a quite of bit of drainage and being the tenth day after surgery, was still bandaged. He commented on the extra long incision I had. As he was leaving, he told me that he would be in daily to check on me. I thanked him and he left for the day.

After he left, the nurse brought in a gait belt, which would be placed around my waist and would be used by the nurses to help pull me up and let me down easily, and to guide me whenever I was to move. Then she gave me a grabber, a hosiery holder, a plastic guide for the back of my shoe, an extra long shoe horn, and a wheel chair. Her next instructions were to have my family bring in clothing as each morning we would be getting dressed. She also told me at this point to send all my nightgowns home, because it was easier for them as well as for me to wear the hospital gowns, but I could keep my leather slippers. [I never got to wear my left slipper all the while I was there, because of the swelling in my leg and foot.] At this time I was informed that I would be dressing myself every day. Next on the agenda was to inform me that there was a huge chalk board right outside my door, and I would have to refer to it to find my scheduled therapy sessions. I was then told that I may not even try to get out of bed alone, only with the help of a nurse. Who did they think they were kidding, I couldn't have gotten out of that bed on my own if my life depended on it. I had difficulty getting in and out of bed even with their help. When they finally realized that I had been a polio victim, my orders became stricter than ever, but I obeyed all the rules that were given to me.

I had gotten there about 11:00 o'clock in the morning, so immediately after this orientation, a nurse helped me into a wheel chair and wheeled me to the dining area, as the other patients were already eating lunch. Randi kept telling me that I would have an eclair for dessert and didn't that sound good! But to me this was not a treat at all because I don't like eclairs. I ate my lunch as I was hungry and the food was pretty tasty.

After lunch the schedule included walking class in the hall for everyone, with the therapists helping each one. The first day I was wheeled out into the hall to watch because they did not have any walking device rigged up for me as yet. They would not allow me to walk with my own forearm crutches because they fail to give any back support, and every time I'd try to take a step, my body would lean over in a bent position. After that class was over, the therapists took me to the therapy room and discussed what they could put together for me.

Randi was very puzzled, but Karen came up with the idea of attaching arm platforms to a walker. It took them until the next day to put this thing together.

A day at the center started off with wake up call at 5:30 at which time I was helped out of bed, and while I was washing up and brushing my teeth, the nurse would make my bed, as once I was up I was not allowed to be on the bed at all during the day, only in the wheel chair.

Next was breakfast, followed by an occupational therapist teaching me how to dress myself, and each day I had to wait to get dressed for the day until a therapist was present. Through the use of the wheel chair, I always had my own clothes out of the drawers and waiting for them.

The therapist would help me remove my nightgown.

Next I'd use my grabber [an instrument that had claws that would close with the movement of the handle], to pick up my under pants from the floor by one leg opening at a time and then the other. The therapist would pull me up to stand and pull my under pants up for me. She'd help me sit back down, and then put my front hooking bra on. Using the grabber again, I used the same method to put on my slacks. Now I put on my long sleeved knit shirt.

Now remember we were restricted not to bend anything more than a 90 degree angle, and so I'd strip my sock over the stocking puller and pull on the strings and up came the sock and the puller opened up and slid out away from my leg. This was a very neat gadget.

Now the shoes were next and we were instructed to wear tie shoes for support. My shoes were pre-tied with elastic shoe laces in them attached by means of two holes in the tongue of the shoe. On the back of the shoe I was given another little gadget that was shaped to the back of the shoe with yarn string attached to it. Now with the aid of a fifteen inch shoe horn I'd place my foot into the shoe, slip out the shoe horn, and presto, my shoe was on. Then I had to take my grabber and catch the yarn of the apparatus on the back of the shoe and pull it off the shoe. Dressing was complete! At times it took me nearly one hour to dress myself, but I did it by myself in the presence of the therapist

Dolly would pick up my clothes and take them home and launder them, then send clean ones back to me when someone would come to visit me.

One day one of the lady therapists was ill, so a substitute filled in for her and he happened to be a young man. This embarrassed me a little and he could sense it, so when it came to my putting on my bra, he told me he would leave the room for a few minutes so I could have a little privacy. But at the same time he instructed me to push my call buzzer when I was finished, as he had to be there when I put on my socks and shoes, so as to avoid any danger for me, and at that same time he had to put my gait belt on for me.

Then after being dressed, I could brush my hair, put on make-up, and I had a few minutes to myself to say my morning prayers.

During the rest of the morning time, were two other classes that I was to attend. I was omitted from two other kitchen help classes because they could see that task was not even feasible for me to try as that would be impossible for me to do at this time, if ever again.

One class that I participated in was conducted as a group engaged in arm exercises. The other morning class was individual therapy.

After lunch was walking class for everyone in the hall, rotating people while the others rested, but each person was expected to walk three times daily. For me, on the second afternoon Karen and Randi had me try this monstrous contraption. As ugly as it looked, it did work for me. After they pulled me up from the wheel chair, one of the six therapists would help me slide my arms through this platform and tighten the strap so my arms couldn't slip out. Then I was instructed as how to step. Due to the restriction of weight that I was allowed to put on my left leg, I was told to lean onto the platforms and place my left leg ahead, then follow with the other leg.

This became very difficult to do because my body had a tendency to fall backwards, but I was not about to give in, I had to concentrate very hard. So each time I walked, I'd try to go a little beyond the last time until after two weeks of being there, I could maneuver about fifteen feet before I had to rest. But believe me, I was absolutely pooped by the end of each try. I did three times of this walking with rests in between, having another therapist follow behind me with the wheel chair.

After walking class was individual therapy class a second time of the day. All of these activities were very strenuous, but I made up my mind that I would do it no matter what.

Even though visiting hours were restricted until after 4:00 o'clock, there were times when Phil would come earlier and I was still in this walking class. No one yelled about that, as a matter of fact, after a few times, they encouraged him to come as he could follow me up with the chair. This freed up one of them to help another patient during that time.

I had the best care ever at this facility, and being that I required extra care due to my affliction, each and every one of them was always there for me.

Every two to three days they would take each patient, one at a time, into the shower using a special kind of wheel chair that was rolled right into the specially built stall. Several times the nurses would get quite wet, but they never minded. They were so efficient about scrubbing us and shampooing our hair. Following the shower, the nurse would wrap a blanket around the patient and after returning back to the room, another nurse would help us get ready for bed as the showering was done at night after visiting hours because the day was so taken up with therapy.

But believe it or not, every night the nurses would pop corn for me and bring it in to me, so Phil would buy pop corn for all the patients on the floor and the nurses would pop it and distribute it to everyone. [Phil and I always had a night time snack at home so I was used to this.] They would also bring me a small can of diet soda, because it was there that it was determined that I was diabetic, but I could have the diet pop.

During my stay there, I was weighed three times. Now this was a hoot! The scale was like a stretcher, and the nurses would help me by sliding me over onto this scale. After being weighed, it was back again and many times this movement was very painful in the hip and back areas, but we were told we had to be weighed.

I was so astonished at the first time I was weighed, and I told the young man who weighed me that his scale was not even close to being correct, because it was fifteen pounds more than my normal weight. But it was good to hear that the metal prosthesis can weigh between ten and fifteen pounds, so this eased my mind.

After the first seven days they had an evaluation on me and they invited me to attend if I cared to. You better believe I went, too. This included an R.N., a physical therapist, an occupational therapist, a counselor, a social worker, and the doctor. Each one would report my progress from their findings in their own respective fields. Then all would make a recommendation of how each one felt my progress was going and how long each one felt that from their standpoint I would have to be there. Then they in turn would ask me what I thought of my progress. It was so interesting and it was so professionally done, that it made one feel like someone really did care about my own well being.

It was rather interesting to note that the nurse had reported that she was concerned that I had trouble having a bowel movement. I told them that If I could have a McDonald Big Mac, my problem would be solved, because they always had that effect on me every time I ate one. So they told me to have Phil bring one in to me. The next day Phil brought one, I ate it, and as I said before it solved my problem. The nurses howled and howled over that one!

On the eleventh day out there Dr. Origines with the

assistance of Nurse Patricia took out my 47 clamps that held my incision together. I thought they would never complete this task as it took so long and I was very uncomfortable having another nurse hold me so I could be on my side. But now I didn't have to have any bandages on any longer.

On the twelfth day, two therapists brought me to my home and they looked over our entire house and had me show them how I would be doing everything in my home. This included transferring from the wheel chair to the upholstered lift chair I had, transferring into and out of my adjustamatic bed, how to transfer to the toilet stool which had an elevated riser on it, how I could back into the shower to sit on my shower stool with someone holding me by the gait belt, and how I could get at and away from the computer. I passed the test but furniture had to be positioned differently in our house so I could manage to get through with the wheel chair.

Then they wanted to know what I would do for meals, and I told them I already had that covered, as my daughters and daughter-in-law volunteered to send meals directly to our house. They were impressed how I had all the problems worked out.

On the thirteenth day, the second evaluation was done and again I was invited. This sounded much better than the first time because all reports were good and I was told that I could go home the next day, but I should call my family and have them buy a diabetic glucose meter and bring it in that evening so they could train me how to use it. What music to my ears! I was going home after two weeks of being in the rehab hospital. I had been away from home for a total of 23 days, and I missed home.

Before I left, Dr. Dussault came in to see me to give me all the do's and don'ts, reminding me not to even think of bending, and not to leave my home once I got there, until he saw me in his office five weeks later. Until he gave me the good word, I was not to leave my home under any circumstances. What a restriction! But anyway I was going home, so this made me happy.

Al, Debbie, and Phil came to get me on a Saturday morning, and after much ado saying goodbye to the other patients, thanking everyone for taking such good care of me, a nurse wheeled me out of the hospital. Getting in and out of a vehicle was so stressful as it was difficult to get down into the car, and later they helped pull me out of the car. Boy, was I glad to be home!

That evening, Debbie and Al brought us each a dinner from the Wheatland Center School's spaghetti supper. What a treat to eat at my own table again!

At home I had nursing care in my home for several weeks. Physical therapy started a few days after being home. I knew the therapist from eleven years ago when I had this hip done the first time. His name was Dick Duerr and he was excellent in his field, he knew what he was doing and he helped me gain strength readily. I will be forever indebted to him for his help. He came to my home for nearly six months, three days a week and whenever I wanted to try to do more and I'd ask him, he would help me.

As time went on during these past two years, the Post-Polio Syndrome is slowly taking over and dictating my life. I still keep as active as possible, and accept each day as one day at a time, and my life goes on.

That was the last of the major worries for Phil and me, but now we each help each other and care for each other. We both keep our medical visits as our doctors prescribe, take our prescribed medications, take vitamins, eat well balanced meals, endeavor to exercise each in our own way, and enjoy life together. Hopefully our stress and worries will be lessened.

Chapter 29
Comes The Time For Retirement

When I was younger, I never even thought of the time that would come for retirement. I was so caught up in raising kids, in teaching, and going on with the activities of daily life, that I guess I never realized that there would be a time of my life to kick back and take life a little easier.

Phil and I had always worked hard, sacrificed for our family, and just went on from day to day taking life in its stride. Phil had some major health problems, was in and out of hospitals involving one heart test after the other, so he decided that he would retire at age sixty-two. He had worked for the Kenosha County Highway Department for twenty-nine years and the years he had served in the military service counted toward his total years as a municipal employee.

When he counted the years he worked and the month he had started, at one point he thought he would have to work perhaps an extra year. This made a difference as to whether I signed another contract or not.

As it turned out, I had really wanted to retire from teaching a few years sooner than I did. It wasn't the teaching that I wanted to get away from, as I loved every minute of my teaching. It was the young principal and the rest of the staff who had treated me very shabbily for the past three years that I wanted to get away from.

It was difficult for me to work under such a person who didn't know beans from bananas about administration, and I could see that the school in general was slipping downhill. This made me very concerned about the future of St. Alphonsus School, as it was a place of learning in which the children had received quality education until she took over.

Then every day after school, the other teachers were all in her classroom, [as she was a teaching principal], cracking jokes, giggling, talking about the students and some of the parish families, and a lot more. I knew they were discussing me because I was always so straight laced and serious about my work. So while they were joking and talking about me, I would sit in my classroom and check papers. This way I didn't have to take any work home. But the sad part of it was that they didn't take any work home either. This was the kind of teaching that was going on in the primary and intermediate grades.

So in 1989 after teaching twenty-five years at St.

Alphonsus, I decided to retire so I turned in my notification that I was retiring. She was one happy person that I was leaving, however at the same time she had turned in her resignation as principal but she wanted to remain on for just the position of teacher. Fine, at least maybe she realized that she wasn't doing a good job in administration, besides she was expecting a baby. Now the school had a chance to pick up and again offer the quality education as in prior years.

I was still concerned about the school, knowing what a mess the next administrator was getting in to. But this no longer was my concern as I was going to retire in June.

In the meantime, two of the school board members, Pat Vos and Dave Richter came over to my house one evening to talk to me. Before they came, my thoughts were that they were going to ask me to sit in on interviews for the next administrator. Wrong!

They wanted me to take the principal's job as a separate job of just being principal, no teaching involved. Well, what a request! We discussed the job and how involved it would be just to straighten the whole situation out again. Pat even volunteered to be my school secretary without any wages.

I told them I really wasn't interested, but they simply would not take no for an answer. So in empathy towards the whole situation, I gave in and accepted it only as a part time job, half days only, for just one year as I wanted to retire. They offered me a wage that was typical for being a parochial school, almost one-fifth of what other elementary school principals were making at the time, so I signed the contract then and there.

I worked all summer long in that office. First of all, it needed cleaning badly, as my predecessor smoked and the whole office was filmy on the walls, the windows, on the mess of papers and books that she had piled up on the floor in every corner of that room. The class that had just graduated, came there many days and helped me during the first few weeks of the summer vacation. The girls washed walls and windows. The boys kept making trips to the dumpster as fast as I could sort out all the old books and papers plus all the other accumulated rubbish that was strewn all over. The kids helped me clean the storage room, but when we were done everything looked really good. I would be forever indebted to that class who stuck with me until the project was completed.

I went out and bought fabric and made window length drapes with a valance over the tops. Now my office was looking like an office, it was neat and it was clean and had a touch of home with everything being so neat and orderly. I even had some plants in my office.

The next project was the making of handbooks. Other schools had long had them and when I was principal for the first time from 1873-1981, I had made up a beautiful handbook for teachers, and through the years, there were no handbooks to be found, someone had destroyed them. Now I really had my work cut out for me. I intended to made handbooks for teachers, one for parents, one for school boards, and one for safety patrol.

I would write up the sheets as I wanted them to appear, and my daughter-in-law, Debbie Lee, did all the typing. Then she and I assembled them and they were ready to be distributed.

Now being that this was supposed to be my first year of retirement, but didn't work out that way, I was back in full force working harder than ever because I had my work cut out for me.

Being that Phil retired in July of 1989, meant that he would be home alone for the school year of 1989-1990, and I'd be working. What a bummer! But I had previously signed a contract and I am not one to break it; once I agree to something I do not go back on my word.

As I sat in my office working, I used to dream about being home all the time, keeping a tidy house, sewing for the children and grandchildren as well as for myself, baking all kinds of goodies, and helping the kids out whenever I could.

Then I would think about taking long trips with Phil, working our Amway business to succeed as we had always planned, visiting and entertaining all our friends, sleeping in every morning until I wanted to rise and shine, and eating out whenever we felt like it. Dreams can be so wonderful if the realities can only materialize.

Our kids planned a surprise retirement party for Phil, and Jim and Dolly had the outdoor party at their house. It was a wonderful party. There were friends, family, other relatives, his immediate boss, and our Amway business associates. Needless to say, he was very surprised after we had gone out to eat with Diane and Rick and then came home to a whole yard full of people.

The kids did such a good job of planning and preparing for the party, but then our kids were always there for us, and Phil was most grateful. As a matter of fact, Phil has always been a most appreciative person for even the smallest of kind deeds.

Phil's days of retirement started off by wanting to stay in bed and rest every morning until he felt like getting up. It was a treat for him to be able to do this at last, because all through the years he had worked hard, sometimes working a regular job and moonlighting two other jobs to keep our big family going. It was heavenly for him having the thought of just ignoring the alarm clock every morning.

When I'd come home in the afternoon, he was on the couch watching TV, hadn't made anything for himself to eat, and so he turned into a couch potato. This was not good, but there wasn't much that he could do as his hands were left without any feeling due to prior strokes. He couldn't take up a hobby, and fishing and hunting were quite seasonal, so this left him with nothing to do.

Now this touched my heart, and then more than ever, I had wished that I would have said no to that job, but I guess there's a part of my heart that will be in that school until my dying day. Oh well, it was only for one year anyway.

Then we couldn't do any entertaining or visiting or going out at night as my job required that I attend many school meetings and functions. Now I could see how this was interfering in our lives and I didn't like what it was doing to us, but I endured for the year, and Phil endured right along with me.

When contract time came around in February, the school board and Father Massey begged me to stay on for just one more year. Father Massey even talked about putting in a bathroom upstairs if I would stay, but I knew how this could end up, and I wanted out before I got caught up in a trap. I gave a definite no and explained that I wanted to go on with my life with my husband. So I retired at age sixty-three.

After interviewing several candidates, Father Massey and I did find them a good replacement for the job, and trained this man for several sessions throughout April and May. I was confident that the school would continue to run smoothly.

Replacement Brian Jones was well informed and well trained and showed a great deal of interest in our school. He had been a Headmaster of a school in Great Britain, as a principal's title was there. He was married and had a son of his own and loved kids Brian was also a very intelligent man with good common sense and a high set of values and standards.

Now with my leaving, the Parish Council planned a retirement party for me. They put a lot of work into this, and the party was a smashing success. Donna Raetzke, whom I have mentioned before, was chairman of the planning.

The day of the celebration was on the feast of Pentecost, so it was started off with a very special Mass in church. During the liturgy, many gifts were presented to me at offertory time. These were given to me by representatives of the student body. Such touching moments!

The homilist for the liturgy was a St. Alphonsus classmate of mine who now was a priest, Father Don Elverman. He was a stitch! He revealed many of the happenings of grade school days, but divulged some of the mischievous things that I had done as a child. This made some of the present student body sit up and take notice and I just know what was going through their minds, 'Mrs. Roanhaus did all those things as a kid, and she was so very strict with us'. But Don told it all!

After church the dinner followed by a reception was held at Marino's Country Aire. So many people were in attendance, that it gave me a feeling of joy, as this showed me that there was gratification on the parts of some people anyway. I know one can't please everyone, but my diligent work must have pleased the majority.

I was presented with a plaque which was to be placed in the school library in my honor as I was the one who started the central library in the school. After this I was presented with another plaque thanking for my years of service. This one was for me to put up in my home.

In the next part of the program, several men of the parish gave tributes to me concerning my major accomplishments in life and in the working world. They were: Dave Richter, president of the school board; Don Vos, trustee; Bill Dale, president of the booster club. After Bill was done speaking, he presented me with a check for one thousand dollars. This was meant for Phil and me to use toward our first trip after retirement, a trip to Las Vegas. I was overwhelmed at this, it's the first real consideration that was ever afforded me, and I was appreciative beyond words.

Then it was my turn to speak, and that I was good at because I always had my vocal cords well exercised. It was difficult for me as this was the goodbye to my teaching career forever, as I thought at the time. It was a time of verbally extending my gratitude to all those good people of the parish who had supported me during all those years. Many families stand out in my mind and they and their children will always hold a special place in my heart. Pat Vos was special because she did the secretarial work for me without a salary.

Many pictures were taken, people were forming a line to congratulate and thank me. My whole family was there except David and Monica, but she had just had a baby in May so it was excusable. This had become a memorable day of my life. At last I've retired from working outside the home and the biggest treat of all would be to sleep in every morning and get up when I felt like it. This meant that I could plan my days as I desired and not have to feel obligated to a job or anyone else except to my dear husband, Phil.

Now I'd be able to keep a tidy house, do all that baking I had planned on before, and Phil and I would be able to take off and go places and do the things that we were deprived of before.

So our first issue on our agenda was planning our trip to Las Vegas. We had discussed long before this time that when we both were retired, the first trip would be to Vegas. Now the time has finally arrived. Dell and his wife Debbie were going to accompany us as they had never been their before, and we needed someone to be with us to help me get around.

Phil and I had been there once before in the mid 80's with Ralph and his wife Dorothy.

We made reservations at Circus, Circus located on almost one end of the strip. We were familiar with this place because that was where we stayed when we went before.

We finally realized that retirement for us meant that we had become busier and busier as time went on. As we look back today, we often remark that it probably was less confusing to go to a job every day instead of our life today with planning each day of our retired life. The good part of it is that we only have to account to each other and not anyone else, and that's what makes it all so enjoyable.

We've had our ups and downs with numerous bouts of illness but we always, with God's help, come through the bad days. We feel that if we can just awaken every morning, then we have to thank God for another day of life that he has granted to us. Yes, in all reality, retirement is great beyond all expectations, and we accept the fact that we are growing older by the day, but we are together, still in love, and these are God's blessings that count.

Arlene's Retirement Party in June 1990
Back L-R: Darlene, Debbie, Diane, Dell, Dolly, Danny, Donna
Seater : Phil holding granddaughter Kelly, and Arlene

Secretary Pat Vos and Arlene

Phil's Retirement party, July 1988
Phil talks to some of the ladies present

Phil is greeted by Amway Associates, Greg and Jenny Wilson

Chapter 30
But My Teaching Continues

Now that I was officially retired from working outside the home, I knew that the domestic chores still would continue on as they had before. I eagerly looked forward to entertaining our friends in our home as we liked to play cards and do the things we hadn't been able to take the time for due to our jobs.

Following June 20, the last day of working in my office and officially the day my retirement started, phone calls started coming in to my house inquiring if I would consider private tutoring. Gosh, I hadn't even thought of how I would utilize my spare time as yet. I was just getting used to the idea of sleeping in and not having to get up for a job every morning and I liked that part of retirement already. Beyond that, I had no immediate future plans.

Then I started to seriously anticipate which directions I wanted to consider before carefully making a final decision about anything. Being that I had done private tutoring all throughout my teaching career during summer months, this was not anything out in left field nor was it something that was unfamiliar to me. The question was: 'Did I want to tie up my time devoting more time and energy to children now that I am retired?'

I thought and thought about it after much pondering, and the more consideration I gave to the idea, I began to perceive this as my career continuing on, but I still hadn't definitely made up my mind. After having taught for thirty-four years, it did seem like there would be a void if I didn't work with children, and already I knew that I would miss teaching in a short while.

In the meantime, one day our parish priest, Father Massey, approached me and asked if I would be interested in teaching adult convert religion, knowing that I had already taught one lady, and prepared two young girls for Confirmation all in February of 1990. Now this really interested me, providing I could continue to have the people come to my house for training, as the other three that I had already prepared had come to my house on Saturdays and in evenings. It was that summer I had just started walking with the aid of forearm crutches and it was difficult for me to ambulate. Father Massey assured me that would be just fine to hold the classes in my home, so I became the R.C.I.A. Director for our parish

Now one of my first tasks following immediate retirement was to research and compile a course of study in religion. This took me two years to complete this course of instruction. It required this much time because every bit of information is authentic and had to be proven by several sources before I would use it. As a matter of fact when I started teaching my first client in 1990, I was still in the process of organizing unit to unit just to keep ahead of the next unit that I would teach, but it worked out so beautifully as this gave me a sense of direction as how to finalize the organization of these materials into units of sequence.

Joanne Ross, Religious Education Director asked me to teach children and younger adults in preparation of some of the sacraments, because they did not have the proper training prior to receiving the sacraments that they hadn't received as yet. So she let me select which text I wanted to use and she ordered them for me out of the C.C.D. fund. Joanne and I work very closely together in the Religious sector of our parish.

Shortly after I committed myself to teach religion, Mrs. Vos, Mark's mom called me on the phone and asked if she could come over to see me as she needed to talk to me. She is one of the dearest ladies in our community who is a professional nurse. She asked if I would take Mark for tutoring as they had just found out that he was dyslexic and needed the extra help in his school work.

Mark was in third grade at the time, and I became very interested in this idea. I had never in all my college days or even in any extra courses that I had taken through the years to keep up with all the latest trends in education, had any training in this type of disability. I felt as though this would be a challenge so I accepted the offer.

Now I was back into the field of teaching once again, making lesson plans and worksheets as I had done previously, except this would be a one-on-one teaching situation and I liked the idea. I always had enjoyed all the tutor work that I had done previously throughout my whole teaching career.

Then I went to see Miss Julie Muellenbach, whom I had worked with previously and who was Mark's third grade teacher. I explained the situation to her that I would be giving him the extra help that he needed, and that I wanted to work closely with her to fulfill his needs, and she was very cooperative. I knew that Julie was a good teacher and that she would have Mark's best interest at heart because she was very dedicated to children's learning. Mark's mom also went to meet with Miss Muellenbach, so it would then be feasible for Mark to stay in the private school because all his friends were there and change would be very detrimental to Mark, academically and socially.

Ron and Terrie had Mark tested by psychologists the very best doctors in the field, to determine how to help Mark in his learning situation. I had gone over the doctor's reports over and over again so I could explore the best means of helping Mark, so now the arrangements were made. Mark would get off the bus every day after school at my house, and we'd work for one hour. This arrangement worked well, so when he'd get off the bus, I'd have a snack ready for Mark, as kids are hungry right after school. After the time was up, one of Mark's parents would come over to pick him up.

On Saturdays Mark would attend Cardinal Stritch College in Milwaukee where he was taught special learning strategies by a specialist in her field of teaching dyslexics. Miss Schulteis was an excellent resource for me as she gave me many hints and suggestions for the best means of helping Mark, so we kept in touch with each other. In conferring with Dr. Newby, I gained much knowkedge from him as to the best means of dealing with Mark's learning disability to help Mark benefit to the greatest extent in the learning process. This really helped me so I could help Mark.

In 1992, I taught a little girl for religion on Saturday afternoons for an hour, followed by a little boy who came for the next hour after she left. Then on one evening a week, I taught religion to a man. The adult course was a seven week course, while the children's was a fourteen week course. I suddenly had become busy, but I enjoyed it.

It was now that word got out that I was doing academic tutoring, and wasn't it some of the same people who called right after I retired and I told them I'd think about it. Well now, I committed myself, so I was teaching four afternoons a week right after Mark left at 4:15. My schedule was getting tighter and tighter and I had to refuse many people, so when summer came, most of my day was taken up from 8:00 until 2:30. So you can guess how many kids I was teaching. The bulk of my teaching was for reading and phonics, but a few in Math. I ordered textbooks from the companies that I had dealt with previously when I was principal.

In this way, I had the best eduactional materials to work with, and I furnished all the materials for the students, and the parents paid me $5 an hour.

I wasn't making money but I was definitely helping kids learn the skills that they were lacking in. In later years I charged $10 an hour, but still wasn't making money like the tutors in the cities were. But I still was not in it for the money. I had self satisfaction in witnessing the progress of the children and how their self-esteem was gradually building up.

One of my favorites was Megan Lois, whom I taught for four summers. Even now she keeps me informed as to how she is doing in school, and she has become very special to me.

Two other children who were sister and brother were Matt and Molly Mowery. These two children worked so hard and it was a joy teaching them. Molly was the little girl who was shown on a TV airing with me, while I was working with her.

Jeffrey Cope was another child whom I worked with, and he became a cherished student of mine also.

As a matter of fact, I became so attached to each of the students I tutored. Each child was a unique individual and each one was willing to work for me in their own way. I can honestly say that I have enjoyed all of the kids whom I have tutored.

In 1993, I taught a class of two ladies in Religion one evening, and a class of six on another night of the week. On April 11, these eight plus the man previously taught were all confirmed in a class together by Father Robert Massey. At this confirmation ceremony, I began to realize the goodness of the righteous work I really was doing, and at that point I suddenly perceived the merits of my teaching. Now more than ever before, I knew that this was God's plan of action for me, and thanks to Father Massey for helping me to find it.

Father Massey left the parish in June of 1993 and Father Thomas Biersack became our pastor. During that year there didn't seem to be any catechumens. I wondered about that and so I approached Father Tom and showed him my course of study that I used during the catechumenate period, and told him that I had been teaching for the parish. I asked if he wished for me to continue and he said yes, I should. So the religious training continued again. Following that time when ever someone needed the Religion course, Father Tom directed them to me.

As time went on during the years of 1994 through 1996, I had taught twenty adults, four elementary school children, and two teenagers. The year of 1996 brought about a new experience for me as I prepared 2 seven years olds, a four year old and a three year old for receiving the sacrament of Baptism. More and more self-satisfaction was being granted to me now, and I knew God's blessings were accumulating for me.

In February of 1997, I had major surgery and was told by my orthopedist that I could not do any tutoring until school started again in the fall of 1997. He didn't say that I could not teach religion, I doubt that he even knew that I did that kind of teaching, and I wasn't about to tell him. Father sent more candidates to me. but he told them that he wasn't sure if I could start teaching then or if they would have to wait a while. I taught three adults and two children during that year.

Throughout the summer of 1998, I had a whole family come for religious training. First I taught two of the children, then the mother for the whole course of religion as they all needed Baptism, and last was the little six year old who I prepared for Baptism. The children who were in third and fifth grades were enrolling in the Catholic School as they were disgusted with the public school where they were attending.

I recently completed teaching four adults and two children as of the end of May of 1999. I will start two adults next week and two children next week and have two teenagers waiting until I can work them in.

At the end of the school year of 1998, I discontinued tutoring young students academically. My age is starting to get to me, and my patience is wearing a little thin so I want to quit on that note. I have an excellent status for tutoring students, and I want to end it that way.

I still have my Mark as he is going to be a senior in High School in the fall of '99. When he started coming to me in third grade, he used to joke about when the day would come that he could drive himself to and from my house. It wasn't that many years after, that he could do just that, as the years flew by so quickly.

Mark will go to college and major in the fine arts and music. His older brothers are also musically talented. Chris, the oldest boy in the family, has his own band called Fresh Water Collins. Brian plays in this same band, and they are sensational and well known. Music is a natural talent for all three of these boys.

Through the years I have tutored starting with the level of Kindergartner through High School all through the school year

341

and during summers. I've tutored children from the following schools: Wheatland Center, St. Alphonsus, Riverview, Salem, Lakewood, Whittier, Westosha Central High, Burlington High, and Catholic Central High.

Each time that I agreed to taking a student, I would contact their teachers in the school system where they attended, and along with their respective teachers would assess the child's needs so I could make the time of teaching really help the students.

My summers got so hectic with kids that I was starting to teach afternoons in addition to the whole mornings. I guess one would call that only semi-retired, but I still enjoyed teaching.

I also helped college students with some of their studies in the areas of whatever subject they needed help with, but mainly working with them in studying for exams.

I helped an adult lady study and prepare for her state board exam in pharmacy. She had a problem figuring out the math and proportions and equivalents, using the metric system in calculating for prescriptions according to age and size. I learned a lot right along with her, and it was fun, she passed her exam, and this was as rewarding for me as well as for her.

I have made many new friends by having taught religion to them, and I have acquired lasting friendships. Nancy Andrews, a very special lady, became a close friend, as we both like to cook and bake and she endowed me with many extraordinary recipes. We share a common bond with our spiritual interests in prayers and religious beliefs.

I'm still presently engaged in teaching Religion. My lasting memories of my teaching career can never be taken from me, they are the wondrous memories stored in my heart forever. But the greatest rewards are God's blessings.

Chapter 31
Awards and Recognitions

In my childhood there were no opportunities for any awards and recognitions as one just did whatever a kid was expected to do and accepted that as face value. I was just happy to get good grades on my report cards and the fact that I knew that I always did the best I could was recognition enough for me. I had always set extremely high standards and goals for myself, and I performed with excellence in mind. I have always been a perfectionist and somewhat of a procrastinator, but it seemed that I always performed the best under pressure to the degree of the best success. Many times this in itself caused me much stress and anxiety, but I always enjoyed doing what ever the task, no matter the cost.

In school, the first recognition I received was in the year of 1940 as I graduated from elementary school. It was a certificate for excellence in handwriting using the old time Palmer method of writing. I was thrilled beyond words to receive this award.

I have won many honors, gold medals, pins, and certificates during my 4-H club membership, and each one has special meaning to me. In 1995, I was awarded the 4-H Club Alumni Award. This is an award that is given at a county level through the means of having been first nominated by someone who knows of your work in the community, then selected by a county committee. I feel very honored to have received this award in the form of a plaque.

While I was back in high school I received many certificates and awards by participating in contests in State of Wisconsin High School Forensics meets and in acting in Thespian Groups. All of this I really enjoyed, as at one point in my life I thought about pursuing a teaching career in acting and wanted to attend Pasadena Playhouse in California for training. This whole idea got scrapped because I was more interested in teaching young children the academics, highly interested in marriage and raising a family.

At teachers' college the extent of awards were mostly in conjunction with teaching methods certificates, athletic awards, emblems, and letters. With the monetary scholarship I was granted from Business and Professional Women's Foundation to further my college education I received a beautiful certificate.

Probably one of the best of recognitions was the congratulatory letter from the dean of the college of education, Lewis W. Stoneking, at University of Wisconsin - Whitewater. It was a letter of commendation for achieving first honors, stating that this was the highest grade category for student recognition. I had wanted to be on the dean's list because studying at age 46 was not so easy but I worked hard and I accomplished that goal.

Many awards I received later in life as an adult and out into the working world. It means so much to earn awards and recognition as life goes on, knowing how much effort was put into working for these achievements in life. But I always felt that anything worth having was worth working for.

A former student of mine, Tim Goodman, entered a contest telling why he had the best teacher. It was a magazine called Happiness. Well Tim won this contest and he was honored with a certificate, and I was honored with the Best Teacher certificate.

In February of 1990, I was honored with a special public service award from the Kenosha County Sheriff Allan Kehl. It was quite extensive in nature and stated: 'Office of the Sheriff, Kenosha County, Wisconsin hereby presents this public service award to Arlene Roanhaus, Principal of St. Alphonsus School, in appreciation and recognition for assisting the law enforcement profession in Kenosha County in the preservation of law and order and public safety. For your unselfish dedication to the St. Alphonsus School District, and the education and welfare of the children of Kenosha County from 1947 - 1990. Happy Retirement. This award is made on behalf of the officers and staff of the department in tribute to the public service rendered.'

I felt so honored to have gotten this award, and I couldn't even go to the presentation that very evening because my dear heart husband was in the hospital with a serious heart condition, so I was with Phil at the hospital during that time. But it is the appreciation from the officers in behalf of children that counted.

When I retired, I received two certificates of gratitude for having worked with children for so many years. One was from Father Darneider from the Archdiocesan Office of Child Ministry and Education, and the other was from Wisconsin Governor Tommy Tompson.

One of my most recent thrills was about a year ago

344

when I received a letter from the Who's Who Among America's Teachers. At that time I was informed that I had been nominated by a former student, who at present is a law student, Amy Lois. Amy had to be nominated by one of her present teachers as the best of students, and in turn she could nominate a teacher whom she felt was worthy and deserving of this recognition, so she picked me. I had been her junior high school teacher at St. Alphonsus School many years ago.

I had to complete the information sheet and my name and accomplishments would be listed in the Who's Who Among America's Teachers. I was elated to think that at my tender age, my name would appear in this great volume.

The information in the book using abbreviations reads as follows: [page 561] :

ROANHAUS, ARLENE LENZ, Tutor, Wheatland, WI. *b;* Phillip M., *c;* Darlene D., Dolly Thuemmler, Daniel P., Debbie Vos, Dell P., Diane King, David M., Donna Dixon *ed;* University WI at Whitewater [BA[Elem Ed, 1973: RKNS Tchrs Coll St Cert Elem Ed 1946: Albert Meyer Inst 1976: Univ of WI Oshkosh 1982: Specialized Courses Lib Sci: *cr.* Randall Oak Knoll Rural 1st - 8th Grd Tchr 1947-1952: Salem Mound Ctr Rural 1st - 8th Gr Tchr 1952-1954: Wheatland Ctr 1st, 2nd Gr Tchr 1955 - 1957: St. Alphonsus Tchr, Prin. Librn. 1964 - 1990: Tutor Low Achievers 1990 -Pres: *ai;* WEA 1955-58: WI Cncl of tchrs, 1978-1983: NCEA 1964-90: Catholic Foresters 1948, Jr Dir: 4-H Club, 1938 - Pres Ldr Alumni Awrd, 1995: BPW Schlsp 1972: Tchr of Yr 1980: Kenosha Co Sheriffs Awd 1989: WI DPI Recognition of Svc 1989.

All of my volunteer work that I've done throughout the years has been appreciated and organizations that I worked with have bestowed honorable awards and recognition for my many hours of time and dedication donated. I have to admit that I have always enjoyed working with youth as much as now when I am working with and teaching adults. Seeing the outcomes of my work has been rewarding to me and has helped me to grow personally.

Just recently I have had another recognition along with a group of other teachers in Burlington on September 26, 1999. A former student of mine, Ray Ziebell, from 1951 at Mound Center School, invited me to be his guest at Teacher Appreciation Day at the Bethel Baptist Church. I was happy to attend and everyone there made all the teachers feel so special, and gave each one of us a gift.

Ray is also a teacher who has been teaching in the Burlington School System for a number of years. Ray's wife, Carol, also a teacher, is a very special lady.

After serving a brunch, the award presentation took place in the church. This has become a memorable event in my life.

On October 8 of '99, I attended a Wisconsin 4-H Recognition Banquet in Madison. To my surprise, I was awarded a state 4-H Alumni Award given in recognition of outstanding service to the community and for continuing commitment to the Wisconsin 4-H youth development program.

I knew that I had been nominated, but I had no idea when I went to the banquet that I would be one of the recipients of the award. Two other ladies receiving awards were Helen Hornby from Vernon County and Elda Hoyt from Rock County. My thoughts were that most likely all the nominees would be invited to attend, and the recipients would be picked from that group.

On the program, was a synopsis of each of us. Mine stated: Arlene Roanhaus has spent more than forty years working with Wisconsin 4-H, first as a member and later as a volunteer leader with 4-H youth in Kenosha County. Arlene has been active in numerous conservation and community service activities throughout her community. She has also received numerous awards for her work as an elementary school teacher and administrator, and is currently writing a book in which she notes, "4-H afforded all these opportunities to help me to grow to become a better person, because to this day in my tender age I still strive to make the best better."

After the presentation of the plaque to me, Kathy Vos [a former 4-H member of our Wheatland Wiling Workers 4-H Club], who is on the state staff, presented me with a beautiful basket of flowers with a congratulatory greeting given to me by friends in Kenosha 4-H and U.W. Extension Office. This was so gratifying to me and my appreciation can never be expressed in words

To me this is a great achievement in my life and I will continue being a 4-H leader in the Child Development Project.

Chapter 32
Our Kids' Accomplishments

Parents aren't the only ones who are worthy of awards and recognitions. Our kids as adults now make us proud of their accomplishments in life upon completion of the goals they have set for themselves.

In the past, Darlene has earned many awards in her line of work, the field of cosmetology. She won a trip to New York to study hair color from a prominent teacher in this field. While there, she was afforded the privilege of the social life of New York as an added bonus.

Darlene was also granted a trip to Canada where she engaged in an advanced hair cutting class at Marvin Parsons School of Hair Design.

During her courses of training in Cosmetology, she enrolled in the James Allen Modeling School in Lake Geneva, to enhance her career and to better herself.

She entered two contests during her time. The first was at a Supercuts franchise district hair cutting and styling contest in Illinois where she placed second. The other contest was sponsored by Cost Cutters Family Hair Care regional competition in which she placed second in the children's category. Her niece, Missy, was her model at age eleven.

Throughout her working days at Cost Cutters Family Hair Care, she became a Paul Mitchell advisor. She actuated many stage presentations and conducted classes to teach the proper uses of these hair care products.

The year of 1998 was a banner year for Dolly. In June, she was awarded the newspaper achiever award for this area. The name of the newspaper is 'Bulletin' and is published weekly. Following is a copy of the article as it appeared in the newspaper.

4-H Benefits From Thuemmler's Work
by Jane Watkins

Being a mother of five would be enough contact with children on a daily basis for anyone, but Dolly Thuemmler doesn't think so. She not only is mother to five children, between ages of 10 and 24, but she is also involved in many community activities that involve children other than her own.

"I have the time. the need is there and I like working with youth,"says Thuemmler

Thuemmler is the general co-leader for the Wheatland Will-

347

ing Workers 4-H Club. She has been doing this for three years now along with Mary Daniels. Besides being the general leader, she is also a project leader in Foods and Nutrition. This year she is doing cake decorating, and is very involved with the fishing project.

Thuemmler was a 4-H member herself when she was younger. "When my kids got involved in 4-H, so did I," said Thuemmler. "You need the parents to help make it work."

Thuemmler also is involved with St. Alphonsus Catholic School in New Munster, where her two youngest children attend classes.

"I help serve lunch and clean up two days a week," explained Thuemmler. "I like it because I get to see the kids, and I'm more involved."

She also will begin her third year as school board secretary at St. Alphonsus School in June. Thuemmler has been an assistant coach in track and field for four years. She has also served as a room mom and a playground mom.

St. Alphonsus Fall Festival is yet another area where Thuemmler is involved each year. One year she served as kitchen chairman, but she had consistently been in charge of children's games for four or five years now.

Thuemmler is a member of the Parent Volunteer Commitee, and also has worked as a food stand volunteer for the annual ball tournament for the past eight years.

She resides in Wheatland with her husband Jim and their children.

"I grew up two houses down," said Thuemmler. "I really love this area."

In October of 1998, the 4-H Alumni Award was awarded to Dolly. She was so thoroughly surprised! She was most deserving of this award as you have just read in the prior news article summarizing her most worthy qualification.

Danny, who from little boy on, has always been a true sportsman who takes after his dad in that respect, engages in fishing and hunting. Of the two sports, fishing has become his favorite. He has always set his goals very high and never gave up until he accomplished these goals he had set for himself.

He has joined the sports fishing organization called Walleye Unlimited, USA having 590 members from all over the nation. He has become a professional fisherman. One of his major accomplishments was winning the award for catching the third largest Walleye in 1998 of Canada, which was seven ounces away from being number one. His accumulated points from 1998 is the second highest in the club's history in 30 years.

Recently he was named the champion and along with being acknowledged for his championship, he received several awards at their annual banquet. The trophy he received was a bit short of Dan's own height of six feet five inches. On this monstrous trophy were the inscriptions for :

BIGGEST MUSKIE OF THE YEAR
BIGGEST WALLEYE OF THE YEAR
BEST FIVE WALLEYE OF THE YEAR
[which was 4 ounces short from breaking a twenty-two year old record]
BIGGEST LOCAL LAKES MUSKIE
6TH PLACING IN THE WALLEYE RELEASE CONTEST

Danny maintains that it pays to go where the big fish are, so he no longer fishes for small fish. In the spring and fall of the year, he fishes at Sturgeon Bay in Wisconsin. Some of his other favorite places for fishing include: Lake Geneva, Lake Erie, Chain of Lakes in Illinois, and on Little Bay De Noc in Saskatchewan in Canada.

He continues to teach his sons, Jake and Grant, the art of fishing and they, too, have been very successful in their catches. It pleases Phil that this art of fishing is being handed down from generation through generation.

Debbie has engaged in helping many children through youth organizations, and was always there for them when kids needed a ride, or morale builder, and any kind of support that was needed.

Her major accomplishment, which would have made my dad, her Grandfather Lenz, very proud of her was her winning the election for the Town of Wheatland Treasurer. She is serving her second term now and likes this job as she meets many new people, and her work is so interesting.

Dell had always tried to better himself as time went on. He is now entered in Andrews Heliax University where he is engaged in academic courses: Electrical Engineer, Microwave Digital Links, Radio Frequency Systems, Fiber Optics, Category Five, and communications.

Diane has recently had the honor of being nominated and chosen to work with the Merrill School System in assisting with selection of educational materials in utilizing the State Chapters' Funding.

Diane, as Assistant Quality Control Manager at Fox Point in Merrill, recently went to classes in Green Bay.

Donna received her certification for preschool and day care teaching after doing volunteer work at a local Day Care Center.

David does custom remodeling work for clients and has the honors of representing various Building Supply Houses in magazines and on TV, for his creativity and outstanding work in this field.

I know that all of our kids' accomplishments have not come back to mind, but I did recall a few of them. [Forgive me, kids, if I neglected to think of your personal achievements, it was not done intentionally, just an oversight]

Phil and I are both very proud of all our kids and the volunteer work that they have engaged in, as we have always felt the worthiness in helping someone else learn and grow through one's personal efforts.

Chapter 33
Lord, I'm Not Ready Yet

"Lord, I'm not ready yet! I still have the work to do that you have laid out for me. There are many children out there who know nothing about God, and so many adults roaming around searching for the true God, and right now I fear that you want me. If you take me now, I don't know who would take over where I would be leaving off, but I'm sure that you will provide someone. Please give this some sincere thought and consideration before you decide to take me now."

And so I went on praying that this was not the hour of my departure from this earth, and yet I placed all my trust in God. My life was in his hands, and whatever he willed was fine with me. But there is tremendous anxiety about death when you feel you are facing it head on, no matter how strong your faith can be.

It was the seventeenth day after a hip reconstruction surgery, and up to that point everything was going well as was anticipated. On the second Sunday that I was at the Sacred Heart Rehabilitation Complex at Lakeland Hospital in Elkhorn, I awakened that morning shivering with chills so I asked the nurse for an extra blanket. She brought it, and then I went into a cold sweat, and didn't want any covering on my bed what so ever. I felt as though a semi truck ran over me and drained the life right out of me. I felt just awful!

Another nurse came in and took my glucose count because it was at this institution that it was determined that I was a diabetic. So each morning and evening someone would take my glucose count. After she left, I felt so nauseous, and dreaded the thought of going to breakfast. But I took each minute as it came, hoping for an improved feeling. It was a Sunday of all days, and I was confident that God wouldn't let me down, especially on a Sunday, the Lord's day.

The nurse who had given me the extra blanket came back and told me she wanted to take my blood pressure and temperature. My blood pressure was sky high and my temp was also elevated. This left her very puzzled. I asked Patricia, who was my nurse in charge, what the heck was going on because now I felt like fainting.

She became very concerned herself and told me maybe I needed food as breakfast would soon be up from the kitchen. I was on the fourth floor of this unit, and we had our own dining area for all the patients on that floor.

It was then that I heard the cart with the breakfast trays coming down the hall. Pat came in and got me and I told her that I just wanted to skip breakfast that day. She told me she would wheel me to the dining area and stay with me and then if I felt that I just couldn't eat, she would bring me back to my room.

I agreed, after all I had promised all the nursing staff and the doctor in charge there, that I would eat a breakfast every single day because prior to that time I never ate a breakfast at home. But now I knew the importance of that first meal of the day, so I tried very hard to eat some of the toast, and drink the fruit juice, and took a few sips of coffee. Now more than ever I felt like barfing and passing out, so Pat could see how miserable I was, so she took me back to my room.

When we got back into the room, she gave me a small container and yes, I upchucked the very little that I did try to eat. Now she and I both thought I'd feel better. But I continued to feel worse and the chills came back more intensely than before. Pat couldn't believe her eyes, I was shivering so badly that the bed shook. She left the room and called the doctor who was an oriental named Dr. Origines. Being Sunday he doesn't make rounds on Sundays, so he told Pat to stay with me and keep reporting any changes throughout the day.

Again she took my blood pressure and temp and my blood pressure was so low that she couldn't imagine that I was still alive. This went on and on, I felt worse as time went on, so I asked Pat to call a Catholic priest for me. Our parish priest, Father Tom, was out of town with the confirmtion candidates from our parish on a retreat so she couldn't call him.

The usual priest, Father Hanauska, who always served Lakeland Hospital was at my home parish in New Munster taking Father Tom's place that Sunday. Pat called parishes in Elkhorn, East Troy, Delavan, and Lake Geneva. After a while a priest who did an extra mass at East Troy said he would come over after the masses were done, but it wouldn't be until after 1:30 P.M. I was some what relieved now as I knew a priest was coming to my spiritual aid.

This feeling of chills, cold sweat, being hot, my whole body trembling, and still feeling nauseous continued, and as time went on these feelings grew worse. The bed still continued to shake when I went into the state of chills and my body trembled. My blood pressure continued to fluctuate up and down like a yo-yo.

My anxiety worsened and I hadn't the slightest idea of what was going on.

By this time when Pat called Dr. Origines, he told her to give me a dose of Darvocet to help calm my anxieties and perhaps I could get some rest. Oh, Lord, here they are giving me some more pain relievers. I don't like to take them any more, but doctor's orders so what could I do? I've already had enough drugs pushed to me during the past sixteen days.

After all, during my nine days at Burlington Memorial Hospital where the surgery took place, the nurses there kept pushing Percocet to me every four hours. Then after I arrived at the Rehab Complex, these nurses also kept pushing the Percocet to me every four hours. I requested that I didn't need all these pain relievers, because I have a high tolerance for pain and I could endure pain without grumbling. Besides, I just wanted my body to stop shaking and trembling, and they want to give me more drugs.

So after the eighth day that I was at Lakeland, the doctor ordered a milder pain reliever called Darvocet. I still begged them not to administer so much to me as I didn't want it, so they cut back immensely on that drug.

Now the time came for the dinner meal and at times I felt a little hungry and at other times the thought of food really nauseated me.

Again Pat took me down to the dining area and I tried to eat some soup, but my hands as well as my whole body were trembling so badly, that I couldn't get the spoon up to my mouth. The other patients started staring at me and Pat noticed this so she took me back to my room again. When we got back to the room, she got my tray and brought it into the room and fed me the soup. We had baked chicken with rice, and a helping of broccoli all of which I really liked, but I could only down the soup.

After this meal episode was over, I had visitors. It was my tutor student, Mark, whom I had tutored for eight consecutive years, and his parents, Ron and Terrie. I was so delighted to see them because I had grown very close to Mark through the years, and I had always regarded him as another grandchild, so to speak. Mark's parents have always been so supportive of their own family and have always treated Phil and me like a king and a queen.

Just this family visit really boosted my morale as I was

353

having this most dreadful day of my life. Terrie is a professional in the nursing field, who not only cares for the well being of patients, but also travels all over United States and abroad, teaching in this profession. Being that she is a nurse, she wanted to know if I was being taken care of in the best fashion possible. I had to admit that I was given the best of care.

Then Ron and Terrie started to tell me that Mark had 'Mrs. Roanhaus withdrawal', and that he missed my working with him so much that he had lost all interest in his school work. He didn't care if he went to school or not, if he did his homework or not, he said he missed me that much.

This made me feel a bit sad because it took a bit of doing way back when to build up his self-esteem and now I was fearful that he may lose it. So I told him that he had to buckle down and his parents, who were very intelligent, were capable of helping him with his work, because due to doctor's orders, I would not be able to work with him until the next school year at which time he would be a sophomore in high school. This also meant that I couldn't help him during the summer months as I had always done in the past.

Being the type of kid that he is, he accepted this graciously, knowing that in the future I would be helping him again. I just wanted to hug him and tell him how much he means to me, and that I would always be there for him, just not right now. After a short visit as they could see that I was upset, and not feeling up to par, they left.

Right after they left, Darlene came in. She was there a short while when the priest came. He was a priest from Marquette University who was helping out at East Troy that day. He was there for a brief time and he left, but momentarily in his presence, I felt a sense of tranquility in hopes that this would contribute to my well-being. I placed my trust is God as my life was in his hands.

This blissful feeling soon left me so again I was in the state of discontentment which accounts for the difficulty in trying to accept one's visit when you feel like the most wretched creature on this planet.

Being Sunday, there was no physical therapy nor any walking class. Being that I was in the dining area and just couldn't eat, the other patients were extremely worried and concerned about me. I was always the one in the group during meal time who spoke to everyone and they all missed me.

Then the other patients had inquired to the nurses as

to what was wrong with me, but all the nurses could tell them was that I was going through unexplainable stressful agitated seizures. Everyone was now concerned, even the other nurses on the floor.

As time went on, I became more and more fearful and it seemed that every time I would have one of these seizures, they were becoming strongly more severe. Pat was very concerned about my blood pressure elevating and dropping at intervals. All that went through my mind was the thought of how bad could the seizures really get, could it be possible that I was nearing my death. Oh, no, Lord, please, I'm not ready yet.

Now the supper meal is here, and Pat informed me that I needed to make my own decision whether I wanted to go to the dining area or not. Immediately I told her no, that I didn't even want to see or smell food, so she agreed and sent my tray back. She asked if anything at all appealed to me, and I told her that I thought I might try a little chicken broth, so she got it for me. I drank about a half glass of the broth and it was the first food to stay down.

Now I started thinking that maybe I was overcoming whatever was wrong with me. Then it started all over again, another seizure. I was to the point of giving up as I became so puzzled. Pat called Dr. Origines again, about the fourth time that day, and he told her he was going to a movie with his family and when he returned he would call the hospital to see how I was.

The next two and a half hours seemed like an eternity, because I knew that the doctor would come to the hospital after he returned home. In the meantime there were no changes, the same-o same-o and I was still in misery and began to panic.

Finally at 9:30 P.M. Dr. Origines called and inquired as to how I was doing and Pat told him that if anything, I was getting worse, and that he had better come over. Then he told her to give me a dose of Percocet. She asked him if she heard him correctly, and he told her to just do it and administer it to me immediately.

When Pat came in and gave me the Percocet pills, I told her I thought that he was trying to kill me, but what did I have to lose, I was in misery anyway. I took the two pills with a full glass of water and all I could think was, 'Sure, now he wants to drug me before I die, but I'm destined anyway, so what's the difference!'

It was only about twenty minutes after taking these percocet pills, all the misery was slowly subsiding, I perked up and I told Pat I was hungry. She ordered down to the kitchen for a tray for me. In the meantime, I asked if she would help me up because I wanted to walk. Nurses aren't allowed to help the patient walk, only the therapists can. But it just so happened that one of the therapists was there doing some book work and she was delighted to help me walk, because she, too, was overly concerned about me.

I ate my supper, and after that the therapist helped me walk in the hall. The other patients now knew that I was up because all along they kept asking the nurses how I was. My dear husband Phil was there visiting me and he, too, had been so worried about me. He watched her help me walk in the hall, at most was about eight feet with a walker with arm platforms attached, but I was up and feeling much improved. She had Phil follow behind us with the wheel chair as the therapists always did this so when I became tired the chair was right there for me to fall into.

Now it dawned on me that I was still among the living and the Lord didn't want me yet after all. 'Oh, thank you Lord, thank you'! But the mystery still remained as to why I had gone through all these seizures, would this mystery ever be solved? I couldn't wait until the next day when Dr. Origines would come in. I slept well that night as I was completely exhausted and worn out from the strain of the day's episode.

The next morning went on as usual. Five o'clock wake up, glucose count, blood pressure check, temperature taken, wash up and brush teeth time. I seemed to be normal once again. I went to breakfast and everyone had a multitude of questions which I, nor Pat, could answer. They were as eager as I was to find out what had happened.

After breakfast, each patient was assigned to attend a special class. My nine o'clock class was arm exercises. At about 10:00 A.M. Dr. Origines made his usual rounds and when he came to my room I couldn't wait to hear what he had to say.

He started off by saying, "So I hear that you had the scare of your life yesterday, eh?" I replied, "Well I certainly did, I thought I was about to die and I wasn't ready for that yet." He chuckled a bit, but I failed to see any humor in the entire scenario. The he admitted that he was puzzled himself for a while until he came to realize what accounted for the situation.

Anxiously, I said, "Well, what really did happen to me?" Then he went on to admit that my body was not satisfied with the Darvocet, but was calling for the stronger drug, Perco-cet. Being that I had been on the lighter medication, Darvocet, my body was not content with that drug. As soon as the drug Percocet was ingested, my body was satisfied and slid back into a normal state. I had been hooked on a drug, and was hooked very innocently. What I had been through was drug withdrawal. I couldn't believe it! Me... drug withdrawal! How obscure! What an innocent victim I had been!

I am one who can endure a great deal of pain and I'd rather have it this way than to be taking so many pills. I would have much preferred the pain than have this happen to me, but it happened anyway under a physician's care. Believe me, after that episode, I totally refused any pain relieving drug and endured on my own.

At the next meal which was the noon dinner, in answer-ing all the questions that were asked by the other patients, I hardly had time to eat. You'll never know how close people can become to each other when you're patients together in an rehab institution. Their compassion for me was unquestionable, and they were all happy to have me back as I was before. I always added a bit of wit and made light of suffering and was an incentive for all of them due to my being in Post Polio Syndrome. I had lots of stamina, and they admired me for my courage. To me this was just another crisis to battle and I could handle it easier than most because of my strong mind and will.

All I can say is I never want to take Percocet or Darvo-cet as long as I live. I don't want to run a risk of becoming addicted again. Never in my wildest dreams did I ever even con-template a thought in my mind of my becoming addicted under a doctor's care. Once in a lifetime is far too much for me. God didn't really want me yet, so I'm still here today.

Chapter 34
Our Long-Awaited Vacations

It seems as though Phil and I were looking forward to having adult vacations after so many years of family vacations. However, we did take two vacations shortly after we were married. We accompanied my brother Bob and his wife Sophie, who took the place of a sister that I never had and so we were very close. We went on our first summer vacation together after our first year of marriage. Actually it was for anniversary celebrations for Phil's and my first and Bob and Soph's second as they were married a year before we were.

We went to Chetek in Wisconsin, and rented a cottage on a lake so the men could go fishing. During the times while the men were fishing, Soph and I would tidy up the cottage, plan, and cook meals. In the evenings, we would play cards. Some evenings we'd eat out and take in a movie, while other evenings we'd stay at the cottage, pop corn and drink beer.We enjoyed these vacations being a time of such relaxation. We did this until they had Regina and Lennie, and we had Darlene. At that point, our vacations together stopped.

When our family was in the stages of getting older, Phil and I, along with Darlene and [at the time] husband Norman, and Jim and Dolly all went to California to attend a wedding of Phil's niece, Theresa. So in 1981 was my first plane ride.

We flew on United Airlines which was one of the major airlines at that time. Now this was an experience of one of a kind for me! The only other time that I had ever been to an airport was the time when I took Dolly to Mitchell International Airport in Milwaukee to fly to Los Angeles to visit with her Uncle Ralph and Aunt Dorothy.

When we boarded the plane, I was amazed at the seating arrangement. As I walked down the aisle to row 26, I kept thinking, "I don't want a window seat, I'll be scared to death to even look out." The plane was a 747 so the seats were in groups of threes. We approached our row and Phil motioned for me to go into a seat, and I looked at him in distress, as he said, " Don't you want the window seat?"

"Heavens, no, anything but that". So Phil took the seat by the window and I sat next to him. Luckily the plane was not filled to capacity so the seat on the other side next to me was vacant. Until the plane was completely boarded, I was in a state of worry about leaving the ground. "Oh, no, they are closing the cabin door".

Many thoughts went around in my head, and I suddenly wondered where the oxygen would be coming from as already I felt claustrophobic and just knew that any moment I'd stop breathing. "Oh, dear, will I ever see my other children again? God, please don't let anything happen to us as we have kids at home who are still depending on us for their survival".

By this time, the stewardess instructed everyone to follow the direction card as she explained all the details that had caused my worry. Umm, maybe this won't be so bad after all. All seat belts had to be fastened as we were ready for take-off. The Captain revved up the engine, the plane started in motion, on down the runway. We were taxiing for a while, and suddenly the captain cut loose, the captain put the pedal to the metal, and we were in fast paced motion. Phil said to me, "We'll soon be off the ground".

"Did you have to remind me?" I grabbed his leg and held on so tight, I'm surprised to this day that he never had a bruise there from my clutching on to it.

Next I hear, "Look, mother [as Phil often addressed me because of the children], we're banking over the ocean, look out the window. It's so neat to see". And at that very moment I had my doubts as to whether the plane was going down into that ocean as it was so tilted.

"I can't look, I'm scared, hold on to me or I'm a goner". As we ascended higher into the atmosphere, I chanced sneaking a glance and saw how minute everything looked, the house and buildings, the roads with vehicles on them, and then there were clouds, and only clouds. The captain announced the altitude, but I was still not in the least bit impressed. As a matter of fact, that added to the anxiety as all I could think of was where would we be if this plane suddenly went off course and down.

Now the stewardesses were taking drink orders, so I ordered an alcoholic beverage in hopes that it may help calm my nerves. I needed a good stiff one at this point. The one young lady asked if this was my first flight. I haven't a clue how she could tell! After serving beverages, she came by me and sat in the vacant seat next to me and assured me that I would be getting to California safely. She gave me a few pointers about chewing gum or popping my ears due to pressure. I guess the drink was taking a hold by now and I started becoming more relaxed and reassured that she was right

Then I felt like my bladder was full and ready to explode.

I had to go and I had to go bad. I staggered down the aisle, not from the drink but from the movement of the plane to get to the lavatory. Darlene went with me. I opened the door and had another surprise being shocked at the smallness of this relief station. I backed in to get in and there was no room to turn, so when I was finished with what I had to do, I walked out. That was the first and last time that I ever used this facility on any plane again.

After a few hours of flight, we heard the information announced that we would soon be landing. Oh, my gosh, now I started all over again in a frenzy about landing. What would it be like? Would we feel a huge thud? Would the pilot get the plane stopped soon enough? I worried about any little detail that you can imagine.

Our seat belts were fastened, we started to descend as you could hear the engines were already cut back. We were getting out of the clouds and back to reality. I could see the terrain and all that's in motion on it so vividly now. I also saw the runway as we seemed to be going too fast. "I hope he knows how to stop this thing to land."

"Oh, no, we touched ground! I felt that. It wasn't at all smooth like everyone told me it would be, but we're here at L A. Airport safe and sound."

Ralph was there to meet us, and after claiming our luggage, we went to his red station wagon, piled in and we were off to the motel.

The next day was the wedding. Theresa and Tom were married in a huge Catholic Church in Oxnard. Ralph had picked us up at the motel, then drove us to church. Then he returned to his home and took the rest of his family to church, returning back for the bride.

After the church ceremony and pictures, we all were taken to the reception. In California most of the wedding receptions are held immediately after church, which meant this is in the afternoon. The buffet luncheon was served, followed by dancing. To us from Wisconsin, it seemed strange to hold a dance in the afternoon because we had evening receptions.

While we were in California, Ralph and Dorothy had tickets for us and his whole family to go to Disneyland. The next day we went to Disneyland in four vehicles because we were so many people. Ralph insisted on paying for all seventeen people.

When we arrived there, we all split up in groups. The younger generation went on their own and Ralph, Dorothy, Phil, and I went together. Trying to explain Disneyland is difficult, but all I can say is that it's like being in another world. The shows were done in the best of style, and the rides were totally awesome. My favorites were Small World, Pirates of the Caribbean, Tiki House, Bear Country and the Hall of Presidents, although I have to admit I liked everything about Disneyland.

On Monday we went to Universal Studios. They were filming Airport at the time and they showed how the ocean scene was done. Then they asked for volunteers from the audience to show how they had filmed the scene with the ambulance. Seeing that not many people volunteered, they selected people and so Ralph was picked to be the ambulance driver. This was so neat to see, but it took a little of reality away from what we see a movie as.

We also saw Hedda Hopper's dressing room and got a glimpse of her wardrobe with all her fine clothing, jewelry, her collection of shoes, furs, hats and wigs. Her dresserette was magnificent with the brightest lighting and every kind of cosmetic imaginable. We only regretted that she wasn't in her dressing room at the time we saw it. We saw how the movie Jaws was filmed. Jaws was not as large and fierce as the movie portrayed but a small animated shark. How those producers can fool the people by their projections of filming is amazing.

Another point of interest was the ship at sea from McHale's Navy. This was also rather a disappointment as it, too, was on such a small scale, the ship looked like a toy.

While riding on a tram, we were driven through the parting of the Red Sea as seen in the film Ten Commandments. This was an awesome sight, and became more thrlling to be able to ride through it.

We saw how an avanlanche was portrayed and we had the opportunity to ride through it. This was phenomenal, but so frightening!

At that time B.J. and the Bear were so popular on TV, and we got to see his semi truck. We also saw the trailer from the series Rockford Files.

It shocked me to see a scenic background move and the vehicle that was supposedly moving was actually standing still. It became a bit confusing in my mind because when I watched TV at home or a movie in the theater, I never would have believed this concept if I hadn't seen it with my own eyes. At that particular time, I thought that never again would I appreciate a TV scene or a movie scene after knowing this.

The next day we went to the Wax Museum. As we entered, there was a sentinel guard standing near the entryway. Dorothy and I both wondered, "Is he real or is he a statue?" As we are discussing this right in front of him, he suddenly blinked his eyes. Our question was answered. But was it really answered, we thought!. With all the animation that had been done, we still weren't sure. We both wanted to touch his hand, but neither of us had the guts to do it. Finally I guess the man couldn't keep a straight face any longer, and he burst out into a chuckle. Now were we ever embarrassed!

In the wax museum were many of the stars, whom you would have sworn were real, only to find out they were just made of wax. Some of the scenes were: Debbie Reynolds as the nun in Flying Nun on her motorcycle, Gene Kelly in Singing In The Rain, a scene from Dr. Zhivago, and the partly sunken ship from the original Titanic movie. I was so impressed in that museum as there were so many other stars and performers.

One day Ralph took us to Hollywood and we saw the famous walk where the stars have their hand prints and names on a star built into the sidewalk. We drove through Beverly Hills where the rich and famous live.

We went from one of the old California missions and on to the next. We went through each one, and this tour made the history of the old missions all add up. I particularly enjoyed seeing these after having taught about them. It is remarkable that these buildings are still standing, but they are old and rather delapitated, although the history is still so interesting.

When we arrived home, we got the news from my mother that the rest of our kids who were left at home had one big party while we were gone. They rented a tent so as to keep it outside and not mess the house inside because they knew if they did, Phil and I would be furious when we returned home. We were informed that they had beer, and David, the youngest was so inebriated that his bed was never to be found that night. He must have slept on the ground outside that night, or maybe even a chair, who knows?

The older kids did look out for him though so he wasn't injured in any way other than a big head and a terrific hangover the next day. I guess this is something that Phil and I had never anticipated would happen, but it did.

A few years later, we learned that the day after their party, when the kids took the rented tent back, Dell was driving the truck and Donna was riding in the back of the truck. Supposedly her glasses fell off in the road, so she jumped out of the truck to get them. She yelled for Dell to stop, and apparently he didn't hear her. I don't know if he really didn't hear her or just wanted to teach her a lesson. To my knowledge she didn't get hurt because Debbie did look out for the kids, and Dell apparently helped her. While the cats are away, the mice play.

In 1986, Phil and I decided to visit Ralph and Dorothy again, so we were off to California once more. This time it was just the two of us, Phil and me, so we stayed at Ralph and Dorothy's house.

The two of them gave up their twin beds for us to sleep in. I chose to sleep in the bed nearest the window, and Phil chose the other bed. It must have been that I had Dorothy's bed because during the night, I had a visit from a cat that wanted to get into the bed with me. Now I absolutely abhore cats much as less say one wanting to get into bed with me.

You have to understand that Dorothy was such an animal lover that she took in any stray cat or dog that came along. At one time she had seven cats and two dogs all living in the house with them.

The next night, I went into the same bed. As I laid my head on the pillow, I started to itch. I couldn't imagine what was wrong, until I turned the light on and the whole pillow was full of cat hairs. How disgusting! I brushed off the pillow and turned it over to the other side to sleep on. Then it was okay.

The next morning when I made the bed, I turned the pillow with cat hair side up as I knew that the cat would take a daily nap on this pillow. I pulled the bed spread as far up as I could so as to cover the pillow. I knew that I would not be sleeping in that bed that night as we were leaving for a few days, but we would be returning.

That day the four of us got ready and packed a suitcase to travel to Las Vegas in their motor home. This would be our very first adventure to Vegas, where I had always dreamed of going. We left early in the morning and it took us all day and into the evening to get there. Traveling through the desert is not very scenic but it is so very hot and the motor home had no air conditioning in it, we suffered but we survived.

On the way there we were involved in a minor vehicle accident just outside of Bakersfield. A semi truck had side swiped Ralph's vehicle on the side where I was sitting, so again I could have met my doom. The semi never stopped to see if any damage had been done so when we got to Bakersfield, Ralph stopped and reported it to the police, but nothing was ever done about it. It all happened so fast.

When we got to Vegas, Ralph had reservations for us to stay in the hotel at Circus Circus Hotel and Casino. He and Dorothy stayed in their motor home in the RV park there. We settled in and went to the casino for a while that evening. They introduced us to nickel slot machines, and so we thought that was really fun. After a while we were so tired so we went to bed for the night.

The next morning Ralph came over to our room and got us for the breakfast buffet there. After breakfast Ralph took us for a drive down the strip so we could see all the casinos and hotels. I was in awe, as I never knew Vegas was at all like this but we never got into any other casino except Slots of Fun located right next to Circus Circus, and the Sands and the Riviera across the street from where we stayed.

Later that afternoon we bought tickets for an evening show at the Sands Casino. We ate supper at the Pink Pony in Circus Circus, and then drove down the strip to the Sands. It was a variety show and it was well worth the money we paid.

We gambled a bit at the other casinos that I mentioned but always went back to Circus Circus as Dorothy liked the nickel slots there. I found dime slots and sat the whole last evening that we were there and played dimes and had a great time.

I did have an uncanny experience while I was playing the dime slots. There were two young kids running around the casino, and there are no children under the age of twenty-one allowed to be in the casino area but they were there. One was about thirteen and the other looked like he could be about fifteen. They had been hanging around me at the machine watching me for the longest time. I really watched my purse because the security guards warned me and they watch very closely if women are watching their purses. My purse was an over shoulder bag that had a long strap on, so I had it wound around my legs and the purse in my lap.

So slyly one of those kids came up to me and started talking to me, while the other was off a short distance from my other side. Being that I have such strong peripheral vision, I kept watching him out of the corner of my eye. The one who was talking to me asked if he could count my dimes that were in the machine tray, and I refused. My, but was he disappointed!

Then I saw the kid drop a dime of his own on the floor and said, "Lady, you dropped a dime on the floor". I responded with, "It's okay, you may pick it up and have it". You should have seen the astonished look on his face. I know that they thought if I had to stoop to pick it up, they'd grab dimes from the tray, but they didn't outsmart me. I pushed the change light on my machine and as luck would have it, it was a security guard that came over, so I reported the kids and he very quickly escorted them out. That was our first experience in Las Vegas, and we liked it so much that we decided that we'd go back at a later time for a vacation. We were eager to see all the casinos that we didn't see, so Phil and I made up our minds that in the future after we both were retired, we would take a trip out to Vegas and see everything on our own.

On our way back from Las Vegas Ralph drove us through parts of the state of California and we visited the places that we hadn't seen during our stay in 1981. He showed us where many Hollywood stars had their hideaways away from the public eye. We saw where many movies were filmed. We stopped at every single gift shop along the way. We saw lemon and orange groves. He pointed out many vegetable fields in which vegetables were grown for the canneries.

In 1987, Ralph and Dorothy wanted us to come back and visit them again, so we did. By now, I was used to flying and so I had overcome all fear and liked that way to travel. This time when we went we stayed at their house again, but now I was ready for the cat ordeal. I knew from the very beginning that each morning when I made the bed, I had to pull the bedspread way up on top of the pillow and overlap a little under the pillow. This way, the cat hair would only be on the spread which I took off at night, so I out smarted the cat.

While we were there, they took the motor home and drove us up to Hearst Castle near San Simeon. After driving for many miles, we finally reached our destination, the property of William Randolph Hearst. It is interesting that this was one of the descendants of the Patty Hearst who was kidnapped, and held for ransom due to her family being millionaires. For years on end this kidnapping was in all the newspapers. Many believe that she most likely turned up dead, but there was never any proof.

Another theory was that she was taken by a gang and got involved with drugs. Some people to this day believe that she liked that kind of lifestyle and didn't want to come home. I guess the whole truth will never be known.

That was an afternoon well spent, and we certainly enjoyed it immensely. On the way back home, we stopped at many other exciting places of interest that we hadn't seen previously. Many nationalities are blended in the state of California, but due to their location the Hispanics actually dominate most of the state.

Many of the restaurants served truly Mexican foods, which was quite a treat for us, as there weren't that many places in Wisconsin at that time that serve the true south of the border type of food.

Now back to the next adventurous vacation. In the year of 1990, after having retired from my full time job in June, Phil and I decided to plan a trip to Las Vegas. Dell, our son, and his wife Debbie, expressed the desire to accompany us, because at that time I was walking with the aid of forearm crutches, and was very limited to the distance that I could walk. They decided it would alleviate many problems for us if they were to go along and help us get around. This was a great idea, so we made plans to go in August.

Never having made any arrangements before this time for Vegas, we decided that we wanted to stay at the newly constructed Excalibur, so we went to the travel agency in Burlington and booked through Fun Jet.

We had the experience of riding in an L 1011 plane which was huge. During the flight, the Fun Jet representative gave a briefing and handed out coupon booklets to use while being in Vegas. This was a booklet that had many coupons for freebies at the various casinos and hotels.

It was a good flight and we enjoyed it until we had landed in Vegas and discovered that we were not in the main proper of the airport, but rather in the back section of the airport. This meant that we had to debark from the back of the plane, down the multitude of steps with no chute for being enclosed. Two attendants employed by the airline, strapped me into a portable seat and carried me off the plane and down the steps.

All the people who were on this plane conjugated in a group until the name of the hotel at which people was staying was called, then we had to board buses that took us to where we needed to go. We finally reached our destination, and there was to be a wheel chair ready for me to get around in during our stay, as at that time walking was already giving me many problems. When we inquired about it at the front desk as we were checking in, they told us that the chairs were all in use. Now I was as upset as the rest of my family with us was, because all of this had been prearranged by the travel agent.

We hadn't even been to our rooms, yet, when Dell and Phil told Debbie and me to go to the rooms with the luggage as the bell hop was waiting for us. They said that they wanted to just look around and they would be up to the rooms in a bit. So we started off to the rooms until we got to Deb and Dell's room, so the porter put all the luggage in their room, we tipped him and he left.

Now I wanted to get our luggage to our room, when I discovered that Phil had the one and only key that was issued to us at the desk. So I called down to the desk and asked what the number of the room was for Phil and Arlene Roanhaus, and she very politely told me that she had no authority to divulge that information. Well, I more than politely told her is so many words that I was Arlene and explained what had happened, after which she responded with the comment that it was her job to protect and to respect the privacy of the guests from being annoyed and bothered by other people who most likely weren't staying at the hotel. I was furious!

As it turned out, Ralph and Dorothy were to meet us at the Excalibur, and we would spend some time together while we were in Vegas. They were long waiting for us, as we had arrived late. In the meantime they located Phil and Dell, and wondered where Debbie and I were.

She and I had no other recourse but to locate the men and when we finally found them, they had been sitting at the dollar slots ever since they got there. They didn't want to leave those machines, so Debbie and I found nickel machines and played them with no luck. We looked for two coin quarter slots and played them for a while. We had luck for quite a long time.

After a while, we went back to where they were playing and told them of the predicament about not getting into our room because Phil had the one and only key that was issued. As we were talking, we heard money fall endlessly from Phil's machine, he had won a $500 jack pot. Now was time to take off the winner and leave, however Phil was reluctant about leaving as he had a hot machine. But we left anyway.

When Ralph and Dorothy heard about the wheel chair deal we all took a cab over to Circus Circus. Being that Ralph had always stayed there, he got a wheel chair for me from Circus Circus for the duration of our stay.

We played slots at Circus Circus, then Slots of Fun, then at Stardust, Westward Ho, Fremont and back to Excalibur for the duration of our first night in Vegas. We never got to bed until wee hours of the morning like to the tune of four o'clock. Finally after all the problems had finally ceased, we had a great time. During our stay we toured the strip and stopped at most all of the casinos, playing slots here and there. We usually took a cab when we wanted to find something off the strip or when we decided to go down town to see what the casinos were like there. One of them down town that we all liked was Fitzgerald's, truly Irish in every respect. I liked it because we could rub the Blarney Stone for good luck. I didn't believe in it but it was fun just to say you rubbed the Blarney Stone from Ireland. Then we went into the Dunes, which by the way is no longer in existence. We stopped at the Sands, also no longer in existence. Some others were Aladdin, Desert Inn, Stardust, Westward Ho, Binions Horseshoe, Silver City, Fremont, Riviera, Slots of Fun, Tropicana, Palace Station, Caesar's Palace, Lady Luck, Hascenda [which no longer is there], Bally's, Main Street Station which is not operating under that name any longer. We always liked the strip better than the down town.

In 1991, Debbie and Dell accompanied us again and this time we stayed at Circus Circus. Again Ralph and Dorothy met us there at the Circus Circus where they stayed in the mobile park in their motor home. As we were waiting for the bell hop to get a wheel chair for me, guess who happened along. It was John and Marilyn Lichter and their daughter Barb. Little did we dream that we would ever see anyone from back home out there while we were there. We talked with them for a while as they, too, were staying at Circus Circus.

This was the year that the Mirage Casino was built, so being new we had to see what it was like. It was a place of beauty with all the tropical flower gardens having a traditional stone walkway giving one the feeling of being in the tropics. Due to all these flower gardens, it was very damp and Debbie and I had problems of congested feelings with breathing difficulties. At that point we decided that we would never attempt to stay there due to this dampness.

As we were tooling along in the Mirage, we happened along a cafeteria and who do you think we saw in person? It was Gabe Kaplan from the Welcome Back Kotter show. We were going at such a fast pace that we never thought of getting his autograph, but at least we got a glimpse of him in person.

We did a bit of gambling there at the Mirage, but it seemed that the only one who had any luck was Dorothy playing the nickel slots. One can hardly realize how those nickels can count up to much of a sum, but they surely did for her.

Across the street was another new casino, the MGM Grand. The front of the building was a huge gold lion in a lying down position facing the people as they entered through his huge mouth, in which the entrance and exit doors were located. Upon emerging into the entry way, one could see the animated picturesque scenes from the Wizard of Oz. In order to get to the gambling part of the casino, one had to take the paths that led through the portrayal of the entire movie. As one looked up, the sky was so blue filled with stars until the thunder and lightning started and the rain fell. This was one of the most dramatic and fantastic phenomena one could ever encounter.

The slot machines were so tight and not even one of the six of us had a payout. The best part of the casino was the refreshments, the most delicious strawberry daiquiri being served while giving the establishment our coins through their machines. This place was a bummer for gambling.

On the same side of the street was the newly opened Luxor. Dell, Phil, and Ralph were so intrigued with the talking animated camels who talked to the people upon entering the place. I was not at all impressed with this casino. It seemed liked it was underground, anyway that was the feeling that one got, and I have claustrophobia anyway, so I was an unhappy camper while we were in there. We didn't stay long as the slots were tight.

We liked the Riviera because it had more class than Circus Circus or many of the other older casinos. Maybe it was that we just had good luck gambling there, but we really liked it so much that we decided that in the future we'd like to stay there.

We had made plans early in the season for our next trip to Vegas. In the meantime, Dolly had won a raffle at our church Smoker event and won the first prize, either $500 or a trip to Vegas. She chose the trip to Vegas, so now it would be even still more fun having six of us going.

In August of 1992, we went to Vegas and not being able to get a straight through flight we had to land in Los Angeles for a stop, then go on to Vegas. This was the year of the terrible forest fires in California, so as we flew over California, we were low enough to see the blazing flames from our plane. It was a dreadful sight to see, knowing of the damage being done.

As we were approaching Vegas, we saw the vast clouds of smoke left from the ruins of the Dunes Casino and Hotel that had just been imploded. Had we been a few minutes earlier, we could have witnessed the whole structure coming down. Now we wondered what would be built there in the future.

This time we stayed at Circus Circus again. Ralph had come to meet us there, but he was alone this time as Dorothy had passed away on March 13 of that year. Ralph's son Bert brought out a van to Vegas that he had sold to Ralph, so Bert spent the weekend with us also.

Being that Ralph now had a van, he drove us all around in Vegas, which eliminated renting a cab all the time. Being that Ralph was more familiar in Vegas then we, he took us to many casinos where we had never been before and saw many casinos down town this time. But after visiting the down town, we decided that we liked the strip much better. The places on the strip were more up to date, cleaner, and you didn't have street people trying to shove smutty publications in your face.

We went to a newly built casino called Boom Town, actually a replica of an old mining town, which was done in good taste. A tour was conducted which took one through the stages of mining, so a fellow dressed up as a miner helped spectators pan for gold. It was the neatest experience ever. Whatever granules of gold that each person panned out, this man put them in a tiny glass jar of water and capped it up so each one could keep it as a souvenir. I couldn't mine because I couldn't stand that long, but I enjoyed watching them as they reached into the water and sifted out the soil particles leaving the gold granules.

We went to the Palace Station which was a replica of an old railroad station terminal. The neatest was the clocks hanging on the walls with all the different time zones of the world. All the helpers were dressed as train conductors and train travel waiters and waitresses. All of the eateries were set up as train cars, long and narrow with seating on each side. The food was outstanding and a sandwich was a real sandwich usually served on an oversized bun, but so delicious.

The quarter machines were quite liberal that day. One of our group would play this particular machine, it would pay out well. Then another of our group would play, and it paid great all the while. Within our group of seven, we just kept rotating on this machine and it kept paying out. What fun! The funny part of it all was that each one would actually walk away from the machine before another would play it, and not one other person in the casino would even try the machine. I don't know what happened when we left, but we had our share of fun and luck.

One evening we went down town to the Lady Luck casino and went to the magic show. This was a fantastic show put on

371

by the world's first female magician called Melinda. She was a very beautiful woman, I'd guess in her early thirties, who was outstanding in that field of magic. We really enjoyed this show.

This was the year that I won a thousand quarters at two different intervals and at two different places, once at the Riviera, and once at the Hilton. How exciting this was to see a red 7, followed by a white 7, and then a blue 7 all lined up in the same row for the $250 win! At the Riviera, the machine ran out of coins, so I had to wait for the attendant to come over and fill the machine so I could get my pay out. At the Hilton, the machine had enough coins in to pay at the time. What a thrill to win this kind of money even though it wasn't high roller stuff!

One afternoon we met Len and Annie on the street. I told them of my winnings and invited them for dinner with us that evening, my treat. That evening we ate at the Hacienda where the food was good and we sat around gabbing for quite some time, then departed and we all went our separate ways.

In 1993, we didn't go to Vegas because we remodeled the exterior of our home and funds didn't allow us to go at that time. Any how work was still being done on our house for months after it was started in July. But when October rolled around, all four of us missed that year of not going, but at the time our house was of greater importance and in need of the new lift.

In June of 1994 we booked and reserved our rooms so we went to Vegas again. Now that Ralph had been a widower, he had remarried so he and his new wife, Trinidad [whom we called Trini], met us in Vegas. He had his van so he took the six of us around Vegas, including them we were now a group of eight, but we managed okay.

None of us had much luck gambling, so we went to a comedy show at the Stardust called Improv. It was okay, but not done in the best of taste, the humor tended to be of a rare nature, and this is not to my liking. I also cannot tolerate when one nationality ridicules another. This is not my idea of comedy.

Dell and Jim were fascinated with the game of Let It Ride, which was a different form of poker. I never played it but it seems that the first two cards are up, then the bets are placed on three different spots, the next card is down, at which time one may pull back one or two bets, but one bet must remain. One more card is dealt, the same procedure of betting continues on, then the fifth card is dealt down. At this time one determines what kind of poker hand he has. Then the hands are shown one at a time, and the bets are all paid off.

It was at the Riviera that Dell had a heart royal flush going for him except he needed the ten of hearts as the last card, but as one would expect, the last card down was not the ten of hearts, but rather a black ten. Needless to say, he was disappointed because the difference in monetary winnings was greatly lessened, although he ended up with a straight flush with which he won $750, but if he had the royal flush, he would have won ten times that amount or $7,500.

Now Dell really had this notion of a real win in his head and he couldn't get it out, so he and Phil went to Vegas in January of 1995. Dell didn't have the luck at Let It Ride that he had anticipated, but Phil on the other hand won on four duces in that same game. The payout was good so he had won about $750 on that game.

Then he decided to play the same slot machine that Debbie Lee always played at Slots of Fun, which was a double diamond and didn't he luckily win on that machine. To make the story more interesting, he took a thousand dollars along to Vegas and came home with a thousand dollars. Not bad, eh? We joke about it today yet, because with this very money, we paid part of our property taxes for that year.

Phil and Dell had stayed at the Riviera, so they got free complimentary tickets for a choice of shows. Being that they were alone without Debbie and me, they chose to see Crazy Girls. Debbie and I will never go to any shows that has nudity in them, we have more respect for women than that. But Dell and Phil enjoyed the show, and of course they kept telling us that it was humorous and the little bit of nudity that was in it was most tolerable. I say to each his own! But not for me!

Then in October of the same year, the six of us went together again and stayed at the Riviera. When we arrived late in the evening, there had been some kind of mix-up and so our rooms had been rented out. To compensate for this inconvenience, because we had those rooms booked for five months prior, they gave each couple their individual suite accommodations for that night. This was plush because we could never afford to rent a thousand dollar a night suite.

At this particular time a movie was being filmed at the Riviera. This was called 'Casino' in which Sharon Stone, Don Rickles, Robert DeNiro, and Joe Pesci starred. It just so happened that when Dell went to meet Darlene and her friend who already were in Vegas, didn't he run smack dab into Don

Rickles. Being that he was short, Dell almost looked right over the top of him before it dawned on Dell who he really was. Debbie and I saw Sharon Stone off in a short distance. Jim, Dolly, and Phil also saw some of the men stars.

Actually due to this filming, there were electrical cords all around the casino taped to the floor. It was difficult getting around in the casino, and at times certain areas of the casino were blocked off due to the filming. We didn't do much gambling there that year, but went to other casinos to gamble to avoid all the congestion. At this point we were in Vegas to have fun and not watch some movie be filmed and we could eagerly wait to see the movie when it would come out.

The next year of 1996, Jim and Dolly didn't go to Vegas with us because they went to Ixtapa, Mexico with their friends Scott and Amy Parfrey in February. Phil and I stayed with their kids at their house while they were gone. In March they went to Vegas for the tile convention and we stayed with the kids again. Then in April, Dolly and Deb went to Washington, D.C. with the eighth grade class from St. Al's. With all these vacations, Jim and Dolly decided not to go with us this time, but would again go with us in the future.

So Debbie and Dell and Phil and I went. I have to tell you what happened on the plane on our way out. The plane had three seats on one side and three on the other side, so Phil, Debbie, and Dell sat in three seats on one side. On the other side was the seat for our party next to the aisle, so I decided to sit there because it would give me a little more leg room. The other two seats were occupied with a couple who were perhaps a few years younger than Phil and me.

I'm one who likes to communicate with people, so I started talking to the man next to me. He wasn't very congenial so I leaned a little forward and started talking to his wife who was a very nice lady. She told me about their taking two vacations a year, and so one was to Vegas, and the other was out east, Massachusetts, to visit their daughter and her family. She was a most enjoyable lady to converse with, while he just sat there like a dud.

So the flight went on and being that it was a Red Eye flight, the main lights in the plane were off, it was dark, and many people fell asleep. I decided that I could use a little shut eye myself, and wanted to turn off the mini light which lit up an advertisement attached to the back of the seat in front of me. I couldn't find the switch, so I leaned over to ask Debbie across the aisle how to put this light out. She said, "Just pull the cord, Mom".

So I pulled a cord, and pulled and pulled harder and harder and nothing happened. So I thought! All this while the man sitting next to me was just cringing and pulling his jacket closer and closer to himself. I even looked at him in a puzzled expression as to what his problem might be, when I discovered what I had been pulling on so tediously. My face must have turned every color imaginable when I realized that it was this man's jacket cord around the bottom of his jacket that I was pulling on so laboriously. Very apologetically, I tried to make amends to this poor fellow for what I had done. I just wanted to sink right out of sight at this particular moment.

Then I leaned across the aisle to tell Debbie what had happened, and she burst out in laughter. When she told Phil and Dell what I had done, they all laughed so hard, and the more they laughed the more I felt chagrined. The sad part of it all was when this man got up from his seat to leave the plane, I noticed that I had actually pulled the cord right out of the one side of his jacket. Now more than ever I felt bad about what had happened. Needless to say, I never did find the light cord.

Again we stayed at the Riviera. This was the year that the movie, 'ConAir,' was in the making. We saw the plane crashed into the side of the Sands Hotel and Casino, as the movie was in progress. The Sands was one of the older casinos and it was to be coming down anyway. Ralph and Trini met us again this year and we all went out to dinner at the Hacienda. Prior to this time the food was always very outstanding, but this time it was in the least bit edible. But what we didn't know at the time was that the Hacienda would soon be coming down.

We ate at a place called The Dive, and it had a submarine theme. Inside as we sat there looking around waiting for our food, there were waves splashing up on the porthole windows. Now this really gave one the feeling of being in a sub, but before entering this place, we had seen that outside there was water forced to splash onto the windows. But the feeling inside was so authentic. The food here was so delicious.

On the last evening that we were there, we went down town to see the newly created laser show. It was absolutely phenomenal to watch the scenes from the Old West go by portraying some of the former cowboys, Gene Autrey, Roy Rogers and Dale Evans gliding along to the tunes of the old West. It even included a cattle round-up and camp fire themes. All one had to do was to just look up and all around you there they were. It really is beyond describing, you had to be there to envision the magnitude of it.

Our vacation to Vegas didn't materialize in 1997, because in February I had my hip reconstructed.. This meant that I would not be able to travel in October of that year, so we didn't make any plans. I didn't miss it that much either, as I was too caught up in recuperating from the surgery.

On the last day of that year on New Year's Eve, there was a TV special so we watched it. The Hacienda where we had many good meals was being imploded at midnight. Phil and I watched it at home in our own house, bringing back the good memories of Vegas; all the good times, all the electric bills we must have helped pay for in the past, and the clinking of those quarters as they rolled into the coin bin, all the noise, and the music. Then we wondered when we would be able to get back to Vegas again with Debbie and Dell, as the new year 1998 started.

Phil and I already knew that he and I were taking an extended second honeymoon in August and into September with Dolly and Jim, who were celebrating their 25th wedding anniversary. Yes, we were stopping in Vegas on our way home.

Even though we had to wait a long time for our vacations, we enjoyed every minute of each one, and always eagerly contemplate the next one.

Chapter 35
Summer Vacations at the Lake

For many years, Jim and Dolly have invited Phil and me to accompany them on their summer vacations in northern Wisconsin. Jim's parents, Barb and Ted Thuemmler bought property in the Waupaca area in 1972. They liked this area because of the numerous nearby lakes. On this property they had a mobile home. It was very nice and well equipped for a comfortable stay and relaxation.

I'll always remember the huge field stone, or I should say boulder that was in the yard which too was so large. Mother Nature had flattened the top of this rock and it was perched on three stones which were a bit smaller. This was the most natural picnic table that anyone could have. Not too far from this rock was a pit in which the Thuemmlers used for bonfires for outdoor cooking and for sitting around the fire at night as a camp fire.

Most of our meals while there were cooked out of doors. After eating we would all sit around the fire. The children would toast marshmallows, and at times the adults would also engage in this toasting, as it brought out the 'kid' in all of us. .

After the younger children were in bed, the adults still sat by the fire indulging in Old-Fashioned cocktails, until the heat of the flames almost mesmerized us. It had to have been the heat, because it could not have been the alcohol, so we like to think. Getting to bed almost always got to be wee hours of the morning, but the men were always ready for another day of fishing at one or the other of the nearby lakes. They went to Wolf Lake or sometimes to Pickerel Lake.

During the day Dolly would take all the children and anybody who were guests at the time to either of these lakes to swim. What a truly relaxing vacation this always was, and this was a week of no phone calls, no mail to get those awful bills, no knocking at our door, just peace and contentment in the midst of all the natural beauty around us.

Dolly and Jim could tell about the first time Barb and Ted invited them there, they were gone quite a while when Dolly asked Jim if he packed the suitcases, and he told her no that he thought she had done it. So this meant that they had to turn around and return home for the forgotten suitcases. Experiences like this could take all the absolute joy out of vacationing.

Renee tells of the time that she and Jason were fly fishing and Jason hooked her in the finger. This will always stick with her as a memory of vacations, although they laugh about it now that they're older.

It was discovered in this area that after Jim and Dolly took the kids to the petting zoo, Renee's eyes swelled up profusely, that they took her to the emergency in the hospital. When they arrived there, the attendant told them to wait but if her throat swelled up, they could see her ahead of others who had been there first. Well, this was certainly frightening news to hear, but as it was the doctor said Renee was allergic to deer hair, so they treated her. It took years and years for her to outgrow this allergy.

On days that we didn't wish to go swimming, we would play outdoor games, like volley ball, croquet, and water fights. We adults played cards on days of inclement weather, and many times we played card games with the children.

The first year that we were invited to go with them was the year of 1982, a few days after Tanya, their third child, was born. Jim drove his Black Ford Econoline van and Tanya was taken in her bassinet, where she was so comfortable. Jason and Renee were their other children who were so enjoyable to be with. We were six people riding in this van in addition to the baby in the bassinet, but we always managed so well, mainly because we were all vacationing together.

One July in the early 80's when Jason was very young, he spent a few days in Merrill with his Aunt Diane and Uncle Rick. Instead of them driving that long drive back to bring him home to Wheatland, they brought him to Waupaca and spent the weekend with us at the trailer. This was a hoot, and at the same time David drove his El Camino there and also spent the weekend with us. We played so many outdoor games, sat around the bonfire at night, talking and having a few drinks.

Many times while we were there, we spent time taking a ride around the countryside to look for Amish farms. The Amish had a religious culture which condoned the use of anything that was run manually. There were no cars, no tractors, no modern farm machinery, so they did everything the hard way.

We enjoyed watching a family going to town by means of their horse and buggy. Many times I envied them because it looked like so much fun riding in that buggy.

We tried to take pictures as we drove by their farms, and if there were any of the females outside they quickly turned their backs that one could not get a photograph while passing by. After a while we respected their privacy and never even tried to

378

take pictures.

Jim's parents had many enjoyable weeks of vacation there and on Labor Day weekend, they invited their entire card club to spend the weekend with them. I can imagine it must have been wall-to-wall people in the mobile home, but they always enjoyed having friends spend time with them.

In 1984, Barb and Ted decided to buy a cottage on a lake, so they sold their mobile home with the property. They bought a beautiful cottage on Lake Shawano. This so called cottage was a lovely year round home, having a huge L shaped living room with a fireplace, two bedrooms, bathroom, kitchen, closets for storage, a back entry way, and an open porch in the front facing the lake.

The lake was only a matter of feet away from the house, and the children could go swimming any time they wanted as the lake was shallow near the shores. There was little danger of drowning due to the shallowness of the water. Fishing right off the pier was good and the kids enjoyed fishing.

Phil and I continued to accompany Jim and Dolly's family ever since the Thuemmlers had this cottage. It is a place of peace and quiet where one could relax and either sit under a shade tree or in the sun for a tan. In the evenings we ladies would play cards with the children, snack, and have a few cocktails while the children were allowed to drink soda; after all, it was vacation.

In the first few years, Deb and Al and their girls would come up for a weekend and have fun with us, although their oldest daughter Missy was always with us on these vacations as a guest of Tanya for many years.

Renee has taken many of her friends along throughout the years. But her stay was usually for the weekend and she went home on the following Monday.

In later years, Diane, who lived an hour's drive away from the cottage, would bring the two boys, Ryan and Ben, and spend the entire week with us. This would mean that Rick would come on Friday night or Saturday morning, whenever we'd get there, and stay until Sunday afternoon when he would return home. He would have to work the next day, Monday, but Diane would always schedule her vacation during the week when we would all be there.

Each year we look forward to this week in Shawano as we do not see Diane and Rick and their boys very often. This is not quite the long drive from Merrill to come to Shawano as it is for them to visit us at our house in Wheatland.

A few years back, Phil got very ill there and we had to have Dolly drive us home. Diane accompanied her so she didn't have to drive back by herself. Being that Ben was so young at the time, Diane took him along and Jim stayed with the rest of the children.

After we got home, and could finally get a doctor appointment for Phil, it was found that he had heat exhaustion plus a bladder infection. It took a while for him to get over this. The weather was extremely hot, and when one is sick, there is no place like home.

This year of 1999, was not a good vacation. On the first day that we arrived, we weren't even there for two hours, yet, and Phil had his wallet stolen at the grocery store. This was a loss of $500. When we got home, the Green Bay Postal Department had mailed the wallet back to Phil. Needless to say, the money was all gone, but he was happy just to get his personal things back that were in the wallet.

Then on Wednesday evening, Ryan fell off his bike and broke both bones in his arm. Diane, Dolly, and Tanya spent the night in a hospital in Green Bay as Ryan had to have surgery on his arm.

After he returned home, his doctor had to operate again to reset the bones.

We called this the vacation from hell, due to all the unfortunate happenings. But still we look forward to next year's vacation there.

Chapter 36
School Celebrates 125 years

St. Alphonsus School, now in its 125th year of operation, held a celebration March 29, 1998. The momentous occasion began with a 10:30 Mass celebrated by the alumni of the school and the faith community of the parish. Past and present students and faculty along with their families were cordially invited to attend this Mass followed by an Open House in the school cafeteria with refreshments being served from 11:30 till 2:00 P.M. This event was well attended accompanied with a great deal of reminiscing of years gone by.

Prior to this celebration, on March 5, I had the honor of being interviewed for the Kenosha News newspaper which was published in that next Monday's paper. Julie Muellenbach, the present principal, made the arrangements for this, so Julie, the reporter, and the photographer from the paper came to our house for this interview. This was something that came up at a very short notice, actually one day. I only had a short while to think about what I would like to say, but when Kathy, the reporter, started with the inquiries, I suddenly couldn't think of what I really wanted to answer. Again I attribute this lack of thinking capabilities to my so called 'tender young brain'. My ability for quick thinking has slowed down at my age.

Following are a few excerpts from the article that appeared in the newspaper.

Student, Teacher, Administrator:
Her Journey Continues

For more than half of that time that the school existed, Arlene Roanhaus has been linked to that school, first as a student, then as a teacher and eventually as an administrator. A lifelong resident of Kenosha County, she has a historical perspective that is tinged with fond memories. She recently shared some of those with reporter Kathleen Troher.

St. Alphonsus School has 66 students in grades one through eight, with two grades taught in each of the school's four classrooms. Tell me about the atmosphere there.

"I would say anyone who enters the school feels most welcomed. Their needs are certainly met. Throughout the school it's like a family atmosphere. You go out on the playground and see the older kids looking out for the younger kids. There's much to be said for that."

When did you start attending classes at St. Alphonsus?

"I started there when I was 5 years old, so that would be back in 1931. When I started teaching there I taught third and fourth grades for eight or nine years, then I became principal in 1973. It was a dual job: teacher and principal combined.

I taught fifth and six grades, and did all my administrative work in the evenings and on Saturdays. When I started there my salary was $1,250 per year, no benefits. That was in 1964. And it was just a verbal agreement between the priest and me. All of my children went to school there, and my grandchildren are there now".

What was the school like when you were there?

"Well we still had the same four classrooms, but a lot of modernizations have taken place. Years ago we had a very basic curriculum. We didn't have any fine arts. The only music we had was choir for church, every Friday afternoon".

What do you think the future holds for the school?

"Well I do not see it closing. When the nuns left [in 1973] and they went to an all-lay staff, people at that time were really in a frenzy, thinking the school might close. But the parents kept it going. They saw to it that we got lay people to staff it".

Tell me about the support from the parents and the parish community.

"The parents wanted the school so much that they upped the church dues. We had no tuition at the school. The church dues paid for the teacher salaries."

There had been no tuition?

"That's right. When the nuns were there they received very little money. Then, when they left, the church dues were upped. Tuition did not start until 1989, except for people who were not parish members".

Can you share with me a favorite memory about the school?

"From when I was a student or a teacher?"

Either one.

"Well, I'm writing a book now. It's called 'Threads of Memories', and it's going to be about my life. Now I'm on the school section of it, and when I sat down the other day to start that part of it I was thinking the thing that impressed me the most was when I was a first grader, and I was 5 years old. I was chosen to have a lead part in the eighth grade play. And of course you know that was big stuff. I think that left a lasting impression on me."

"And I think the other impression...maybe I shouldn't tell you this...but I was always kind of a high-flier in school. Things came easy, so I had fun you know. If you look at my knuckles, I have big knuckles from the nuns rapping them with a ruler. And the nuns would pull you ears, so I have big ear lobes".

So you're writing a book?

"Yes, I'm doing it mainly for my grandchildren, because I was born and raised on a farm, and things are so different now. Sometimes when I tell them stories they say, 'Oh, grandma, that's so interesting.'

But I'll tell you who really gave me this idea-- my last graduating class that I had at St. Al's. One of the girls said, 'Oh, Mrs. Roanhaus, you've got to write a book, and don't forget to put us in it'. That's really what gave me the incentive".

When you consider the school's history, what do you find interesting?

"One thing that stands out in my mind was the cost the school was built at. It cost about $10,000 to build the school in 1916."

What else would you like to see at the school?

"Well, I'd like to see that they have a kindergarten and a day care program which they are working for. I see a need for that in the community. I'd also like to see a huge multi-purpose room accessible for handicapped people. And they really need to work on the teacher's salaries. Those teachers are deserving of much more that what they are getting now".

Immediately after this interview came out in the Kenosha Newspaper, I received many congratulatory responses from former students, parents of students, friends, assembly men, senators, and people who didn't even know me.

I received one very negative response from a nun, whom I did not know, because she didn't have the backbone to identify herself in the letter she wrote to me. She criticized me greatly for speaking out the truth, and she outright called me a liar. I wish that I could meet with her personally and I'd like to tell her what a good education I received from these teaching nuns. By no means did I intend to discredit or demean them in any way, as I had eminent respect for them and still do, but I spoke the truth.

The history of the St. Alphonsus School is unique and exceptionally inspiring as to how the founding fathers established the beginnings of Catholic Education in our community.

In 1863, education began in a most informal way with classes being taught in a home. Quite eccentric in nature for this time frame, school was taught by two laymen teachers, Henry Toelle and another parishioner named Lampe, who volunteered their services. This arrangement continued for nine years.

The first building erected as a school was constructed during the pastorate of Father Nicholas Zimmer in 1872. This initial school was staffed by the School Sister of Notre Dame, who remained for four years.

Years later, a chapel was added to the school to accommodate the winter weekday Masses. Franciscan Sisters of Charity staffed the school with a seventy-one student enrollment. Grades one to four were in one room and grades five to eight in another room. Some of the subjects were reading and writing in German, Arithmetic, Catechism, Bible History, and Spelling. Special classes for girls were: knitting, darning socks, and carpetbagging. Special classes for boys were: picture framing, cross-stitching, and darning socks.

Many children walked to school or came by horse and buggy. Other students who lived farther away stayed at the nun's house for the week and went home on weekends. These families would pay by either money or food and milk. There was no such thing as graduation, when children received their First Holy Communion, that usually was the end of school for some children, while others went on for a few more years to school.

A new four-room school was built of solid brick construction in 1916, having dining and kitchen facilities and a chapel on the lower level, plus an auditorium above the main floor. This same structure, which is presently known as St. Alphonsus School, was built for an approximate cost of $10,000. [I remember so well, the part of the kitchen which was once a monstrous coal bin, and the unsightly green curtains that divided the cooking area from the dining area.]

The hot lunch program for students didn't evolve until 1961 for student cost of forty cents. Up until that time, students had their daily menu of sandwiches, fruit, and a homemade cookie that Mom packed in a famous lunch bucket. If you were lucky, you even had a thermos filled with milk from the farm. This school was dedicated in February of 1917.

School Sisters of St. Agnes were engaged for staffing the school in 1934 with an enrollment of one-hundred twenty students. This order of nuns remained here for thirty-nine years. Athletics have always held a priority in the area of extra-curricular activities, as back in the 40's, Father Michels was manager, head coach, and referee of a parish young people's basketball team. Father Michels was responsible for many major improvements in the school, and indoor lavatories were installed as well as plumbing in the hall on the main floor. Now students could wash their hands before eating lunch and after using the lavatory.

In 1959 the kitchen and cafeteria were modernized with the building of new cupboards, two sinks were installed, a huge refrigerator was put in, several stoves were installed along the back wall, which used to be the coal bin in years gone by. A central workspace with a butcher block type top was arranged in the center of the kitchen. This kitchen was now much easier for the ladies to work in for the turkey dinners served at the fall festival.

During this time, after so many years of an all-religious staff, the first lay teacher ever since the beginning of the school, Mrs. Rachel Herda, joined the teaching force. In 1969 the first school board was organized with the official title of School Commission on Education, by Sister Mary Ellen Johnson. Members were Richard Elverman, Stanley Lois, and Lillian Robers.

In 1973, the sisters were retrenched from duties here so Mrs. Arlene Roanhaus, who had been teaching here for eight years, became the first lay teaching/principal with a complete lay staff. She was instrumental for many changes being introduced: physical education and music classes were taught by special teachers, band instrumental lessons were taught, but a school band never materialized due to lack of interest on the part of the students. Costs of individual lessons might well have been a factor.

At this time all library books were pulled from the classroom shelves and a central library was started. More sports were made available for the students: softball, volleyball, basketball, and track and field for boys and girls, and cheerleading for the girls. Enrollment was now one hundred students.

In the 1978 -1979 school year, Mrs. Roanhaus resigned from principal duties, so was replaced by Harriet Kaluva. After she worked there for three months, she was not doing a good job so Father asked her to leave. Mrs. Roanhaus got the principal job right back again.

In 1981 Mrs. Roanhaus resigned as Principal due to health reasons but continued to teach the junior high school students. In 1983 the school became accredited under the principalship of Mrs. Carol Degen. It was at this time that the school mission statement and philosophy was established by the faculty composed of Carol Degen, Arlene Roanhaus, Betty Justman, and Sara Peroutky. This staff put in long tedious hours on composing this and researching information for the reports for accreditation

St. Alphonsus School Philosophy

The philosophy of St. Alphonsus School is the provision of experience and understanding in a Catholic environment, so as to enable the student to develop personally, physically, morally and Spiritually, intellectually, and socially: that the student may build upon;
-faith to become rooted in Christ,
-hope so he may meet the challenges in our ever-changing society,
-love for Christ and for his neighbor,

that he may become an effective individual, regardless of race, color, or religion, in a productive and satisfying role in society and in the church community.

Mission Statement

St. Alphonsus School, a community of faith, will provide the best opportunity for the realization of the three aspects of the mission: proclaiming and teaching God's word, celebrating the sacred mysteries, and serving the people of the world. Students shall graduate from St. Alphonsus School having intellectual knowledge, sound morals, effective decision-making abilities, loyalties to God, to the parish community, to their families, and to one another, through specific defined objectives.

In August of 1982, the classrooms were remodeled and the tall windows that had been there previously since the building of the school, were blocked off and new roll-out windows had been installed. This enhanced the looks of the classrooms.

Of special interest was a project that Mrs. Roanhaus and her seventh and eighth graders took on. We sent an order to NASA to do an experimental project. Thus involved planting tomato seeds that had been taken into space and left there for one year. When the seeds were brought back, they were shipped in September to be planted and cared for and a log of progress kept as as to report back to NASA on the class findings.

In April 1989, Carolyn Miller Chambers resigned as principal and Mrs. Arlene Roanhaus finished her term for her. Mrs. Roanhaus,who was retiring from teaching accepted the principal job for the 1989 - 1990 school year. For the first time ever, was the principal job separated from the dual position of teacher/ principal. Mrs. Roanhaus hired out for part time but it became more extensive than that. It became a full time position due to the many jobs that she was responsible for., for part time pay. At this time Mrs. Pat Vos volunteered to do the office work for Mrs. Roanhaus to help free up some time for her to do her administrative work.

After she retired from all duties, Mr. Brian Jones was hired as principal and remained there from 1990 until 1992. He was replaced by Sister Roserita, who only lasted in her position for three months and was asked to leave. A Dr. K. from Illinois finished out her year.

In 1993 Kurt Lundgren was hired as Principal until 1995. The school suffered during some of these years until Miss Julie Muellenbach accepted the position of Principal. She prefers to do some of the teaching along with this administrative job, but she has the time because she has a secretary employed.

Some of the later changes within the school that Julie was responsible for starting include the building of a computer lab, installing new playground equipment, and implementing German and Spanish Language classes taught to the students. Extra curricular activities include the Yearbook, and class trips to Washington, D.C. There are two new fund raisers held annually, a Breakfast during Catholic Schools Week, and a Fish Boil prior to the season of Lent.

The staff now includes six teachers and two classroom aides. Four teachers are employed for full time teaching and the remaining two are special teachers who are employed for part time. One teaches physical education and the other teaches music. The full time teachers continue to work within those same four original classrooms.

Being that the nun's house is no longer rented out as a private home, new carpeting has been installed and the music classes are held in that building. This offers plenty of space and these classes do not disturb the remainder of the school during the times that music classes are held.

There are many needs and concerns within the school that need to be addressed yet today as well as in the near future. One of the present urgent needs is to provide a facility with ample space for holding parish functions that are wheel chair accessible. The community needs a Day Care and our school could provide it along with a Kindergarten.

Of utmost importance is the need to offer fair wages to the teachers along with other benefits, if our school intends to keep quality teachers employed. Many top notch teachers have left the system due to the wages and lack of benefits.

Even today St. Alphonsus continues to offer quality Catholic Education with a professional staff who practice the Philosophy and Mission Statement of St. Alphonsus School. These teachers, along with Julie Muellenbach are to be complimented for their dedication and loyalty to our parish school.

Chapter 37
My Second TV Appearance

Not long after the school celebrated its 125th anniversary on March 29,1998, I received a telephone call from a man named Bob Daugherty from WIN TV Station representing southeastern Wisconsin. The studio was located in Burlington. When I answered the phone, he identified himself to me and stated, "I suppose you are wondering why I am calling you". Being so puzzled, I replied, "Yes". He went on to tell me that he had read several articles in the newspapers about my having been a student, teacher, and administrator at St. Alphonsus School, and he was interested in doing a feature about me relating my past experiences in affiliation with the school.

This particular TV station focused on a person in the community who had been engaged in something notable or outstanding on the Forever Young segment. This was aired for two days in a row every hour at 25 minutes before the hour.

Bob then asked if I would consent to participate in this endeavor, that it would be taped right in my own home. A portion of the tape would be dedicated to viewing one of my tutor students being taught by me. It would be someone I was working with at the time of this taping.

Without a doubt in my mind. I told him that I would be honored to participate in this outstanding venture. He set up an appointment with me and told me that the name of the young man who would be doing the interview and the taping was Chris Marchiando who was the stations' technician. In the meantime he wanted me to contact my tutor student's parents and inform them that their little girl would be on TV with me, her tutor.

The little girl I was working with on that particular day and time was Molly Mowery. She had difficulty with some of her school subjects so she came to my house twice a week for remedial help.

Now I have to describe Molly. She had long dark hair, had the most beautiful dark expressive eyes surrounded by the longest lashes, and was just a beautiful nine year old. It was indeed a pleasure to work with Molly because she put her all into learning, wanted so badly to succeed, and this extra help did her the world of good. Actually I loved this little girl as my own grandchildren, that's the close relationship that Molly and I had.

This second time for my TV appearance was very different from the first time I made my TV appearance for homemakers back in the 50's. Being in the studio was completely different than being in my own home. Chris came to my house and only had one bright spot light on me for taping. He asked me questions and I'd more or less answer them and elaborate on the questions asked. This is what he had instructed me to do beforehand. However I had no idea of what he was going to ask me.

After a half hour of my personal taping, we waited for the school bus to stop and let Molly off. When she was settled, I brought out the lesson for the day, which was Language [Grammar usage]. Molly was going to have a test on that next Friday at her school, so I had made up worksheets for her. I explained the concept for each lesson to her, then had her do the worksheet.

Immediately following the lesson, I'd go over it with her and if she had any errors, we'd work on that same concept until she understood it.

After Chris had the footage that he wanted, he told us when this feature would be aired on the Forever Young viewing. Molly was so excited and couldn't wait until she got to school the next day to tell her classmates and friends that she was going to be on TV the next Wednesday. Most of the kids thought she was joking until they saw for themselves, Molly was now a celebrity!

I taped the airing on a tape so I could have it for a remembrance.

In late August of 1998, I was watching the CNN news and a little later I heard this voice say, "Mrs. Arlene Roanhaus, a dedicated retired teacher still feels the importance of teaching so she does private tutoring in her home. This will be coming up soon as a special feature for the opening of a new school year approaching rapidly.

Here is a copy of the Thank You note, dated April 8, 1998, that I sent to Bob after all was completed.

Dear Bob,

Thank you for the recent coverage on Win TV on the Forever Young segment. It was an enjoyable experience for me as well as the little girl whom I tutor. I thought you did a great job of editing because the day Chris was here, I was a little nervous about express-

ing myself, as you can realize this tender aged mind does not think as quickly as in the past. I was a little concerned as to how it would all turn out until I saw it on TV. Many people saw this segment on TV and commented as well as complimented on the good job you did. Molly, the little girl, was simply ecstatic about being seen on TV. Again, thank you so very kindly for providing this marvelous experience for both of us.

Gratefully,
Arlene Roanhaus

Bob responded back to me as follows:

Dear Arlene,
Thank you for your kind note about the Forever Young feature. I really had little to do with producing it and have passed your note on to Chris Marchiando who put it all together. I'm glad you enjoyed it and thanks for allowing us to showcase your good work.
Sincerely,
Bob

This was another great experience in my life and I will treasure the memory of this adventure for the rest of my days.

As a student at St. Alphonsus School, I have to credit the Sisters of St. Agnes for an excellent quality education that they afforded to me. I wasn't always in tune with being such a *goodie* because I was as full of mischief as anyone could be. Things came easy for me, so I had fun. Enough said...............

After having taught in public schools for many years, I stayed home for a time to mother our eight children. I missed teaching so much that I started teaching at St. Alphonsus School. At that time, I was hired by Reverend Peter Grabauskas with a handshake and verbal agreement, with no benefits granted, for a salary of $1,250 per year. I was happy, however, because I was back into teaching.

As a teacher there, I was a very strict disciplinarian, who treated the students with respect, fairness, and a great deal of love. I demanded quality work from the students and they reciprocated. When the students would become mischievous, I knew exactly what they were up to. Often times, they would remark, "Mrs. Roanhaus, how did you know that we were up to that?" I never divulged myself, but remember what I have just told you about myself as a student, I was full of the dickens so consequently I could predict their every move by just relating back to my own days as a student. But I never used a ruler on knuckles nor did I pull ears as had been done to me. All I needed was a stern look or a raised eyebrow, and they knew what I meant.

Now, in my tender age, as a retired teacher, I feel that I have touched lives in a positive way, because former students approach me yet and express their gratitude. This, in itself, makes all the sacrifices and lack of a reasonable salary, all worth it. I loved my students and my job.

Now, on the other side of the coin, so to speak: as a principal at St. Alphonsus School, I have always dealt fairly with the students endeavoring to bring out their best qualities to help them develop personally to become productive individuals. Many times I was confronted with issues involving student needs. This gave me the opportunity to guide them, make them aware of good morals and values, and in many cases to help them build their self-esteem. Students were very open to approach me with their problems and needs, because they realized that I would listen, discuss, and help them. One of the greatest attributes of St. Al's School was the respect that the students showed for themselves, their peers, and for authority.

St. Alphonsus School has come a long way from its beginning 125 years ago until now. We have a most capable principal, Ms. Julie Muellenbach, who shows love, concern, and loyalty to the students. Julie sets the best example for all the students as well as for her staff. She has a supportive staff of teachers. Another member on staff is the dedicated Mrs. Treasure Besch, who contributes to student learning with her nutritious hot lunches that she prepares daily for the students. She is a truly dedicated lady who, like Julie, takes her tasks seriously and performs in an expertise manner. My real hope is that Julie can become a full-time principal, who has her classroom teaching eliminated, except for a few specialized subjects for which she is so apt. No one can realize how much work, time, and sacrifice there is involved in carrying out administrative duties. Our whole parish needs to support her in her work and ideals so our school can continue to grow. Catholic education is such a vital entity in young people's lives, that we all need to cooperate in keeping our school active to continue to give quality education in the future as it has in the past.

Closing thought for the future.

May God in His almighty power and goodness, grant St. Alphonsus School the continuance to grow to endure another 125 years of service affording quality Catholic education in our faith community

Submitted by Arlene [Lenz] Roanhaus, class of 1940.

Chapter 39
Our Second Honeymoon

I guess after fifty years of marriage a couple deserves a second honeymoon, and this is exactly the way Phil and I felt about it. After living together for fifty years, we grew to know each other very well. We shared everything together, enjoyed all the good times together, helped each other survive the bad times, but with the help of God we always made it through.

Having raised eight kids and helping them as adults along the way, listening to and guiding them and sharing in many of their good times as well as their bad times, it was now our turn to get away and enjoy time together. And that we did!

About a year after celebrating our 45th wedding anniversary, our son-in-law Jim told us one day, "Save your money, mom and dad, because the year you are married 50 years, Dolly and I will be married 25 years and we're all going together on a cruise, and we'll stay two weeks."

At the time I thought, "Sure, talk is cheap, but I'll be dreaming about a cruise long after our 50th wedding anniversary had gone by". This statement proves that I felt that in my mind this plan could not and would not materialize.

But being the person of great faith that I am, I did start saving money with hope. All the while I saved, I also dreamed. I had always wanted to go to Hawaii but knew that I never would have the opportunity to go there. My dreams as well as hopes continued for the next couple of years.

When it got to be June of 1997, I asked Dolly on the phone one day if Jim was really serious about taking a cruise. She told me that she believed that he really and truly was serious, but he never had mentioned any more about it.

A few days later, Jim approached us and told us that we had better start making anniversary plans. He had thought about it for some time and suggested that perhaps we could either go to Hawaii where Dolly and I wanted to go, or we could go to Alaska where he and Phil desired to go. At that time we told him to make plans with the travel agent and whatever he came up with was agreeable to us.

A couple of months later, he had a first set of preliminary plans drawn up by the travel agent. When he showed them to us, I was in awe. He had planned a four day cruise with stops off in Catalina Island and Encinata, Mexico. Then we would fly to Oahu and stay for four days, and fly on to

Maui for a four day stay, then on our way back home we would stop for a few days in Las Vegas before returning home. We both liked these plans and told Jim to proceed on as this was great with us.

In the autumn of that year we made our first down payment on the entire trip, and by January of 1998 we had our total vacation paid in full. All we needed now was the spending money. Now I knew my dream was coming true after all these years, we were taking a cruise and we were going to Hawaii.

Time went on and before we knew it, the end of August had come. Darlene was going to stay with Dolly and Jim's kids while we were gone, and our neighbors Marty and Chris were going to keep an eye on our house.

On Sunday, August 30, 1998, the limo picked us up at home at 1:00 P.M. After loading all our luggage which consisted of four large bags to be put in baggage and two carry ons, plus my huge purse, my forearm crutches and my wheelchair. Jim and Dolly's luggage was already in the limo, and after they helped us, we all got into the limo and we were off to O'Hare Airport in Chicago.

We left Chicago on Reno Air enroute to Reno, Nevada, where we had to transfer planes to fly to Los Angeles. From the L.A. Airport we took a station wagon cab to Days Inn where the travel agent had reservations for us to stay overnight as it was close to the port from where we would board the ship.

After getting settled in at the motel, we ordered out for food to be delivered. So at 10:55 at night we were eating as we had traveled non-stop and were very hungry by that time. Days Inn was located on East Pacific Coast Highway

The next morning, Monday, August 31, after check out time, the Days Inn Van took us to Port San Pedro, from where we would embark for our cruise. After reading so many brochures, we were cautious about which porters we allowed to check our luggage with. We wanted to be sure that we checked with porters affiliated with the ship or we would have not had our luggage on the ship.

Then we had to go through customs and provide proper identification. After we had our drivers' licenses and birth certificates checked, our boarding passes were stamped and we were instructed to proceed to the next desk to receive our Sail and Sign cards and our cabin keys. We had our marriage certificate with us, but we didn't have to show it at all.

These Sail and Sign cards were like a credit card, showing our name, identification number, name of the ship, the name of our dining room and the time we were to be seated, and our table number at which we were required to sit. These Sail and Sign cards were to be used to buy gifts on the ship and for beverage purchases and gratuities. Everything else on the ship was included in the initial charge.

Finally at 2:00 P.M., we were allowed to board the ship through means of a long ramp. Jim wheeled me up the ramp and onto the ship. As we boarded, there were two mates greeting everyone, a male and a female mate. As I was about to roll down the incline the male mate, who by the way was very handsome, extended his arms out and said to me, "Shall I catch you?" I could only reply back to him with, "I'd love that!" He just smiled back and a "Welcome aboard, folks" greeting.

We went on to find our assigned cabins, as Jim and Dolly were in Cabin M110 and Phil and I were in Cabin M90, because ours was a handicapped cabin. The door to our cabin was wider, and the bathroom facilities were set up for a handicapped person. When we approached our cabins, our luggage was already in there for us.

After we saw our cabins, we looked around the ship which was called the Holiday from the Carnival Line. The ship was huge, having ten decks. Starting from the bottom on up, there were the Deck 3, then Riviera, Main, Upper, Empress, America, Promenade, Lido, Verandah, and top most deck was the Sun Deck.

By this time we were hungry so we went to the Wharf Bar and Grill and had some hot food at 3:55. I had chicken stir fry and a salad, and the food was delicious. After eating, we scouted around the ship to see what was all on it.

The Information Desk was on the Main Deck just around the corner from the hallway where our cabins were. Also on this Main Deck, which was located midship, were the Video Diary/Snorkel Desk and also the Shore Tours Desk.

Elevators were located fore, midship, and aft on each deck, which made everything on the ship easily accessible for everyone no matter where your cabins were.

Below the Main Deck was the Riviera Deck where more cabins were located. Below the Riviera Deck was the Tender fore, and the Infirmary aft.

On Upper and Empress Decks were strictly cabins, and nothing more. But there were stairs on every deck located near the elevators.

On America Deck in the fore were: Americana Lounge, Galleria Shopping Mall, Beauty Salon and Union Square. Midship on this same deck were: Carnegie's Library, Rick's Cafe, and the Four Winds Dining Room. On the aft of the ship on this same deck was the Seven Seas Dining Room, where we were assigned to take our meals, but we ate all over the ship and didn't always go to the dining room. The Children's Playroom was also on this deck.

On the Promenade Deck in the fore was the Americana Lounge upper level, Photo Gallery, and Times Square. Midship was the Gaming Club Casino, Bus Stop Bar, Cappuccino's, Tahiti Lounge, Reflections Dance Club, and Broadway. In the aft were the Blue Lagoon Game Room, and the Children's Pool.

On Lido Deck in the fore was the bridge, in the midship were the Patio Bar by the Pool, the Wharf Bar and Grill, and the Pizzeria. In the aft was another bar by another Pool.

On the Veranda Deck were the V1- V10, Radio Room, Nautical Spa and Gym, and Volleyball Court. At the upper most part was the Sun Deck.

At 6:00 P.M. which was the first seating for eating, and we were assigned to that time, we ate in the Seven Seas Dining Room. The service was great and the meal was a five course meal. Each time we had our own waiter Alan and our own beverage server for our table was Roberto. The menu choices were so unbelievable and so different, but we didn't have anything that we didn't like as the food was tasty and of such variety and served in such a delectable manner.

Aboard on this ship were 1400 guests, 600 crew members, and 40 different nationalities of young people employed on this ship. Shortly after we were on board, everyone was called to a certain point of the ship as was posted on the back of each cabin door, to meet at that particular designated place for a safety drill. All people in wheel chairs had to meet at a certain point and the person's relatives or traveling companions were allowed to stay with them. We had to put on our life jackets and then were instructed where to go if there was an emergency. I was impressed at this drill at how well it was handled.

Our cabin steward was a French fellow by the name of Fidel Guevara. He was very nice, hard to understand, but he kept our cabin neat. Every evening after dinner, the cabin steward had turned down the bedding, and had left a 'Sweet Dream' message with a candy mint on each pillow. A clean

398

bath towel was folded into a different shape every day. Some were in animal shapes, but the cutest was an elephant and he perched Phil's sunglasses on the elephant's trunk.

Each day he folded my nightgown into a shape also, from a flower to an anchor. This was so creative.

Many afternoons we'd spend at the Bus Stop Bar and have cocktails. We usually had a bar waitress who came from Slovakia, whose name was Yana Mokikova. She was such a sweet young girl.

We always managed to have the drink of the day, as each day it was different. I stuck to my Pina Coloda's though, as a half a slice of fresh pineapple was served with every drink, and I liked that. Phil and Jim always had the drink of the day, But Dolly had her own choice as I did.

The first night we were there, we were already out to sea, so the gambling casino was opened, and we took advantage of that. At midnight, we went to Doc Holiday's buffet. That night we retired at 1:05 A.M. In our cabin was a printed agenda of the next day's activities, so we could select what we wanted to do.

On Tuesday, September 1, we were in port of Catalina Island at 7:30 A.M. In order to go ashore, we had to board a tender at the gangway located at Deck 3, Forward. We had to remember to take along our Sail and Sign Cards, our boarding pass and a photo ID, in order to get back on the ship.

Catalina Island has a rich and colorful history. Native Americans who lived there were first visited by European explorers who named the island 'Santa Catalina' after St. Catherine of Alexandria. During the Mexican Era, Catalina was a haven for Yankee smugglers.

In the 1880's Catalina was discovered by vacationers, the town of Avalon was founded as a resort in 1887. It is a beautiful island with great water sports, hiking, snorkeling, kayaking and much more!

In more recent times, Catalina Island is a famous Hollywood playground, located just 24 miles away from Los Angeles. Formerly the city of Avalon was a hideaway for the Hollywood stars, and at present is a popular escape for the rich and famous.

The island is 28 miles long and is owned by Wrigley. Two notable facts are that it has one bank, and the children do go to school. The main street runs right along the beachhead. Off in a distance was the famous Casino Ballroom, and

Museum. One of the attractions there is the horse drawn carriage rides. While there, we took the glass bottom boat ride, and saw the variety of fishes, and the kelp in the waters that is used in the manufacture of vitamins and hair care products. Abalone is common in this area of the ocean. This tour took us on the cliffside of the surrounding hills where many forms of fascinating wildlife can be found including American buffalo.

While there, we did our fair share of shopping and looking, and it was so much fun. We spent a total of $87.77 with the tax rate of 7.66%. The last tender back to the ship left at 4:30 so we went back a half hour before that time, as we left the beautiful Catalina Island.

When we got back and went to our cabin to place all our purchases, our cabin was decorated with anniversary decorations hung all over from the ceiling of the cabin. In the center were attached two Carnival key rings. On the wall was the greeting, Happy Anniversary. All the while we thought that it was complimentary but later found out that Dolly and Jim were responsible for ordering and paying for it. How nice of them to do that. If I had only realized at the time, we should have done the same for them for their 25th anniversary, but at that time I hadn't read all the brochures and didn't know that this type of thing was available.

After this time the ship started moving again and so the gambling casino was opened, so we went to play slots and Dolly and I learned how to play Roulette. Jim played table games and Phil played slots. Nothing big was won, you could win a little and keep playing and lose the same, but it was fun.

We didn't go to the Captain's dinner that evening as we were all too tired from the day's outing on the Island, so we ate at the buffet and had steak. Later before retiring, we went to the pizzeria and took pizza back to the cabin along with a drink.

The next morning on Wednesday, September 2, we had room service deliver coffee, milk, croissants and muffins at 7:35 A.M. Later at 10:00, we had a real breakfast at the buffet.

We went on to the gangway to debark for Encinato, Mexico. We were always instructed through means of the Carnival Capers daily news bulletin, to be sure to carry our Sail & Sign card, and Photo ID with us to be sure to get back on the ship. All guests were subject to handbag inspection when leaving and returning to the ship. They weren't strict about this at all. At this point we had already decided that we were not going to take any of the tours.

After Jim wheeled me down all those ramps and we left the ship, we waited for a cab to take us to the downtown area of Encinato. When the cab stopped, I turned to Dolly and asked, "Dolly, where is the downtown shopping section?" She politely responded, "Mother, this is it". We hadn't even gotten out of the cab when a little girl who couldn't have been more than five or six years old approached us and wanted us to buy Chicklet gum.

I was in amazement at how run down and shabby the buildings were, how poor the streets were as they were putting in new streets, and everything was torn up. The work of building new streets was all done manually by the people, as there was no road construction equipment of any kind. After about three blocks, the streets, shabby as they were, seemed to be in tact, but none of the buildings compared to ours at home.

As we got farther into the shopping district, there were vendors on every corner of the streets. It was nothing at all to see a young mother sitting and breast feeding her baby right out in public, and at the same time wanting to sell something. Vendors became a nuisance, but I realize this is their way of life.

Shopping in the stores was great because the value of 10 pesos in Mexican money was worth one dollar in American money so we had the advantage of real shopping. I made a haul in The Leather Shop. I picked out a Louis Vuitton purse for Darlene that was priced back here at $445 and they were asking $69 for it, so I kept wheeling and dealing with the clerk telling her that it was too much, and she quoted $50, and I said it was still too much, so after about ten minutes of this dealing, she sold it to me for $30. Wow!

Now I wanted one for myself, so I picked out one that sold for $335 here in the states, and again I started wheeling and dealing and got it for $18. Then Phil wanted a lambskin fanny pack and it was $21, again I told her it was too much and after a few minutes, she asked what I would give her and I said $7. She said, "Sold". Immediately I told her that I would take a second one for the same price, and she sold it to me. In Mexico there is no tax, so I really made out great!

We shopped in many other stores, and in all the stores together in Mexico, I spent 966.76 pesos which was $96.68 in American money. The shopping was the good part of Mexico, but we were warned not to drink any water, and to be careful of eating food there, so we had bottled soda or beer, and ate nothing except what was in a bag processed commercially.

The last tender left at 3:30 so we left about 3:00 P.M. and after returning back to the ship, we went to the Buffet and ate. Following this we made way to our favorite spot, the Bus Stop Bar where Yana always waited on us.

We went out on the Pool deck and had cocktails and enjoyed the lazy life out there in the ocean breezes. The ship was moving enroute to San Pedro.

After dinner we went to the show in the Americana Lounge that evening, and the show was great.

Thursday, September 3, was the fun day at sea. At 11:00 A.M., we were directed to go to the Americana Lounge for debarkation instructions by Cruise Director Larry Garlutzo and to learn the debarkation procedures. Luggage handling, Tipping and Gratuities, how to fill out our customs cards for U.S. Customs and Immigration were the topics of importance.

Luggage had to be tagged according to colors and debarkation waiting areas were announced. We were instructed to keep out clothing to wear on Friday in the room, as all luggage had to be outside our cabin doors by midnight on Thursday night. Anyone having purchased over the designated amount had to declare with customs.

We spent most of the day meandering around the ship and enjoying the pool side atmosphere with cocktails. Later that afternoon, we went to our favorite spot, the Bus Stop Bar. That evening we went to the dining room and paid our dues, the gratuities to both our waiters and to the Matre D. At this dinner each of us couples, Dolly and Jim and Phil and I, was presented with an anniversary cake and all the announcements were made that it was our 50th and the kids' 25th anniversary. Everyone applauded and congratulations were coming from all around us.

Later that evening we went to the Americana Lounge, played Bingo, saw another show and later packed our luggage and put it outside our cabin doors. We spent the rest of the evening at the Gambling Casino before we retired.

The next morning, Friday, September 4, we left the ship and went to Los Angeles Airport to fly to Honolulu Airport in Oahu. The gate for us to fly out of was changed twice, but we just made our flight as people were already boarding on United Airlines. It was close!

When we arrived in Honolulu, the MTI representative greeted us with a fresh flower lei and gave us instructions for the orientation to be held the next morning at the Imax Theater. Jim went to get the rented van from Alamo while we waited at the airport before going to our destination, Hilton Hawaiian Village Resort on Waikiki Beach.

When Jim arrived with the van, we started off to our destination and when we arrived there we discovered this place of sheer ecstasy, the Hilton Hawaiian Village where we had reservations. This village is Wakiki's most contemporary and unique resort, a perfect paradise with lush tropical plants and flowers, wildlife, cascading waterfall and a wide range of activities.

We were escorted to our rooms, where we had adjoining rooms. Phil and I had number 3239 and Dolly and Jim had 3240. After settling in our rooms, Dolly discovered that she had forgotten her carry-on case at the airport, so she and Jim drove back to the Honolulu Airport. Luckily it was in the United Airline unclaimed baggage.

When they returned, we went out to a pizzeria in the village and had supper. On our way back to the room, we stopped at the cocktail bar and had a new kind of drink called Lava Flow. It had strawberries, ice cream, and rum blended as the basic ingredients with a half slice of pineapple on the glass, and it was the most refreshing drink. We got hooked that first time we tried it and from then on, that was our favorite drink. Jim and Phil tried many new kinds of drinks while we were there. It seemed as though every drink had a half slice of fresh pineapple served with it.

The next morning on Saturday we boarded a bus and went to the Imax Theater for our orientation. Here we had a continental breakfast of fresh baked sweet rolls, coffee, and fresh fruit juices, We had our pictures taken and it was here where tickets could be purchased for different tours while on this island. After deciding what we would do while in Oahu, we bought many gifts to take back home.

As we left the Imax, we rode a trolley and were taken through the streets of Waikiki with the intent of going back to the resort to get the van. However, we were taken to the famous Hawaiian shopping mart called Hilo Hatti. After shopping there, we rode another trolley back to the resort where we got the van and went through the streets on our own. We saw many places of interest. the Honolulu Academy of Fine Arts, the Federal Building and Court House were two that impressed me.

We stopped at Planet Hollywood and at Hard Rock

Cafe where we ate lunch, and did some shopping at both places.

On our way to the Polynesian Cultural Center we enjoyed the beautiful scenery and many times we stopped to take pictures. We could see two other islands which we thought might be Kauai and Molikai.

Islands represented at the Polynesian Cultural Center were: Tahiti, Samoa, Fiji, New Zealand, Tonga, Marquesas, and Hawaii. This visit gave us the opportunity to experience native-life styles and habitats from centuries ago. The images, history and hospitality of these seven Pacific cultures came alive at the 42 acre Cultural Center.

The islanders reenacted war dances and wedding cere-monies, rubbed sticks to create fire, carved tiki figures, and climbed coconut trees with bare feet. They presented intriguing details of tribal tattooing, ancient transoceanic navigation, and the preservation of history without a written language. They spear fish, they climb 50 foot trees to find fruit, they roast pigs underground, they walk on fire, they tattoo each other with mal-lets, they wield wooden clubs, they make clothing out of bark, they make fire from coconuts, they make jewelry from leaves, yet they are the most spellbound and friendliest people on earth.

We enjoyed their cultural food for supper and later we attended their spectacular show called Horizon. I marvel at how these people have preserved their culture and how proud they are to be who they are.

On Sunday we attended Catholic Church services at one of the conference halls right in the hotel. The priest from a parish called Sts. Peter and Paul from Honolulu said the Mass.

Later that afternoon we drove to Pearl Harbor to see the memorial of the U.S.S. Arizona. On the way we saw sugar plantations and pineapple fields. We stopped to view the pine-apples in their stages of growth, as it was so interesting. We had seen many fields of sugar cane and some of them had already been burned off.

The natural scenery was wondrous beauty in itself, truly magnificent workings of our creator, God. The flowers and trees were absolutely awesome, and the waters were gently splashing against the sands of the beaches.

When we arrived at the U.S.S. Memorial, we had a preliminary viewing of what the tour included. This memorial is kept through the National Park Service, and is property of the

U.S. Department of the Interior.

We had to go to the memorial by boat, but the rangers were very helpful to the people. Words cannot begin to describe this phenomenal memorial. The memorial wall with the multitude of names was edifying and lamentable which made one saddened, and it was difficult holding back the tears. So many families lost all their sons because as we were told that back then when one boy in a family enlisted, all the brothers would enlist and request to all be together. This is what happened at Pearl Harbor on December 7, 1941.

We viewed remains of the ship that were brought to surface. The gunners' turret was quite visible but rusty from age. Outside the display area was the anchor of the ship, ever so huge. I don't like narrating about this whole episode, as it is too woeful. Viewing this makes one appreciate what all these men did for the sake of our country.

On Monday, September 5, we flew to Maui. This is the isle of one-of-a-kind sightseeing, luxurious resorts, great shopping, spectacular sunsets, or just a place to hang loose. We stayed at the Embassy Suites Resort on Maui's sunny west coast of Kaanapali on the seventh floor having another ocean view.

After Jim picked up another van, we went to our destination. We drove around to view the sights. Renting a vehicle allows for one to really see the beauty of the island, and to stop at the places that one wants to see.

On Tuesday we took the drive to Hana. The road to Hana is an unforgettable multisensory experience. It is 52 miles of a winding escapade, with 617 turns and 56 one-lane bridges and takes three hours to get there. Hugging the ocean, this jungle drive passes waterfalls, scenic parks and pools, and the higher elevation allows one to view the beautiful valleys down below. There is no way that one can go around the island with an ordinary vehicle so after reaching Hana, one refreshes with food and drink and makes your way back again. Exciting, but scary in places!

Jim put the camcorder on the dash of the van and taped several miles of this winding road so we could show this to everyone when we got home, as it is so unbelievable. The Seven Sacred Pools of Kipahulu was an awesome breathtaking sight. This was a full day of adventure!

On Wednesday, we went shopping in Maui and ate lunch at Planet Hollywood. We found a place from where we could ship many of our purchases back home. We saw the Bubba Gump Shrimp Store from the movie Forest Gump.

In the evening we went to Lahaina to a Luau. As we entered the grounds we were each greeted with a fresh flower lei and were handed a cocktail, after which time we had our group picture taken with two of the native waiters. Then a picture of each couple was taken. Later we had the option of purchasing the pictures.

Two of the native waiters escorted us to our table The pig [Kalua Pua] was roasted in the ground since early morning and it was now evening. Everyone was escorted to the [Hale A'i] the eating house for a bountiful buffet. A variety of salads, fresh fruits, banana bread, chicken long rice, baked Mahi Mahi. [Pulehu] grilled chicken and ribs, Hawaiian specialities like [Poke] marinated raw Ahi tuna, [Lomi Lomi Salmon] salmon bits with tomatoes and onions, [Haupka] coconut pudding, rice, sweet potatoes. Many coconut and fruit desserts were served with coffee. Our personal waiter who served the cocktails was named Kalipa.

After the meal was completed, they put on an excellent show. Their hula dancing is really an art, and looks like it would be difficult to perform. The program started with Ote's , the festive drum dance of Tahiti. Next was the Kahiko, the ancient hula. Then the missionaries and the Merrie Monarch, was followed by Auana, the modern hula, and the finale was Old Tahiti.

One of the interesting features of Hawaii is how the islands were formed, and how the people refer to each island. The island of Hawaii is called the Big Island, Oahu is the Gathering Place, Maui is the Valley Isle, Kauai is the Garden Isle, Molokai is the Friendly Island, Lanai is the Pineapple Island, Kahoolawe is the Target Island due to military forces using it as a target, and Niihau is the Coral Island.

Millions of years ago fiery basalt rock erupted through a crack in the floor of the Pacific Ocean. Gradually the lava cooled and formed great undersea mountains whose summits protruded from the ocean. Over the centuries the action of wind,water, fire, and ice on the chain of volcanic peaks created the islands that became the state of Hawaii - a land of exotic flowers, shining beaches, and majestic mountains.

The first inhabitants of Hawaii were Polynesian sea-farers who came to the islands in sturdy outrigger canoes more than 1,500 years ago. When the British sea captain James Cook discovered the islands in 1778, he found a preliterate but thriving people who bred fish for a better catch and irrigated their taro fields, Today Hawaii has a population more varied than that of any other state: its inhabitants include descendants of the original Polynesian population, of 19th century sailors and traders, of the New England missionaries who brought Western ways to the native people, and of the Asians and Portuguese who came as field hands to work on the islands' sugar and pineapple plantations - mixed with the service personnel from the United States mainland who arm the great Hawaii-based naval and air fleets.

In many ways the 50th state and last state in the Union is the most unusual one, and lies entirely in the tropics. Separated from the United States mainland by the world's biggest ocean, the Pacific, it is the one state that does not fall within the continent of North America. It is the only state that was once an independent kingdom and the only one with a royal palace. It is the only state composed entirely of islands, and the only state not dominated by Americans of European ancestry.

The nickname of the Aloha State comes from a late 19th century Hawaiian word, Aloha, for love that is used as a greeting and to say farewell.

The Hawaiian alphabet has twelve letters Of these twelve letters five are the vowels a,e,i,o,u, and the consonants are H, K, L, M, N, P, and W. There are three basic rules observed in spelling Hawaiian words of non foreign origin. [1] Every Hawaiian word must have at least one vowel. [2] There are non consonant clusters and words cannot end in a consonant. [3] A kahako which is a straight line over the letter, occurs only over a vowel Hawaiian vocabulary.

We soon were taught to say Aloha, which means hello or good-bye and mahalo which means thank you. So 'Aloha'!

On September 10, we flew back to Honolulu Airport to fly back to Los Angeles enroute to Las Vegas for the remainder of our vacation. When we got to Los Angeles, we waited in the airport there for five hours before we could get a flight out, as our scheduled flight had been canceled due to a delay as a result of inclement weather.

When we finally arrived in Vegas, we hired a limo to take us to Treasure Island, where we had reservations. Phil's brother Ralph and Trini were waiting for us as our flight was so late and it was already late at night.

In Vegas we did the usual gambling, but we didn't get to many casinos due to Phil having difficulty walking due to a sun burn he acquired in Maui. His legs and feet were baked, and he was hurting. But this gave us an opportunity to visit a lot with Ralph and spend time with him and Trini.

On September 13, Sunday, we went to church at the Guardian Angel Catholic Cathedral on the strip.

While we were in Vegas, we saw the show called Mystere, Cirque Du Soleil. It was an awesome performance

On September 14, Monday we flew back to O'Hare in Chicago and the limo took us back home, at about 5:30 P.M.

This vacation was more extensive than our first honeymoon, and we enjoyed it immensely.

Phil and Arlene in the Seven Seas Dining Room
on the Holiday Ship
Carnival Cruise Line

Old Lahaina Luai
Phil, Arlene, Dolly, Jim with two table waiters
"Hang Loose" in Maui

Chapter 40
Former Students' Contact

Somehow or other it seems that fond memories of people whom I have taught in the years gone by never fade. As ironic as this may seem, it must be the teacher-student bond that draws us together many years later.

As a matter of fact, many of my past students have become teachers, the fact that makes me proud in hopes that I may have touched their lives somewhat in the past.

From my very first teaching job there was a girl named Donna Weiler, who was so intelligent for her age, and was bored with the level of work in the grade in which she was in. In conferring with her parents, together we decided that Donna could very easily skip the grade that she was in and go a level beyond. So this is what we did for her, and she proved herself to everyone that we had made the right choice in her behalf.

She became a teacher, decided to marry, and when she was expecting her first child, she approached me to inquire if I would like to take the long term substitute job for her at one of the schools in Randall Township where she was employed at Wild Rose School.

At that time, I was home raising a family, and accepted substitute work in Kenosha County whenever I was needed. So I agreed to taking this temporary sub job and enjoyed every minute of it. My mom was always there to babysit for me, so I had the liberty to accept all this sub work, which made me very happy to keep in touch with my profession.

Donna was a very good teacher, well organized, well versed on her subject matter, a good disciplinarian, and was very successful in her profession. As a matter of fact, she has taught in the same school district for all of her years of teaching. We keep in touch at Christmas time, and her note this year stated that she is soon ready to retire. I enjoy hearing from her, and on occasion several years back, I would see her occasionally at the same store where I was shopping.

She has always held a special place in my heart, because at times I could envision her as a younger version of myself. I am flattered that she cared enough to keep in touch with me even at my tender age. This speaks well of her home training due to her having wonderful, caring parents.

Another former student from my first teaching job was Ray Cates. Today he is truly an asset to the whole community.

411

He has and still does hold prestigious positions for helping improve and maintain various organizations through his leadership. His own children. Lori and Tim, are grown now, but Ray still works with children of the community helping them to develop skills and morals through his own love of sports. He is of such fine character, and by his own good life, he portrays good examples for the kids.

At one time he was a member of the St. Alphonsus School Board, during part of my years as principal there. I'll never forget how he stood by me when a member of our parish wanted to home school her son who had been a student for two years in our school. This mother couldn't accept the fact that her son was having difficulty in his work and in his social interactions with other children. Instead of allowing the staff to help her son socially and academically, she wanted him to be home under her wing. Ray stood by me when I tried to explain how detrimental this would be to her child, but there was no reasoning with her because her decision had been preconceived.

On the lighter side of our relationship, I see Ray and Lois every year at the annual church activity, the Smoker. They always make it a point to come to our table and talk with us, and of course I inquire about their children.

Also at this Smoker church function, Ray's brother Jim, who was also a student of mine, always comes up to me and talks a while. He has the nicest wife, and I appreciate that they bother to even acknowledge me at my age.

At this same function, Gale and Gerry Lois, who are parents of two of my former students, always clue me in on the latest on Amy and Brad.

Amy is now a lawyer and I'm sure she is a good one, because she was very well spoken even in elementary school. Brad has his own lawn care and snow plowing business. He was one of the eighth grade graduates of my last class taught.

Another former student of mine who became a teacher is Ray Ziebell. He teaches in the Burlington School System, and at one time taught fifth grade at Waller School, and now teaches strictly Science in the School System. He has a special interest in photography and developing, so he has sent me several pictures from an operetta that I wrote and produced at the school where I had him as a student at Mound Center. He, by the way, had one of the leading parts in this production and played the part like an old timer in the acting field.

A few years ago, he came to our house to visit us during the summer vacation, at which time we did much reminiscing. It was rather sociable for both Phil and me as Phil knew Ray's dad well from trucking in the excavating business. Ray is a very knowledgeable person and so we had much to talk over.

Loretta (Ellingson) Fox is another former student who is a very successful teacher. She has started off as an elementary teacher, went on to school and became a reading specialist. Recently she moved to Florida where her mother had moved to many years ago. Loretta is now teaching Kindergarten in a parochial school in Florida.

Another former student was Tim Hubbard. In later years he came to me for private tutoring to help him prepare for applying for a driving license. He passed the written test and got his license.

Many former students of mine are ushers or lectors in church. I often see Larry Lois, Lennie Vos, Ray Vos, Steve Robers, Tim Lois, and Dennis Poepping ushering at church. This group of young men usually usher at the 10:30 Mass, and when they usher on the side of the church where I sit, they always talk to me after Mass is over at which time they hand me a church bulletin. I'm sure there are many others who usher at different Masses, but it seems so nice that these young men take time to talk with an older lady, me.

Kelly Riley Wilson is one of the best lectors we have in our church. Kelly was a student of mine for many years at St. Alphonsus School. She speaks so fluently and uses expression which makes listening to the readings a pleasure because they are meaningful in the way she presents them to the people.

Barbie Lois, who now lives in Burlington and teaches at the Junior High, comes to church here occasionally and I get to talk to her at those times. Not long ago, I asked her if I could dedicate my book to her, and she agreed to it immediately. I think she was really elated about it. Recently Barbie became engaged to marry.

Another student from St. Alphonsus School in the third and fourth grades classroom during the 1974-1975 school year at which time I was Principal, is David Kreutz, who now teaches at Burlington High School. When he first was employed there, he asked my daughter-in-law, Debbie, if she knew a Mrs. Roanhaus that used to be at St. Alphonsus School. Debbie replied, "Yes, she is my mother-in-law".

Then David went on to tell her how strict I was at school back then. He told her of the time when the kids were coming in from recess and were lined up outside the school, he had the top buttons open on his shirt. When I saw that I called him a Hooligan and told him to button up his shirt. I remember this incident so vividly, and apparently he does too. Now I hear that he's a truly an outstanding science teacher and coach.

I wish that I could have the opportunity to see David in person, I'd like to visit with him and reminisce some of the days from back at that time in school. He had such a wonderful mother and often times I wonder what happens to many of these parents of students who attended St. Al's.

Another former student of mine, Jane Richter Peterson, worked in the office of the high school. When Debbie told her that I was writing a book, she indicated to Deb that she wants to read it after it is published. Jane works in schools within the Burlington School District.

During my course of teaching religion I taught a husband of another former student, Dawn Polawaczk. She married the nicest fellow and they have a son who is very intelligible. At times the world seems to become much smaller than it really is, when incidents like this happen.

Back at St. Al's, I had a young girl work for me through the youth program whose name was Rose Meyer. She sends me a Christmas card ever so often. She did odd jobs like putting library books on the shelves, dusting the shelves, and other little jobs around my office. She was genuinely a nice girl.

Not so long ago, I had a phone call from John Robers, a former student of mine from St. Alphonsus. He lives at Clear Lake, Wisconsin. John was hit by a car after he left our school, and was hurt badly . Our students wrote to him many times and prayed for him at that time. He was tutored privately during his earlier high school days, as he wasn't able to attend school. I was so happy to hear from him as now he is married and has a daughter. John sounds so happy.

Recetly I saw some of the Banas children at my brother's funeral. I had a nice long talk with Christine, whom I taught when she was in fourth grade at St. Alphonsus. I talked with her brother, Steven, who always was so personable and friendly, although I never had him as a student, but he was in the same school.

I also met one of the twins there also, but as per usual, I never could tell one apart from the other, as they were identical twins, David and Danny. When I said hello to him, I told him that some things never change, I didn't know which twin he was.

I knew that he expected me to say that, but it was David. It was so neat as he said, "Remember, Danny is the smart one, and I am the good looking one". I replied, "But I know that you have both these qualities, smart and good looking". It was so nice meeting them again as their family was so special, but they had such wonderful parents, Dorothy and Wally Banas.

I didn't see Danny, but the truth of the matter is that Danny also was smart and good looking. These twins were the nicest kids and always had such good manners along with being so friendly.

I can't forget the Elverman kids. I see them at church and once in a while at church functions. I had all these children in my classroom at one time or another: Diane, Jackie, Joanne, Dan, and Ron. Diane was always so helpful when she was in my classroom. Whenever I was teaching one grade, she would get out my teacher's manual for the next class that I would be teaching. Diane was such a Miss Efficiency Plus, and I did appreciate her help. Her two children now go to St. Alphonsus School.

For the past few years, Dolly takes Phil and me to the Kenosha County Fair in Wilmot. We like to see the 4-H exhibits, the open class exhibits, the booths in the educational building, the commercial buuilding, and see our grandchildren's rabbits on exhibit.

As I was looking at the photography that was displayed, I met another former student of mine who had been a first grader when I taught at Wheatland Center School. Her name was Lola Karow Stubblefield. I hadn't seen her since she was in grade school, but somehow I recognized her right away, as she recognized me at the same time. We both caught up momentarily on what our lives are like now, and it was such a joy to see her as I always liked her.

Often times I see another former student, Patti Johnson Huston, who works at Sentry's Store in the floral department. Occasionally I see her in church with her mom, and sometimes I see her sister Karen with them.

Not long ago, I received a note in the mail from Patti. In the note she had thanked me for the good education that I had afforded her while she was a student of mine. She aslo stated that she was so grateful that she knew how to spell because so many people whom she worked with didn't know how to spell. I actually felt elated about getting this note. So many years later, she bothered to take time out of her busy

415

schedule to make her feelings known to me.

Last, but not by any means the least, I have to relate the importance of my relationship with Keli Jo Lenz, who is my great niece. She was in fifth grade during my last year as Principal. She is and always has been a great kid. She is very sports oriented and now is in college in Alabama utilizing a full scholarship which she earned through her years of playing high school baseball. She is a good student along with being such a great athlete, and carries a 4.0 grade point average.

She works very hard on her school subjects as the book learning doesn't come easy for her, but she puts her all into her education. This is not always easy for her, because when she travels on the road to play all the games she plays, she still has to study even enroute to and back from games.

After she graduated from elementary school, she had difficulty with a couple of her subjects, due to having an inexperienced teacher. So Keli Jo came to me during the summer months and I helped her to understand the concepts that were not presented to her properly. She is very bright and is certainly an asset to any ball team.

Now she has grown to be a beautiful young lady, who is very poised, friendly, lovable, and is fun to be around. She is witty and humorous and well spoken. Keli Jo is so special to me.

There are so many more students with whom I have had contact, but these are the ones that come to mind now.

I treasure all these memories of the past of my former students, who have all been special to me.

Keeping in touch with friends and other people whom we were in touch with in the past is as important today as it was back then, so we try to some how keep in touch if it is only once a year, perhaps at Christmas time. In the case of some of the people, it's more often.

Some of these I refer to at only Christmas time include a fellow from Phil's past who was in the armed forces at the same time Phil was. His name is Earl Ollinger who lives in West Bend, Wisconsin. Earl, who likes to be called Bud now, is retired and lives together with his wife Sally. Their five children are either away at college or married with families of their own. We communicate by a card and a letter annually. They have stopped in here once to visit a long time ago and now they are so involved with their family that they find it difficult to find the time to visit us.

We keep in touch with Carol Nickel, whom we used to accompany on our numerous fishing trips. When they moved into the house next door, we were so happy becuase we became good friends and had so many good times together. We visited back and forth all the time, and played a lot of cards together.

She and her husband Gene divorced a few years after they moved away from our neighborhood. We always remember Carol's birthday in January with a greeting card. When we have special celebrations we still invite her to enjoy with us. Not long ago, she and her mother, Vivian, stopped in and we had a lovely visit. She lives in Waukegan, Illinois.

Another person who is very special in our lives is Georgiana (Lois) McNamera whom we all call Jan. Jan and I grew up together on neighboring farms, although she was more of my older brother's age than mine, we always kept in touch. Her mother and dad were so special in my life as they were the ones who opened up their home to me when I needed a foster home in Kenosha so I could attend the Orthopedic School. Their names were Kate and Ed, who to me were my parents of second nature.

During the past years, our friendship has been rejuvenated, because Jan comes to visit us and stays with us a few days during the summer. After she leaves here, she visits my sister-in-law Helen as those two used to work near each other at local restaurants in this area.

When Jan is here, we take a ride to places that she has known from her past. We view places where she used to live when she was in this area. Many things have changed in the vicinity, so we drive by places of her and my past as friends. This summer during August, she stayed with us and the three of us reminisced our days gone by. We enjoyed that visit so much as neither of us are lost for words. It was fun.

Jan had an older brother named Russell. His wife's name was Eleanor. They used to come to visit us whenever in the neighborhood. Russell passed away several years ago, and Eleanor remarried. A year ago last summer, Eleanor and her daughter Patsy and her husband Norman visited us one sunny afternoon, and we had the most enjoyable visit. It was before we were to take our extended vacation. They had been to Hawaii, and they briefed us on sights worth seeing, and especially not to miss the road to Hanna on the island of Maui. I had been very excited about this trip before talking to them, but after they aroused even more excitement and I started counting the days until we'd leave. This past year Eleanor passed away.

Another couple who have been very influential in our lives are Paul and Charlotte Jaeger from Kenosha. They are now retired, but in the past they were both Extension Agents; Charlotte a Home Agent and Paul an Agricultural Agent. They had touched our lives through 4-H and through Homemakers Groups in such a positive way.

After their retirement, we saw them at the county fairs and really only communicate at Christmas time through means of a Christmas card letter, but we value their friendship.

Another person with whom I communicate is Marjorie Graetz, the lady with whom I rode to Wisconsin University in Whitewater. She, too, I hear from at Christmas time and she often times sends pictures of herself and her family.

My room mate, Lynette, with whom I spent a great deal of time in the Kenosha Hospital as she was also stricken with Polio. We write periodically during the year, but it is so difficult for her to write as her hands are so arthritic. I type all my letters to her on my computer, or she would never be able to read my writing due to the Polio settling in my right hand that is now full of arthritis. We often times send pictures and greeting cards for different holidays. There is a certain bond between us from sharing so many times of distress while ill.

Another person with whom we keep in touch only on occasion is my sister-in-law, Helen Roanhaus, who lives in Burlington. We mostly keep in touch by phone and see each other sometimes. She and I have always been friends from the past in addition to becoming sisters-in-law.

Two people who are very special in our lives are Phil's niece and her husband, Jan and Herb Weinaug. Whenever we have a special event in our family, we invite them to share the joys with us. We have had many good times together in the past.

They used to come down and stay overnight at my mom and dad's house. We have done some crazy things while we were engaged in played cards. Many nights of laughter have been shared with them along with my parents.

One night my parents went back to their house right next door to ours, while Jan and Herb stayed and we talked until wee hours of the morning. When they went to go to bed next door, my mom had thought that they were already in, so she locked the door and turned the lights off. So they came back here, and told us about it. We did not want to wake up my parents, so we told them we'd make room here.

We stayed up until four o'clock in the morning arguing who would take Phil's and my bed. We wanted them to take our bed and we'd sleep on the couch, and they insisted other wise. After much discussion, it ended up that I changed the sheets on our bed and persisted they sleep in our bed and Phil and I slept on the couches. We had younger children at home yet, so the bedrooms upstairs were occupied by our children. What a night!

The next morning, when mom discovered that they were not in her house, she came over early and knocked at our door, to apologize for her mistake. Mom never forgot that episode, and needless to say, Herb being the jokster he was didn't let mom forget it either. We have shared many good times in those days.

Jan and Herb usually try to get to see us a couple times a year, and Phil and I always look forward to seeing them.

Jan's brother, Bob, and his wife Linda usually visit us once a year. They attend a dinner and show at Fireside in Fort Atkinson during the first week in November. On their way home after the show, they stop in to visit us. We look forward to this annual visit.

Some people whom we haven't seen in years, are Phil's nephews and niece, Ralph and Dorothy's children. They used to visit us every couple of years as a family and would stay with us for an extended visit. Being that their kids were pretty much the same ages as our kids, they had so much fun together.

For many years, as they were in college, then off to jobs, we hadn't the opportunity to see them at all. Phil and I visited Ralph and Dorothy back in the 60's, but we didn't get out to California until 1992 for Dorothy's funeral, at which time we saw all the kids.

Being that Ralph passed away in early March of 1999, Phil and I didn't get out there to his funeral. Ralph's death was very difficult for Phil emotionally. Ralph's passing meant that Phil was the last survivor of his family, as well as I am now the last in my family. This hits pretty hard.

In May we received a call from Michael telling me that the whole family was coming to Wisconsin for a visit on the week end of June 26, which happened to be Phil's and my 51st wedding anniversary.

It was great seeing the kids. Eric, the oldest, came from Clovis, New Mexico. Michael, his wife Dea and daughter Becca, came from Cupertino, California. Bert, his wife Jeannie, and two daughters, Rhawnie and Randi, came from Henrietta, Texas. Teresa and husband Tom Shannon, came from Oxnard, California. Tom and his wife, Pam, and two chidlren, Carolyn and Derek, came from Colorado Springs, Colorado. The youngest daughter, Janie, had passed away some time back.

They came in on Friday, stayed at a motel Country Inn at Highways 50 and I94, so they were only about fifteen miles from our home.

On Saturday, our family and their family got together at Debbie and Al's place in New Munster. Danny roasted a pig, smoked a turkey and had fish smoked. The rest of us brought dishes to pass, and Dolly made a huge anniversary cake. We had plenty of food.

What fun it was reminiscing about the times when they came out to visit us when they were small children. Many stories were exchanged and much singing was done, and we had a blast to the tune of three o'clock the next morning.

On Sunday, they all stopped in to say good-bye to their Uncle Phil and of course, me. These kids made their Uncle Phil's day. We are going to keep in touch with them.

Friendships are so valuable and now in later life, it is amazing how one embraces the precious memories of friends and relatives from the years gone by, while still seekig new friendships.

420

Jan and Herb Weinaug help Phil and Arlene
celebrate our 50th wedding anniversary
Back: Jan and Herb
Front: Arlene and Phil

Chapter 42
Never To Be Forgotten

There are some people who have touched our lives in the past and so we look upon them as too worthy to ever be forgotten. I refer here to losing some of the people closest to our hearts through their deaths. Death in a sense is a frightful thing, but when searching for true beliefs, one finds comfort in the fact that death is only the beginning of life, which in turn is one's eternal spiritual life. This is a life of true happiness and a state of well-being in a different context from what mortal life is.

Many of Phil's and my relatives have been long gone, only to be remembered for the memories of the happy moments of their presence in our lives never to be forgotten. I'll always treasure these times and consequently continue to pray for them

My Grandma Elizabeth Lenz, a petite little lady, died after suffering the pain that accompanies colon cancer. Her pain and suffering had lingered for such a long time, until God liberated her from these perils of mortal agony. I was twelve years old at the time.

On December 22,1942, Grandpa Nicholas Barbian, who had worked so hard all his life engaged in farming, became ill with pneumonia at the age of 81 years. His lungs gave out from the illness and old age, so he went to his eternal rest. He had always been a very distinguished looking man with the disposition of a saint. I never heard my grandpa ever raise his voice at anything or anyone.

The next of my relatives Grandpa Joseph M. Lenz lived to enjoy many years of life on this planet, as he finally went to his eternal rest on March 29, 1950. at the age of 83 years. Grandpa was a man of tall stature, having a broad frame, and I'm sure that he would have been a successful prize fighter because of his physical build. But like most of the people in his community, he chose the all popular occupation of agriculture.

In the year of 1955, it was Grandma Mary Barbian who was laid to eternal rest at the age of 83 years. Grandma was the one who taught me how to bake at my early age, and I used to like spending time with her as she always took time to explain things to me, and let me do all the baking in her house that I wanted to. She was a feisty woman who never allowed anything to get her down, and I don't think that much ever bothered her, as I never heard of her doing any worrying. If only I could take after her in that respect. She was humorous and enjoyed life, and loved to entertain people.

One of the most traumatic experiences in my life that I cannot forget is the recall of how my younger brother Ardell, at age 25, had been taken to the hospital by ambulance time and time again. The anxieties of not knowing whether he would ever come home again or not, was like waiting for a bomb to go off. This, being so difficult for my parents to endure, put much added stress on them as Ardell's genital heart condition was worsening steadily as time went on.

In my own heart I knew that this was bound to be his last trip to the hospital as he was suffering severely and the look on his face told a whole story, because he knew it too.

On July 28, 1958, after being in the hospital for four days prior, our whole family was called in to be with him. It was very early evening, and we were all at his bedside praying for him. At about ten o'clock the doctor told my parents that we should all go home, as Ardell could linger a while and everyone needed sleep due to previous days and nights being at his side. The doctor promised us that he would call immediately if there was any change.

My mother absolutely refused to go home, and insisted on my staying there with her. The doctor did not want me to stay but mother was persistent. So my older brother, Bob, went home and Phil took my dad home with him, being that mom and dad had built their retirement home next door to ours.

After they left, the doctor told my mother that he was going to take me to the doctor's lounge to rest as I had no business being there in the first place, and that if anything happened he would call me immediately to be with her. After a bit of convincing, she finally agreed.

What mom didn't know was that I was pregnant but the doctor knew because he was my doctor also. I didn't tell her about my pregnancy because she always worried so much about me every time I was p.g. due to the ordeal I had with Danny's birth. I didn't want to burden her with any more worrying as she had enough anxiety and stress over my brother's condition.

I had been in the doctor's lounge for about two hours when all of a sudden I heard a woman's voice screaming as she was hysterically running down the hospital corridor, yelling my name as she was looking for me. It was my dear distraught mother, but I was already up because the doctor had already told me it was a matter of minutes.

I left the room abruptly and went to comfort her until we

reached the room where my brother was. As we entered the room, mother and I each held one of his hands, whispered softly in his ears, letting him know how much we both loved him and that it was time for him to be freed from all his previous suffering as Jesus was calling him to come home. I will never forget the half smile on his face as though he understood and was willing to go peacefully, as he breathed his last breath.

Mom and I were allowed to be with him for as long as we wanted. After a short while of being there, I witnessed the most horrendous thing ever in my life. Blood streamed from my brother's nose until it had expelled about one pint, then it ceased. Mother and I were both bewildered at this sight, but luckily the doctor was with us and explained that this is not uncommon with heart patients as the clogged artery finally gives way from the pressure within.

Mother was always thankful that we were both with him in his last minutes. After a while, the doctor politely told us that we should be on our way home now because there was nothing we could do, and he would make arrangements from there on. He requested that our family all come into his office the next day. At this time, I drove mom home.

When we arrived at my parents' house, I went in with mom to talk to dad. Mother was shattered with grief, and dad had not slept a wink. I stayed with them the rest of the night, or rather early morning hours, trying to calm them both, but what a dreadful time!

Phil was home with our children, so I had to wait until later to let him know, but he already knew as his heart told him so. I have to say that our neighbor lady, Beaty, always watched our children for us every time we had to be at the hospital. We always appreciate what she had done for us.

Mom took this whole ordeal very hard and weeks and months went by before we could even get her to eat again. She was running down physically due to grief. She felt as though her whole world caved in right before her very eyes. It was a long period of adjustment for her, but finally it was our children and my brother's children that helped take her mind off the situation and her deep loss, by showering their grandma with their innocent sincere love and affection. This helped ease her pain somewhat but the pain of the loss never really went away for the remainder of her life.

Seventeen years later, my sister-in-law, Sophie, passed away very unexpectedly on October 26,1975. It was on a Sunday morning, and she was taking a bath before getting ready for church, so she slumped away right in their bathroom at home. My brother gave her CPR in strife to retain her breathing, but to no avail. When the rescue squad got there, she was gone.

My niece, Reggie, came running over to our house just two doors away and awakened me, as our family always went to the late mass, and Bob and Soph and family went to the early mass.

Here was Reggie, standing at my bedside, shaking and calling to me, "Auntie, wake up, it's mom, come quick, it's urgent. I think mom's dead".

All I could say was, "That can't be, you made a mistake, but I'll hurry and go over to your house with you."

Oh dear God! What a shock! It really did happen! How can this be? It was a massive heart attack, being fatal. No one ever knew that Sophie had a heart condition, but I recall how she used to get a distressed look on her face and fold her arms across her chest as if in dire pain. But she was never a complainer, and just took it in its stride. In those days one didn't go to a doctor unless there was something direly wrong, and like the rest of us, she didn't run to the doctor for every little thing.

We called the rectory at St. Alphonsus but the priest was in church saying mass, immediately after church was over, Father Grabauskas came to the house.

Later that afternoon Phil and I went with Bob and his kids to the McCarthy Funeral Home to make funeral arrangements. This was such a sad and distressing task but it had to be done.

I will never forget her, because she was the sister that I never had, even if it is sister-in-law. We got to be very close and did many things together especially shopping. She and Bob and Phil and I went out together many times eating out, and going to dances. To this day I still miss her almost as much as Bob did.

Phil's brother, Marvin, passed away on February 19, 1978, at age 63, due to a terminal illness. He is also so missed by us, as we did many things with Marv and Helen too. Both of them have always been so good to me even when I was little.

Marvin had such a deep low voice, and at times it sounded like he was grumbling and mumbling. At one of the Sheboygan weddings, he made his voice heard very distinctly. People were waiting in lines at the bar to get cocktails and being so crowded, the man and his wife behind the bar waiting on customers were so busy and got behind in many orders. The man yelled at his wife to hurry and get those drink orders out faster, and he kept yelling and yelling at her.

Finally, Marv had enough of the bartender's yelling at her and in his deep low-toned voice shouted, "Get off her G_ _damned back". With that there was instant silence, one could have heard a pin drop. Needless to say, everyone turned to see where that voice came from, and dear little Helen was so embarrassed. I believe that was the last wedding in Sheboygan that they attended.

The next grief that Phil and I shared together was the passing of Phil's dad Joseph Roanhaus on May 8, 1983. He lived an extended life of 95 years and had very few illnesses in his entire life. His cause of death was due to old age. He spent his last few years at the retirement home, Lakeview Terrace, at Brown's Lake where he was actually happy.

In order to be accepted at this retirement home, one had to be self-sustaining. Phil's dad could pretty much take care of his own needs except he was unable to get into or out of a bath tub, so this meant that twice a week Phil had to go to the home and give his dad a bath. Never once did I ever hear Phil grumble about having this responsibility as he took it in his stride to help his elderly father. As time went on, the nursing staff there suggested to Phil that due to his dad becoming incontinent, it would be necessary for him to wear protection. Phil was about to get Depends for him when in the meantime, he died suddenly, as he reached the age of 95.

Lucille, the only girl in the Roanhaus family, who had become the wife of Walter Guse, lived on a farm in Sheboygan Falls, Wisconsin. It seemed as though it was her turn next to go to her eternal rest.

Her death became extra sad due to the date, October 20, 1984, the day Lucille's grandson Ken Weinaug was getting married. It was when the kids went to her door to take her along to the wedding, there was no answer. Upon their going into the house, they had the shock of their lives. Lucille was all dressed ready for the wedding and they found her limp which meant death.

Now my mother who had gone through such hardship during her life suffered many serious illnesses and had undergone several major surgeries. This put much stress and strain on me because mom and I were always very close. I was her only daughter, obviously she was my only mother, and such a beautiful lovable woman that she was, the greatest mom that ever lived. She was always there for me, so I made sure that I was always there for her.

When I was teaching at Salem Mound Center School, mom had a hernia and became seriously ill. This pain came on her very suddenly and so my dad called me at school and said he had called the ambulance to come and take her to the emergency unit at the hospital and how quick could I come home? Well, this was not as easily done as it was said, so I called the wife of the school board president and asked her if at all possible I could comply with my dad's wishes. She immediately told me that she would come right over to school and that she could handle the situation, and I would be free to leave. So after Mrs. Ellingson arrived, I was off to the hospital.

As I reached the hospital, they were prepping mom for emergency surgery so I had arrived in time. After the numerous tests they took, it was diagnosed as a strangulated hernia. This became a very serious matter and she was in the hospital for twelve days. In the meantime, I made arrangements for a leave of absence so I would be home to take care of my mother when she was released from the hospital. I knew that she would have many restrictions as to lifting and even caring for the house, because this surgery took the starch right out of mother, even though she was a fighter.

The Ellingson family again came through for me and handled this matter. Being my second year of teaching there, this went on until the end of the school year, so I didn't sign another contract. In the meantime I became pregnant with our second child and went through a daily routine of constant nausea that would have interfered with my teaching anyway, so it all worked out for the best, and I put my name on the substitute list in Kenosha County.

Through the years I can remember mom having gall bladder attacks, until she finally had it removed. Mom never got sick often but when she did, it was always the most serious illness that one could have, it seemed as though she never contracted the less serious illnesses.

She had diverticulitis, and this meant that her diet was restricted from eating anything with small kernels or seeds. Being that she loved pickles and cucumbers, she got to the point where she had to have an end of bowel removed. She had waited too long and so she had what the doctor called a blow-out and her body became so infected and was full of poisonous matter caused by peritonitis. She had a pump hooked up to her body in which the poison was taken off, and in the meantime,

428

her life was hanging on a thread. We prayed and prayed for her, but God was again good to us and spared her life. After mom came out of this surgery she discovered that she had a colostomy, the surgical construction of an artificial opening to the colon to the outside of the body, permitting passage of intestinal contents into a pouch that had to be emptied often and that whole area had to be kept sanitized and clean. Mom was not happy about this and she told the doctor, "I'd rather be dead than to have this bag, as I had no idea you were going to do this and now I want this bowel put back".

The doctor promised that as soon as her colon went through the healing process and he was sure that all was functioning properly and her body could withstand another surgery he would put the end of the colon back. Even though he was reluctant to perform this surgery, Mom held him to his promise, as two months later, she went through another surgery to have this all put back. She was fortunate because this was such a delicate situation. I admire my mother for all her courage it took to go through all this as she got through so many surgeries that no one else could have ever survived. We often commented how mother had been at death's door so many times, but each one was not the right time for God to take her back, but through God's will and everyone's strong faith is what helped her through.

All through mom's life, she had many serious illnesses and so in her last years of life, she endured the frailties of heart failure. Little by little she needed more and more oxygen until the final stages of her life ceased after years of suffering and struggling to live. I was with mom at the hospital during these final days, and she was in a state of relief knowing that she would soon be relieved of her sufferings. This last day was such a difficult time as mother was in a coma, and I endured just to keep my emotions bottled up to make those last moments as comforting as possible. My beautiful mother was at last allowed to rest void of all the pain and suffering she had endured in her 85 years of life on December 4, 1984.

On August 10, 1990, exactly two months after I retired, my dad Joseph Lenz was called to his eternal rest.

My dad's health problems never caused any degree of worry or stress. as he was most healthy. I think his daily early morning Coffee Royal [a cup of hot coffee with a shot of brandy in it] kept his resistance as an immunity to disease. He was one to doctor up everything by himself with the rubbing of

Vicks Vapo-Rub, and the amazing thing is that this salve kept his feet from excessive swelling. He went to his final rest due to natural causes, old age. My dad always said that he wanted to live as long as Phil's dad, Joe Roanhaus. Well, dad almost lived up to that statement, as he reached the age of 94.

The only time dad was ever in a hospital was the time he fell and broke his hip. He gave those nurses one hell of a hard time there with his grumbling and complaining because to him nothing was ever right. He was dissatisfied with the food, with the service as he called it, and he thought he had the poorest of care, but you had to know my dad to understand all this. Mother went to the hospital every day to stay with him all day long, and he had her waiting on him hand and foot, and still he was as ornery as a bear because nobody or nothing could please him there.

All this chasing took its toll on mother as she was wearing down from all the stress. He complained to mother so much that she asked the doctor if dad could have his Coffee Royal every day while at the hospital. With compassion for her, the doctor ordered this as a medication as long as mother would provide the brandy. This made him happy to a certain extent, but everything else was not so good in his eyes.

When he came home, we all tried to help mother care for him, but mother became just about as stubborn as dad. I guess he started rubbing off on her. The greatest hurt for Phil and me was the fact that so much of our help was resented by mother. Every Sunday morning we offered to take mom and dad along to church with us as dad was walking with the aid of a walker and we wanted to assist mom with helping dad in and out of the car, and to pack the walker away after. Mom very indignantly refused saying, "I can take care of Joe, my husband, by myself, and I don't need your help".

So at church she would park the car in the handicapped parking stall at the church, and whenever Phil wanted to help her get dad out of the car or back into the car again, she would tell us she knew how to handle my dad without any help. But by the same token, when other parishioners would come along to help her, she accepted their help. I often wondered what Rita and Art Vos thought of us, because they were two people whom mom would allow to help, and to this day I'm sure they still don't understand the whole situation. At times, mother had her own ways of belittling people, but no one is perfect as we all have our own faults; we are human beings and I forgave her many times over.

A few years later in 1987, one of the worst episodes of my life was the day I had ridden in the Medix ambulance with my dad whom had just been discharged from the hospital. He never got back to his own home again. We rode directly to a nursing home in Kenosha where he was to become a resident. How perplexing it was when dad thought he was returning home and we didn't even go near his house, but directly to the nursing home.

To top it all off, this was the day of my birthday and such a terrible memory of placing my own dad, who had been so good to me all my life and so near and dear to me, in a nursing home. From that day on every time we went to visit him there, the amount of stress kept building up to the point of wondering how much longer I could maintain my sanity, because I knew he was not nor could ever be happy there.

Prior to this time, my brother and I shopped around for a nursing facility that we thought was appropriate for dad. We were cautious that it was reputable for obtaining the best of care, so we decided on the Claridge House. It was the best of the lot which was affordable out of the five homes we investigated and it seemed clean and did not have the odor of urine when entering the building. That was always one thing I loathed about nursing homes, they always had a foul smell. Bob and I had conferred with dad's doctor and he recommended that we make arrangements to take dad to the nursing home from the hospital. He said that if we took dad to his own home, he would never want to leave and he was not capable of living alone any longer.

The memory of that day will always be a thorn piercing in my heart with a dreaded thought in my mind, but trying to help him live alone at his home had become so hazardous, as we never knew if he was safe or in jeopardy of a home accident. His living at home created a constant worry as to the dangers involved if he would fall. Did he leave the stove burner turned on? Was the coffee pot still plugged in? Did he take his medication during the day?

Finally the Midwest Home Nursing Care provided a nurse for dad's morning bath and breakfast, Meals-on-Wheels delivered his noon lunches, and I sent over his evening meals and evening snack. Margaret Bastrup, the visiting nurse would come back and help him to bed. Our daughters and daughter-in-law Monica, helped keep his house clean by rotating weekly, changed

431

his bed sheets, and daughter Deb did all his laundry. Then this arrangement alleviated much worry and stress in addition to the work load.

Being in the nursing home eased some of the worries that I had before because now he was in a safe environment where he had round the clock nursing care, and his medication was administered to him professionally so he got the right prescription medicine at the right time. He was a resident there for about three years.

I wasn't with my dad when he was in his final stages of life, but my brother Bob, daughters Darlene and Dolly, had been with him earlier in the day. Phil and I were out of town visiting our daughter, son-in-law, and children in Merrill. The last one to be with my dad was our youngest daughter, Donna. She wanted to stay with her grandpa until the very end, but the staff at the nursing home ordered her to leave. This left emotional stress on her because she wanted to be there to comfort him in his last moments and breaths.

I always felt sad that he had to be alone at that particular time, but in all honesty I was relieved that I was not there because I had been in two prior traumatic experiences with my younger brother and my dear mother. I knew then at that time I could not have withstood another distressing moment of death.

Just recently, Phil's brother became terminally ill with a condition that had never before been knowledgeable to him nor his family. His first signs appeared in December and by March 1 he had passed away. Ralph's second wife, Trini, kept us posted as to Ralph's daily condition. When she knew it was nearing the end of time for him, she called us and allowed each one of us to say Goodbye to him on the phone. His voice was already quite weak, and at times due to his slipping in and out of a coma as she said, he seemed to be quite coherent on this day, Phil and I feel that this last message is something that no one can ever take away from us, this goodbye memory will always remain close to our hearts.

On June 10, 1999, my brother Robert [Bob] Lenz, passed away at Mount Carmel Nursing Home in Burlington. Phil and I had just been in to visit him shortly before. He was not at all like himself, as he was so starry eyed, and was very confused in what he was saying in conversation, so not much that he uttered made sense at all. We knew at this point that he would not live to see his next birthday which was on June 23.

Making funeral arrangements was somewhat complicated,

being that Bob had named Annie, [Lennie's former wife], as power of attorney. Bob and Annie had made prior funeral arrangements when he was alive, but there were many details still pending. When Annie called me to tell me of Bob's death, she was away on a mysterious vacation and no one knew where she was. This added to the confusion as she gave me a number of a person named Brian who was her companion, and had a cell phone through which means I was to keep in touch.

Later that morning, I received a call from this Brian, Annie's assumed gardener, requesting that I call the funeral director and give him information for the obituary. The funeral director told me that I would have to be the person in charge for further arrangements, and that he would keep in touch with me instructing me as to what needed to be taken care of.

In the meantime, Annie called Dick Elverman and told him that Bob didn't want any pall bearers, and what should she do? I was hurt when I heard about this, because Bob was my brother and she didn't confer with me about it at all, so I contacted Reggie and Lennie, Bob's children, and asked what they thought about the deal. All three of us did not want strangers to carry our loved one to his grave so they told me to go ahead and line up pall bearers, so I did. Annie was not happy about this, but we did it anyway.

Our daughter, Debbie, and our son-in-law, Al, helped us plan the funeral mass. Al selected all the songs with tender loving care. Keli Jo was to do the readings at Mass, Ashley and Josh Thuemmler would serve Mass, Marilyn Uhen would direct the choir, Lennie and Keli Jo would take up the offertory gifts, I called Father Tom and he approved everything

The next issue was getting in touch with the ladies of our parish, Dorothy and Evelyn Kerkman, who hosted the funeral luncheons and planned the meal. Shortly after I had called Dorothy and talked everything over with her, she called me back and told me that Annie had called her and told her that chicken was to be served at the luncheon as this was Bob's wishes. I can't conceive this idea at all and I truly doubt that this is even true, because I'm sure when one makes funeral arrangements ahead of time, one doesn't give a hoot what will be served at the luncheon after your own funeral.

Then after the luncheon was over, Annie picked up the left-over chicken and left. When I went into the kitchen to thank the ladies for putting on such a good luncheon, Dorothy asked me what to do with the left over food, as it is always given to

433

the family. I knew better than to take left over food, so I told Dorothy that I just wanted to take the two things home that Dolly had made, a salad and a cake. I told the ladies to divide up the food and take it home, because I knew what Annie would say after all was said and done, so I played it cool. There was only a small portion of beef and ham left so Dorothy sent that and all the relishes and rolls with me.

Later on, I asked Annie for thank you cards to send to the ladies who donated food and helped with the luncheon, and she brought eleven. This was not near enough so I had to use my personal thank you cards to write the notes to the ladies, and to our friends who sent money to our house for masses. I don't know if thank you notes ever got sent out to people who donated monetary or floral offerings or not. Phil and I didn't get one, but I didn't expect one. I offered to help her write out these thank you notes, but she refused.

I will say one thing for her, she was very good to my brother, but why shouldn't she be, she had everything to gain from his personal property. Lennie and Reggie got nothing, not even a memento of their father. I have forgiven her for all the grief she put me through and the nasty things she said to me during the whole bereavement process. I have been taught that one must forgive the transgressions of others as we are all human beings, and no one is perfect. The Lord's Prayer clearly states this concept.

All of these deceased people who were such an intricate part of our lives are now mortally gone but they all live on in our hearts, until we are all reunited after the close of history when we all reach our own eternal destiny. I remember all these people in my daily prayers, and used to visit my parents' and my brother's grave sites but now it is very difficult due to my being confined to a wheel chair. Death is evident but I embrace the memories of the times we all shared together here on earth.

My younger brother, Ardell, at age 18

My Mom Dorothy and Dad Joseph

My sister-in-law Sophie and my Brother Robert
on their 25th wedding anniversary

Chapter 43
Life Continues On

Yes, life goes on with its many variations as the years go by. Even though life is what you make it, one has to learn how to cope with these numerous changes, mentally and physically, in order to age gracefully. This is just a forewarning of what it can be like after reaching the age of seventy.

Forgetfulness. This is one of the first notable changes, forgetting. Golly, it can't be Alzheimer's disease because I don't drink my soda from an aluminum can, nor do I use deodorant that has aluminum in, so it just can't be that. But many times I would leave one room to go to another to complete a task. To my sudden surprise, when I arrived in that next room, didn't I forget what I had come into that room to do? Oh, yes, this still happens all too frequently.

At the first signs of this, I stopped to ponder and think, 'Am I losing my mind?' Then by giving myself a little trial test, I realized that I still knew my name, that Phil is the love of my life, I could add and subtract, I knew that I was in my own house, I could still appreciate our God given natural beauty, and convinced myself I really and truly was okay, I hadn't lost my mind.

I do many mind boggling activities like crossword puzzles, word searches, and fill-ins. I find that all of these help develop skills and keep the mind aware of my former mastered skills. I play Scrabble on my computer and this is challenging as the computer is my competitor and it takes an abundance of thought to keep ahead of the computer who functions under the name of Maven.

I also work Algebra problems on my computer, as well as play two different forms of Solitaire. One game is Klondike and the other is Eight Off. Both these games afford many challenges to keep my mind in functioning gear.

I take Ginkgo Biloba vitamins daily to enhance my thinking capacity. It has been helping me in writing this book as many happenings and events are coming back to me quite readily. I consider myself fortunate. Thanks to those good Amway vitamins! I am proud of myself that I was able to remember most of the focal points of my life. Even through all the stress that I am still experiencing, I consider myself quite apt.

Memory was probably the worst of the mental part of aging. Now let me tell you about the physical dilemma of the aging process.

One of the first notable modifications for me was the sagging breasts. Sometimes I felt like my boobs were hanging on my knees making peculiar sounds, only to find out that it was my arthritic knees creaking and not my breasts clacking on my knees at all. What a relief that was!

Being that I have been endowed with ample sized breasts, my kids and grandchildren always kidded me about my food falling on my natural table. My sons-in-law always made a joke about mom hitching up the team. They knew that I was full of wit and humor myself so I thought nothing of it and I laughed right along with them, because not one of them said it maliciously. Oh, but how they all liked to tease me!

The next notable dimension is the bulge around the middle, my spare tire which never went flat like the tires on a vehicle. I used to get kidded about that. Again the kids teased me that if I ever had a blowout, I'd always have a spare. The humor in my family is unbelievable. But this makes growing old, a conversation piece, so I enjoyed their humor right along with them.

Then there is the problem of hearing or rather what you cannot hear. When I was teaching school, I had the best ears for hearing that anyone could have. The kids in the far corner or back of the room would whisper to each other and I could repeat what they said, word for word. That faculty has lessened quickly through these past few years.

But the phenomenon of it all is the fact that the ears grow larger and longer with age, but the hearing grows lesser as time marches on. At times my kids tell me that I have selective hearing, and I am inclined to agree with them as at times I hear every word that I shouldn't be hearing. Oh, well you can't win 'em all.

I can't forget to point out the balding spots found on my head. Phil can share this loss right along with me, as he is thin and almost shiny on the top and on the back of his head. I have had two totally hairless spots on my head to the point of scaring daughter Darlene and granddaughter Renee, both hair stylists, as to what could account for this. So because they both insisted, I inquired about it to my doctor, and after results of tests, Dr. Smith told me to use Neutrogena T/Gel Shampoo. I did and still do, so the spots are starting to fill in. So there is still hope of not being totally bald, even though they found three more bare spots on my head.

Speaking of hair, this is another story. That is the graying around the temples and the salt and pepper look on the back of my head. Again Phil and I both share in this together. Being that he wears a flat top, gray doesn't show as much on him as it does on me, even though I wear my hair very short. So about every six weeks, I have my hair colored. Then for a time it looks shades darker than my usual normal color and it becomes noticeable beyond what I had expected until it starts lightening up a bit. But I take it all in stride and graciously accept how I look.

Another sign of aging is the degeneration of the eyes. They not only look all blood-shot, but they sink and give off the visage of two peep holes in a snow bank. If it weren't for the glasses that we each wear, one could hardly tell that we even have eyes. Just to let you know, I have dark blue eyes, and Phil has bedroom eyes.

Needless to say, below our eyes can be seen dark circles or rather dark saggy bags. Sometimes it appears that we may have had a shiner in its healing stages. This is another dead give away that one is experiencing the age-old process of aging.

I hate to admit, but if I don't hold my head absolutely upright and high into the air, you may see my double chins. I like to think of it as my neck is growing thick and is lifting upward. But I don't know if others perceive it the same way as I do, but I use this as a legitimate excuse.

Another facet of aging is evident by looking at and feeling my skin. As we age, our skin's cell turn-over rate slows down, letting environmental effects catch up with us in the form of brown spots, lines, and larger pores. Somehow or other this aged skin starts to have tiny notable creases or puckers. Some call them wrinkles but I like the terms tiny creases or puckers instead. I try not to put emphasis on this trait even though it's so visible to the naked eye.

Then there is the contrast of legs. Skinny legs for men and plump legs for women is the next noteworthy feature. Phil's emaciated legs are like that of just bone with a little epidermis pulled over them, so he tries avoiding wearing shorts. My legs, on the other hand, are plump with arthritic bulgy knees protruding. We are very much a contrast in that respect. The sight of my knees does not stop me from wearing shorts, because when it's hot, I want to be comfortable, no matter what the looks are.

I always thought the best part of aging would be when the kids all left the nest and we would be all alone, just the two of us together, Phil and me. But our lives didn't work that way. While we both were still working full time at our jobs, our oldest daughter decided to change jobs with the intent of moving to New Mexico with one of her girl friends. So she asked if she could move back home until she relocated. We complied with her request, she moved in with us temporarily, which turned out to be permanently because her plans never materialized.

Getting back to the aging process, it is a time of our lives to accept these many modifications, as our marriage changes right along with all the other variations. It is a time for returning to couple hood after decades of our being in a family frame of mind, and rejuvenating our relationship from our earlier days while progressing on. We come to realize that we are somewhat a different type of couple than we were in our twenties, but all those years of life experiences made our love for each other grow to a capacity far beyond its original state when we first fell in love with each other.

We are not only a couple but we are each other's closest friend and we enjoy our time together. Even though the capacity of the deepness of intimate love-making falls somewhat short of what it had been in our youth, due to age and medical difficulties, our marital intimacy has been intensified by our sharing not only our physical bond, but our feelings and also our thoughts.

This brings us back to our state of marriage in which we joined together on our wedding day, "And the two shall become one". This is significant in our lives today and our love which has grown stronger through time, still proves to be the genuine kind of love.

I must admit having Darlene living with us actually seems to be a blessing in disguise as there are times when we feel so alone and having a younger person around lightens up our lives. Her friendly greetings when she gets up in the mornings, when she leaves for work, when she arrives home, and when she retires in the evening, make it all so worthwhile which adds a touch of her special love for us.

During football season, she watches the games on TV with her dad, and they enjoy conversing throughout the game, almost replaying many of the bad plays on the part of the team, with "Why didn't he...", "He plays like a...", "Go, go go...", or "Another fumble...". Many times I'm in another room and I hear them discussing the dumb plays of the teams, and at times they get so annoyed and so excited, that I hear them both yelling as if they were sitting right in the stadium watching the games. They are both truly Packer backers. I feel this is their quality time together and it becomes quite obvious they both enjoy this.

She volunteers to take me shopping on most Wednesdays as this is her day off work. This is our quality time together, as we both like to shop. We don't always buy, but there is significant difference in shopping and buying. She very patiently takes tender loving care of me during these pleasure trips.

Our usual excursion is to Southport Shopping Plaza in Kenosha. This is a relatively new mini mall and has some of our favorite stores. We usually start at the Card Factory and stock up on greeting cards for the next two or three months for the family members' birthdays, anniversaries and special days of the year. This totals up to thirty-nine members in our immediate family.

Next stop is the Dollar Bill Store which is the neatest place just to shop around, but we usually end up buying many dollar items. In all reality we purchase things that we hadn't even thought of buying.

From there Darlene takes our purchases to her car and drives down to park nearer to Kohls, our favorite store in the mall. During this time I wheel myself down the sidewalk and most of the time we arrive at that destination at the same time. That is if I don't have to stop too many times to rest my arms. Along the way every time I do this, many people both young and older, stop by me and ask if I need any help. Heaven forbid, that I should accept any of these kind and thoughtful people's help! I'm not being persnickety about this but I want to remain as independent for as long as I am able to do just that.

We never miss purse shopping at Kohls because they have the neatest styles in leather as well as any color imaginable. We each pick out our favorite purses then we decide if we are going to buy them or not, but their leather purses are so reasonable. When one or the other of us decides to buy, then the other will buy too. Sometimes, we decide that it's not in either of our budgets to buy on a certain day, so we convince each other that we didn't need it in the first place.

Of course we can't leave the store without going through the clothes there. So she heads for the misses department while I wheel off to the plus size section. If and when we each find something we like we get the other's approval before purchasing. Sometimes we buy, depending on the sales, sometimes we put it all back, but this constitutes the fun of shopping.

Next and last stop is Target, for the stock up on Pepsi and Mountain Dew, Viva paper towels, Charmin big roll toilet tissue, Kleenex, tooth paste, and what ever else we may need at the time. Then we mosey around the store to see if there is anything we might like, again we honor each other's approval. This kind of shopping lends itself to finding many things that are on sale, that one never thought of buying before because of cost factor. I'm referring to one of those gotta-have-it items. At times we ponder over these values and at other times we buy.

After shopping in so many stores, I'm fatigued and so is Darlene, so we head on home. .

When we return home Phil helps carry in our purchases of the day. He doesn't like to shop but occasionally he does take me and helps pick out groceries. We usually shop at Woodmans Market which is so huge, that grocery shopping consumes a great deal of time. He pushes the grocery cart while I wheel down the aisles picking out what we need and he puts everything in the cart. When things are too high on a shelf, he gets them down from the shelves for me.

Phil and I don't go out much anymore and we're quite contented staying in our humble abode. On the nights when I teach, Phil watches TV and answers the telephone in the living room while I'm engaged with a student at the table in the dining room.

When I finish, we usually retire to the bedroom, get ready for bed, take our nightly prescriptions, get some sort of snack and a couple of sodas from the kitchen, talk to each other while we watch TV, set the sleep timer on the remote, turn out the main light, turn on the ceiling fan for circulation of air, continue to view TV until we fall asleep. Not too exciting, is it?

We go to church every Sunday together, unless either of us is sick, then we watch Mass on the religious channel on TV. After the church service is over, we meet and talk with our friends. We both enjoy people, so this becomes a good way to socialize with other people of the parish. We miss out on other activities of the parish which are held in the school cafeteria or hall, due to my inability to enter the building with a wheel chair, so we are deprived of many hours of fellowship with other parishioners.

The one extensive regret that lingers in my heart is this: after devoting twenty-six years of work, service, and dedication to the school, I am not able to attend Grandparents' Day during

Catholic Schools Week, to be with my grandchildren like other grandparents can be. Phil goes without me so the kids have someone there with them. To me this is quite a deprivation, but several weeks after that day is over, the hurt lessens until the next year.

We both look forward to the parish function, the Smoker. This event is held at Marino's Country Aire prior to the season of Lent. This building is accessible for handicapped persons. Deb and Al always pick us up and take us home after.

We play a card game called Screw Your Neighbor, in which you get one card, and if you have a low card you can pass it off on your neighbor by means of trading cards, that is if he doesn't have a King. Many times you can get burned by getting a lower card than the one you traded, so if you lose you have to put a quarter in the pot. You start with three quarters, and when they're gone you're allowed to play on your honor for as long as you don't lose. Whoever stays the longest wins the pot. We all like this game because it's a no-brainer, and requires no concentration, so we can talk without fear of losing concentration.

During the evening, there are many raffles of donated items, and chances are sold for one dollar a ticket or seven tickets for five dollars. Each raffle has an average of fifty items. Later in the evening is the larger raffle in which the items are of far more value. Throughout the evening, beer and soda are served with pretzels and popcorn on each table. Later a lunch is served including a hot ham and cheese sandwich, potato chips, a dill pickle, and a dessert. The admittance charge is five dollars, but you surely get your money's worth.

Always the first Saturday in April, St. Francis Xavier Parish in Brighton has their Smoker. Deb and Al pick us up for that one too.

The other extent of our going out includes mostly having cake for grandchildren's birthdays at the homes of their parents. Occasionally some of our kids invite Phil and me to their houses for a special meal. This is something else we enjoy. Many times Deb and Al invite us to their home parties that they have with their friends, so this keeps us in touch with the younger people, and it's amazing how we are accepted by this younger generation.

Now that we are retired, we do occasional babysitting for the grandchildren if the mom wants to work or if there is a special occasion where the children are not invited, Phil and I then watch the grand kids. This is done in our own home as the

443

children are brought to us.

We are always on hand if any of the grandchildren get ill at school, then Phil picks them up from school if their parents cannot be reached at their places of employment which prevents them from leaving their work. Then the sick one stays with us until their parents come to get them. At times when a grandchild has had an accident at school, we have even taken them for medical care to a doctor.

For the past four years, Jim and Dolly go to a tile convention in Las Vegas. Phil and I move into their house and care for their children while they are away. This is quality time for us with their kids. This always happens the end of January. This year I did more card playing with the children in the evening when the homework was completed. They enjoyed this as much as I did.

Phil and I care for each other's needs, as Phil's hands were left incapacitated after having suffered a few strokes. My right hand, being useless due to my past polio, gives problems also, but we work together on the household chores that need to be done. Phil usually makes the bed daily, because I can't manage with any kind of ease, to be able to make the one side of the bed, but many times we do this task together.

Phil does all the vacuuming as I get all caught up in cords under my wheels when I attempt to do this, but on occasion I have done it but it takes me two hours to do four rooms and two hallways. While he vacuums, I dust the furniture and straighten anything that is out of place putting it back where it belongs.

I do all the cooking, baking, laundry, and the reminder of the cleaning. The bathroom cleaning is the most time consuming, although loading and unloading the dishwasher and putting the clean dishes away is another time-consuming chore. But I live up to my own philosophy, 'You can do anything that you want to do, if you just put your mind to it'. This philosophy I have always instilled in my students during my teaching career Now they come back and tell me how true it is, and how they have succeeded by using this helpful information.

The biggest joke around our house is watching me peel potatoes. After peeling twelve potatoes, I have the equivalent of six. We often laugh about it together, and I always tell Phil that he knew this about me before I married him at which time he assured me that he had no problems with how the potatoes would ever be peeled. My kids always want me to use a peeler, but every time I try using the darn thing, it slips right out of my hand, so I do it by the only means that works for me, a paring knife. I usually have proof of having peeled the potatoes by just looking at my hands with all the cuts on.

Many years ago this potato peeling episode really bothered my dad, so he would come over to our house, collect the peelings out of our garbage and plant them. Quite a few years in a row, he had a fairly good potato crop by just planting the discarded peelings. This then became another family joke, and many people riddled me about this, but I used to laugh right along with them.

Being on a fixed income, there are many ways in which one learns to cut corners. The one aspect of this theory that I found troublesome was how to cook for three people when all those years I was used to cooking for ten. Actually it was quite recent that I have finally learned how to cut down in quantity, and eliminate so many leftovers.

Some times I think some of my mental powers are temporarily going astray because they fail me and then I begin to hope that I'm not losing my faculties. It's like my brain doesn't give off the right message to the rest of my body creating a physical problem. I say this because some nights I retire with so much discomfort in my back and hips so I find need to pop a pain reliever called Hydrocodone which has been prescribed by my doctor for pain.

At times the wires that the doctor put around the bone in which the prosthesis has been placed bother me a great deal. But the wires are there to stabilize the bone, because being the second time the bone is not as strong as was the first time when the prosthesis was inserted. When I'm in such discomfort, I can't fall asleep so the Hydrocodone helps me get a few hours of sleep. It seems every time that I need to take one of these pills, I constantly dream wild dreams all night. When I awaken after my first stretch of sleep, three hours at the most, I wonder where I am and what has happened to me. Am I on another planet? But when I awaken I come to realize that I was only dreaming this horrible stuff. This also proves to be another facet of aging.

Then the problem starts all over again as the pains return. But very rarely do I ever give in to taking a second pain reliever in a night, as I do not want to become addicted to them. Now it's a bummer to fall off to sleep again. Many nights I look at the clock and see the hours pass slowly by before my very eyes, as I can hardly wait until my alarm goes off at 6:00 a.m. at which time I arise for the day, feeling very fatigued due to lack of sleep. Often times about three o'clock in the morning I find that I cannot go back to sleep. so I get up and play games on my computer. After a while of not being able to fall back to sleep, I find that this becomes most annoying to me but as time goes on, I am becoming adapted to the whole situation and life seems more tolerable again.

When I awaken in the morning, I take time to thank God that he has granted me another day of precious life. Next I head for the bathroom, take my glucose count because I am diabetic, then I go to the kitchen and put on a pot of coffee. My next move is to read a magazine article, or a chapter in a book, or play a game of solitaire on my computer while enjoying my first cup of coffee. On some days for variety, I work a couple of fill-in puzzles.

Ten minutes before my scheduled time to eat, I start for the kitchen and get a fruit ready, and toast two slices of cinnamon raisin bread. This is the only food that I can get down as I only eat breakfast because I have to. I do find this to be difficult as I never have been a breakfast person.

I'm on a diet of 1500 calories a day due to the Diabetes. So I have to plan my meals very carefully, and try to eat on time, as this is so important when one is diabetic. At eleven a.m. I must have another serving of fruit. Phil and I both eat lunch at 1:00 p.m., and dinner is at 6:00 p.m. At 8:30 I'm allowed to have a snack, usually we both have pop corn or any snack that is sugarless and low on calories.

I'm used to my style of eating now, but it took some time to get adjusted. So many foods that have been favorites in the past are totally eliminated from my diet now. I am so happy that Phil is so understanding about it all, and goes along with the schedule that has been set for me.

My daily shower is usually put off until after my mid-morning fruit snack, so I finally get into the shower about 11:15 a.m., but during the summer months when I teach in the morning, I take an earlier shower.

So many major changes have occurred during this time of graceful aging, but I try to keep a positive attitude and life doesn't seem too bad at all. When the chips seem down, I just think how lucky I am to have all five of my senses and all four of my limbs because many people don't have these faculties, so this means that there are so many humans out there in the world who are so much worse off than I am, and I don't have to look very far to find one of these less fortunate people.

I have much difficulty trying to walk mainly due to my inability to hold my back erect, so this causes a great deal of pain whenever I attempt to walk. For years I have not been able to walk without the aid of forearm crutches. Now I can only walk a limited short distance with the aid of a walker and try to endure the pain in my back. However at night when the batteries on my power chair are charging, I use the walker to get into the bathroom located just around the corner from our bedroom. This I can maneuver and endure for that brief while.

In addition to my walking limitations, ever since Polio I can not raise myself up from an ordinary chair without having to push myself up from it, so this causes another problem. Each time that I need to rise from my chair, I have to use full strength of my arms to push myself up or to let myself down again. Many times I can't control my sitting down, so I plop down into my chair, but this is very hard usage on my power chair, but at times this is beyond my control.

Still another limitation I have to cope with is the inability to lift my own legs, so I can no longer walk up steps. When I want to get upstairs in my house, I crawl up the steps. What an unsightly scene this is so I never crawl up them when someone is around with the exception of Phil or Darlene, who are behind me so I don't slip and fall backwards. At times, granddaughters Missy or Tanya will follow behind me up stairs if they happen to be around.

In our bathroom I have a potty extender to elevate me when I am sitting on the toilet stool. Without the aid of this and the bar attached to the wall, I would never get down on the seat nor up from it without pulling myself up using the bar. In the shower, I have a stool to sit on to take my shower, as my back is not strong enough for me to stand in there. To get out of the shower, I have another bar on the wall to pull myself up and out.

I have a power wheel chair that is motorized with a hand control and this alleviates the arm and shoulder pain that I suffered so badly when I had to push myself around the house. This pain was rapidly traveling up to my neck and at times the pain was so severe and went on into my head, that I had to give in and take pain relievers just so I could keep motivating.

The other problem I had with the manual chair was locking the wheels whenever I wanted to stand up and so many times there went the chair. It's a wonder that I never fell flat on my fanny, but I am so cautious about falling because if I do take a fall, I'd never be able to help myself again. The power chair locks automatically when it stops, so this avoids any undue accidents for me.

Without this power chair, I'd never be able to keep up with my housework. It was difficult before I had this chair. How does one wheel both wheels and carry something to clean with?

I tried to solve this problem by buying my long sleeved tee-shirts in a much larger size than what I needed. In this way, I could put something up my sleeves and the other items I put on the bottom of my shirt and folded the fabric up and around these items in order to carry things from room to room. Many times I have glass cleaner or furniture polish soaking through my shirt, but it dries out eventually. Anyway this proves where there is a will, there is a way.

All in all, I am lucky to be who I am, and I appreciate that fact. I don't have any complaints because I take life as it comes and I am one of the happiest people on earth. I can honestly say that I enjoy life in my own way. The greatest fear that I have is that the day may come that I would have to move from my blissful domain, and one thing that I never want to do is to go to a nursing home. I want to be independent and not have such a structured and dull life.

I beg my family never to put me in a nursing home, because ever since my brother, Bob, was admitted to one, he has gone down in his morale as well as his physical condition. He had given up hope of regaining any strength. I feel that he was merely existing, without any real pleasures of life left for him to enjoy. He didn't live long after he was put into that home, and he passed on. I never want to be put into a nursing home to deteriorate like my brother did.

I'm sure that anyone who is in our age bracket can attest to the facets of aging that all I have said is so very true.

Phil and I are so thankful to almighty God that we are still together enjoying life in our own way. We share the joys and woes that are bestowed upon us, deal with problems from day to day trying to avoid any added stress of daily living and look on the bright side of happenings around us. We accept the aging process as that special part of life which gives us the feeling of togetherness as a couple, still in love.

Chapter 44
Accepting Who I Am

Accepting who I am causes me great difficulty, anguish, and even pain at times when I stop to realize that I started out in life as any healthy normal child and at age nineteen, this changed overnight. Often times, I ask God...."Why, why me?". My strong faith in him answers this question for me, but facing up to the reality of it all is not as easily accepted and can be challenging and more often hard to understand, even though I know the answer.

Now that I am approaching another year older, I keep thinking more deeply in searching for my true feelings, and try to understand how it could have all been different if it had not been 'Me', the chosen one. Then I ask myself this question, "Why not me?". At this point, I then have a feeling of contentment as I realize that I am so fortunate to be who I am. I could be one of those poor helpless creatures who are so much less than the average person, but I'm not and I thank God daily for that.

In evaluating myself I find that I have always had a bright mind, a brain of logic and intelligence, and the opportunities to develop the qualities of life that some people were never even given a chance to develop. My heart has always reached out to them and many times over I have thanked God from the bottom of my heart for allowing me to be who I am.

Being that some days are better than others, I need to constantly remind myself that each morning when I awaken, I have another day and another chance at life, which I must make the most of. This begins my day on a positive note and then I can overlook all the negativity around me and in the world, including my own negative feelings that I sometimes encounter when I'm in a down mood and I have to turn them about into the positive, but I can do it because I am strong-willed and determined.

I belong to a Post-Polio Support Group of Milwaukee, but I never get to any of their functions but as long as I pay my dues, they continue to send me all the good literature on how and why to accept an affliction and ways and means of dealing with the day to day living in the best manner possible. This monthly news letter is called Spirit. In the most recent issue there is a prayer that is so true to life.

449

Morning Prayer

So far today, God
I've done all right,
I haven't gossiped,
Haven't lost my temper,
Haven't been greedy, grumpy, nasty,
Selfish, or overindulgent.
I'm really glad about that.
But in a few minutes, God,
I'm going to get out of bed,
And from then on
I'm probably going to need a lot of help.
Amen.

I always keep asking God for favors, and most of the time he grants them to me, but I keep wondering how long will he continue to hear me and all my pleading. Will he so graciously keep granting my requests? I sincerely hope and trust that he will, in fact I know that he will, because he loves me as much as I love him.

Each month I faithfully read this Polio newsletter as it contains many helpful hints on how one can preserve the strength that we still have left in us, and need to utilize it wisely. The humor and wit printed in these newsletters helps one to perceive an affliction as acceptable, perhaps even a gift from God.

An example of this: '"On the lighter side, you know you have Post Polio Syndrome when instead of taking half a day to do nothing, it now takes me all day to do nothing and I have to rest up the next day from the exertion". This may sound a little extreme but I have many days like this, then two days later I have to work harder to make up for the lost time, this is so true to life and so typical of my own life style.

I'm learning though to take each day at a time, and what gets done, gets done, whatever doesn't get done, doesn't get done, and I have learned to accept this as such. I like the saying that was in a recent Post-Polio newsletter: "One day at a time, this is enough, do not look back and grieve over the past, for it is gone. And do not be troubled about the future for it has yet to come. Live in the present and make it so beautiful that it will be worth remembering". Such words of wisdom!

I am trying to learn what my strengths are and what my weaknesses are so I can deal with this Post Polio Syndrome.

In the letter from the editor are listed some practical suggestions for people who are in PPS.

-Lay that body down. Hit the polio wall every afternoon, so try to rest even if you don't sleep.

-Give yourself at least one day off a week. Whether you need it or not, plan to do something special or nothing at all. Have that second cup of coffee, blast the stereo, sleep late, work a puzzle, or whatever.

-If you are fortunate enough, let someone give you help.

-Become someone you love. Try to be a simpler you, someone you will love and understand.

-Don't wait for a friend to come to you or call, you do it first.

-Learn or find out what resources are available to you to help improve your life.

-Live each day to the fullest.

-Don't let a day go by on you and your loved ones with anger between you.

-Tell those you care for that you love them every day. Life is so precious and so short here on earth.

-Be kind and gentle with yourself.

I find that if I don't thrive on the things that I can't do, and elaborate on the things that I can do, I am a happier person. I am special in my own right. I am worthy of receiving love and respect because I give love and respect to others. I have great self-esteem because I have earned that quality all throughout my life and this is the contributing factor toward my self-worth. I know my self-worth and I humble myself to others. I treat others as I want to be treated, with kindness, integrity, loyalty, and understanding. All these qualities have helped me in accepting who I am.

451

Chapter 45
Advice For Happiness

Did you know that there are so many sayings that can influence our lives? Many wise people have extended these renowned sayings on to us.

I have always enjoyed these and there are some that impressed me as an expression of well-being, desirable standards of living, enhancing fine morals, boosting morale, giving helpful hints, and being sound guidelines notable for an extension of happiness and success.

Here are some of my favorites

-Yesterday is a cancelled check and tomorrow is a promissory note.

-Today is the only ready cash you have to spend, so spend it wisely,

-Anyone who thinks he knows all the answers isn't quite up-to-date on the questions.

-A Christian is not necessarily a person who is better than someone else, but one that is better than he would be if he were not a Christian.

-He who buys what he does not need will often need what he cannot buy.

-It isn't the people who tell all they know who cause the most trouble, it's the ones who tell more than they know.

-Wisdom is not knowing all there is to know, but knowing what to do with what little you do know.

-Those who go against the grain of God's laws shouldn't complain when they get splinters..

-There are two ways to stop malicious gossip stop listening and stop talking.

-There is no right way to do a wrong thing.

-If you think you are becoming more forgetful, you are simply becoming more selective in what you remember.

-An old-timer is a person who remembers when a person who wanted something saved UP for it instead of paying DOWN.

-The world would be full of good people if anybody was half as good as they expected others to be.

Life is so worthwhile but everyone needs friends. These quips and sayings are all about having friends. . Life would become so empty without having friends.

Friends

-Nothing but heaven itself is better than a friend who really is a friend

.-Many things can bring us wealth but only friends can bring us joy.

As a closing thought :

A B C's For Successful and happy living

Avoid negative sources, people,places, things, and
  habits.
Believe in yourself.
Consider things from every angle.
Don't give up, and don't give in.
Enjoy life today, yesterday is gone, and tomorrow
may never come.
Family and friends are hidden treasures, seek their
advice.
Give more than you planned to.
Hang on to your dreams.
Ignore those who try to discourage you.
Just do it.
Keep trying no matter how hard it seems, it will get easier.
Like yourself as a person and the rest will fall into place.
Make it happen.
Never lie, cheat or steal, always strike a fair deal.
Open your eyes and see things as they really are.
Practice makes perfect.
Quitters never win and winners never quit.
Read, study, and learn about everything important in your
  life.
Stop procrastinating.
Take control of your own destiny.
Understand yourself in order to understand others.
Visualize it.
Want it more than anything.
EXecute your efforts.
You are unique, nothing can replace you.
Zero in on your target and go for it.

Keep this special alphabet in mind and put it into practice in your daily living for a happier **YOU.**

To order additional copies of **Threads Of Memories** complete the information below:

Ship to: (please print)

Name:_____

Address:_____

City, State, Zip_____

Day Phone_____

_____ copies of   **Threads Of Memories**   @ $16.95 each $_____
                        Postage and Handling @ $5.00 per book $_____
                              WI residents add 5.5% tax $_____

Make checks payable to   Arlene Roanhaus

Send to: Arlene Roanhaus
6301 - 328 Avenue * Salem, WI 53168